Mr. Muhammad Speaks An Invincible Truth:

The Pittsburth Courier Articles Collection

Mr. Muhammad Speaks An Invincible Truth: The Pittsburgh
Courier Articles Collection

2015 First Edition

Compiled and Arranged by Demetric Muhammad

The Nation of Islam

Printed in the Nation of Islam

ALL PRAISE
IS DUE TO ALLAH

This volume is dedicated first to The Honorable Minister Louis Farrakhan and Mother Khadijah Farrakhan. They are two of the most magnificent human beings who have modeled the way for the believers in so many critical areas. They are luminaries. Their model proves that dutifulness, committment and long suffering are the fruits of love and the seeds to greatness. I thank them both for sharing with me their rich personal connection to these articles.

This volme is also dedicated to all of the brothers and sisters of the FOI and the MGT who helped the Most Honorable Elijah Muhammad in the early days to spread his message through the Pittsburgh Courier Newspaper and other Black Newspapers of that time period. We thank you. We salute you. We are indebted to you. Our heart is filled with love for you.

NOTE: Every effort was made to present the words of the Most Honorable Elijah Muhammad exactly as he published them in the original Pittsburgh Courier Newspaper. There are no changes to his spelling of words or to the content of his articles. The only editing involved was our team working to ensure that what we typed from the original articles is exactly as it appeared in the original articles. We are taught that mistakes shall not exist among the laborers, so if there is something that escaped our careful proofing and review, please contact us at *invincibletruthofmuhammad@gmail.com* and we will correct it.

Table of Contents

TABLE OF CONTENTS I

INTRODUCTION XII

PITTSBURGH COURIER HISTORY XIX

THE SEMINARY OF MINISTER LOUIS FARRAKHAN XXVIII

JUNE 9, 1956 1

JUNE 16, 1956 3

JUNE 23, 1956 4

    PERSECUTION FOLLOWS 4

JUNE 30, 1956 7

    THE BIBLE AND QUR-AN 7

JULY 7, 1956 9

    'HOLY QUR-AN AND BIBLE' 9

JULY 14, 1956 13

    HOLY KUR-AN AND BIBLE (CONTINUED) 13

JULY 21, 1956 15

    HOLY KUR-AN AND BIBLE (CONTINUED) 15

JULY 28,1956 17

    WHO IS THE ORIGINAL MAN? 17

AUGUST 4, 1956 19

    IF THE CIVILIZED MAN FAILS TO PERFORM HIS DUTY WHAT MUST BE DONE? 19

AUGUST 11, 1956 21

    CIVILIZED MAN FAILS TO PERFORM HIS DUTY WHAT MUST BE DONE? 21

AUGUST 18, 1956 23

    IS THERE A MYSTERY GOD? 23

AUGUST 25, 1956 25

    WHAT IS ISLAM? 25

SEPTEMBER 1, 1956 27

WHAT IS ISLAM?..27

SEPTEMBER 8, 1956...**29**

PRAYER SERVICE OF ISLAM...29

SEPTEMBER 15, 1956...**31**

THE GREAT IS FALLING (Rev. 18:2-4)...31

SEPTEMBER 22, 1956...**32**

COME OUT OF HER, THE GREAT IS FALLING (REV. 18:2-4)...................32

SEPTEMBER 29, 1956...**34**

THE GLORIOUS HOLY QUR-AN SHARRIEFF 34

OCTOBER 6, 1956...**36**

THE HOG AND HIS EATER...36

OCTOBER 13, 1956...**40**

THE HEREAFTER...40

OCTOBER 20, 1956...**42**

THE ONE HUNDRED AND FORTY-FOUR THOUSAND....................42

OCTOBER 27, 1956...**44**

NOVEMBER 3, 1956...**46**

NOVEMBER 10, 1956...**47**

"ISLAM - DIGNIFIES"..47

NOVEMBER 17, 1956...**49**

"THE GRIEVOUSNESS OF WAR"..49

NOVEMBER 24, 1956...**51**

"KNOW THYSELF"...51

DECEMBER 8, 1956..**52**

ISLAM IS FOR THE BLACK MAN..52

DECEMBER 15, 1956..**53**

"IF GOD WAS YOUR FATHER, YOU WOULD LOVE ME" - (JOHN 8:42)......................53

DECEMBER 22, 1956..**54**

THE COMING OF ALLAH (GOD)...54

DECEMBER 29, 1956..**56**

I AM ALLAH THE BEST KNOWER (Holy Quran Sharrieff 32:1) 56

JANUARY 5, 1957...**60**

ANSWER TO MR. R. R. DEROUGEMENT 60

JANUARY 12, 1957 .... **61**

ANSWER TO MR. R. R. DEROUGEMENT (Continued) 61

JANUARY 19, 1957 .... **63**

"CHALLENGE ELDER MCCOY TO PROVE HIS CHARGE OF FALSITY OF MY ARTICLES AND
THE REVELATION OF GOD TO MUHAMMAD." 63

JANUARY 26, 1957 .... **64**

FEBRUARY 2, 1957 .... **65**

"THOSE WHO LIVE IN GLASS HOUSES SHOULDN'T THROW STONES" 65

FEBRUARY 9, 1957 .... **67**

"ISLAM FOR THE AMERICAN SO-CALLED NEGROES" 67

FEBRUARY 16, 1957 .... **68**

ISLAM THE TRUE RELIGION - HOLY QUR'AN 61:9 68

FEBRUARY 23, 1957 .... **70**

ISLAM FOR AMERICAN SO-CALLED NEGROES 70

MARCH 2, 1957 .... **71**

ISLAM FOR THE SO-CALLED NEGRO 71

MARCH 9, 1957 .... **74**

"AND MIX NOT UP THE TRUTH WITH FALSEHOOD, NOR HIDE THE TRUTH WHILE YOU
KNOW." (HOLY QUR-AN 2:42) 74

MARCH 16, 1957 .... **75**

"ISLAM FOR THE SO-CALLED NEGROES OF AMERICA" 75

MARCH 23, 1957 .... **77**

ISLAM FOR THE SO-CALLED NEGROES 77

MARCH 30, 1957 .... **79**

ISLAM FOR THE SO-CALLED NEGROES (Continued) 79

APRIL 6, 1957 .... **81**

"SALVATION FOR THE SO-CALLED NEGROES IN ISLAM" 81

APRIL 13, 1957 .... **83**

AMERICA IS FALLING - HER DOOM IS SEALED 83

APRIL 20, 1957 .... **86**

SALVATION FOR THE SO-CALLED NEGROES IN ISLAM 86

APRIL 27, 1957 .... **88**

"THE SO-CALLED NEGROES' SALVATION IS IN ISLAM, THE ONLY TRUE RELIGION OF GOD"...88

MAY 4, 1957... **90**

"THE SO-CALLED NEGROES' SALVATION IS IN ISLAM - THE TRUE AND ONLY RELIGION OF GOD"...90

MAY 18, 1957 .... **91**

THE AMERICAN SO-CALLED NEGROES' SALVATION IS IN ISLAM, THE ONLY TRUE RELIGION OF GOD 91

JUNE 1, 1957.. **93**

UNITY 93

JUNE 8, 1957.. **95**

SOLUTION FOR THE NEGROES' PROBLEMS 95

JUNE 15, 1957... **97**

JUNE 22, 1957... **99**

SALVATION IS ISLAM 99

JUNE 29, 1957... **101**

"THE BLOOD SHEDDER" (REV. 16:6)... 101

JULY 6, 1957 .... **103**

JULY 13, 1957.. **104**

ISLAM THE TRUE RELIGION, THE SO-CALLED NEGROES' SALVATION AND ETERNAL LIFE. ACCEPT IT AND LIVE.. 104

JULY 20, 1957.. **106**

ISLAM, THE TRUE RELIGION, THE SO-CALLED NEGROES' SALVATION 106

JULY 27, 1957.. **108**

THE HISTORY OF JESUS (CONTINUED)... 108

AUGUST 3, 1957 .... **110**

THE HISTORY OF JESUS (CONTINUED)... 110

AUGUST 10, 1957 .... **112**

JESUS' HISTORY FROM THE MOUTH OF ALLAH (GOD).. 112

AUGUST 17, 1957 .... **114**

JESUS' HISTORY, BIRTH AND DEATH.. 114

AUGUST 24, 1957 .... **116**

JESUS' HISTORY BIRTH AND DEATH – FROM THE MOUTH OF ALLAH(GOD) MARY FLEES TO EGYPT 116

AUGUST 31, 1957 .... **117**

HISTORY OF JESUS' BIRTH AND DEATH 117

SEPTEMBER 7, 1957 .... **119**

JESUS IS KILLED 119

SEPTEMBER 14, 1957 .... **121**

THE MAKING OF A RACE OF DEVILS 121

SEPTEMBER 21, 1957 .... **123**

JESUS' BIRTH AND DEATH 123

SEPTEMBER 28, 1957 .... **125**

RELIGION OF ISLAM: JESUS AND HIS MOTHER A SIGN 125

OCTOBER 5, 1957 .... **128**

THE SO-CALLED NEGROES' SALVATION IS THEIR OWN TRUE RELIGION, ISLAM, UNDER
THE GUIDANCE OF ALLAH (GOD), TO WHOM BE PRAISE FOREVER 128

OCTOBER 12, 1957 .... **129**

OCTOBER 19, 1957 .... **131**

JESUS, A SIGN AND EXAMPLE 131

OCTOBER 26, 1957 .... **133**

CHARACTERISTICS OF A REAL DEVIL 133

NOVEMBER 9, 1957 .... **135**

JESUS' HISTORY MISUNDERSTOOD BY THE CHRISTIANS 135

NOVEMBER 16, 1957 .... **137**

THE COMING AND PRESENCE OF "THE SON OF MAN" 137

NOVEMBER 23, 1957 .... **139**

THE COMING OF THE SON OF MAN - THE GREAT MAHDI 139

NOVEMBER 30, 1957 .... **142**

THE COMING OF THE SON OF MAN: WILL YOU BE THE WINNER? 142

DECEMBER 7, 1957 .... **144**

THE COMING OF THE SON OF MAN - THE INFIDELS (ANTI-CHRISTS) ARE ANGRY 144

DECEMBER 14, 1957 .... **145**

THE COMING OF THE SON OF MAN (THE GREAT MAHDI) AND THE GREAT DECISIVE
BATTLE IN THE SKY 145

DECEMBER 21, 1957 .... **147**

THE GREAT DECISIVE BATTLE IN THE SKY THE SON OF MAN (GOD IN PERSON) AND THE
DEVILS 147

DECEMBER 28, 1957 ....**148**

THE GREAT DECISIVE BATTLE IN THE SKY BETWEEN GOD AND THE DEVILS 148

JANUARY 4, 1958 ....**152**

ISLAM SUBMISSION TO ALLAH (GOD) TO DO HIS WILL 152

JANUARY 11, 1958 ....**153**

ISLAM VERSUS CHRISTIANITY 153

JANUARY 18, 1958 ....**155**

ISLAM - SUBMIT TO ALLAH AND ENTER INTO PEACE 155

JANUARY 25, 1958 ....**158**

CHRISTIANITY VERSUS ISLAM 158

FEBRUARY 1, 1958 ....**160**

ISLAM - SUBMIT TO ALLAH AND ENTER INTO PEACE 160

FEBRUARY 8, 1958 ....**162**

THE PRAYER SERVICE OF ISLAM 162

FEBRUARY 15, 1958 ....**164**

TIMES FOR PRAYER 164

FEBRUARY 22, 1958 ....**166**

PRAYER SERVICE 166

MARCH 1, 1958 ....**168**

THE SIGNIFICANCE OF PRAYER 168

MARCH 8, 1958 ....**170**

MUSLIM PRAYER SERVICE AND ITS MEANINGS 170

MARCH 15, 1958 ....**172**

PRAYER IN ISLAM 172

MARCH 22, 1958 ....**173**

PRAYER IN ISLAM 174

MARCH 29, 1958 ....**175**

THE SO-CALLED NEGROES' SALVATION IS IN THE TRUE RELIGION, ISLAM 175

APRIL 5, 1958 ....**178**

TIME 178

APRIL 12, 1958 ....**179**

TRUTH TO BE PROCLAIMED AT ALL COSTS 179

APRIL 19, 1958...**181**

WE ARE THE SEED OF ABRAHAM REFERRED TO IN THE BIBLE, AND NOT THE ISRAELITES. 181

APRIL 26, 1958...**184**

"YOU MUST ACCEPT ALLAH AND THE TRUE RELIGION OF ISLAM OR SUFFER THE CHASTISEMENT OF ALMIGHTY GOD ALLAH."...184

MAY 3, 1958 ....**185**

THE TRUTH (ISLAM) IS REJECTED BY THE BLACK PREACHERS OF CHRISTIANITY 185

MAY 10, 1958..**187**

MAY 17, 1958..**188**

MAY 24, 1958..**189**

MAY 31, 1958..**191**

WHAT SHALL WE EXPECT TO SEE? A SPIRIT OR A MAN?..191

JUNE 7, 1958..**193**

GOD CAME FROM TEMAN, AND THE HOLY ONE FROM MT. PARAN (HABAKKUK 3:3). IS HE A MAN OR A SPIRIT?...193

JUNE 14, 1958..**194**

GOD CAME FROM TEMAN AND THE HOLY ONE FROM MT. PARAN (HABAKKUK 3:3) 194
IS GOD A SPIRIT OR A MAN?...195

JUNE 21, 1958..**196**

THE ORIGIN OF GOD BEING A SPIRIT AND NOT MAN. 196

JUNE 28, 1958..**198**

WILL AMERICA REPENT? 198

JULY 5, 1958..**200**

THE BIBLE AND HOLY QUR-AN 200

JULY 12, 1958 ....**201**

THE BIBLE AND HOLY QUR-AN 201

JULY 19, 1958 ....**203**

THE BIBLE AND HOLY QUR-AN 203

JULY 26, 1958 ....**204**

THE BIBLE AND HOLY QUR-AN 204

AUGUST 2, 1958..**206**

AUGUST 9, 1958..**208**

WE MUST HAVE SOME OF THIS GOOD EARTH THAT WE CAN CALL OUR OWN! 208

AUGUST 16, 1958 ....**210**

WE MUST HAVE SOME OF THIS GOOD EARTH THAT WE CAN CALL OUR OWN 210

AUGUST 23, 1958...**211**

WILL THE WHITE CHRISTIANS ACCEPT ISLAM? 211

AUGUST 30, 1958...**213**

SEPTEMBER 6, 1958...**215**

SEPARATION SOLVES THE PROBLEM 215

SEPTEMBER 13, 1958...**217**

ROBBED AND SPOILED (ISAIAH 42:22) 217

SEPTEMBER 20, 1958...**218**

ROBBED AND SPOILED (ISAIAH 42:22) 218

SEPTEMBER 27, 1958...**220**

DISAGREEABLE TO LIVE WITH IN PEACE 220

OCTOBER 4, 1958...**222**

CHRISTIANS' DEVIATION FROM THE TRUTH 222

OCTOBER 11, 1958...**224**

WE MUST HAVE A HOME 224

OCTOBER 18, 1958...**225**

THE SO-CALLED NEGRO PREACHERS, WILL THEY ACCEPT ISLAM? 225

OCTOBER 25, 1958...**227**

THE FINAL WAR 227

NOVEMBER 1, 1958..**229**

NOVEMBER 8, 1958..**231**

"WHO IS LIKE UNTO THE BEAST? WHO IS ABLE TO MAKE WAR WITH HIM?" (REV. 13:4) 231

NOVEMBER 15, 1958..**233**

NOVEMBER 22, 1958..**235**

THE DREADFUL AND TERRIBLE BEAST WHO IS ABLE TO MAKE WAR WITH THE BEAST? (DAN. 7:7, REV. 13:4) 235

NOVEMBER 29, 1958..**237**

"THE BEAST" 237

DECEMBER 6, 1958...**240**

DECEMBER 13, 1958...**242**

'THE WOMAN AND THE BEAST' (REV. 17:4) 242

DECEMBER 20, 1958...**244**

GOD ATTACKS THE TERRIBLE BEAST...244

DECEMBER 27, 1958...**246**

GOD ATTACKS THE BEAST 246

JANUARY 3, 1959 ....**249**

THE THIRD ATTACK ON THE BEAST FOR HIS EVIL ATTACKS AGAINST THE RIGHTEOUS
....249

JANUARY 10, 1959...**250**

THE BLOOD SHEDDER (Rev. 16:6) 250

JANUARY 17, 1959...**252**

THE FINAL JUDGMENT OF THE BEAST..252

JANUARY 24, 1959...**253**

THE FINAL JUDGMENT OF THE BEAST..253

JANUARY 31, 1959...**255**

FINAL WAR AGAINST THE BEAST..255

FEBRUARY 7, 1959...**257**

THE FINAL WAR AGAINST THE BEAST, THAT OLD SERPENT, THE DEVIL AND SATAN
(Rev. 18:4)...257

FEBRUARY 14, 1959 ....**259**

BEAST, THAT OLD SERPENT, THE DEVIL AND SATAN (REVELATION 18:4)...........................259

FEBRUARY 21, 1959 ....**261**

THE FINAL WAR AGAINST THE BEAST, THAT OLD SERPENT, THE DEVIL AND SATAN, THE ARCH-
DECEIVER OF BLACK MAN...261

FEBRUARY 28, 1959 ....**263**

"MYSTERY BABYLON, THE GREAT" - (Rev. 17:5) 263

MARCH 7, 1959..**265**

"THE REVELATION'S BEAST" (Rev. 17:8)..265

MARCH 14, 1959 ....**266**

THE REVELATIONS BEAST (Rev. 17:8)...266

MARCH 21, 1959 ....**268**

MARCH 28, 1959 ....**270**

COME OUT OF HER, MY PEOPLE, "THE BEAST, THAT OLD DRAGON, THE HUMAN SERPENT." (Rev. 18:4-
8) 270

APRIL 4, 1959 ....**271**

IF ANY MAN WORSHIP THE BEAST AND HIS IMAGE (Rev. 11:9, 10).......................................271

APRIL 11, 1959 ....**273**

"DIVINE CHASTISEMENT FOR ANY MAN WHO WORSHIPS THE BEAST, THE HUMAN SERPENT" (REV. 14:9 - 10) 273

APRIL 18, 1959 ....**275**

UNIVERSAL CORRUPTION 275

APRIL 25, 1959 ....**276**

COMMON SENSE APPEAL TO UNITE 276

MAY 2, 1959 ....**278**

THE TRUTH HAS COME 278

MAY 9, 1959 ....**280**

BROTHERHOOD OF BLACK MANKIND 280

MAY 16, 1959 ....**281**

THE DEVILS GOING RAMPANT 281

MAY 23, 1959 ....**283**

THE DEVILS INCITE THE HYPOCRITES AND DISBELIEVERS 283

MAY 30, 1959 ....**284**

UNIVERSAL BROTHERHOOD 284

JUNE 6, 1959 ....**286**

THE DANGER OF TAKING ENEMIES FOR FRIENDS 286

JUNE 13, 1959 ....**288**

JUSTICE 288

JUNE 20, 1959 ....**290**

THE SO-CALLED NEGROES OF AMERICA 290

JUNE 27, 1959 ....**292**

THE WHITE RACE'S FALSE CLAIM OF DIVINITY 292

JULY 4, 1959 ....**294**

THE WHITE MAN'S CLAIM TO DIVINE SUPERIORITY 294

JULY 11, 1959 ....**295**

THE WHITE RACE'S FALSE CLAIM TO BE DIVINE CHOSEN PEOPLE 295

JULY 18, 1959 ....**297**

THE WHITE RACE'S CLAIM TO DIVINITY 297

JULY 25, 1959 ....**299**

THE WHITE RACE'S FALSE CLAIM TO DIVINITY 299

AUGUST 1, 1959 300

FOR WHERESOEVER THE CARCASS IS, THERE WILL THE EAGLES BE GATHERED TOGETHER. (MATT. 24:28)
.... 300

AUGUST 8, 1959 302

THE ST. NICHOLAS ARENA NEW YORK CITY 302

AUGUST 15, 1959 304

TRUTH AND JUSTICE FOR THE SO-CALLED NEGROES.. 304

AUGUST 22, 1959 306

JUSTICE FOR THE AMERICAN SO-CALLED NEGROES.. 306

APPENDIX 308

THE IMPACT OF THE MOST HONORABLE ELIJAH MUHAMMAD AND THE NATION OF ISLAM 308

ACKNOWLEDGEMENTS.. 355

BIBLIOGRAPHY 358

INDEX 361

It is my desire that this volume of magnificent articles written by the Most Honorable Elijah Muhammad will help to re-introduce him as the great man that he is, one who is worthy of respect, admiration and love. In this way, this volume can be considered as complementary to the work of the Honorable Minister Louis Farrakhan whose tour de force ministry has put the Most Honorable Elijah Muhammad and his teachings on the hearts and minds of men and women around the globe. Both men have been so terribly maligned by the mainstream media and many in the academic world. There are many, particularly those who are dubbed the millennial generation, who really don't know who the Honorable Elijah Muhammad is. And they are woefully ignorant of the enormous good that he produced and is producing among Black people that also positively impacts American society as a whole. I am personally offended by this grievous treatment of the Most Honorable Elijah Muhammad and Minister Farrakhan. I consider it to be unacceptable that such wonderful leaders, teachers and guides have to suffer being marginalized and evil spoken of.

Every year during February-Black History Month I am reminded of the deliberate plan at work to hide the Most Honorable Elijah Muhammad. During this month where many great luminaries, revolutionaries and accomplished Black men and women are remembered and celebrated, one man is skillfully omitted-the Most Honorable Elijah Muhammad. He is hidden from the masses while academics and historians crucify his reputation on the pages of academic journals and history textbooks.

As someone who's religious, cultural and moral awakening is as a result of the teachings of the Most Honorable Elijah Muhammad, his mishandling, and the abuse given to his name, is not something I can ignore. I am compelled therefore to fight against this kind of injustice. In some of his commentary on the Biblical scripture, the Most Honorable Elijah Muhammad identifies the constituent categories of knowledge and component parts of scripture to be

> "histories, predictions, stories of rulers, people and nations, poems, parables, rules and laws."(Message To The Blackman p.89)

Scripture therefore, containing such a critical and broad range of content, becomes the perfect lens through which to view the world in which we live. And its historical and predictive portraits of the ancient prophets and their enemies serves as a perfect model for the phenomena surrounding the life and work of the Most Honorable Elijah Muhammad. In the pages of the Bible and the Holy Qur'an, the desire of the enemies of the prophets and messengers of God was to get rid of them. They wanted to kill the Prophets, and many of them they did kill. Yet prior to the actual physical assassination, these enemies found it necessary to perform a thorough character assassination first. So the omission of the Most Honorable Elijah Muhammad and the falsifying of his reputation are two main aspects of the overall wicked strategy to eliminate him and to destroy any interest in his message.

Such assassination of the character of the Messengers and Prophets of God is what gave rise to the verses or ayats in the 68th Surah of the Holy Quran which read:

> (By) the inkstand and the pen and that which they write! By the grace of thy Lord thou art not mad. And surely thine is a reward never to be cut off. And surely thou hast sublime morals. (Holy Qur'an 68: 1-4)

In this passage from the Holy Qur'an, Allah (God) Himself defends His messengers against their enemies. Close reading of this verse/ayat reveals that this is a dual defense. Allah defends the prophets against the criticism of their being nothing more than "mad men" going about the land spouting hate-filled false teachings. And He also defends them against the charge of being immoral.

This verse/ayat of the Holy Qur'an is a part of Allah's (God's) response to the enemy's strategy known as "Smite the Shepherd, Scatter the Flock."

Jesus in the New Testament of the Bible introduces this strategy in the book of Mark:

> And Jesus saith unto them, All ye shall be offended because of me this night: for it is written, I will smite the shepherd, and the sheep shall be scattered.-Mark 14:27

This strategy has involved the character assassination and the physical assassination of the Prophets and Messengers of Allah (God) as well those revolutionary leaders who are, in truth, also special servants of Allah (God) worthy of honorable mention right after the Prophets and Messengers. Some might not agree that the revolutionary leaders, who are found among the oppressed peoples of the world, are special servants of Allah (God). But I would argue that it is a mistake to consider those who labored, suffered and died to alleviate their people's suffering as a purely secular group. We have been blessed to have many of these types of men and women during the Black man and woman's 400 plus years of sojourn in the "hells of North America." What supports my belief in the inherent nobility and even the divinity of revolutionary leaders comes from a verse of scripture in the Holy Qur'an that I first heard Minister Farrakhan cite many years ago.

> So they put them to flight by Allah's permission. And David slew Goliath, and Allah gave him kingdom and wisdom, and taught him of what He pleased. **And were it not for Allah's repelling some men by others, the earth would certainly be in a state of disorder**: but Allah is Full of grace to the worlds. Holy Qur'an 2:251

This verse clearly says that it is Allah (God) whom we are to attribute as producing "men to repel men." When viewed like this, it is easy to see such men as manifestations of Allah (God) in his attribute of justice (al-Muqsit). They are actors being animated by Allah's (God's) intention to fill the earth with justice just as it had prior to been filled with injustice. Injustice in the form of slavery, colonialism and imperialism served as the environmental conditions that birthed for our benefit strong Black revolutionary leaders like Marcus Garvey, Dr. Martin Luther King Jr., Paul Robeson, Malcolm X and many others.

The Honorable Elijah Muhammad and his work of repelling injustice is similar in nature to these other great and worthy leaders. He and his student – the Honorable Minister Louis Farrakhan-differ however in that both men are both messengers of Allah (God) along with being at the same time revolutionary leaders. It is in their person and in their teachings where we find the harmonious and beautiful synergy of the "secular" and the "sacred" paths to revolutionary change. In them converge the prophets and revolutionaries in the same way merging streams converge into a mighty river.

In today's world both the prophets and the revolutionary leaders are subject to the Smite the Shepherd Strategy. Popular writer Robert Greene, author of *48 Laws of Power*, writes in his book the following:

> One resolute person, one disobedient spirit, can turn a flock of sheep into a den of lions...Do not waste your time lashing out in all directions at what seems to be a many-headed enemy. Find the one head that matters-the person with the willpower, or smarts, or, most important of all, charisma. Whatever it costs you, lure this person away, for once he is absent his powers will lose their effect. His isolation can be physical (banishment or absence from the court), political (narrowing his base of support), or psychological (alienating him from the group through slander and insinuation). Finally, the reason you strike at the shepherd is because such an action will dishearten the sheep beyond any rational measure."-Robert Greene, 48 Laws of Power

The Smite the Shepherd strategy is aimed at keeping Black people in America from arriving at their true destiny. Scripture, when rightly interpreted, powerfully communicates that the ultimate destiny of the Black man and woman of America is to become a righteous nation- a holy nation of priestly people. We are to be as Joseph was in the Bible wherein he became the ruler in the land that he was once sold as a slave.

To arrive at this destiny, Allah (God) has furnished us with great examples and great leaders-great shepherds. But today, ugly narratives have been attached to the "shepherds of Black sheep." And the masses are left to scatter and wander in the veritable wilderness of America. It has been a wickedly effective strategy. This strategy has branded Marcus Garvey as a lawless and fraudulent con-man; Dr. King as an adulterer; Booker T. Washington as an Uncle Tom and Malcolm X as a bi-sexual.

The character assassinations carried out against the great heroes and heroines of our struggle in America have the effect of de-magnetizing them and causing Black people to look upon them with a jaundiced eye. In the case of the Most Honorable Elijah Muhammad he is not only hidden and omitted from the Black History conversation, but is also falsely accused of killing Malcolm X and being the anti-white Black supremacist leader of the Nation of Islam.

Imam Mikal Saahir discusses how historians have ill-treated the Most Honorable Elijah Muhammad in his wonderful book entitled The Man Behind the Men: The Most Honorable Elijah Muhammad. He argues that:

> The dismissal of the contributions of Elijah Muhammad seems to be a conscious effort even amongst many African American historians. He was a contemporary of Dr. Martin Luther King Jr., but when African American history writers compare the Civil Rights Movement with the Nation of Islam, Malcolm X is juxtaposed with Dr. King in place of Elijah Muhammad. The minimizing of Elijah Muhammad's role in Black History and the lifting up of Malcolm X above him is thievery. How much longer will his positive contributions be overlooked? When will Elijah Muhammad be properly rewarded in history for his labors with the poor and rejected Black man and woman of America?

Again, this mistreatment of the Most Honorable Elijah Muhammad is unacceptable.

Imam Mikal Saahir discusses an interview with former Nation of Islam member and Native American health professional Diane Williams about how this mistreatment of the NOI leader effects students of the Honorable Elijah Muhammad whose vocations place them in professional circles.

Diane hopes that one day Elijah Muhammad will get the credit he deserves. Very much aware of how the current world of professionalism operates and the reality that most in the professional world are unfamiliar with the excellent work achieved by Elijah Muhammad, Diane acknowledges that the name "Elijah Muhammad is still a dirty word and dirty name." In the professional world and other sectors of society, there still exists an inaccurate perception of Elijah Muhammad that Diane Williams believes makes it difficult for many former Nation of Islam members to receive the "understanding and respect for the time that we spent in the Nation." She further explained, "In other words, it's not something you put on your resume in the professional world. I'm just saying it like I see it..."

Special Appendix

So this volume of articles written by the Most Honorable Elijah Muhammad in the Pittsburgh Courier Newspaper includes within its pages a powerful appendix made up of a never before seen compilation of accolades, honors, tributes and testimonies that document just some of the tremendous impact of the Most Honorable Elijah Muhammad.

The broad cross-section of persons quoted will show the staggering gulf between the false propaganda that for too many is the only available narrative with which to view the Most Honorable Elijah Muhammad and the truth of his enormous impact on the most well-respected, prominent and legendary men and women in America and around the world. We intend with this section to clear the Most Honorable Elijah Muhammad of the false charges of his enemies; enemies which are really the enemies of all Blacks in America. We pray that this section will serve to ameliorate the hearts of those who believe in the Honorable Elijah Muhammad. This section will educate all in properly understanding the scope and depth of his impact throughout America and the world. Such an education is quite strengthening for the believer.

We also want the young of the millennial generation to read this section and ponder questions such as "Why have I not been told about this man before?" And "why has what I have been told about Mr. Muhammad been so negative?"

And, "could he really be the evil man that I have heard of while at the same time be honored, admired and emulated by those whom I respect and look up to?"

It is our hope that the special appendix section will be of value to persons such as Diane Williams and really what she represents of the hidden students of the Honorable Elijah Muhammad. There are many who are like her. They are situated in diverse fields and professions, most occupying a place of eminence as a result of their professional excellence. These are they who will privately acknowledge as did Diane Williams that

> "I know what I know not because of anything U.C. Berkeley (University of California Berkeley) taught me, but because I learned what I learned in the Nation of Islam. I learned it from the sisters who learned it, basically, from Elijah Muhammad- and it worked!"

But due to the public perception of the Honorable Elijah Muhammad, they would rather keep their being a student of his a private matter. I would hope that they too would enjoy this section and strengthened by its contents.

May Allah bless the reader with joy, peace and happiness-all of which are beneficial effects of becoming a student of the teachings of the Most Honorable Elijah Muhammad.

In presenting the Pittsburgh Courier articles of the Most Honorable Elijah Muhammad it is helpful to offer the reader some background information on the history and value of the Pittsburgh Courier Newspaper and its relationship with the Most Honorable Elijah Muhammad.

The Pittsburgh Courier began in 1907 in Pittsburgh, Pennsylvania and was printed through 1965. It was began by Edwin Nathaniel Harleston who worked as a security guard for Heinz food packing plant. He was succeeded in ownership by Attorney Robert Vann. Author Andrew Buni writes of Van that,

> Under his leadership, The Courier developed into one of the leading black newspapers of this era. By the 1930s it was one of the highest circulated black newspapers in the United States. As many as 14 different editions were circulated throughout the country. (Buni, 1974)

After Vann passed in 1940 he was succeeded by Ira Lewis. Under Lewis the paper reached its largest circulation of 350,000 per week. Ira Lewis, who had worked for the paper since 1914 passed away in 1948 and the paper was sold to John Sengstacke who also owned the Chicago Defender newspaper.

Historically, The Pittsburgh Courier has been a newspaper that not only offered news and information about Black people, it was also an activist organ that championed the causes of Black people and our collective struggle. As an example, writer James Jaap describes the Pittsburgh Courier's partnership with A. Philip Randolph and the Brotherhood of Sleeping Car Porters.

> The Courier was smuggled throughout the South by a network of black Pullman car porters, who would hide the paper in the floors of railroad cars and drop off approximately 100,000 copies each week outside of every major Southern city. (Jaap, 2015)

Over its long history the Pittsburgh Courier took strong stances with respect to the major issues affecting the Black community. In the 1930s, the Pittsburgh Courier joined the campaign against the radio program Amos n'

Andy to protest its portrayal of negative Black stereotypes. During this time PC writers also strongly criticized Republican President Herbert Hoover for not doing more to end the depression. Other news campaigns executed by the Pittsburgh Courier included the fight for Black military servicemen who fought in World War II. Blacks in the armed forces were fighting for the freedom and liberation of foreign nations and afterwards returning home to America and getting denied the very freedoms their blood, sweat and tears had just secured for America's allies. This campaign was known as the "Double V" campaign and was one of its most popular campaigns. The "Double V" within the campaigns title was a symbol for America's need to win victory at home against racism and anti-black discrimination just like it won victory abroad in foreign wars for "democracy." The activist nature of the paper was also on display in the writings of sports writer Wendell Smith. Writer David Kenneth Wiggins writes on the significance of Smith's role in Jackie Robinson's integration into Major League Baseball:

> Wendell Smith, who became the paper's sportswriter in 1938, used his column to denounce segregation in the major leagues. His efforts contributed to Jackie Robinson's signing with the Brooklyn Dodgers in 1947. In the early years of Robinson's baseball career, Smith traveled and roomed with Robinson on several Dodger trips, and arranged his travel and housing itinerary, because in some cities Robinson could not stay with the rest of the team in segregated hotels. (Wiggins, 1983)

Professor James Jaap continues in his history of the Pittsburgh Courier on the legendary giants of the Black struggle who helped the Courier maintain a strong activist posture and tone:

> To present these controversial stances, the Pittsburgh Courier employed many of the leading African American writers and intellectuals as columnists. George Schuyler, author of the satirical novel Black No More, was the Courier's leading editorialist and one of its most popular columnists. He joined the staff in 1925 and wrote a weekly column, "Views and Reviews." Late in 1925, Schuyler began on a nine-month tour of the South and wrote a series of columns he called "Aframerica Today." Other prominent African American figures who contributed materials to the Courier include Joel A. Rogers, Marcus Garvey, W. E. B.

Du Bois, Zora Neale Hurston, and Elijah Muhammad. Rogers, a prominent African American journalist and historian, became the first African American war correspondent in U.S. history and wrote a regular column that focused on African American history. Marcus Garvey contributed a serialized autobiographical column beginning on February 15, 1930. In 1936, Du Bois, after his resignation from the National Association for the Advancement of Colored People (NAACP) and The Crisis in 1934, wrote to Robert Vann stating his desire to publish a column of his observations. Du Bois's weekly column, "A Forum of Fact and Opinion," ran from February 8, 1936, to January 23, 1938, and covered a wide range of topics, from politics to Europe to African American history. Du Bois also traveled to Berlin to cover the 1936 Olympic Games for the Courier. In 1952, Zora Neale Hurston was hired by the Courier to cover the trial of Ruby McCollum, a wealthy, married African American woman who murdered her lover, Dr. C. Leroy Adams. (Jaap, 2015)

The Most Honorable Elijah Muhammad had a regular weekly article in the Pittsburgh Courier from June 9, 1956 through August 22, 1959. This collection of articles exists as his first major body of writings and teachings to the masses of Black people in America. Various ones of these articles appeared in books that were later published by the Nation of Islam, namely Message to the Blackman in America; The Fall of America; Our Saviour Has Arrived and How To Eat To Live I and II. But this collection of his Pittsburgh Courier articles has never been published as a stand-alone collection of articles.

The relationship between the Nation of Islam and the Pittsburgh Courier can best be described as mutually beneficial. According to Nigerian born University of Chicago Professor Essein Udom,

> The relationship was beneficial to both parties, for in 1958 followers of Muhammad sold 1,164,110 copies of the Courier and realized a total of $23,282.20 in commissions at two cents per copy. Until the severance of relationship between the Pittsburgh Courier publishers and Muhammad, the paper sold for 15 cents. The company received thirteen cents per copy. On this basis, it grossed $151,334.30 in 1958 from sales which were made by the Muslims. (Udom, Chicago)

In fact the Most Honorable Elijah Muhammad and his followers proved to be a great asset to the Black press throughout the country. He published his profound writings in the Pittsburgh Courier and other African-American Newspapers of that time period. Some of which include the Los Angeles Herald Dispatch, the Chicago New Crusader and the New York Amsterdam News. Former Muhammad Speaks editor John Woodford described how Mr. Muhammad impacted the very survival of many struggling Black papers with his popular articles and the sales force comprised of the men and the women of the Nation of Islam.

> Malcolm had written a column for the Amsterdam News, following a precedent set by Mr. Muhammad himself, who had published a column from time to time in many African American newspapers for the previous dozen or so years. (Black newspaper publishers found their circulations rose dramatically when the Messenger's column ran, because Muslims bought all available copies and resold them, at no markup, to disseminate their faith. Mr. Muhammad probably saved or prolonged the life of many a Black newspaper, although White advertisers and politicos occasionally succeeded in intimidating the Black publishers into dropping the column because of its vilification of "the Devil.") (Woodford, 2014)

In the case of the Pittsburgh Courier, which was the longest and most significant of these types of relationships, the Honorable Elijah Muhammad's articles were considered indispensable. In 1957 circulation manager A.D. Gaither gave the Most Honorable Elijah Muhammad the Courier Achievement Award for the matchless benefit he brought about in the sales, distribution and profit of the Pittsburgh Courier. In describing how important the Mr. Muhammad Speaks column was for the Pittsburgh Courier (PC), former PC staff writer Nadine Brown said:

> I can remember the Messenger's column, it was really great. When I look at what's happening today and I remember what the Messenger was saying in those days, then I know what a wise man he is. Without a doubt, his column was the best thing that ever happened to the Courier. (Mosby, 1974)

Ms. Brown's experience proves that the Most Honorable Elijah Muhammad's impact was not purely financial in nature. She clearly sees what we would consider to be the Honorable Elijah Muhammad's intended impact, which was to impart knowledge, wisdom and guidance to the PC readers that would empower them and assist them in escaping the dangerous days ahead in America's future. While newspapers, as a rule, report on events and on goings that have already happened, the articles of the Most Honorable Elijah Muhammad gave the Pittsburgh Courier predictive capabilities. In other words, readers of the Mr. Muhammad Speaks articles were not just reading about events and occurrences that already happened, they were reading about the things that would take place in the future. The Mr. Muhammad Speaks articles were therefore enabling its readers to have foreknowledge of the critical, important and sometimes dangerous events taking place in the world long in advance of those events actually happening! Ms. Brown's delightful commentary on the predictive value of the Messenger's writings call to mind the Holy Quran's Surah 25 ayat 27 that includes the reaction of those who did not follow the Messenger after it had become manifestly clear that all that he forewarned about had come to pass.

> And on the day when the wrongdoer will bite his hands, saying: Would that I had taken a way with the Messenger!

Controversy Over Elijah Muhammad's Articles
With such a positive impact on the Pittsburgh Courier, it is intriguing and rather sad that this relationship was severed as a result of external pressure on the PC from the white community. In a letter dated April 10, 1961 J.B. Stoner, Arch leader of the Christian Knights of the Ku Klux Klan wrote to the Most Honorable Elijah Muhammad the following threats.

> I pressured the Pittsburgh Courier into dropping your weekly column and I forced them to fire their managing editor for being too friendly to you. I have hired many niggers to put pressure on The Chicago Defender, The Afro-American and other nigger papers to expose you and scare Christian darkies away from you Muslims.

Professor Udom's research into the Nation of Islam does not cite Stoner as the root cause for the Pittsburgh Courier ending its immensely beneficial relationship with the Most Honorable Elijah Muhammad. But he does document that outside pressure from the White community drove the decision to end the Mr. Muhammad Speaks weekly column. From a September 5, 1959 Pittsburgh Courier article written by Pittsburgh NAACP branch executive secretary Derrick Bell, Professor Udom records the following:

> In the time since the Muslim group has been brought to the nation's attention, the local NAACP office has been advised by several sincere individuals that we must denounce the Muslims in non-uncertain terms...They advised full-page ads in local newspapers, and some even offered money to help underwrite the project. They further urged that The Pittsburgh Courier, which each week publishes a column by the Muslim leader, Muhammad, be condemned for this action, and that we use our influence to get the column removed. (Udom, Black Nationalism: A Search For An Identity In America, 1962)

Professor Udom is bold in his analysis of the shortcomings of many Black newspapers in their handling of the Most Honorable Elijah Muhammad. And what he describes is consistent with the fear of loss that evil forces have historically used to threaten those who show courage in embracing the Prophets, Messengers and Revolutionaries. Professor Udom writes:

> Most Negro newspapers have acted with duplicity and opportunism regarding Muhammad's movement. So long as Muhammad had not become a nationally controversial figure, the Negro press supported implicitly a growing opinion which Muhammad represented in his "Messages." They denied, however, any responsibility for opinions expressed by Muhammad; acting from the "highest of motives," they hoped nevertheless to increase circulation of their papers by "going along" with him. The Pittsburgh Courier, which has consistently opposed the "Buy Black" campaign in New York, went along with Muhammad for nearly four years, and it was not until the white press "exposed" him, that it severed the relationship. There is no question that it was actually pressured into doing so. (Udom, Black Nationalism: A Search For An Identity In America, 1962)

That many in the white community would threaten Black newspapers for their relationship with the Most Honorable Elijah Muhammad fit perfectly with the characteristics ascribed to the devil in scripture. For the Holy Qur'an says of the devil in Surah 2 Ayat 268 that,

> The devil threatens you with poverty and enjoins you to be niggardly, and Allah promises you forgiveness from Himself and abundance. And Allah is Ample-giving, Knowing

We should recognize that noted scholar and author C. Eric Lincoln discussed the positive impact of the Most Honorable Elijah Muhammad on the Pittsburgh Courier's sales and revenue. According to his book *The Black Muslims in America*, Dr. Lincoln writes:

> For several years, Muhammad's column in the Pittsburgh Courier attracted wide attention among Negroes and stirred a lively debate between those who supported his views and those who were indignant that he was granted space in the paper. During his tenure as a Courier columnist, no other single writer drew as many letters to the editor; and the newspaper, which had been steadily losing readers, suddenly found its circulation increasing. This was partially due to the fact that the Muslims took to the street corners and the housing projects to hawk the papers each brother being assigned a quota.

Professor Lincoln's work also gives the Pittsburgh Courier credit for pushing back and defending the Most Honorable Elijah Muhammad against his critics. On page 142 of *The Black Muslims In America*, Professor Lincoln writes:

> The Courier's editors and columnists also came frequently to the Muslims' defense. For example, George S. Schuyler, New York editor of the Courier and one of the most widely read Negro journalists in the world, wrote in his column, "Views and Reviews":
> "The recent uproar over Mr. Muhammad's movement . . . seems to me to be quite superficial. . . . There is no point in inveighing against Mr. Muhammad's followers as anti-white when the whole climate surrounding them is anti-black. . . . Mr. Muhammad may be a rogue and a charlatan, but when anybody can get tens of thousands of Negroes to practice economic solidarity, respect their women, alter their atrocious diet, give up liquor, stop crime, juvenile delinquency and adultery, he

is doing more for the Negro's welfare than any current Negro leader I know."

In October 1959, the Courier took Time magazine to task for "flippancy" in its treatment of the facts in an expose of Muhammad. The Courier said editorially:

"Time magazine ... is relentless in its frenetic search for le bon mot. It seems frequently more interested in the good word than in the good reputation. If it can get its writers to turn a good, or bad, phrase, so long as it "clicks," Time's editors do not seem to be concerned. They have the same penchant for "facts" unadorned or unexplained."

The Courier was complaining about Time's unamplified reference to Elijah Muhammad's arrest on a charge of contributing to the delinquency of a minor in 1934 and to Time's assertion that the Muslim leader was jailed for draft-dodging in 1941. The Courier editorial pointed out that the charge of contributing to the delinquency of a minor" was brought against Muhammad for refusing to withdraw his children from the sect's parochial school and send them to public schools. With reference to Muhammad's alleged draft-dodging, the Courier pointed out that Muhammad was forty-five years old in 1941 and, therefore, ineligible for the draft. It did not offer the further clarification that Muhammad was jailed for exhorting his followers not to register for the draft.

Ultimately the severance of the relationship with the Pittsburgh Courier was a bittersweet episode in the Nation of Islam's history. It was bitter that such a mutually beneficial relationship had to end due to pressure from the very same community that enslaved Black people in America. And in this case of exercising such gross paternalistic fear based control of the potential power of the minds, hearts and pens of Black writers and publishers it is especially bitter for all Black people. It reminds me of a quote from the great freedom fighter David Walker who in his Appeal postulated over the value of future Black writers and historians.

"When the Lord shall raise up coloured historians in succeeding generations, to present the crimes of this nation, to the then gazing world, the Holy Ghost will make them do justice..." (Walker, 1829)

Might the real fear of the Mr. Muhammad Speaks articles lie in the nature of these articles to serve as a herald of the long awaited and much anticipated scripture's "Day of Justice"? It is certainly the opinion of this writer that these fears are the familiar fears of those who sow the seeds of evil who fear the season of reaping of the harvest that they have sown.

The end of this relationship with the Pittsburgh Courier is sweet because as many great evangelists have preached, "with God, a setback is a setup for a comeback." In the case of the Nation's work of the publishing and distribution of Muhammad's Message, this particular setback was the setup for the Nation to comeback with its own publication; its own newspaper. So in October of 1961, Mr. Muhammad Speaks became no longer the title of an article or column in a newspaper owned by others. It became the title of the Nation of Islam's own newspaper.

When we say that this was a mutually beneficial relationship we mean exactly what we have discussed thus far. The benefit to the Nation of Islam was to get the message of the Most Honorable Elijah Muhammad before the readers of Black/Negro newspapers that had an established readership and trusted reputation. There was also a small sum of financial consideration produced by commissions earned from the tremendous volume of sales produced by the brothers and sisters of the Nation of Islam. The Pittsburgh Courier benefitted by an increase in sales revenue, profit and by being plugged into a broad distribution network comprised of all cities where Nation of Islam mosques existed. As already discussed, the benefit that the Most Honorable Elijah Muhammad and the Nation of Islam brought to the Pittsburgh Courier was indispensable. Determining from the available literature on the history of the Pittsburgh Courier, we conclude that without the Mr. Muhammad Speaks articles, the Pittsburgh Courier would not have been as widely circulated, as widely read and possibly would have gone out of business.

But there remains one critically important benefit that the Nation of Islam received from its relationship with the Pittsburgh Courier that I would like to explore and document.

That extra special benefit that the Nation of Islam received which has also been an equally beneficial blessing and benefit to millions of people throughout the world is the profoundly inspiring and soul-stirring ministry of the Honorable Minister Louis Farrakhan.

The Pittsburgh Courier articles written by the Most Honorable Elijah Muhammad gave to us the magnificent ministry of the Honorable Minister Louis Farrakhan. What I mean by this, has to do with words to me from the Minister on how important these articles were to him in his development as a young Minister in the Nation of Islam.

In December of 2010, I was blessed to ask the Honorable Minister Louis Farrakhan about the Pittsburgh Courier Articles during a meeting with him and a group of us that he had assembled earlier in the year to serve as his research team. This meeting was held on December 28, 2010 at the National House in Chicago.

Prior to that meeting, and beginning sometime during the spring of 2009, I was asked by Student Minister Anthony Muhammad of Muhammad's Mosque No. 55 in Memphis Tennessee to locate for him several articles written by the Most Honorable Elijah Muhammad. Specifically he wanted a series of articles that had been referenced by Minister Jabril Muhammad in his column in The Final Call Newspaper. At that time in one of Minister Jabril's weekly articles called Farrakhan: The Traveler, he made reference to a 22 article series written by the Most Honorable Elijah Muhammad on the subject of Jesus. The article series had been published in The Pittsburgh Courier newspaper.

As an assistant to Minister Anthony, I often tracked down research materials that he wanted to use in the preparation of his lectures. This time was no different and I began to search for the requested series of articles.

After finding this series of articles, I was pleased to read them for myself and to be able to give them to Brother Minister Anthony. And even though I had read all of the books written by the Most Honorable Elijah Muhammad, there was information contained in these articles that I had not read before. I wondered at that point, what all I had been missing. I wondered what else of the matchless wisdom of the Most Honorable Elijah Muhammad awaited me if I could read and study every article that he wrote in the Pittsburgh Courier.

This was the beginning of my relationship with the Pittsburgh Courier articles written by the Most Honorable Elijah Muhammad. The more I read these articles and studied them, I felt that they should all be compiled and published.

During that December 28, 2010 meeting I expressed to the Minister my desire to compile the Pittsburgh Courier articles into a book. He looked at me joyously and he shared with me these words.

> "So here's a work. I'd like to see it completed, because it is a great study. I'm telling you that I fed from those articles, I read nothing else. I'm not a book reader[per se], I'm an Elijah Muhammad student. That's the God's truth. You can't give me, I got books everywhere now. Ask me how many of them I read. But my father I read Him and where he guides me, that's where I go. You see. It looks like I read all the books, but in reality He's the book that I read. And He is the only book that I really desire to read from. I read that book (The Secret Relationship Between Blacks and Jews) and I read companion things you know. I read every one of those articles, they are my base, my root. But I want to see what he has in mind. That's going to be a heck of a book!"

Thus began a project that has taken 4 years and 2 months to complete. I have approached the handling of the precious words of the Most Honorable Elijah Muhammad with fear and trepidation. This is because I am a believer in the teachings of the Most Honorable Elijah Muhammad. And I see his words as words from Allah (God) coming through him for the benefit of the suffering masses of our people. Through my study of his words and the matchless representation of his teachings provided by the Honorable Minister Louis Farrakhan I have grown to believe in him as Allah's Messenger-Messiah. I see him more and more as the fulfillment of the prophecies regarding the exalted Christ of the Bible.

My fear was borne out of the awe and reverence for the Most Honorable Elijah Muhammad, and not seeing myself as worthy for such a task as to handle and compile the words of a man who looms so large in my mind- one whom Allah(God) raised from among us to be His Messenger –Messiah to the world. My fear was also of not wanting to make a mistake in the work that would need to be done of re-typing his words for the purpose of publishing them all together as a collection in book form. During this period of time there were periods where my fear would not allow me to make too much progress. And there were alternating periods of time when I could get quite a bit done. After prayer and reflection on the task at hand, I decided to put together a team of skilled believers to help me accomplish this assignment. Their collective work was invaluable to me in helping to bring this work to fruition. Their names appear in the acknowledgements section of this volume. I am grateful and thankful to them all for their work and sacrifice. As the completion of this project nears, I have also come to appreciate the fact that Allah (God) decreed that it take this long to come to fruition. For had I completed it earlier, there is much of what is included of supporting material and contextual histories that I would not have been able to provide. The compilation of the testimonies, quotes and commendations received by the Most Honorable Elijah Muhammad was only recently compiled and made ready in the first and second month of 2015. I also would not have been able to provide the direct commentary from the Honorable Minister Louis Farrakhan that we now present in this part of our preface.

The more I reflected on the Minister's words to me, I began to see these articles as being much more valuable than I had previously understood. I began to see that these articles constituted what would become the ministerial training or seminary education for a man that has become the greatest student that the Most Honorable Elijah Muhammad ever produced, which has resulted in him being the most popular speaker, teacher and leader that Black Americans have ever had!

Minister Farrakhan as Honorable Elijah Muhammad's Greatest Student
First of all to say that the Minister is the greatest student of the Most Honorable Elijah Muhammad should not be considered as hyperbole on my part. I mean I love the Minister. He is the father of my consciousness and he is a man that I adore. I see him as an illuminated figure who is being raised by the one true God

Allah that I believe in and submit to. And I fall more and more in love with Minister Farrakhan the more I study him and seek to carry into practice the principles that he both teaches and represents. But my love for him has nothing to do with my identification of him as the Most Honorable Elijah Muhammad's greatest student. That declaration, that some might consider bold or in error, has the necessary actual facts to back it up.

I have taken it as my work and mission to, out of my passion and love, commence to research for the purpose of defending the Minister against the propaganda of his and our enemies. Within all that I have been blessed to compiled, we have provided in our articles, books and lectures rich amounts of both qualitative and quantitative data to support the Minister's venerable name and person. I am not going to go through all of that in this space. I do however feel it vitally necessary to compile just some of what is available in the form of direct quotes wherein the Honorable Elijah Muhammad himself, identified the Minister's value to him.

It is helpful to share the following passage from an article written by Minister Jabril Muhammad from his *Farrakhan: The Traveler* article entitled *Learning How to Learn* dated June 29, 2006. He describes with authoritative detail the Most Honorable Elijah Muhammad's expectation that Allah (God) would send to him a "special helper." Minister Jabril is one who spent 6 years living with the Most Honorable Elijah Muhammad in his home. He has always emphasized the great value that awaits the students of the Honorable Minister Louis Farrakhan if we delve deeper into the teachings and writings of the Most Honorable Elijah Muhammad.

> The Honorable Elijah Muhammad sought a helper from God to assist him with major aspects of his assignment. His brother Charlie was the first one he thought would be that helper. I know that because I heard him say that. He said that they were very close.
>
> It's a fact that by the time 1954 came around he knew that the time was close when he would meet that special helper and start his preparation, with Allah's help.
>
> Consider his words when he delivered his Savior's Day address (as it was then called) in February 1954. At one point he stated: "We have been so greatly misunderstood that I desire that Allah send to me a little helper."

Master Fard Muhammad sent Minister Farrakhan to the Honorable Elijah Muhammad the next year; on Saviour's Day.

Captain Yusuf Shah told me, in the course of a four-hour interview I conducted of him in June of 1971 in New York City, that Brother Malcolm told him where and how to help position Minister Farrakhan on February 26, 1955, so the Honorable Elijah Muhammad could recognize him, in the physical sense of the word. Brother Malcolm had already informed the Honorable Elijah Muhammad of the impressions that Minister Farrakhan had made on him.

The Honorable Elijah Muhammad saw through Brother Malcolm's words of the Brother to that which Brother Malcolm did not see. It was the seating arrangement that would enable the Honorable Elijah Muhammad to see what his future "helper" physically looked like.

Throughout the years of the close teacher-student relationship between the Most Honorable Elijah Muhammad and the Honorable Minister Louis Farrakhan, there are several statements and declarations made by the Honorable Elijah Muhammad that we now cite for the benefit of the reader.

Elijah Muhammad Says, Farrakhan Is Best Helper
Allah couldn't have given me a better helper... They can't help but to follow a man like that! Got the whole big city New York all stirred up!...

If I was all the other Ministers, I'd take pattern [after him]. Like the Disciples did Paul. Paul was one of the greatest preachers the Disciples had. Well, he wasn't one of the Disciples, but he came up and beat all the other disciples...

Source: Sultan R. Muhammad, Table Talks of the Honorable Elijah Muhammad - The Transcripts: Volume One, Second, ed. Table Talks Project Editorial Board (Chicago, IL: MUI Press, 2013).

Elijah Muhammad Says, Farrakhan Puts Everything In Its Proper Place
The Hon Elijah Muhammad (THEM): "Well, my Brother Minister [Farrakhan], you've got-a lot-of-things lined up in the right and the most best way."
Minister Louis Farrakhan (MLF): "Thank you, Dear Apostle."

THEM: "I love to see you wise because that gives me pleasure because I'm your teacher...and I made such wise ministers."

Group of Ministers: "Yes, Sir!"

Dr. Salaam (DS): "Yes, you gave birth to all of us."

THEM: "So when I see you acting and speaking wise I have rejoice in my heart. I say this is the ONE (i.e. MLF) the world can't bother. I want to prove to Satan that my minister is a greater light to the world of man than you and your world's man---the whole of them."

MLF: "Yes sir. Bless you Dear Apostle."

THEM: "It's wonderful"

******

THEM: "Well, that's what I'm saying I can sit here and listen to you (MLF) and then I can step back and smile. I just need you to be Paul, you know. Go ahead on and put it out just like you are doing. You'll put it out, sometimes I sit here— we all sit here and get a chance to listen at you, I listen at you brother, preaching Brother, and you'll be surprised just to take a peek at the room through your spiritual eye and look at us. We enjoy it!"

MLF: "All praises due to Allah."

THEM: "You [MLF] put everything in such proper place wherein it belongs. It's beautiful! So we all is very happy over you, from Allah—that Allah made a helper."

Source: *Sultan R. Muhammad, Table Talks of the Honorable Elijah Muhammad - The Transcripts: Volume One, Second, ed. Table Talks Project Editorial Board (Chicago, IL: MUI Press, December 1973, 2012).*

Elijah Muhammad Says, Continue To Hear Farrakhan

I want you to remember, today I have one of my greatest teachers here. We have with us today our great national preacher. The preacher who don't mine going into Harlem, New York, one of the worst towns in our nation or cities. He is our brother in Detroit or Chicago or New York.

I want you to remember, every week he's on the air helping me reach those people that I can't get out of the house. I want you to pay good attention to his preaching. His preaching is a bearing of witness to me and what God has given to me.

This is one of the strongest national preachers that I have in the bounds of North America. Everywhere you hear him, listen to him. Everywhere you see him, look at him. Everywhere he advises you to go, go. Everywhere he advises you to stay from, stay from.

So, we are thankful to Allah for this great helper of mine, Minister Farrakhan. He's not a proud man. He's a very humble man. If he can carry you across the lake without dropping you in, he doesn't say when he gets on the other side, "See what I have done?" He tells you, "See what Allah has done." He doesn't take it upon himself.

He's a mighty fine preacher. We hear him every week and I say, continue to hear our Minister Farrakhan.

Source: Elijah Muhammad, "The Theology of Time (Lecture Series)," Vols. July 30, 1972 (Chicago, IL: MUHAMMAD Mosque No. 2, 1972).

Elijah Muhammad Says, Farrakhan Full of Allah's Spirit
You know, Brother Farrakhan is a very good minister. He has been with us for a long time and he's a man full of fire. The fire of the Holy Spirit of Allah. Wonderful minister, wonderful.

Source: Elijah Muhammad, "The Theology of Time (Lecture Series)," Vols. July 16, 1972 (Chicago, IL: MUHAMMAD Mosque No. 2, 1972).

These excerpts are a few of the many that support my position of Minister Farrakhan being Elijah Muhammad's valedictorian. And the Minister's value to the Most Honorable Elijah Muhammad must be acknowledged as the highest of honors conferred upon the Minister. But we must also give due reflection and appreciate the honorable position he holds in the Black community at large.

Farrakhan As Greatest Teacher and Guide of the Blackman
When the Honorable Elijah Muhammad dispatched ministers to various cities, he did so using the guidance and wisdom he received from his teacher Master W. Fard Muhammad. And New York City was a special city in his estimation.

He expressed an understanding of the value of New York City to the overall work of resurrecting and awakening the Black man and woman of America to the truth that he was teaching. New York City, with its Black Mecca being Harlem is where he dispatched Minister Farrakhan to in 1965, commissioning him to be his minister and representative there. A quote from an August 1959 article in the Pittsburgh Courier tells us what he thought of New York and from that we see the confidence and faith he had in Minister Farrakhan's ability to be the minister there.

> "Once Harlem is united into the Brotherhood of Islam, she could command the whole 20 million American dark people. She only needs to rid herself of worthless orators who have no constructive program for this half a million dark people. We the Nation of Islam have been given that constructive program and by all means, **we intend to give it to our people in Harlem, New York**. The readiness in the eyes and actions of the people of Harlem tell you and me that these people are now ready..." Hon. Elijah Muhammad, August 1959 Pittsburgh Courier

From a base in New York City, we see the Honorable Elijah Muhammad having the expectation that his Minister Farrakhan would ultimately impact, effect and "command" all of Black America. And in my research of the life and work of Minister Farrakhan, I bear witness that he has done exactly what his teacher expected of him. This was the subject of our previous work entitled *Who Do They Say I Am: The Vindication of Minister Louis Farrakhan*.

In that book we documented the tremendous impact of the Honorable Minister Louis Farrakhan, particularly on the sea of prominent men and women of this country and around the world, whose testimonies as to how they personally feel and in what estimation they hold the Minister, is in and of itself an obliteration of the propaganda aimed against him. Persons like the esteemed ethics experts Don Wycliff have noted the impact of the Minister in grand terms. Don Wycliff, according to his bio is:

> a long time editor for the Chicago Tribune and nationally recognized expert on ethics. Don Wycliff joined the School of Communication fac-

ulty in Fall 2008. He teaches Reporting and Writing, Ethics & Communication, Feature and Opinion Writing, Historical and Critical Issues in Journalism and Journalism in Race.

Before he joined the Loyola School of Communications faculty, Wycliff served as the vice-president for News and Information at the University of Notre Dame. Before that he served as public editor of the Chicago Tribune from 2000-2006, and as editorial page editor from 1991-2000. His distinguished career also included stints at the New York Times, the Chicago Sun-Times, the Dallas Times-Herald, and the Chicago Daily News. Don will be teaching, reporting and editing for us this fall. Wycliff has previously taught courses at Notre Dame, Roosevelt University and Columbia College. He was a finalist for the Pulitzer Prize in editorial writing in 1996, has been inducted into the Chicago Journalism Hall of Fame and received a lifetime achievement award from the Chicago Journalists Association.

Don Wycliff reacted strongly and passionately about what he witnessed of the Minister's ability during the Million Man March:

> Not since the death of Martin Luther King, Jr., in 1968, has black leadership spoken in a genuine, effective way to the souls of black folk. Not, that is, until October 16 and the Million Man March. The genius of the event—which is to say the genius of Louis Farrakhan, who conceived it--was to couch its purpose in religious terms: atonement, reconciliation, recommitment to God, women, family, and community. In so doing, he spoke to the souls of black folk in a way that not even Jesse Jackson had managed to in the twenty-seven years since Dr. King's death. In so doing, he transformed the Million Man March into an occasion for re-fusing a cord, for reconnecting with the hopeful, faith-filled religious tradition that King represented and that seemed to fall into decay after his murder.

It is clear to me that in Professor's Wycliff's mind, he sees Minister Farrakhan as comparable to and the contemporary version of Dr. Martin Luther King Jr. Dr. King has been considered by many to have been the 20th century's greatest communicator and his speeches are to this day studied, examined and recited. His words were and are inspiring, motivating and soul-stirring.

So for Professor Wycliff to compare Minister Farrakhan to Dr. King is a good comparison, in my opinion. I see in the reactions of many people to the Minister's words a similar reaction to the words of Dr. King. They both have enjoyed wide popularity among the masses of the people. They both have had huge mass gatherings at the Nation's capital in Washington D.C. Both are known for the eloquence, force, power and inspiring qualities of their speeches.

And while much has been written about the formal education of Dr. King. Very little has been written about the formal education of the Honorable Minister Louis Farrakhan. Dr. King attended Morehouse College and was a student of the great theologian Dr. Benjamin E. Mays, author of the very excellent book *The Negro and His God*. From there he went to seminary at Crozer University in Chester, Pennsylvania and on to graduate work at Boston University in Boston, Massachusetts.

Minister Farrakhan had no such formal seminary training. He did go for 3 years at Winston-Salem Teacher's College in North Carolina. But he often has described that his own high school education was so advanced that when he went to Winston-Salem, he never had to purchase a book. I am intrigued that the Minister attended and graduated from Boston English High School which is one of the first high schools in America. He also attended Boston Latin School for only a year and it is also a premier and historic school being the first public school in America.

Minister Farrakhan As Seminary Student of Elijah Muhammad
Collins defines the word seminary as an academy for the training of priests, ministers, rabbis, etc. Merriam Webster says of the word seminary:

> The English word seminary and its Latin source seminarium, a derivative of semen, "seed," both originally denoted a nursery for young plants. Roman authors sometimes used the Latin word figuratively, but English has gone much further in extending the meaning of the word, while the old sense "nursery for plants" is now obsolete. The use of seminary in reference to training schools for Roman Catholic clergy dates from the 16th century. Today the word refers equally to Catholic, Protestant, or Jewish colleges for training priests, ministers, or rabbis. Seminary has also been applied to other kinds of schools. When they

were first formed in the 19th century, colleges for women were called "female seminaries" or "seminaries for young ladies."

A seminary, therefore, is essentially a seed-bed for the ideas of God and religion; a nurturing ground for young ministers who might grow to become the "planting of the Lord." This is the function of the Pittsburgh Courier articles of the Most Honorable Elijah Muhammad in the developmental growth of the ministry of the Honorable Minister Louis Farrakhan. Certainly other factors were used by Allah(God) to produce 'Farrakhan.' But up until this point, it has not been publicly known just how valuable the early writings of the Most Honorable Elijah Muhammad were to Minister Farrakhan's early learning and development.

From a chronological perspective, it is easy to see the Minister's dependence upon the Mr. Muhammad Speaks articles in the Pittsburgh Courier. The Minister joined the Nation of Islam in 1955. He became a minister in 1957. But it was in 1956 that the Most Honorable Elijah Muhammad began a weekly article series in the Pittsburgh Courier newspaper. And from 1956-1959, the Mr. Muhammad Speaks articles served as the primary vehicle for the dissemination of the teachings of the Most Honorable Elijah Muhammad. And outside of the lectures delivered in the temples by Nation of Islam ministers, it was the primary means by which the believers in the Nation of Islam related to the teachings of Muhammad. So for the lay believer, the Pittsburgh Courier became a de facto religious text. This is especially the case when we consider the millions of the papers that were sold by the brothers and sisters of the Nation of Islam. And the fact that the time period under discussion is well prior to the popular books of Muhammad being first printed. Message To The Blackman was the first major book of the Most Honorable Elijah Muhammad and it did not get published until 1965. The other books came out as follows: How To Eat To Live Book 1-1967, How To Eat To Live Book 2-1972, The Fall of America-1973, and Our Saviour Has Arrived-1974.

I was pleasantly surprised to learn that Mother Khadijah Farrakhan was a part of the sales force who worked to help spread the message of the Most Honorable Elijah Muhammad. She told me "brother I used to sell that paper." She said brother "I was a soldier and still am." I do not know how many other sisters participated in the distribution of the Pittsburgh Courier, but for the Minister's wife to have had this relationship with these articles is further support for my thesis that this series of articles helped to give birth to the most profound representation of Elijah Muhammad and the Nation of Islam that has ever been.

Dr. C. Eric Lincoln described the vital role of the Pittsburgh Courier to the Muslims during the 1950s. He writes on page 142 of *The Black Muslims in America*:

> The Pittsburgh Courier, with a circulation of 300,000, is the largest Negro newspaper in the country. It has a nationwide coverage, implemented through several regional editions (such as the New York Courier), and it was the first paper to give any significant coverage to the Black Muslim Movement. **For about three years, from 1956 until the summer of 1959, it served in some ways as a spokesman for the Movement.**

For Dr. Lincoln to describe the role of the Pittsburgh Courier as a national **"spokesman"** is an intriguing description. Especially as we are here discussing the role of this paper in the development of the man who would go on to become the Most Honorable Elijah Muhammad's and the Nation of Islam's National Representative and Spokesman.

I like this description put forth by the great Dr. Lincoln because it calls to mind the Bible in the Book of John, wherein it reads "in the beginning was the word." The first chapter of the Book of John goes on to say that *the word was God and was with God and that the word ultimately became flesh and dwelled among men(paraphrase).* And we can say that who and what Minister Louis Farrakhan became is the actual embodiment of the words and teachings of the Most Honorable Elijah Muhammad, that he first began to intensely study them as weekly articles in the Pittsburgh Courier Newspaper.

The Most Honorable Elijah Muhammad had many ministers. But there is only one man that people all over the world think of when the phrase "The Minister" is uttered. Minister Louis Farrakhan is the man who grew to become "The Minister." Minister Farrakhan is victorious in producing agreement with the truth even among those who prior to listening to him were averse to his message. The effectiveness of his ministry powerfully demonstrates that Minister Farrakhan has the key to open up and touch the hearts and minds of a broad cross-section of humanity. He is literally magnetic. The Most Honorable Elijah Muhammad said to him "brother through you I will get all of my people." In guidance that the Minister shared with the research team he described the uniqueness of his delivery and his effectiveness.

> How did the Minister arrive at where he is? See, that's the path that you must follow. And if you cannot see the value of the way the Minister phrases things. My phrasing of words is the heart of God. That's why I win and you lose. Because if I phrase like God, then the heart of the man that is seeking God will gravitate toward me. Because it's not me. That's why emptying yourself of yourself is critical for God to put Himself in you.
>
> Now each of you are going to express God in your own way after a season. But the first step is like the child. Daddy says it this way. Mommy has an accent. So I'm listening and so I develop the same accent as my mom. Because she's my first teacher.

The Minister was encouraging us to do as the Most Honorable Elijah Muhammad said that all his ministers should do and that is to "take a pattern after" Minister Farrakhan. It is no secret; the Minister has no peer. And I believe that if one wants to be successful in communicating God's word to God's people, using Minister Farrakhan as a model or pattern is the way to success.

In appreciating the impact of the Pittsburgh Courier on Minister Farrakhan's growth and development it helps to be aware of his impact on the prominent persons throughout society. Hip-Hop generation activist and journalist Kevin Powell said of "The Minister":

> God knows, when I heard Farrakhan, I had never heard a black man talk like that. It blew my mind, absolutely blew my mind. It was intoxicating, as intoxicating as crack was for a lot of people in our community in the '80s.

In an interview with the Final Call Newspaper, Archbishop George Augustus Stallings said of Minister Farrakhan:

> Speaking to fellow pastors following Minister Farrakhan's message, ACLC-USA's national co-president Archbishop George Augustus

Stallings, remarked that he noticed many taking "copious notes," probably in preparation for Sunday morning sermons. Archbishop Stallings said Min. Farrakhan had a "Triple A rating" meaning "anointed, appointed and approved" and was "a prophetic voice for our time and age."

"I wish that we as Christian ministers would know the Qur'an the way the Minister knows the scriptures. I wish that we as Christian ministers would get out of our Eurocentric, hegemonic superiority attitude, embracing a religion that is a stolen legacy, rather than celebrating its Afrocentric roots," said Archbishop Stallings.

"I wish that some of us would seek to purify our Christianity. We cannot purify our Christianity until we study the Qur'an. I know that's a shocking statement to some of you Christian folks, but you and I cannot appreciate the true heritage of Christianity until we know the Qur'an, until we know Muhammad (PBUH) until we can articulate the principles of the Islamic faith the way the Hon. Louis Farrakhan articulated the principles of the Christian faith, and not only the Christian faith but also the Jewish faith," Archbishop Stallings added.

Theologian and former Morehouse president Robert Michael Franklin said of "The Minister":

But what is Farrakhan's role in the political realm today? First, he is a prosecuting attorney on behalf of this nation's poor and oppressed minorities. He understands his role to be one of forcefully pointing out discrepancies between American political rhetoric and the reality of black American life. His eloquence and analytic gifts, extraordinary memory, and refined debating skills uniquely qualify him to represent the cause of the unemployable masses which most civil rights organizations and churches have not consistently advanced. Farrakhan speaks to black audiences in a manner that resembles old southern preachers who preach for two or three hours without notes, modulating their presentations between impassioned intensity and humorous, mischievous conversation. One has to sit in his presence to appreciate the quality of his dramatic performance. Many young blacks have been motivated (some would say seduced) by Farrakhan's charisma. Unemployed young people have banded with him, and he has given them hope. Many cannot read or write and are therefore ineligible for the job opportunities which Rev. Jackson and other civil rights leaders generate through protest and bargaining. Farrakhan demonstrates to such young people that after they have been rejected by the wider society they have a chance to become self-respecting persons within their own community.

He has gone into prisons and helped to reform numbers of America's most troublesome population. He has preached family stability and male-female mutual respect in a way that makes him sound more like Jerry Falwell than Malcolm X. But the black underclass has embraced his conservative ethical teachings and his Dale Carnegie-style lessons on personal hygiene, dress, manners, and salesmanship...

Second, Farrakhan is a prosecuting attorney for the Islamic faith and Afro-American Muslims. No other non-Christian leader in black America has so forcefully indicted the Christian tradition for its tacit and explicit racism, classism and hypocrisy, and still managed to command large audiences in the most prestigious churches across the nation. Farrakhan knows the Christian tradition intimately from his years as an altar boy in the Episcopal Church. Indeed, I think that he is drenched with the Anglicanism of his formative years. He believes that all things should be done decently and in order, that religion is a matter of rational understanding and that religious authorities, hierarchy, and traditions should be respected-all motifs which are emphasized in most quarters of the Episcopal community. Farrakhan also reminds us that Islam is not a parochial Arab tradition but a world-wide religion that creates a global community of Muslims who worship Allah.

In 1995 after the Million Man March, Professor Henry Louis Gates interviewed several Black pastors to offer a professional assessment of the Minister's Million Man March speech. Here is an excerpt:

Henry Louis Gates, Jr., asks five masters of black sacred oratory to give a strictly professional assessment of a colleague's delivery. THE REVEREND WYATT T. WALKER (Canaan Baptist Church, Harlem): Even though I have my quarrels with Louis Farrakhan, I would say that on a scale of ten he was about a twelve, oratorically speaking. THE REVEREND JAMES A. FORBES (Riverside Church, Harlem): As a piece of communication, it was an extraordinary moment. In terms of style, especially in his public condemnation of the President and whites, and so forth, there was a balance of courtesy and critique that I liked.

We document these and more in our previous work entitled Who Do They Say I Am: The Vindication of Minister Louis Farrakhan.

The Education of Moses and Farrakhan

There are so many aspects of Minister Farrakhan's life that draw strong parallels to the lives of the Prophets written of in the Bible and Holy Qur'an, this is also the case with his teacher the Most Honorable Elijah Muhammad. Examining these parallels are helpful to develop a thorough appreciation of the example that Minister Farrakhan displays that I argue is at least partially the product of the Mr. Muhammad Speaks article series in the Pittsburgh Courier-a major part.

Every true Prophet that there ever was, was raised to be a Prophet by Allah (God) Himself. And at a certain point in their growing relationship, the Most Honorable Elijah Muhammad told Minister Farrakhan, "I didn't make you brother, Allah (God) made you for me." It therefore follows that when a man is made by God for such a purpose as was Minister Farrakhan, then it becomes incumbent on believers in God to study every aspect of that man. His character, his words, his spiritual make-up are all critical studies that from a believer's perspective are both valuable and comprise a duty to express gratitude to God for making such a man for us.

In the case of the Pittsburgh Courier articles of the Most Honorable Elijah Muhammad, our examination is of some of the factors that went into the making of Minister Farrakhan for the Most Honorable Elijah Muhammad and his people. Such study identifies a divinely ordained path that Minister Farrakhan "traveled" to arrive at the destination that he is at currently. That path also forms what some we could describe as the model, recipe, template or pedagogy to reproduce in one's own self all the magnificent characteristics, capabilities, and qualities that are found in Minister Farrakhan and which please Allah (God).

One parallel between Minister Farrakhan and the Moses of the Bible is in his formal education. The Bible says of Moses in Acts 7:22 that

> "Moses was educated in all the learning of the Egyptians, and he was a man of power in words and deeds."

There is some worthwhile commentary on this verse that is also of value in understanding the parallel between the factors that went into the "making' Minister Farrakhan and those that were characteristics of the Prophets. From Gil's Exposition of the Entire Bible we read:

> Philo the Jew says (e) that he learned arithmetic, geometry, and every branch of music, the hieroglyphics, the Assyrian language, and the Chaldean knowledge of the heavens, and the mathematics; yet was not a magician, or skilled in unlawful arts, as Justin suggests (f): and was mighty in words; he had a command of language, and a large flow of words, and could speak properly and pertinently upon any subject; for though he was slow of speech, and of tongue, and might have somewhat of a stammering in speaking, yet he might have a just diction, a masculine style, and a powerful eloquence, and the matter he delivered might be very great and striking: and in deeds; or in "his deeds", as the Alexandrian copy, the Vulgate Latin, Syriac, and Ethiopic versions read: he was a man of great abilities, and fit for business both in the cabinet and in the field.

Not only is there the parallel between the Minister and this aspect of Moses life. America is also paralleled with Egypt in that the Bible records Egypt enslaving Hebrews for 400 years and America enslaved Black people for 400 years. The Minister's "Egyptian" learning at Boston Latin and Boston English is therefore quite a significant factor in his make-up.

Boston Latin being the oldest public school in America produced many prominent historical figures. Five signers of the Declaration of Independence went to Boston Latin including: Benjamin Franklin, Samuel Adams, John Hancock, William Hooper and Robert Treat Paine. The Minister only went to the 7th grade there and left due to a racist climate. But in that year he would have been exposed to their curriculum component called oratorical declamation. Oratorical declamation is defined as

> the rhetorical device of adopting the persona of an ancient figure to express a particular viewpoint or perspective. It is described as vehement oratory; a speech marked by strong feeling; a rhetorical or emotional speech, made esp. in order to protest or condemn; tirade. In classical music it is the artistry or technique involved in singing recitative passages

From the school's website we read that for Boston Latin students

> declamation is the most time-honored of the school's traditions. Pupils in the 7th to 10th grade are required to give an oration in their English class three times during the year. There is also Public Declamation, where pupils from all grades, or classes, are welcomed to try out for the chance to declaim a memorized piece in front of an assembly. During Public Declamation, declaimers are scored on aspects such as "Memorization" "Presentation", and "Voice and Delivery", and those who score well in three of the first four public declamations are given the chance to declaim in front of alumni judges for awards in "Prize Declamation".

What impact did oratorical declamation at Boston Latin have on the Minister in the 7th grade? Might an environment where he would have been exposed to the techniques and processes necessary to speak passionately with eloquence, force and persuasion have left him with skills that he could "reach for" once the task was before him to speak and "declaim" on behalf of his suffering people as a representative of the Most Honorable Elijah Muhammad? I think so. I think that this was an ingredient in the production of what has become his peerless ministry. From my vantage point, this exposure was a part of the path that Allah(God) was bringing his Minister along.

In some of the most important guidance I ever received from the Minister is when he shared with us some of the critical aspects of his pedagogy. The Minister shared the following guidance with us during a research team retreat to his farm on December 18, 2012. (emphasis added is mine)

Look let me say this. **All that I'm doing was put in me**. I asked myself this question and maybe you can help me with it. My father said, "Brother you don't have to study." But the words of the Saviour is, "you all get busy and study young and old." Now, to contravene something as germane to success as study, is he contradicting God? No. Then when he said, "oh Brother you don't have to study, you just stand up and let God speak through you." **This is after** I would take a week to write a half hour broadcast. I would search every word and then economize on words to see if I could say a sentence better and sharper by using different words. This is the truth. I did this for 3 years.

I went in a studio that I made in my garage at 2311 97th Street in East Elmhurst which was the home that Brother Malcolm lived in. I had the garage soundproofed. I took my Nagra recorder, which was the best in the world at that time. I went in that studio with my script. Nobody in there but me and a microphone and the spirit of God and my love for Him. I didn't need an audience. I just dealt and **I've got this down to a science where if you said to me you got 20 seconds, I could develop my point in 20 seconds and be off**. I mean that's how refined it got.

Then I was telling the Messenger you know how I did it. Of course he knows. "Well brother you don't have to study. You get the thought that you want to build your talk on and then stand up and let God speak through you." **So for the next 3 years I developed the thought, came out, put a few scriptures down and then went. Now the 3 years prior to that being so exact, because I remember as a little child I would look up and it said from Bacon. "Writing maketh a man exact." So, the more I wrote the more exact my language became.** Francis Bacon, that's right. So, I'm saying that to say this. He knew that at a certain time He was going to put stuff in me and I would not have to go in a book; I go up in my head or to the soul that He had written on. And the book is already there. And we find that.

As a lecturer, writer and student minister, this commentary from the Minister is invaluable. For it reveals the synthesis of some of the factors that combined to produce the effect we see whenever we behold the majesty of his delivery of the word of Allah(God). In other words, the Minister is saying in the passage above that Allah(God) put into his make-up certain leanings and innate capabilities and strengths. His formal education gave him tools he used to cultivate what Allah(God) put within him. His love for what he was reading from the Most Honorable Elijah Muhammad in the Pittsburgh Courier and elsewhere caused him to discipline himself to being the finest representation of the man and the word that he so loved. And that discipline plus love plus the spirit of Allah(God) forged a young man who once had a stammering tongue into one whose preaching of lectures has the effect of music on the ears of audiences often large enough to fill stadiums.

It was Allah(God) who put the thought in the mind of the Minster's mother to seek for him the best of education, the best available education in America the modern Egypt. She initially sought Boston Latin, but in hind sight, the Minister was to be there for only 1 year. The Minister left Boston Latin and attended for the duration of his formal education Boston English, another old and prestigious educational center for the modern "Egyptians." According to the Encyclopedia Britannica:

> English High was created originally to educate working class schoolboys in preparation for business, mechanics, and engineering trades as opposed to "latin-grammar" schools like Boston Latin that prepared schoolboys for the college, ministry and scholarly pursuits, and private academies that were open only to affluent residents. Its original curriculum consisted of such courses as English, surveying, navigation, geography, logic, and civics as well as a strong emphasis on mathematics.

During the time of the Minister's schooling at Boston English, he was exposed to a very well-rounded education that included physical education, military drill, commerce, history, chemistry, physics, typewriting, algebra, trigonometry, plane geometry, meteorology, navigation , economic geography, commercial law, merchandising, economics, bookkeeping, English, German, French, Spanish and Latin languages.

One of the course descriptions for English 7 (E7) describes it as an oral expression class.

> This course provides an opportunity for the student to understand the nature and function of speech, to eliminate any factors which tend to keep him from expressing his ideas most effectively, and to form new and successful habits of expression and communication. Proper pronunciation and enunciation are stressed. Presentation of principles; discussion and illustration from the experiences of the student and others; self-analysis and auditor analysis by each student.

Such a course is an example of the early educational environment that Allah(God) placed the Minister in. Allah (God) was directing the Minister's development from the start. It is as the Bible records in the book of Jeremiah:

> "I knew you before I formed you in your mother's womb. Before you were born I set you apart and appointed you as my prophet to the nations."(Jeremiah 1:5)

The Minister's ultimate stellar success in using the English language to communicate the word of God, found recorded in the Hebrew, Greek and Arabic languages, is evidence of the hand of Allah(God) being involved in his preparation.

Again, the scriptures commentary on Moses (Musa) is illuminating. Musa of the Holy Qur'an is a liberator of an enslaved people. And as a prerequisite to that difficult task, Allah (God) chose to furnish him with a basic yet broad exposure and education at the hands of the Egyptians. Consider some of the commentary of legendary translator of the Holy Qur'an into English Abdullah Yusuf Ali.

> Footnote 64: Thus Moses was brought up by the enemies of his people. He was chosen by Allah to deliver his people, and **Allah's wisdom made the learning and experience and even cruelties of the Egyptian enemies themselves to contribute to the salvation of his people.**
> Footnote 1073: Moses was raised up with a threefold mission again (a) **to learn all the learning of the Egyptians and preach Allah's Truth to them as one who had been brought up among themselves,** (b) to unite and reclaim his own people, and (c) to rescue them and lead them to a

new world, which was to open out their spiritual horizon and lead them to the Psalms of David and the glories of Solomon.

Footnote 2557: Long after the age of Joseph, who had been a Wazir to one of the kings, there came on the throne of Egypt a Pharaoh who hated the Israelites and wanted them annihilated. He ordered Israelite male children to be killed when they were born. Moses's mother hid him for a time, but when further concealment was impossible, a thought crossed her mind that she should put her child into a chest and send the chest floating down the Nile . This was not merely a foolish fancy of hers. **It was Allah's Plan to bring up Moses in all the learning of the Egyptians, in order that that learning itself should be used to expose what was wrong in it and to advance the glory of Allah.**

Footnote 3334: This was the Plan of Providence; that the wicked might cast a net round themselves by fostering the man who was to bring them to naught and be the instrument of their punishment-or (looking at it from the other side) that **Moses might learn all the wisdom of the Egyptians in order to expose all that was hollow and wicked in it.**

To be sure, there are aspects of what the Bible and Holy Qur'an describe as the history of Moses that parallels with the life of the Most Honorable Elijah Muhammad. In fact we might ascribe more of the scriptures prophecies with respect to Moses or Musa to being fulfilled by the work of the Most Honorable Elijah Muhammad. But when we consider the Bible and Holy Qur'an's emphasis on the formal education that Musa received and his using it to bring to naught the power of Pharaoh to enslave his people that, as we have shown, is fulfilled in the life and work of the Honorable Minister Louis Farrakhan.

English Speaking Messenger of God

It also bears noting the language emphasis within Minister Farrakhan's formal education. He attended Boston "English" High School. English is the language of America, the modern Egypt. America is also the world superpower nation. As a result the English language which Minister Farrakhan masters in order to communicate the wisdom and will of Allah(God) to the world, carries a tremendous power in influence among the nations of the world. Statistically English literally reigns supreme among the world's languages mediums of communication. According to the PBS documentary The Story of English:

- English is the most widespread language in the world and is more widely spoken and written than any other language.
- Over 400 million people use the English vocabulary as a mother tongue, only surpassed in numbers, but not in distribution by speakers of the many varieties of Chinese.
- Over 700 million people, speak English, as a foreign language.
- Did you know that of all the world's languages (over 2,700) English is arguably the richest in vocabulary; and that the Oxford English Dictionary lists about 500,000 words, and there are a half-million technical and scientific terms still uncatalogued?
- Three-quarters of the world's mail, telexes and cables are in English.
- More than half of the world's technical and scientific periodicals are in English
- English is the medium for 80% of the information stored in the world's computers
- English is the language of navigation, aviation and of Christianity; it is the ecumenical language of the World Council of Churches
- Five of the largest broadcasting companies in the world (CBS, NBC, ABC, BBC and CBC) transmit in English, reaching millions and millions of people all over the world.

The Holy Qur'ans Surah 14 Ayat (verse) 4 sheds light on the issue of languages spoken by the Prophets:

> **And We sent no messenger but with the language of his people, so that he might explain to them clearly**. Then Allah leaves in error whom He pleases and He guides whom He pleases. And He is the Mighty, the Wise.

Accordingly then, there should be an expectation for an English speaking messenger of Allah (God). Religious adherents living in English speaking countire may self-identify as Jews, Christians or Muslims. But those religions and the Prophets around which they developed emerged out of the Eastern Hemisphere, specifically a region of the world referred to by scholars as the Ancient Near

East or ANE. And at the time in history when Abraham, Moses, Jesus and Muhammad preached and taught, there was no such language as English.

In order for the will of Allah(God) to be preached to an English speaking world, the Holy Qur'an leads us to believe, Allah (God) would use a man who speaks English who can clearly do what is the job of all Prophets and Messengers to do. And that is to give guidance to all, preach good news to the faithful and issue a warning to the wicked.

This is exactly the work that the Nation of Islam has been performing in America and throughout the world. Master W. Fard Muhammad, the Most Honorable Elijah Muhammad and today the Honorable Minister Louis Farrakhan are three who act as one. They are united in spirit, mind and purpose. As the Holy Qur'an says of the 3 sent to a rebellious town in Surah 36 ayats 13-17:

> And set out to them a parable of the people of the town, when apostles came to it.
> When We sent to them two, they rejected them both; then We strengthened (them) with a third, so they said: Surely we are sent to you. They said: You are only mortals like ourselves, nor has the Beneficent revealed anything — you only lie. They said: Our Lord knows that we are surely sent to you. And our duty is only a clear deliverance (of the message).

In a future work we will look at more of the pedagogy of the Honorable Minister Louis Farrakhan. For now, we hope that the reader will be encouraged, inspired and uplifted by what you have read so far in these introductions. The real treat awaits you inside this rich collection of articles penned by the beloved of God, the friend of God, Allah's Messenger-Messiah to us and the world, The Most Honorable Elijah Muhammad

As-Salaam Alaikum,

Your Brother In Islam
Demetric Muhammad
February 2015

1956

His great teaching and warnings to us (the so-called Negroes) is BE YOURSELF. What is our own self? He answers that "Your own self is a righteous Muslim, born of the Tribe of Shabazz."

He taught us that we are the original people of the earth who have no birth record.

He calls on us to SUBMIT to HIM that He would sit us in heaven at once. He made it clear what constitutes heaven on earth, freedom, justice, equality, money, good homes and friendship in all walks of life.

This Christianity cannot give us (not the Christianity that has been taught to us).

HE GREATLY rejoiced over us and was real happy that He had found us.

He said that He would make a new people out of us who submit to Him by causing us to grow into a new growth, not an entirely new body but a reversal of the old decayed body into a new growth, which He said would make us all as we were at the age of 16.

There will be no decay in this new growth of life. He also stated that the next life is a life of unlimited progress.

He taught us the things that were and are and a glimpse of the things to come.

HIS FIERY warnings of the judgment of this world makes one feel as though there would be a very very narrow chance for any life to survive such a destruction.

He taught us that our fore-parents were deceived and brought into America by a slave trader whose name was John Hawkins in the year of 1555.

Just what happened to our fore-parents and we their children after landing here in the Western Hemisphere would make a dog weep and fight if her pups were treated in such manner as our forefathers and their children were treated.

OUR FIRST parents who were brought here, He said that, they were killed after giving birth to their first babies, to prevent them from teaching their children anything of self or of their God and people.

This act of murdering our forefathers by the slave masters left their children to be taught and reared in whatever pleased the slave masters and we are from those children.

That made us blind, deaf, and dumb to the knowledge of self or anyone else and it stands true today that, the American so-called Negroes don't know themselves or anyone else and the worst of all they don't know that they don't know themselves or others.

We can't be considered a free people as long as we are in the white slave masters' names; this the white man never advised the so-called Negroes to do, but yet claims that we are free. He also refused to teach us the truth of our kind, their civilization before bringing us into slavery.

THE KNOWLEDGE of Allah, the Supreme Being, the true religion (Islam) has never been taught us by anyone before the coming of Allah, in the person of Master Fard Muhammad.

The whole of the Western white civilization is opposed to Islam, the only true religion of God, therefore they (devils) don't teach of Allah and Islam to us. He said Christianity was organized by the white race and they placed the name of Jesus on it as being the founder and author to deceive the black people in accepting it.

After our first parents landed here they saw that they had been deceived by this devil John Hawkins.

He brought them here on a ship named Jesus, this ship when on its way back for another load of our people, our fore-parents stared at the old slave ship as it departed and begged to be carried back, but to no avail and they said that "You can have this new Western world but give us the ship Jesus back to our people and country," which now has become a song among our people, which goes something like this, "YOU CAN HAVE ALL THE WORLD BUT GIVE ME JESUS."

But, our poor fore parents did not know at that time, that it would be 400 years from that day before the real ship Jesus (GOD HIMSELF) would come and get them in their children and cut loose every link of the slave chain that holds us in bondage to our slave masters by giving us a true knowledge of self, God and the devil and wipe away the 400 years of tears, weeping, mourning and groaning under the yoke of bondage to the merciless murderers.

THE SLAVEMASTERS' children are doing everything in their power to prevent the so-called Negroes from accepting their own God and salvation, by putting on a great show of false love and friendship.

This is being done through integration as it is called, so-called Negroes and whites mixing together, such as, schools, churches and even intermarriage with the so-called Negroes, and this the poor slaves (the so-called Negroes) really think that they are entering a condition of heaven with their former slaveholders, but it will prove to be their doom.

Today, according to God's Word that we are living in is the time of a great separation between black and white.

The members of every nation must go to their own and the American so-called Negroes are the most handicapped in the knowledge of just what they should expect at this time.

June 16, 1956

IN LAST week's lecture I said that mixing and intermarriage between the whites and blacks (so-called Negroes) will prove the doom of the so-called Negroes. Today, according to the word of God, the time that we are living in is of a great separation between black and white. The prophesied 400 years of slavery that we would have to serve this people was up in 1955 and not anything will help solve this problem but a return to their own. The divine power is and will continue to work in favor of the so-called Negroes' return to their own. The separation would be a blessing for both sides.

All nations know and love their members, but the so-called Negroes, they, are even afraid to act too friendly towards each other. They are educated in everything but the love and knowledge of self; therefore they will never enjoy love and unity until they are taught the knowledge of self and kind.

The judgment of the world has arrived and the gathering together of the people is now going on. Why should there be a judgment of the world? Why was there a judgment of the people of Noah and Lot's people? The

Bible says, "That day shall not come except there comes a falling away first, and the man of sin revealed, the Son of Perdition," II Thessalonians 2:3. This man of sin is now being revealed. The man of sin is the devil in person, who was made of sin, not any good was in the essence that He was from. Since He was made of sin, what good can one expect of the man of sin? Why has he been hidden from the eyes of the righteous people and only revealed today? The answer is; how could the man of sin rule the righteous for six thousand years if He had not been veiled to prevent the discovery of his true self? According to II Thessalonians 2:9 the man of sin had a work to do and God wouldn't interfere with this work of the man of sin until the time given the man of sin was fully up.

The eighth verse in the same chapter reads that the Lord shall consume with the Spirit (of Truth of the man of sin) of his mouth, and shall destroy with the brightness of His Coming, which means that the truth of the man of sin is so clearly made by God that there can be no doubt, that he is really the man of sin who has and is causing all the trouble among the righteous. The Great Deceiver, liar and a murderer by nature. The great sin and straying of the righteous is, when the man of sin is revealed instead of them refusing to follow such a man further they disbelieve in God's revealing of this man and give God the lie for His revelations and continue to follow the man of sin to his doom, because they receive not the love of truth concerning the man of sin. II Thessalonians 2:10. This is now being fulfilled. The so-called Negroes must know the truth, but surely they will and are rejecting it.

June 23, 1956

PERSECUTION FOLLOWS

He (MR. FARD MUHAMMAD, God in person) chose to suffer three and one-half years to show his love for his people, who have suffered over three hundred years at the hands of a people who by nature are evil, wicked, and have no good in them.

He was persecuted, sent to jail in 1932, and ordered out of Detroit, Mich., May 26, 1933. He came to Chicago in the same year, arrested almost immediately on his arrival and placed behind prison bars.

He submitted himself with all humbleness to his persecutors. Each time he was arrested, He sent for me that I may see and learn the price of TRUTH for us, the so-called American Negroes (members of the Asiatic nation).

He was well able to save himself from such suffering, but how else was the scripture to be fulfilled? We followed in His footsteps suffering the same (persecution).

My people are yet sound asleep to the knowledge of the good that is being carried on for their deliverance. The whole world of our kind awaits the awakening, and our awakening is the last step in the Resurrection and Judgment of the world.

It is a SIN that we were put so soundly to sleep. The end of the world has arrived and most of us know it not, and our enemy's greatest desire is that we remain asleep. My people fight and oppose the God of our own salvation.

(Allah) chose for us Islam as a religion. He desires to sit us in Heaven at once, on condition that we submit to Him and accept the religion of Islam, the religion of God and His prophets. In this religion (Islam) He offers us Universal Friendship, and we, who have submitted to Him, know this to be true.

We know white people have and will continue to persecute anyone who offers help to us, the so-called American Negroes (Asiatics). Should persecution or even death stop the worthy help that will save the lives of the so-called Negroes? NO, it shall not.

The so-called Negroes are absolutely friendless and have sought in vain friendship from their enemies, due to the ignorance of self and their enemies. NOW they are offered universal friendship if they will only accept their own (Allah and Islam).

Seek FIRST the friendship of your own people and then the friendship of others (If there is any friendship in the others.)

We have made the grave mistake of Lazarus and the Prodigal Son, St. Luke: Chapter 15, the one who was so charmed over the wealth and food of the rich man that he couldn't leave his gate to seek the same for himself.

Regardless to the disgraceful condition in which the rich man put him, even to sending his dogs to attack him. The angels had to come and take him away.

The other (Prodigal Son) being tempted by the loose life of strange women, drinking, gambling and adultery, caused him to love the stranger's way of life so much so that it cost him all that he originally possessed (self-independence and Divine guidance). His Father (God in Person) had to come and be his representative, to again meet his brothers, family and friends.

Nothing fits the description of us better, the so-called Negroes (Asiatics). Many of us today are so lazy that we are willing to suffer anything rather than go for self. It is true that our God has come to sit us in Heaven, but not a Heaven where-in we won't have to work.

FEAR is the worst enemy that we have, but entire SUBMISSION to Allah (God) and His MESSENGER will remove this FEAR. The white race put fear in our fore parents when they were babies, so says the Word of Allah.

We must have for our peace and happiness (the seventeen million so-called Negroes) that which other nations have.

This aforementioned peace and happiness can't come under any other flag, but our own. If God desires for us such joy, why shouldn't we give up begging and be real men, and sit with the rulers of the earth, ruling our own?

Our first step is to give back to the white man his religion, Christianity, church and his names. These three are chains of slavery that hold us in bondage to them. We are free when we give up the above three.

The so-called Negroes must know that they have been deceived and be brought face to face with God and the devil. They must get away from the old-slavery teaching that Jesus, who was killed two thousand years ago is still alive somewhere waiting and listening to their prayers.

He was only a prophet like Moses and the other prophets and had the same religion (Islam). He did his work and is dead like others of his time, and has no knowledge of their prayers to him.

Since Islam over-ran mankind in the seventh century after Jesus and is still a power over man, why didn't the translators of the Bible mention it?

Why didn't they give us the name of the religions of the prophets since they claim a religion for Jesus?

June 30, 1956

THE BIBLE AND QUR-AN

WHICH ONE IS RIGHT? I don't know of any scriptural book or religion that doesn't contain some good. What Allah (God) demands today is a book or religion that is all good, not a mixture of truth and false, not a book or religion that is or has been tampered with by His enemies.

The Bible is called a Holy Book, and is often referred to as the Word of God. The present English Bible is said to be translated out of the original tongues, into the present English language by the authority of one King James in 1611.

What is the original tongue or language that the Bible was written in? What language did Moses speak? Originally, the Torah (Old Testament) was given to Musa (Moses) 2000 B.C., who spoke ancient Egyptian Arabic, and the second half (the New Testament) was revealed to Isa (Jesus) 2000 years ago (who spoke both Arabic and Hebrew).

The Holy Qur-an was revealed to Muhammad in the seventh century A.D. over 1300 years ago who spoke Arabic. The believers and followers of these three Scriptures are referred to as follows: (1) Hebrews or Jews, believers in Musa (Moses) and the Torah; (2) Christians, followers of Isa (Jesus) and the Injil or gospel revealed to Isa (Jesus); (3) Muslims, believers in all of the Prophets of God and the Scriptures revealed to His Prophets. The Torah, Injil, Qur-an, the Muslims make no difference in any of them, as long as it is from Allah (God).

The Jews or Hebrews believe that Musa (Moses) was a Jew, who brought them the Torah. The Christians believed that both Musa (Moses) and Isa were Jews. Muhammad, an Arab, was a member of the black nation. The Jews and Christians are of the white race, and they don't believe in Muhammad as a Prophet of God. Naturally, they don't believe in the

Scriptures (Holy Qur-an) that Allah (God) revealed to Muhammad. Muhammad and his followers believe in Moses and Jesus also the true Scriptures that these two prophets brought to their people.

The Arabs or Muslims have tried and are still trying to get the white race to believe and recognize Muhammad as a Divine Prophet of Allah (God) and the Qur-an, a Divine revelation, as they recognize Musa (Moses) and Isa (Jesus) and the Bible as coming from Allah (God). This is sufficient proof to the worship of Allah (God) Himself; if Allah desires to make the black nation the equal or superior of the white race. Again their objection proves beyond a shadow of a doubt that there is no such thing as a divine relation of brotherhood between the black nation and white race. God forbid. The history of the two people is a proof, for six thousand years the two (black and white) have been and still are unable to get along together in peace. This is due to the fact that the God of the two people is not the same.

The Bible is now being called the POISON BOOK by God Himself, and who can deny that it is not poison? It has poisoned the very hearts and minds of the so-called Negroes so much, so that they can't agree with each other. From the first day that the white race received the Divine Scripture they started tampering with its truth to make it to suit themselves, and blind the black man. It is their nature to do evil, and the book can't be recognized as the pure and Holy Word of God. It opens with the words of someone other than God trying to represent God and His Creation to us. This is called the Book of Moses and reads as follows: "In the beginning God created the Heaven and earth" (Gen. 1:1). When was this beginning? There in the Genesis the writer tells us, that it was 4,004 B.C. This we know, now, that it refers to the making of the white race, and not the Heaven and earth. The second verse of the first chapter of Genesis reads: "And the earth was without form and void; darkness was upon the deep and the spirit of God moved upon the face of the waters." What was the water on, since there was no form of earth? As I see it, the Bible is very questionable. After God had created everything without asking for any help from anyone then, comes His weakness in the 26th verse of the same chapter (Gen. 1:26). He invites us to help Him make a man. Allah has revealed THE US that was invited to make a man (white race). A man is far more easy to make than the Heavens and earth. We can't charge these questionable readings of the Bible to Musa because he was a Prophet of God, and they don't lie.

If the present Bible is the direct Word of God, why isn't God speaking rather than His Prophet Musa (Moses)? Neither does Moses tell us here in the first chapter of Genesis that it is from God. No, we don't find the name Moses mentioned in the chapter. The Bible is the graveyard of my poor people (the so-called Negroes) and I would like to dwell upon this book until I am sure that they understand that it is not quite as holy as they first thought it was. I don't mean to say that there is no truth in it, certainly, plenty of truth, if understood. Will you accept the understanding of it? The Bible charges all of its Great Prophets with evil, it makes God guilty of an act of adultery by charging Him with being the father of Mary's baby (Jesus), again it charges Noah and Lot with drunkenness, and Lot getting children by his daughter. What a POISON BOOK.

The HOLY QUR-AN, it is holy because it is the Word of Allah (God) speaking Himself directly to His Servant. HOLY means something that is PERFECTLY PURE and we just can't say that of the Poison Bible. Al-Qur-an the Qur-an means according to the Arabic scholars of the language in which it is written, that which should be read, which was revealed to Muhammad in the month of Ramadan 2:185.

July 7, 1956

'HOLY QUR-AN AND BIBLE'

WE, THE so-called American Negroes, are mentioned in the New Testament under several names and parables. I will name two, the parable of the Lost Sheep and the Prodigal Son (Luke 15:1-11), of which we could not be described better under or in a parable.

Before the coming of Allah (God) we, being blind, deaf and dumb, had mistaken the true meanings of these parables to be referring to the Jews. Now, thanks to Almighty God Allah, Who came in the Person of Master Fard Muhammad (to Whom be praised forever), Who has opened my blinded eyes, and unstopped my ears, loosed the knot in my tongue, and has made us to understand these Bible parables are referring to us, the so-called Negroes and our slave masters.

THE ANSWER(Luke 15:4-6) to the charges made by the proud and unholy Pharisees against Him (God in Person) for eating with His lost found people whom the Pharisees and their people had made sinners, can't be better. It defends Him and His people (lost and found sheep). He proved their wicked and hatred for His love for His people who were lost and He (God) had found them. They (the Pharisees and their people) had more love for a lost and found animal of theirs than they did for the lost and found people of Allah (God).

Regardless to our sins that we have committed in following and obeying our slave masters, Allah (God) forgives it all today, if we, the so-called Negroes, will turn to Him and our own kind. If the wicked can rejoice over the finding of his lost and strayed animal, or a piece of silver, or a son who had a desire to leave home to practice the evil habits of strangers, how much more should Allah and the nation of Islam rejoice over finding us, their people, who have been lost from them for 400 years following other than our own kind? We, being robbed so thoroughly of the knowledge of self and kind, are opposed to our own salvation in favour of our enemies, and I here quote another poison addition of the slavery teachings of the Bible: "Love your enemies, bless them who curse you, pray for those who spitefully use you, him that smiteth thee on one cheek offer the other cheek, him that taketh (rob) away thy cloak, forbid not to take (away) thy coat also (Luke 6:27-28-29)." The slave masters couldn't have found a better teaching for their protection against the slaves' possible dissatisfaction of their masters' brutal treatment.

It is against the very nature of God and man, and other life, to love their enemies. Would God ask us to do that which He, Himself can't do? He hates His enemies so much that He tells us that He is going to destroy them in hell fire, along with those of us who follow His enemies.

THE MISUNDERSTANDING of the Old and New Testament by the so-called Negro preachers makes it our graveyard and must be resurrected therefrom. NOTE - Moses didn't teach a resurrection of the dead nor did Noah, who was a prophet before Moses. The New Testament and Holy Qur-an's teaching of a resurrection of the dead can't mean the people who have died physically and returned to the earth, but rather a mental resurrection of us, the Black Nation, who are mentally dead to the knowledge of truth; the **TRUTH** of self, God and the arch-enemy of God and His people.

This is that **TRUTH** (John 8:32) that will make us **FREE**, whereof John 8:32 doesn't say what truth shall make you free; therefore leaving it questionable and to the advantage of the enemy. Oh, that my poor people, the so-called Negroes could understand, they would sit in Heaven at once. The enemy is alert, wide-awake and ever on the job to prevent the so-called Negroes from believing Allah and the true religion of Allah (God) and His Prophets, the Religion of Islam. The enemy is well aware that Allah (God) is the Rock of our Defense and Islam the House of our Salvation. Woe to you who try to hinder the teachings of Islam and the truth of God and the devil, also ever planning the death of the Messenger of Allah and His followers. It would have been better that you were not born. The chastisement of Allah shall abide upon you until you are brought to shame and disgrace.

REMEMBER THE disgrace suffered by Pharaoh and his people for their opposition against Moses and His followers, just because Pharaoh feared that Moses would teach this people the true religion, Islam? Pharaoh set his whole army against Moses only to be brought to aught. Pharaoh had deceived his slaves in the knowledge of Allah and the true religion **ISLAM**, and indirectly had them worshiping him and his people as God.

The poor so-called Negroes are so filled with fear of their enemy that they stoop to helping the enemy against their own salvation. **BE AWARE** of what you are doing lest you be the worse loser. If they had only been taught the **TRUTH**, they would act differently. The Bible, church and Christianity have deceived them. I pray Allah to give them life, and light of understanding.

The Holy Qur-an, the Glory Books should be read and studied by us, the so-called American Negroes. Both the present Bible and Holy Qur-an must soon give way to that Holy Book which no man as yet but Allah has seen. The teachings (prophecies) of the present Bible and Qur-an takes us up to the resurrection, and judgment of this world, but not into the next life. That which is in that Holy Book is for the righteous and their future only, not for the mixed world of righteous and evil. The preparation for that unseen life is now going on in the few believers of Islam in America. Islam the **TRUE** religion of Allah (God) makes a distinction between the lovers of righteousness and lovers of evil. It is that which Allah (God) is using today to separate the righteous from the evil-doers.

THE PRAYER service and its meaning is so beautiful that I am having it put into a small book for my people who believe.

Let us take a look at the opening of the second chapter of the Holy Qur-an, here Allah addresses Himself to us as being the Best Knower and that we must not entertain any doubts about the purity of His Book (the Holy Qur-an).

"I am Allah, the Best Knower. This Book (the Holy Qur-an) there is no doubt in it, it is a guide to those who guard (against evil)" Chapter 2:1-2 . . . not as a prophet representing Allah (God) and His Scripture as in the words of the Prophets of the Bible, "Thus says the Lord," but actually Allah (God) speaking Himself. Allah challenges the disbelievers of our people and the devils combined to produce a chapter or even a verse like it. I quote another verse of the same chapter 2:285.

"**THE APOSTLE** believes in what has been revealed to Him from His Lord, and so do the believers, they all believe in Allah, His Angels, His Books and His Apostles. We made no difference between any of His Apostles; and they say, "WE hear and obey, our Lord, Thy forgiveness do we crave, and to Thee is the eventual course." Verse 2:285.

Can the proud Christian say with truth the same? No, they don't believe in Allah not to mention His Prophets and the Scriptures of the Prophets; but they like to make a difference in the Prophets. All the old Prophets are condemned as being other than good, but Jesus they go to the extreme in making Him a Son and finally (God). Yet they say that they killed Jesus, the Son of God because He made Himself the Son of God.

The history of this man Jesus has been gravely misunderstood by us, the American so-called Negroes.

HOLY KUR-AN AND BIBLE (Continued)

THE POISON BOOK and the enemies of black mankind, who accuse the righteous daily of being other than righteous, then charge me, and my followers with teaching hatred, overlook the hatred taught by others. According to the Bible (Luke 14:26), "no man could be His disciple unless he hate his father, mother, children, brethren, and sisters, even his own life."

There are many people and especially my people saying that they love everyone. One who loves everyone is not a true lover of anyone, not even himself or herself.

If a righteous person loves an unrighteous person he or she is also unrighteous. Who could trust one who loves everyone? Jesus could not have loved His enemies (the white race) and died that they may be saved, with His knowledge of that people being the children of the devil (John 8:44) and guilty of persecuting and killing the Prophets of Allah (God).

How could Jesus have love for such people who were bent upon killing Jesus Himself, and had lied and caused bloodshed in Paradise four thousand (4,000) years before Jesus was born? Could God Himself be so weak that He couldn't produce a righteous nation, but was able to produce a righteous Son (without the agency of man) and then had to sacrifice His righteous Son, to the delight of His enemies, to bring about a reconciliation between Him and His enemies?

This same enemy who had raised hell in heaven, upset the peace there, and on earth, put angel against angel, sent them to war against each other, divided and scattered the holy people throughout the earth, and still doing the same today, but were so loved by God and His Son, Jesus, that they can't give this race of enemies up to be destroyed for their evils? Oh, how you have and still gravely misunderstand the scriptures.

The only people whom God will give a son's life, so they may be reconciled is the American so-called Negroes. They are the ones who have sinned by following this race of people (the man of sin), without knowledge of either.

It is useless to think otherwise. We, are the only people who left our own native country to follow strangers (the white race) and become trapped by them for the past 400 years, and now we must have some place (a country) to ourselves like other nations to survive.

The entire earth belongs to black mankind. Shouldn't there be enough of it for you and me to live on independently? There are 57,255,000 square miles of land out of water on it, and 29,000,000 square miles of that is producing land.

Seventeen million of us from slavery should not rest until we are really free and on our own. It is sheer ignorance for us as a nation in such number to be satisfied with anything less, but we can never be a free and recognized people until we give back or drop our slave masters' names, their religion and churches.

I must keep repeating this to you, because these are your invisible chains of slavery that are and will hold you more securely as a slave than visible chains.

Everything loves its own kind, the fowls of the air, after its kind, the beast and animals, all by nature after their own kind. It is now very disgraceful for our people to be imitating our slave masters and our women trying to look like them with paint and dye. Educators of our people should help in reforming our women into Islam.

The religion of Islam OPENS your EYES to self and your kind, and you feel and see yourself the equal of mankind for the first time. It makes a new person of you altogether, and again for the first time you are in love with your people.

It is a religion of UNITY and brings you into unity with Allah (God) and His creatures. Islam teaches heaven and hell while you live, and this is true. How can one suffer hell or go to heaven after death? Our own nature is against such SLAVERY belief. After the return of our bodies to earth, what would you have left to send to heaven or hell?

The great time of a separation is now on between the righteous and the devils (black and white), but the American so-called Negroes, my people, don't understand who they are or anyone else, and we must teach them regardless to the cost. Go to our temples, one may be in your city, or write me for the addresses at 5335 South Greenwood Ave., Chicago 15, Illinois.

HOLY KUR-AN AND BIBLE (CONTINUED)

"Set your face upright for the religion in the right state. The nature made by Allah, in which He has made man." Holy Qur-an 30:30.

The so-called Negroes (descendants of the Tribe of Shabazz) are good people, very religiously inclined by nature (Divine members of God) and for the first **TIME** have the privilege of accepting the right religion in the right state. Islam the religion of Allah, is the religion of the so-called Negroes, though their enemies may be adverse. Allah (God) Himself is on their side to save and deliver them. They are inclined to righteous worship so much so, until they are constantly seen disgracing themselves in their ignorant way, due to the lack of knowledge of their God and His TRUE RELIGION, ISLAM.

FOR THE past 100 years since the slave masters have opened the door of his church to them, they have gone insane over it. They have not taken a sane thought that, if there were any saving power in the white race's churches of Christianity for them, why hasn't the POWER freed them from the slave masters' children? Why are they begging them now for civil rights, which are supposedly given to any citizen by the Constitution? A slave or a free slave is not His master's equal; therefore it is silly for the so-called Negroes to think of being granted equal rights with their slave masters' children.

Think over it, a people and their religion who beg you to become a member and after accepting it with your whole heart, then you must pray to them for recognition. They are ashamed to even call you a brother or sister in their religion, and their very nature rebels against recognizing you.

AGAIN I REPEAT: "Set your face upright for the religion in the right state." Islam recognizes equality of Brotherhood; a Muslim is the brother of another Muslim, regardless to how black the skin or kinked the hair. He is welcomed with sincere and open arms and recognized by his light skinned or copper-colored Arab brother. He is also recognized in the same

way by his brown or yellow-skinned Japanese, Chinese and Indian brothers. Can you say this for your Christianity? In Islam you are not a believer
until you first love for your brother that which you love for yourself.

If the white Christians had meant good for you and me, why did they
make slaves of us and why are they still subjecting us to the most severe
and ugliest injustice?

EVERYONE LOVES good for self: then should not he love the same
for others? If such love were practiced, there would never be a need for
an army, neither a police force. Believe it or not, this is the kind of love
and Brotherhood of Man, that Allah (God) is now bringing about under
the religion in the right state (Islam) by pushing off our Planet Earth those
opposes of the right religion (Islam) and the Universal Brotherhood of
Man.

Let us ask: "When is a religion in the right State"? A religion is in the
right State when its author is the All Righteous Being and that religion
believed and practiced according to the Will of God (it's author). It must
apply to our nature in which we were created. That is the right religion.

IT IS NATURAL for man to want to be the equal of man. It is natural
for man to love the Brotherhood of Man (except the man devil). It is natural that man love FREEDOM for himself, for freedom is essential to life.
It is also natural that man love JUSTICE for himself, for without justice
there is no joy in freedom and equality. Can you say that you are enjoying
freedom, justice and equality in Christianity? Islam, the religion in the
right State is most surely the right religion. Islam uses for its sign the Sun,
the Moon and the Star. These three (the Son, Moon and Star) are most
essential for our well-being. These signs represent a physical work of
Freedom, Justice and Equality, while the Cross (the sign or emblem) of
Christianity represents the physical workings of that religion. The Cross
is far from being a sign of a true religion. If a religion's base (foundation)
or sign is not found in the universal order of things, it cannot be called the
religion of Allah (God), nor can it be called a religion in the right State.
The so-called Negroes should never wear a cross or take such an emblem
as a sign of his or her salvation for it is just the opposite.

It is time that the so-called Negroes have Freedom, Justice and Equality. Join on to Islam if you love to enjoy the Brotherhood of Man.

WHO IS THE ORIGINAL MAN?

THE above question is now answered from the mouth of Allah (God) to us, the so-called Negroes, for the first time since our straying away from our own nation.

This secret of God and the devil has been a mystery to the average one of mankind, to be revealed in all of its clearness to one who was so ignorant that he knew not even himself, born blind, deaf, and dumb in the wilderness of North America.

All praise is due to the Great Mahdi (Allah in Person), Who was to come and has come the Sole Master of the Worlds. I ask myself at time, "What can I do to repay Allah (the Great Mahdi, Fard Muhammad) for His coming, wisdom, knowledge and understanding?

Born in the Southern part of this Wilderness (Wilderness of Sin), where the Man of Sin has always manifested himself to us, the so-called Negroes, that he was really the evil one by the way he treated us. Yet, we were made so dumb that we still couldn't recognize him.

The truth of him is now being told and taught throughout the world to his anger and sorrow. He is losing no time trying to hinder this truth of the above question, who is the Original man?

He is setting watchers and listeners around me and my followers to see if he can find some other charge to put against us to satisfy his anger of the truth that we preach from the mouth of Allah, Who is with us in Person.

THE ORIGINAL Man, Allah has declared is none other than the Black Man. The first and last, maker and owner of the Universe, from him came all brown, yellow, red and white. By using a special method of birth control law he was able to produce the white race.

The true knowledge of the black and white mankind should be enough to awaken the so-called Negroes, put them on their feet and on the road to self-independence. Yet, they are so afraid of the slave masters that they even love them to their destruction and wishes that the bearer of truth would not tell the truth even if he knows it.

The time has arrived when it must be told the world over for there are millions who don't know who the Original Man is. Why should this question be put before the world today? Because it is the **TIME** of judgment between the two (black and white) and without that knowledge of the Original Man, it means to be without knowledge of the rightful owner of the earth.

ALLAH (to Whom praise is due) is now pointing out to the nations of earth their rightful places and this judgment will bring an end to war over it.

Now it is so easy to recognize the Original man, the real owner of the earth by the history of the two (black and white). We have an unending past history of the black nation, and a limited one of the white race.

We find that history teaches that the earth was populated by the black nation ever since it was created, but the history of the white race doesn't take us beyond 6,000 years.

Everywhere the white race has gone on our planet, he either found the Original Man or a sign that he had been there previously. Allah is proving to the world of black man that the white race actually doesn't own any part of our planet.

THE BIBLE and Holy Qur-an bears witness to the above said, if you are able to understand it. The Holy Qur-an, the beauty of Scriptures repeatedly challenges them to point out or show the part of the heavens and earth that they created?

It further teaches that they are not even their own creators. We created man (white race) from a small life germ, the soft pronoun "we" used nearly throughout the Holy Qur-an makes the knowledge of the Original Man much clearer and of a more intelligent knowledge of how the white race's creation took place.

In the Bible referring to their creation we have **US** (Gen. 1:26) creating or rather making the race, the **US** and **WE** used show beyond a shadow of a doubt that they came from another people.

A KNOWLEDGE of the white race removes once and for all times the mistakes that would be made in dealing with them. My followers and I can and are getting along with them in a more understandable way than ever, because we know them.

You can't blame one for the way he or she was born, for they had nothing to do with that. Can we say to them why don't you do righteousness when Nature did not give righteousness to them? Or say to them why are you such a wicked devil? Who is responsible; the made or his maker?

Yet this doesn't excuse us for following and practicing his evil, or accepting him for a righteous guide just because he is not his maker.

READ next week's issue - If the civilized man fails to perform his duty, what must be done?

August 4, 1956

IF THE CIVILIZED MAN FAILS TO PERFORM HIS DUTY WHAT MUST BE DONE?

THE CIVILIZED MAN - his duty is to teach civilization to the uncivilized, the arts and sciences of civilized people and countries of advanced civilization.

A Divine Messenger of God (Allah) raised among his people with the Divine Message is held responsible for its delivery. His message teaches spiritual civilization which is important to the success of a nation and society. According to history, the people who refuse to accept Divine Guidance or His Message sent by His Messengers are classified as uncivilized or savages.

A well-educated, cultured and courteous people make a beautiful society when it is spiritual. Good manners come from the civilized man who doesn't fail to perform his duty.

There are several civilizations, we have a wicked and a righteous. It is a righteous civilization that is in the workings now. We all have been well trained into the wicked civilization, now we must be trained into the knowledge of the righteous one. We **MUST** have a righteous, trained civilized man, who will not fail to perform his duty to us in guiding and teaching us.

My people in America (the so-called Negroes) are under the search-light of the righteous, who are offering to them the right guidance to a supreme civilization of righteousness, never witnessed before on earth. The white race has failed to perform its duty of civilizing the American so-called Negroes. Of course, they have been their slaves for many centuries, and the slave masters have rights over them, as long as they are his slaves; however, if the slave masters free their slaves - not in words, but in deeds - the slave masters should provide the once-slaves with the right civilization and with everything necessary for them to start an **INDEPENDENT** life as their slave masters have.

Certainly, the so-called Negroes are being schooled, but is it the equal of their slave masters? No, the so-called Negroes are still begging for equal education. After being blinded to the knowledge of self and their own kind for 400 years, the slave masters **REFUSE** to **CIVILIZE** the so-called Negroes into the knowledge of themselves of which they were robbed. The slave masters also persecute and hinder anyone who tries to perform this most **RIGHTFUL DUTY**. I will continue to say: That as long as the so-called Negroes don't know who they really are and do not have the knowledge to free themselves from their slave masters' names and religion, they can't be considered free or civilized. To this, their slave masters will agree. Some of the so-called Negroes are ignorant to this important advantage of having their own nation's names, they think there is nothing to a name (it isn't to the ones they are using), but the Bible says a good name is better than gold. To continue to bear the slave masters' names makes them the property of their slave masters and they can never hope to receive equal recognition in the civilized world.

Will a free people accept slaves as their equal? The so-called Negroes must be truly civilized and the right civilized man has not performed his duty until this is **ACCOMPLISHED**. However, the so-called Negro is free to receive his or her own, if they just don't allow **FEAR** and **IGNORANCE** to stand in their way.

It has been seen from the little chance they have had to get a little education, they have shown and proven that they are the original people, who are only asleep and in great need of the right civilized man who will perform his duty of awakening them. The so-called Negroes' fear of being deprived of food, clothing and shelter, also the usual smile of the white slave masters' children, prevents them from seeking the true knowledge of their own nation's civilization. They **MUST** drop the slave masters' names and religion, of which both (names and religion) they have and don't understand, which means nothing but slavery. Of course, some (not all) preachers and politicians, who live off the ignorance of their people, are opposed to the right civilization of our people (the so-called Negroes). Our people are taught to eat the wrong food and drinks, games of chance (gambling), going half-dressed, looking for salvation after death, and not giving a hoot for salvation in this life, as right civilization teaches us.

C O M E and **FOLLOW** the right guide and be rightly civilized.

A u g u s t   1 1 ,   1 9 5 6

CIVILIZED MAN FAILS TO PERFORM HIS DUTY
WHAT MUST BE DONE?

YOU MUST know that you have been rightly civilized. No one can enslave another who has equal education (knowledge). My people (the so-called Negroes) lack science (knowledge) of the right kind. Allah (God), to Whom praise is due, is here to give you and me a superior knowledge of things and a country to ourselves. Separation of the so-called Negroes from their slavemasters' children is a MUST. It is the only solution to our problem. It was the only solution according to the Bible for Israel and the Egyptians and it will prove to be the only solution for America and her slaves, whom she mockingly calls her citizens without granting citizenship. We must keep this in our minds at all times, that we are actually being mocked.

I think it is a DISGRACE to us for ever being satisfied with only a servant's part. Should not we, as a people, want for ourselves what other civilized nations have? It takes a true friend or friends to help another or others to enjoy equal FREEDOM, JUSTICE and EQUALITY. Today for the first time in our history we have that TRUE FRIEND in Allah (who came in the person of Master Fard Muhammad) and the Nation of Islam, if we only would submit and accept Him.

IT IS WRITTEN (Rev. 14:1) that 144,000 of us will accept and return to our God and people, and he rest, 16,856,000, would go down with the enemies of Allah(God). For this sad prophecy of the loss of my people, I write what I am writing, hoping perhaps that you may be able to beat the old prophets' predictions by making the truth so simple that a fool can understand it. You must be RIGHTLY CIVILIZED. You must go back to your OWN PEOPLE and COUNTRY, but not one of you can return with what you have. You must know that this is the TIME of our separation and the JUDGMENT OF THIS WORLD (the Caucasian race) that you and I have known. Therefore, Allah (God) has said to me that the **TIME** is ripe for you and me to accept our OWN (the whole Planet Earth). What are you waiting for, the destruction? Come let us reason together, but you cannot until you have a thorough knowledge of self. Who are you waiting on to teach you the knowledge of self? Surely, not your slave masters who blinded you to the knowledge. (The white race's civilization will never work for us.)

They taught you and me to eat the wrong food, both physically and mentally. Allah (God) has blessed America with plenty (not because she is good), all kinds of foods enough to spare for every hungry person the world over.

AFTER RECEIVING this great blessing she eats and drinks the divinely forbidden food and drinks and at the same time blessed with the best. Millions of pounds of beef, lamb, chickens and fish of all kinds, yet she eats the dirty, filthy hog to Allah's (God) dislike, and almost forces the so-called Negroes to eat it, or I would say everyone. She drinks more alcoholic drinks than anyone else. She is blessed with so much wheat that she can hardly find room to store it, and will even burn it to raise the price, yet she teaches the so-called Negroes to eat **CORNBREAD** and the **HOG**, both of which are a slow death to people in the Southern part of this country (America).

My people have been reared on such poison foods and now all the doctors in the world can't tell them that it is not good for them. All hogs contain trichina (called pork worms), whose larvae infest the intestines and muscles of hog eaters. This animal (hog) is one of Allah's (God) most hated and never was intended to eat.

HE IS MADE for medical purposes. God made him for the white race, because of their physical weakness, which came from being grafted from the Original Nation, thus making them a prey to attracting germs (disease); therefore they demand a superior poison germ for medical purposes to cure the many diseases that they attract. This Allah (God) has taught me, and much more on the subject, but space won't permit me to go further on it.

Jesus was wise to this race, according to John 8:44, see Matt. 8:31. The hog is for the white race, but not you and me. The hog is grafted from cat, rat and dog, says Allah. See Isa. 66:17-65:4. The Holy Qur-an says of them, those who refused to obey Moses, Allah cursed them, and made them apes, and swine. Take yours and give them theirs.

August 18, 1956

IS THERE A MYSTERY GOD?

WHO IS that MYSTERY GOD? We should take time and study what has and is being taught to us. Study the word, and examine it, and if it be the TRUTH, lay hold to it.

To teach people that God is a mystery God, is to teach them that God is UNKNOWN. There is no truth in such teaching. Can one teach that which he himself doesn't know?

If one teaches a thing that he himself doesn't know, he can be charged with lying to the people. The word MYSTERY, according to the English dictionaries, is - something that has not been, or cannot be. Something beyond human comprehension. The unintelligent, or rather one without divine knowledge, seem to delight themselves in representing the God as something mysterious, UNKNOWN.

Such teaching (a mystery God) that God is a mystery makes the prophets' teachings of God all false. There should be a law made and enforced upon such teachers until they have been removed from the public.

ACCORDING TO Allah, the origin of such teachings as a mystery God, is from the devils; it was taught to them by their father, Yakub 6,000 years ago. They know today that God is not a mystery, but will not teach it. He (devil), the god of evil, was made to rule the nations of earth for 6,000 years, and naturally he would not teach obedience to a God other than himself.

So, a knowledge of the true God of Righteousness was not represented by the devils. The true God was not to be made manifest to the people until the god of evil (devil) had finished or lived out his time which was allowed to deceive the nations (read 2 Thessalonians 2:9-10;Rev. 20:3- 8-10).

The shutting up and loosing of the devil mentioned in Rev. 20:7, could refer to the time between the A.D. 570 - 1555 when they (John Hawkins) deceived our fathers and brought them into slavery in America, which is near 1,000 years that they and Christianity were bottled up in Europe by the spread of Islam by Muhammad (may the peace of Allah be upon him) and his successors.

Their being loose to deceive the nations of the earth would refer to the time (A.D. 1555 to 1955) which they were loose (free) to travel over the earth and deceive the people.

Now their freedom is being interfered with, by the Order and Power of the God of Righteous through the Nation of Righteous.

For the past 6,000 years, the prophets have been predicting the coming of God who would be just and righteous . . . This righteous God would appear at the end of the world (the world of the white race).

Today, the God of Truth and Righteousness is making Himself manifest, that He is not any more a mystery (unknown), but is KNOWN and can be SEEN and HEARD the earth over.

This teaching of a mystery God enslaves the minds of the ignorant. My poor people are the victims of every robber. They are so pitifully, blind deaf and dumb that it hurts but I am going to prove to them that I am with Allah (God) and that ALLAH is with me.

In spite of their ignorance of Allah and myself whom He has sent, for I am not self-sent, and the world shall soon know who it is that has sent me.

Allah (God) loves us, the so-called Negroes, so (Tribe of Shabazz) that He will give lives for our sake today. **FEAR** NOT, you're no more forsaken. God is in person, and stop looking for a dead Jesus for help, but pray to Him whom Jesus prophesied that would come after Him. He, who is alive and not a SPOOK.

Do you hate me because I represent Allah, the Living God, your Lord and my Lord? Can you, who believe in a mystery God (unknown) trust your mystery to bring you bread, or to defend you against your open enemies (the blood-thirsty lynchers)? If so, on what occasion did he help you?

If God is a mystery, you are lying to the world when you say that you know Him.

READ YOUR OWN Bible and see if you can find wherein God ever said to the people that He was a mystery God.

He wants to be known, it is His enemy (the devil) who doesn't want God to be known to you and me. Do you refer to God as He, Him? These pronouns refer to a man.

Do you say that Allah (God) hears, sees, speaks, walks, feels, smells, tastes? Then He is a man.

No spirits can do such things. Did you say that you want to be like Him? Surely, you don't want to be a spirit without form, as spirits have no material form. Your God and my God is a material Being, and the Supreme of Beings.

WHAT IS ISLAM?

IT CAN BE ANSWERED in one word (righteousness). Briefly, it is the religion of Allah (God) and His Prophets. Islam is as old as Allah (God) Himself of whom Allah (God) is the author. Islam, the religion of Adam, Noah, Moses, Jesus and Muhammad (the last). Islam the religion of entire submission to the will of Allah (God). ISLAM is the religion of which the Holy Quran teaches.

Allah (God) says: "This day I have perfected for you your religion and completed my favor on you, and chosen for you Islam as a religion (Chapter 5:3). Allah (God) also says in another chapter of the Holy Quran: "Surely the true religion with Allah is Islam," (Chapter 8:18).

The significance of the name "Islam" is peace, the true religion. It is a religion of eternal peace. We can't imagine Allah (God) offering to us a religion other than one of peace. A religion of peace coming to the righteous after the destruction of the wicked is also mentioned in several places in the Bible - read (Psalms 29:11), "The Lord will bless His people (so-called Negroes) with peace (Islam)"; also, "He will speak peace unto His people and to His saints" (Psalms 85:8), and also, the Lord of Peace give you peace always (II Thess. 3:16).

Islam is the religion referred to in the above-mentioned Biblical verses. It is the only religion that gives the believer a peace of mind and contentment. It removes grief and fear at once on believing: "Yea, whoever submits himself entirely to Allah, and he is the doer of good to others, he has his reward from his Lord, and there is no fear for him, nor shall he grieve" (Holy Quran 2:112).

ALLAH INVITES to the abode of peace (Holy Quran 10:25). Can you imagine a divine prophet being sent with anything other than a religion of peace to his people?

As Mr. Muhammad Ali says in the preface of the Holy Quran (Reference, page 6) on Islam: Peace is, therefore, the essence of Islam, being the root from which it springs and the fruit it yields, and Islam is thus pre-eminently the "Religion of Peace."

Our people, the so-called American Negroes, will love Islam when they learn more of it. For it is the religion of their fathers, and it is the last of the three great religions of earth. The other two, Buddhism and Christianity cannot give us a lasting peace. We have tried them to our disappointment.

Christianity is one of the most perfect black slave-making religions on our planet. It has killed the so-called Negroes completely mentally.

Now it takes Allah (God) Himself to revive and restore our people back into their own. Though, I am His Messenger, and Allah can use my life as He pleases for them. They are my people and many lives - while I am only one life.

ISLAM WILL give them the heaven while they live. Islam has more to offer than the white-controlled Christianity. Islam is universal. The true believers of Islam equal in number that of the total population of the whites on our planet (400,000,000).

By nature all members of the black nation are Muslims (lovers of peace) of whose number is over the billion mark.

We must have Islam as our religion to restore our peace after suffering under the slavery, persecutors and the grievous of wars for 6,000 years. The so-called Negroes of America never known the way of peace, no love or mercy was ever shown to them, have today Allah (God).

THE GOD of mercy on their side in the religion of Islam, freedom, justice and equality.

But they are so dumb to it that it hurts my very heart. I am not surprised at what disbelievers think and say of me, but when a supposed Brother Muslim joins the disbelievers in what I write, then I am surprised.

For no true Muslim will speak against another Muslim to the delight of the disbelieving people of Allah and His Prophets and religion of Islam. If your door today is open to all which include human devils whom Allah is angry with and threaten them with total destruction I leave it to Allah to judge between you and me.

WHAT IS ISLAM?

HE IT IS who sent His Apostle with the guidance and the True religion, that he make it overcome the religions, all of them, though the polytheists may be averse; Holy Qur-an (61:9), according to the Holy Qur-an (the right Scripture for the Time).

In the above verse Allah (God) in the last days of this present world (wicked infidel) states that he must destroy false religions with the True religion (Islam). It (Islam) must overcome all other religions that teaches us that Allah in the judgment of the world, will not recognize any religion other than Islam.

Take to task all the learned teachers of religions and they will admit that God is One and that He will have only one religion in the hereafter.

Search the Scriptures of the Bible and Holy Qur-an and be convinced. There are two other religions today that oppose the religion of peace (Islam) namely: Buddhism and Christianity. These two opposing forces will be removed from the people so completely by the light of Islam, TRUTH, guided by Allah in the person of the Great Mahdi, Fard Muhammad. I am His Apostle. It will come to pass that you won't even find a trace of them. Christianity is already dying a natural death. We want a religion of peace, FREEDOM, JUSTICE and EQUALITY. We want it from the Divine Supreme Being Allah, and not a religion prepared by the hand of His (Allah's) enemies.

They desire to put out the light of Allah with their mouths, but Allah will perfect His light though the unbelievers may be averse. Holy Qur-an (61:8). Regardless of the efforts to put out the light of truth (Islam) today, their efforts will be a complete failure. Think over the slavery teachings of Christianity, the three gods, and the worship of Mary, the disciples of Jesus, the many gods of Buddhism; the incarnation taught by both, and other ignorant practices. Islam teaches an eternal heaven for the righteous, but hell is not eternal.

These (heaven and hell) are not necessary places but conditions. Islam teaches that if a brother kills a brother the murderer must be killed, or anyone that murders a Muslim.

The Christian goes to war against each other daily killing their own brothers and others. The righteous must be rid of such people. Make Islam to overcome all other religions whether the disbelievers like it or not. Our God is ONE GOD. Can one God believe in more than one religion and be true to Himself and others?

If the other religions were true religions surely Allah (God) would not send an apostle to overcome them with another religion. "Is it other than Allah's religion that they seek to follow, and to Him submits, whoever is in the heavens and earth, willingly or unwillingly." (Holy Qur-an 3:82). We all bear witness to the TRUTH that everything of Allah's creation obeys Him, regardless to size or numbers.

But the proud wicked MAN of SIN he refuses, and goes about teaching ignorant people not to believe in Allah and His religion Islam.

The TRUE religion with Allah (God) is Islam. (Holy Qur-an 3:18). The emblem of Islam represents the sun, moon and stars; the meaning: FREEDOM (Sun), JUSTICE (Star), and EQUALITY (Moon).

No nation's religion other than Islam have the sun moon and stars as their emblem, no religion is worthwhile if its roots are not found in the universal order of things, and no nation can use the sun, moon and stars to represent their government or religion, but the nation that owns it (the nation of Islam).

We are the sole owners. It was our father who made it. The prayer service of Islam is not equal by any other religion, five prayers a day is made with the face turned in the direction of the SUNRISE.

Prayer at sunrise, at noon, mid-afternoon, at sundown, and before retiring, and if awakened through the night another prayer is made. In fact, two prayers should be said during the night, making a total of seven prayers a day. There is no worship of a Sunday or Sabbath in Islam, all the days are worship days. The Muslims wash and clean all exposed parts of their bodies before prayer early at the gray dawn of day.

September 8, 1956

PRAYER SERVICE OF ISLAM

STUDY the Muslim's way of worship, and you will agree with me, that there is no better way of divine worship.

First, he washes and cleans himself before communication with Allah (God).

In order thus: **FIRST**, clean the body, and then invited the clean Holy Spirit to come in, for your house (body) is made fit. He rinses his mouth, cleanses his ears for hearing, the exposed hands are washed up to the elbows (if exposed), because he is about to spread forth those hands to Allah, the Supreme Being.

WHAT EVIL those hands have committed, he has washed them with water and now said Allah to wash them in the Spirit of Forgiveness.

He stands erect before Him with his hands spread forth, ears cleaned from the hearing of evil, and eyes closed from seeing evil, with face toward the only HOLY spot on our Planet (the Holy City of Mecca).

The city wherein Abraham made an attempt to sacrifice his son Ishmael, under a trial of Allah (God), which was also a sign of what would take place in the Last Days on finding and returning the lost-found people of Abraham and his son, Ishmael. The, Muslim now opens his mouth in prayer.

DECLARING THATALLAH is the **GREATEST** and that he bears witness that there is no God but **ALLAH**, and that none deserves to be served (worshipped) but **ALLAH**, and that Muhammad is His Last Apostle (an Apostle whom Allah would rise from that lost and found people of the seed of Abraham in the Days of Judgment).

Then he (Muslim) further declares, **"That he has turned himself to Allah, being upright to HIM WHO ORIGINATED the HEAVENS and the EARTH,** and that he is not one of the Polytheists (a believer in more than one God).

No religious worshipper could beat such preparation for his prayer service or use more honor and submission to his Maker. The words of the prayer are the best to be used by the so-called Negroes in America, for they fit his condition more than any other people on earth.

We have been turned from our God (Allah) towards the devil, believing and worshipping a trinity of Gods, with our faces down or upward towards the sky, and our thoughts of God in the sky.

THE TURNING, the bowing, prostrating of the Muslims in their prayer has a beautiful meaning which space won't allow me here.

The Muslims are in accord with the whole Earth's turning; it revolves on its axis eastward toward the sun, being attracted by it. Eastward is where we look to daylight, it is in that direction came the prophets and civilization of man.

It is also in that direction which we are told to expect the coming of the Son of Man (God in Person) in the last days of the wicked. The Muslim is taught to pray five (5) times a day and two (2) at night if he awakens, a total of seven.

Do we not have seven inhabited Planets, and the seventh thousand-year after the six thousand years of the devil's rule?

Are we not reminded of this in the six work days of the week (the six thousand years of the workings of the devils), the seventh to rest which belongs to the Lord (the original owners, the Blackman)?

THE PRAYER service of Islam, as I have said, is beautiful. The Muslims' oft-repeated prayer is as follows: "In the name of Allah, the Beneficent, the Merciful; All praise is due to Allah, the Lord of the Worlds, the Beneficent, the Merciful. Master of the Day of Requital.

"Thee, do we serve, and Thee do we beseech for help, Guide us on the right Path, the Path of those upon whom Thou hast bestowed favours, not of those upon whom Thy, wrath is brought down nor of those who go astray."

The Muslims seek in the above prayer the Path to trod that will bring to them Divine help, and for so-called Negroes, this (Islam) is that Path which will get divine help on your side.

Set your face upright for the religion in the right state. The nature made by Allah in which He has made man; there is no altering of Allah's creation. That is the right religion, but most people do not know. (Holy Qur'an 30:30.)

THE GREAT IS FALLING (Rev. 18:2-4)

"COME OUT of her my people, that you be not partakers of her sins, and receive not of her plagues."

The so-called Negroes know not that the above warnings are directed to them, and that they are living in the country where all the prophecy of this chapter (Rev. 18) has been and is being fulfilled.

They are poor, spiritually blinded, and do not know it. Why should the **GREAT BABYLON FALL?** The second verse answers: because she has become the **HABITATION OF DEVILS**, and the hold of every **FOUL SPIRIT**, and a cage of every **UNCLEAN and HATEFUL BIRD** (Rev. 18:2). Nothing could fit the description of North American better.

The country is the habitation of every type of human wickedness. Ancient Sodom, Gomorrah, Nineveh, Babylon and Roman sins were only children's acts compared with the modern sins of America. The wicked cry and rage for more freedom to commit more sins.

THEY PRACTICE the worse kind of filthy wickedness that it takes scientists to think up and invent. This people have done and will do worse.

This race (Caucasian) hates the truth, when that truth is in the favor of her slaves (the so-called Negroes).

Gambling is a common sin in America, drunkenness, use of drugs, adultery, lovers of self, sweet hearting with one's own sex, and murder are the order of the day. Sodom was rich with plenty, her people passed away their time in idleness, but not as much nor as rich as modern Babylon (America), her equal is not found in the past.

America committed suicide when she brought the so-called Negroes from their native land and into slavery. This can't be forgiven her, though the so-called Negroes would gladly forgive, for the promise of social equality, but it is not left to the slave to forgive his master.

REMEMBER THE BIBLE'S parables of Lazarus and the rich man, and Abraham acting as the spokesman for Lazarus and the rich man, and Abraham acting as the spokesman for Lazarus. Abraham knew that Lazarus would have been foolish enough to try making an attempt to save his Master who was in hell to his own destruction.

Not one time did the rich man ask Abraham to bring him water, but he knew the weakness of his servant Lazarus, and was fully aware of the consequences of Lazarus' attempt to aid him after being engulfed into the Divine chastisement.

September 22, 1956

COME OUT OF HER, THE GREAT IS FALLING (REV. 18:2-4)

THE REVELATOR saw (Rev. 18:1) an angel come from Heaven (from the Holy Land) having **GREAT POWER,** and the earth (the so-called Negroes) was enlightened with His Glory (wisdom, knowledge of the truth).

This angel can be no other than Master W. F. Muhammad (the Great Mahdi), who came from the Holy City Mecca, Arabia, in 1930.

He is the most wise and powerful being on earth or ever will be (God in Person). He, who with a strong voice announced the immediate doom of America.

He said that there was no punishment great enough to repay the slave masters for their evils done against the so-called Negroes of America. He also said that the country is filled with devils and every kind of evil.

His voice was strong and mighty, and to everyone who believed and accepted the **TRUE** religion, **ISLAM**, he gave them a holy name of Allah's (God). Every word that he said is true. He came for the salvation of the so-called Negroes, warning them to join on to their **OWNKIND** (the nation of Islam).

ALL NATIONS are charged with committing fornication with her (America) and are now angry with her. The merchants of the earth were made rich in trade with her.

America, the richest of all countries, pays the highest wages, therefore she must charge a high price for her merchandise, and those who buy her merchandise for resale must sell for a profit, and they too, are made rich from such deals.

They shall weep and mourn over her (America), for no man buyeth her merchandise anymore (11th verse). When people are rich and powerful, they can't see themselves being brought to an ought overnight.

Who can remain in power if God has decided against him? He (Allah) exalted whom He pleases and whom He pleases, He brings to an ought.

WHAT DOES the Bible teach us were the sins of Nebuchadnezzar and Belshazzar that God disgraced and broke the power of one, and outright killed Belshazzar? Was it not for those silver and golden vessels that were the property of the Temple of God?

It is the Temple's property now (the so-called Negroes) that God is after today. Nebuchadnezzar was charged with bringing them away from their Temple of God, so is England today charged with bringing into America the first black people to be sold into slavery.

She has and still is losing her power over the World of Black mankind, and she will be left only a stump of her power in what is called the British Isles.

America has poured wine into those sacred vessels (the so-called Negroes) and makes mock of them.

Let no man fool you concerning the American so-called Negroes, they are sacred in the eyes of Allah (God) today. The Negroes will have to be chastised into the knowledge of Allah, the God of their Salvation.

FEAR NO MORE for your God is on your side to avenge you of her. We are in a cage. Islam is the key for us all.

There are several prisoners writing to me, wanting to accept Islam. Just send your slave name saying that you want to join on to your own Holy Nation of Islam, and to serve and obey Allah, and His Apostle. When you are free, report to one of our nearest temples, but be sure it is one that I am the leader.

In the meantime, we will record your name here on our book as a registered Muslim.

I like to read what anyone of you have to say for the Truth, of which I am writing in this paper. Flee to Allah for refuge.

THE GLORIOUS HOLY QUR-AN SHARRIEFF

The book that the so-called American Negroes (Tribe of Shabazz) should own and read, the book that the slave masters have, but have not represented it to their slaves, is a book that will heal their sin-sick souls that were made sick and sorrowful by the slave masters. The book will open their blinded eyes and open their deaf ears. The book that will purify them, the book that makes a distinction between the God of righteous and the God of evil, the book of guidance, the book of light and truth, the book of wisdom and judgment.

But the average one should first - be taught how to respect such book, how to read it, how to understand it, how to teach it. The Qur-an Sharrieff contains some of the most beautiful prayers that one ever heard recited or read. It is called the Glorious Qur-an and without mistake that is just what it is. This book is not from a prophet, but direct from Allah to Muhammad (may peace and the blessing of Allah be upon him) not by an angel, but from the mouth of Allah (God). The Great DISTINGUISHER between TRUTH and falsehood in the judgment of the world, of whom the enemy of truth has ruled the nation of black mankind with falsehood for the past six thousand years.

This book pulls the cover off the covered and shows the nation for the first time that which deceived 90 per cent of the people of the earth without the knowledge of the deceiver. The revelation of the book is from Allah, The Mighty, The Knowing (Chap. 40:2), according to the above chapter and second verse. Allah is the Mighty ONE over all other beings, and is the Knowing ONE. Therefore He knows what is best for every living thing. And the book (Qur-an) that he has revealed there is no doubt about it, for the All Knowing ONE, the Best Knower has revealed it. One who has no equal, the All Wise.

Man makes himself a fool to try attacking Him in arguments. So, we have no doubt the Holy Qur-an is from the Lord of the Worlds. It is one of the cleanest reading books you ever read. The God that revealed the Holy Qur-an Sharrieff to Muhammad (may the peace and blessing of Allah be upon him) is the same that revealed the scriptures to the other prophets according to the Holy Qur-an Sharrieff, "Surely we have revealed to you as we revealed to Noah and the prophets after him, we revealed to Abraham, Ishmael, Isaac, Jacob, the Tribes, Jesus, Job, Jonah, Aaron, Solomon and we gave to David a scripture, and to Moses Allah addressed His words speaking to Him. And we sent Apostles we have mentioned to you before, and Apostles we have not mentioned to you; (4:163, 164)." Some people whom the devils have deceived in regards to the Holy Qur-an, call it the work of Muhammad - (may peace and blessing be upon him).

Some call the religion Islam a dream of Muhammad, though the Bible doesn't say it is from God, but from the prophets, and is dedicated to King James of England. The white race does not like to worship a black god and his black prophets. They are too proud to recognize a black prophet or god. The so-called Negroes should know this by this time. The Holy

Qur-an's readings are not the kind that will lull one to sleep, but to get a real Qur-an one should know the Arabic language in which it is written. However, you can find a good translation of it by Yusuf Ali and Muhammad Ali.

EDITOR'S NOTE: The opinions expressed in this column in no manner reflect the editorial policy or beliefs of The Pittsburg Courier. The views are the author's own writings.

THE HOG AND HIS EATER

ACCORDING to a letter published in the editorial section of The Courier, Sept. 15, a Mr. M. Majevsky (white) of Brooklyn, N.Y., charged me with being mixed up in my facts on the black and white people. Great offense was taken because I said that one is superior to the other, and whom the hog was intended for. I am far from being mistaken in what I write pertaining to these two (black and white), and I don't need to study the theory of evolution to learn them.

Theories don't always prove to be the truth. I have the **TRUTH** from the **ALLWISE** One **ALLAH** in Person, to Whom praise is due. He has raised the curtain of falsehood which kept the true knowledge of the black and white (especially the white race) from the peoples of the earth for 6,000 years.

This **ALLWISE ONE** appeared under the name of Mr. Fard Muhammad, and most of the time was known only to His enemies as Mr. W. D. Fard. He came without observation.

Mr. M. Majevsky further says, I am a preacher of racial hatred, but like all of his race, don't like the **TRUTH** especially if the truth is against them. This, we have known all of our lives.

The manifestation of either God or the devil is the manifestation of the other, the devil being a deceiver of the nation of black mankind doesn't like to be revealed, even in his **TIME**. The guilty fares better before a Court of Justice on confessing his guilt, or even keeping quiet than to put up an argument trying to cover up. As it is written, "The bed is too short, and the cover too narrow."

The **TRUTH** of this race (white) of mankind has come. Take it or leave it. To fight it is like darkness trying to fight light, Mr. Majevsky, and if I am a preacher of race hatred, I wonder how you heard me over your whole race of preachers . . . **HATE THE NEGROES?**

Created from Adam to hate and murder all black mankind, and you are that by your very nature in which you were made. Never have I heard white mankind teaching his people to love the so-called Negroes (the Tribe of Shabazz), but one can hear them almost daily (the so-called Negroes) preaching the love of the "Caucasian race."

They are ignorant to the knowledge of that race and in such ignorance you, Mr. Majevsky, would like them (so-called Negroes) to remain. Authoritatively, I can say that they won't because it is a **MUST** for God (Allah) to make the Caucasian race known to them.

Why should the poor so-called Negroes love or preach love for such people who enslave them and their own kind, subject them to every evil and brutal treatment imaginable? The white race is openly haters and enemies of the so-called Negroes; but for the sake of ruling the so-called Negroes in ignorance, and any one of them who opens his or her mouth to teach the **TRUTH, LOVE** and **UNITY** among the so-called Negroes, that one is hated by Mr. Majevsky and his race. He or she is labeled by them as being the worse among the so-called Negroes. They know that they can get the foolish, scared Negroes against such a person, among them, that they (white race) don't like.

I warn you my people, be very careful of siding with them against me and my followers, lest you find yourselves in the chastisement of Almighty God. Allah (God) and I are your friends and they are not. Take us for friends and not as your enemies. I am offering you **LIFE** eternally and they are offering you slavery and death. Their own Presidents, Congress and armies will not force their brothers to give you and I, **FREEDOM, JUSTICE** and **EQUALITY** with them.

In many of their places they won't allow you to eat or drink, not even allow you into their public toilets. They will also shoot you in some places if you dare ask for **JUSTICE**, and teach you to shoot the one among you who seeks **JUSTICE** for you.

It is a terrible thing for such people (Yakub's grafted race) to charge me with teaching race hatred when their feet are on my people's neck and tell us to our face they hate the black so-called Negroes. Remember now they teach you that you must not hate them for hating you.

The Negroes don't need to fear any more if they will believe in Allah (God) and follow me.

Now, for the **HOG**, he was truly made as I said for the white race, for medical purposes and regardless to who eats the hog he was not made to be taken as a food. I made this very plain, also God and His Prophets are my witness, and are with me.

Have you read your own history? Your Bible? The Holy Qur-an? The 2,000-year history of the Caucasian race in Europe before the birth of the Prophet Musa (Moses)? You should surely do so if you haven't. I don't care if all of the whites on earth eat the hog. I am only concerned with my people who don't know, nor do they understand. I know that not one of my poor people will go to Heaven (see the Hereafter) who eat this **POISON HOG** after being given the knowledge.

The white race knows that eating swine flesh, committing acts of adultery, robbing, murdering and lying shall not be recognized as Servants of God, and won't see the Hereafter, if such one doesn't repent today. We see the white race in the South fighting to keep the so-called Negroes from even voting for one of their own (white race) to rule them.

They even fight their own laws to prevent the so-called Negroes from sitting in classrooms with their children. Although it is better for us to not allow ourselves to be destroyed by mixing with them. Get an equal education, but stay to yourselves today. It is too late in the evening to try mixing the races.

The hog is called khanzier in the Arabic language, which means, khan - "I see, zier -" foul and very foul. This animal is so foul, ugly and filthy that it is known to the medical profession that eating the hog sounds the mental power. There is a small opening in the inside of its front legs out of which flows a mass of corruption and the Medical Science says: "The opening is an outlet of a sewer."

See the Monitor of Health by Dr. J. H. Kellogg, M.D., pages 117 - 124. The hog is shameless. Most animals have a certain amount of shyness, but not the hog and his eater; they are similar. The hog-eater will go nude in the public if allowed, their temper is easily aroused and under such conditions they will speak the ugliest and vilest, most filthy language one has ever heard, spoken in public.

Their mouths are full of cursing and swearing. The hog is not a peaceful animal and can't get along in peace with each other. He is the greediest of all animals. He will not divide his food with his young, only the milk in their bellies. The hog is the cause, the very root of most of our sickness. **STOP EATING THEM** and see for yourself.

The Bible forbids you to eat them, Mr. Christian, it is forbidden by God through the mouth of His Prophets. Do you think that you can clear yourself with God by eating the swine and claiming it is all-right?

I will give here some of the places in your Bible where you can read of this Divinely forbidden flesh (the hog). "Of their flesh shall you not eat, nor touch their dead carcass." Deut.: 14: 8. "I have spread out my hands all the day unto a rebellious people who eat swine's flesh and broth of abominable things is in their vessels," Isa: 65:2-5. In the heathen sacrifices some offered swine blood and burneth incense to an idol. Isa: 66:3: "They that sanctify themselves (call themselves sanctified and holy) in the Garden behind one tree (in the church behind the pastor of it) eating swine flesh, the abomination and the mouse, shall be consumed together, saith the Lord." Isa. 66-18 which says, "Stand by thyself, come not near to me, for I am holier than thou." (Such is said by the hog-eating Christians.) These are a smoke in my nose, a fire (anger) that burneth all the day 65:5, "Of their flesh thou shall not eat, and they that saw it told them how it befell to him who was possessed with the devils, and also concerning the swine. Mark 5:11-16. Go and ask my followers who were once possessed with the devil and the swine, how they feel since their release from such by Allah, to Whom praises are due.

The poison swine is a scavenger and lives and thrives from filth, and the tissues of the hog swarms with parasites, worms, which are 99 per cent poison. Allah (God) hath said: "They shall not eat the **SWINE**." Allah says in the Holy Qur-an3:168, 169, 173: "O men, eat the lawful and good things out of what is in the earth, and do not follow in the footsteps of the devils" (the devil referred to is no other one but the white race). Surely, he is your open enemy.

He only enjoins upon you evil and indecency, and that you may speak against Allah, that which you do not know. When it is said to them (meaning our people the so-called Negroes) follow what Allah has revealed, they say, "Nay, we follow what we found our fathers upon," though their fathers had no sense at all, nor did they follow the right way. He (Allah) has only forbidden to you what dies of itself, and the blood and flesh of the filthy swine, and that over which any other name besides Allah has been invoked. (Holy Qur-an).

Allah says that the Caucasian race, having once been a savage people living in the caves and hillsides of Europe, they ate almost everything like meat and ate it raw for 2,000 years. Their cave days to be exact was 4,000 B.C. Naturally, they know good, but just haven't the nature to do good, and you can't make them good unless they, are returned into that which they were taken from. You, who have the Divine Nature of God, do the thing that is right. Unite, live and die for each other in the name of Allah and His Religion of peace, Islam. Do not let the Caucasians attract you to do evil things that you see them doing.

THE HEREAFTER

AFTER WHAT? Maybe the question asked. The HEREAFTER means after the destruction of the present world, its power and authority to rule. The Bible and Holy Qur-an Sharrieff are filled with readings on the HEREAFTER of which I will leave to you to read for proof. This subject wouldn't be necessary if it were not for that Man of Sin being permitted to RULE.

Since he (they) was given ruling authority to try him (them) for 6,000 years, the word "Hereafter" is used, meaning: After the present rule of the Man of Sin, because his (theirs) time is **LIMITED** to a certain time 6,000 years. Some say, after the judgment, after the Man of Sin and his people have been judged and sentenced to death. May I say here, that this present world was sentenced to DEATH when the Man of Sin was made and all who follow him.(**"Whoever of them will follow you, I will certainly fill hell with you all."** Holy Qur-an 7:18.) The Bible says: **"These both were cast alive in a lake of fire."** Rev. 19:20. The Man of Sin and his people deceived the righteous by making them believe that he (they) also is one of the righteous. He (they) claims one father is the father of all, while that is not true.

We all look forward to a **HEREAFTER**, to seeing and living under a ruler and a government of righteousness, after the destruction of unrighteousness. The people of the Man of Sin (the devils) even are worried, disgusted, dissatisfied with their own world and wish to see a change to a better world; but they desire to be the ruler in that **better world**. The **HEREAFTER**, some believe after the **GREAT WAR** of **ARMAGEDDON**, or HOLY WAR

A religious war between the two great religions of the earth and their believers namely: **ISLAM** and **CHRISTIANITY**, of course **BUDDHISM** will also be involved. The **HEREAFTER**; there the righteous will make an unlimited progress; peace, joy and happiness will have no end. War will be forgotten, disagreement will have no place in the **HEREAFTER**. The present Brotherhood of Islam is typical of the life in the **HEREAFTER**, the difference is that the Brotherhood in the **HEREAFTER** will enjoy the spirit of gladness and happiness forever in the Presence of Allah. The earth, the general atmosphere will produce such a change that the people will think that it is a new earth. It will be the heaven of the righteous forever; no sickness, no hospitals, no insane asylums, no gambling, no cursing and swearing will be seen or heard in that life. Fear, grief and sorrow will stop on this side as a proof. Every one of us who accept the religion of Islam and follow what God has revealed to me, will begin enjoying the above life here.

I never felt the like before. Islam is heaven for my people, they will see their God in truth, the righteous meet and embrace them with peace. (As-Salaam Alaikum.)

The life in the **HEREAFTER** is an image of the spiritual state in this life. Just think how good you feel when in the Divine Spirit for a while, you are so happy that you don't feel even the pain of sickness, no trouble or sorrow, and that is the way you will feel always in the next life.

We, the so-called Negroes who accept Allah and Islam will reap this glorious joy and happiness. You will be clothed in silk interwoven with gold and eat the best of food that you desire. This is the time when you enter such life, for your God is here in Person, and you will never be that which you cannot be any more, after believing in Him. My people have been deceived by the **arch deceiver** in regards to the **HEREAFTER**. They think the **HEREAFTER** is a life of spirits (spooks) up somewhere in the sky, while it is only on the earth, and you won't change to any spirit beings. The life in the **HEREAFTER** is only a continuation of the present life. You will be flesh and blood. You won't see spooks coming up out of graves to meet God.

No already physically dead person will be in the **HEREAFTER**, that is slavery belief, taught to slaves to keep them under control. This is taught also so that they won't be thinking over the wealth of their slave masters while under the slave master. The slave is made to believe his will come after death, and his master knows that death settles all, and that you can't return to tell him whether he lied or told the truth.

Read the Scriptures carefully on the life in the Hereafter, and you try understanding it, and you won't find that it actually means what you have been believing. No one is going to leave this planet to live another. You can't, even if you try. You can't reach the moon and live on it, so be satisfied and believe in Allah, live where you are on this good earth, but be righteous.

I must quote these beautiful verses here of the Holy Qur-an, it says: "O soul that is at rest, return to your Lord, well pleased with Him, well pleasing. So, enter among my servants, and enter into my Paradise". (Holy Qur-an 89:27-30).

October 20, 1956

THE ONE HUNDRED AND FORTY-FOUR THOUSAND...

THIS number is mentioned in the Bible (Rev. 14:1) as being the number of the first believers in Allah (God) and His messenger.

The messenger is called a lamb due to certain characteristics of his (the messenger) being similar to that of a sheep, and the tender love of Allah for him like that of a good shepherd towards his sheep.

Though the love of Allah (God) for the so-called Negroes is not equaled by anyone. Describing us as sheep is about the best way of putting it, as sheep are dumb, ignorant and humble, not aggressive.

They will not fight even if attacked by the wolf. So, are the so-called Negroes and Allah has to do the fighting for them.

Let us understand what we are reading. It is prophecy in symbolic of the future that was seen in a vision by Yakub, the father of the white race, which he saw on the Isle of Patmos or Pelan 6,000 years ago. He was warning his people of that which would come to them at the end of their time.

THE NUMBER (144,000) in mathematics means a **SQUARE** which is a perfect answer for the spiritual work of Allah (God) with that number of people.

They are the first (Negro) converts from among the wicked to Allah (God) and His Messenger, referred to as the first ripe fruit (the first of the righteous) unto God and the Lamb, in verse 4 of the same chapter. They are righteous enough (ripe) to be picked out of the wicked race to be used for the purpose of squaring the nations of earth into righteousness.

After the righteous black nation has labored under the wicked rule of the devils for 6,000 years, the return to a righteous ruler, under the God of Righteousness, the people must be reorganized to live under such government.

The All wise God Allah to Whom praise is due, Who came in the person of Master W. F. Muhammad, seeking us, the lost and last members of a chosen nation, is building a new world of Islam out of the old. Therefore, He lays the base of His Kingdom with a square number of **MATHEMATICSTRUTH.**

His New World of Islam (Kingdom of Peace) can be proven mathematically step by step, which we all know that mathematics is truth.

He (Allah) uses the square made of them (the so-called Negroes) who He redeemed from among men (the Caucasian race); they were not defiled with women (the women other than their own kind).

This number (144,000) will be made up of all the so-called American Negroes who have been the merchandise of the American whites for 400 years.

They now must be redeemed by Allah (God) for them to be free according to the Law of Justice, and become the Servants of their Own God (Allah) again. The so-called Negroes should shout to learn of this **DIVINE TRUTH**.

The Revelator didn't see a single one of the Caucasian race in the number (144,000). He (Allah) gave the number of the beast in the previous chapter (Rev. 13:18) as the **NUMBER SIX**, which is the true number of the Caucasian race, or the Man of Sin.

The Bible says, "Let him that hath understanding count the number of the beasts." After the coming of Allah (God), the symbolic beast and his number has been revealed, it is now understood.

THE NUMBER 144, the root is "12" and there are 12 Tribes, the 12 Imams the real answer.

Allah said we once had 13 Tribes, but one got lost. The number 144 will be the Stars of the Nation, and this number (144) multiplied by 12 equals a cube.

This number (144,000) so-called Negroes, under the guidance of Allah (God) Who came in the Person of Master W. F. Muhammad, will cube the whole nation of black mankind, into a nation of righteousness.

Write and get your name on the Nations Book of Life, as one of the brothers or sisters on the SQUARE (144,000).

October 27, 1956

REDEEMED from the power and curse of the slave masters, who have condemned and killed them (the so-called Negroes) and they didn't resist (James 5:6), so doubly true it is. We are denied justice and are put to death by the hands of the enemies daily without even a protest, except by a few. 144,000 out of over 17 million so-called Negroes will actually give up the murdering beast, his name, way of worship and go back to their native people and country. It is a sad picture.

They must have a belief in Allah, and His religion of peace (Islam) for our return. Therefore, the number is small, because the beast (devil) put fear into us when we were babies. The devils seek to destroy the 144,000 as soon as they heard the **TRUTH**, while only babies in the knowledge of it (Rev. 12:4). They also seek to kill any so-called Negro who has enough nerve to speak the **TRUTH**, as the **TRUTH** hurts the devil, and **FALSEHOOD** hurts us and brings us down to the devil's doom.

A LAMB stood on the Mount Sion and with Him a 144,000 having His Father's name written in their foreheads (Rev. 14:1).

First, **SION**, according to the Bible dictionary, is one of the various names of Mount Hermon (Deut. 3:8). Second, the Greek form of the Hebrew name Zion, the famous Mount of the Temple, Mount Hermon. A mountain on the northeastern border of Palestine (Deut. 3:8). Hermon is the most conspicuous and beautiful mountain in Palestine or Syria. If Sion means the Mount or the- Temple in **JERUSALEM** or the land now called Palestine, in this prophetic prophecy of the place for the 144,000 redeemed, then it is a good place to begin, or land for the squaring of the nations, as at present a dispute reigns over who the owner is. Putting them on the square with the God of the LAMB (Messenger or Apostle) to move eastward, because the Lamb's job won't be completed until He and His company have convinced the old world that His God, who delivered them from the beast, is the God of the worlds, and only **HE**, should all nations serve and obey.

It is written (by Sir William Muir on the Life of Muhammad) that Muhammad had 144,000 sincere followers with him on his last pilgrimage to the Holy City Mecca, and not one hypocrite or infidel was among them.

The second and third verses (14:2-3) make mention of the of many people (many water) over the Lamb and His followers' victory over the beast (the devil). The fourth verse says that the 144,000 were not defiled with women, that they were virgins. These women must refer to the beasts, for they are forbidden to the righteous; and if the 144,000 would make love with those whom God (Allah) had come to destroy, their victory over the beast would be impossible. It is the women who the enemy will use to attract the 144,000 to go down to hell with them. She was used in Paradise to bring about the fall and exile, to trick Moses' people, to trick Samson.

They had the name of their Father, not the beast's name (slave masters), which was of no value. His name and works are to be destroyed from the earth. The beast's name was not a name of God or His attributes, but this the so-called Negroes don't know, but I am telling you now. All Muslims' names have a beautiful meaning and 99 of them are divine attributes. Remember my people Jones, Johnson, Smith, Hog, Bird, Fish, Bear, Woods and such names as Roundtree will not be accepted by your God and mine (Allah).

To make up that square (144,000), to be truthful with you, God has said to me that, He will not accept any white people in His Kingdom. The mark, according to the Holy Qur-an that will be in their foreheads will be from prostrating. The Muslims prostrate in their prayers on rough floors or rugs, which produces a mark on the forehead. Some of my followers have such sign now produced by the five prayers a day obligation. The righteous is always marked by his righteousness, as the wicked is marked by his or her wicked acts. They are actually marked by nature and are recognized by both parties.

The 144,000 were not afraid of the beast, as God is on their side and they put their trust in Him alone.

The **LAMB'S** (the Messenger) only weapon was the **TRUTH** (the sword that proceedeth out of his mouth) and it stands true that truth alone is sufficient to destroy **FALSEHOOD**, as light destroys darkness. The ninth verse of the same chapter (Rev. 14) warns us against worshiping the beast, his image or to receive his mark on our head or in our hand, and the small shall drink the wrath of God poured without mixture, and shall be tormented with fire and brimstone in the presence of the Holy Angels and the **LAMB** (Apostle).

The so-called Negroes have great love for their slave masters, their church, religion, color and works. This love must be lost or cast away to become one of the 144,000. You, who believe literally in the physical resurrection of the dead, must remember the Book here teaches that the first righteous to be saved (the 144,000) is redeemed from among men (Rev. 14:4), not out of the grave. It is a sin that you are so blinded that you cannot see, nor will you accept plain **TRUTH**. Surely, there is a resurrection of the dead. It is one of the principles of Islam, but not the physically dead in the graveyards. It is the mentally dead, the ignorant, whom the devil's falsehood has killed, to the knowledge of truth, the **DIVINE TRUTH** which must be preached to them to awaken them into the knowledge of Him again. You and I know that it can't refer to a physically dead person, because that one won't and can't rise again. What is left to rise from a body that has gone back to the earth, or up in smoke, or eaten by some wild beast or fish of the sea? People who died before the flood and after? Even Adam? They have nothing to rise from. Remember the old Testament (the Torah) doesn't teach of a resurrection of the dead, according to Job (chapter 7:9), "he that goeth down to the grave shall come up no more." He must be right as we haven't seen one come up yet from the grave that was really dead. Surely, if it had meant a physical death, God would have taught it to Adam, Noah, Abraham, Moses, and all of the ancient prophets would have had a knowledge of it, even Job, but not so.

Write in and join on to the 144,000. Islam is your right religion, hurry, join your own before it is too late.

"ISLAM - DIGNIFIES"

Why I stress the religion of Islam for my people, the so-called American Negroes.

FIRST - and most important, Islam is actually our religion by nature. It is the religion of Allah (God) not an European, organized white man's religion.

SECOND - It is the original, the only religion of Allah (God) and His Prophets. The only religion that will save the lives of my people, and will give them Divine protection against our enemies.

THIRD - It dignifies the black man; gives us the desire to be clean internally and externally, and for the first time to have a sense of dignity.

FOURTH - It removes fear and makes one **FEARLESS**; it educates us into the knowledge of God and the devil, which is so necessary for my people.

FIFTH - It makes us to know and love one another as never before.

SIXTH - It destroys superstition and removes the veil of falsehood. It heals both the physical and spiritual by teaching what to eat, when to eat, and what to think, and how to act.

SEVENTH - It is the only religion that has the Divine Power to unite us and save us from the destruction of the War of Armageddon, which is now. It is also the only religion in which the Believer is really divinely protected. The only religion that will survive the Great Holy War, or the final war between Allah (God) and the devil.

Islam will put the black man of America on top of the civilization. So, why not Islam? Some people say, "Why so much religion?" It is very much necessary for me to teach the knowledge of that which is the only KEY to the HEREAFTER for my people. After this final war between right and wrong, the lucky ones will be in the Government of Righteousness. Therefore, without the knowledge of it, we can't qualify to live in it.

Islam makes hell and heaven not two places, but two conditions of life, which is very easy to understand. For there could never be either unless it was brought about by our own efforts or making. The earth is our home and we can make it a hell or heaven for us. If we follow and obey Allah and his prophets, we make it a heaven; if we follow and obey the devil and his prophets, we make it a hell.

Islam brings about a peace of mind and contentment to the believer for the first time love for our own black brother and sister. What one loves for himself, he must love for his brother. I will say here that, this alone is salvation to you and me, just learning to love each other as brothers. Islam, unlike Christianity, is doing this right in your midst.

Regardless to how long and how hard you try to be a good Christian, you never have a sincere true love for your own black brother and sister as you should. Islam will give you true brothers and sisters the world over, and this is what you need.

A people subjected to all kinds of injustice need to join Islam, as you are sure of Allah's (God) help in Islam. Why don't the preachers of my people, preach Islam? If they would, overnight they could be on top.

Are you proud to submit to Allah and sit in Heaven while you live, and have His protection against your open enemy? Take it or leave it. You will soon wish that you had. God is drying America up by degrees, little by little. Write and join by mail, the time is at hand and hell is kindling up. Islam is the right way.

"THE GRIEVOUSNESS OF WAR"

"Corruption has appeared in the land and the sea, on account of what the hands of men have wrought" - (Holy Quran, 30:41).

The prevailing corruption is everywhere on account of men's own evil doings. Their hands have built their own doom and never before has such prophecy been fulfilled any clearer than today.

If we take the spiritual side of the above verse from the Holy Quran, 30:41, we will find that it is equally true. The world today is so evil and corrupted that people do not pay any attention to the preaching of good. Their whole hearts, minds and souls are going after evil and bloodshed of each other.

No peace among them, hatred and disagreement are universal. A change of rulership must take place in order to save the nations from self-destruction. They have corrupted the land and sea with all kinds of deadly arms; weapons of destruction which their own hand have built.

They delight greatly in war and not in peace. Who then can enjoy peace in the midst of such a mad world? Who can be trusted? The alarm of war is heard and possibly designed to wipe mankind from the face of the earth. The land is charged with every type of man-made weapons of destruction of each other's lives.

The sea, he has filled with deadly surface ships and undersea crafts (submarines). The sky has been filled with planes loaded with death to drop on his fellowman. Yet they say PEACE. Where is any peace with such evil forces free to spread death and destruction on the poor innocent human beings of the earth? They glory in killing and are not satisfied with the prosperity they have enjoyed. Their thanks to God is to destroy His people. This evil people have worked all of their lives making trouble, causing bloodshed among the peaceful people of the earth and themselves.

Their greed in ruling the black people of the earth is unequaled. They send all their armed forces against you to make you bow to their rule. Even in your own home they want to rule according to their desire and not to yours, although it is your HOME.

Once they have access to enter your house, they will go to war with you before they will leave in peace. They will take over your property and call it theirs. "Allah will scatter them who delight in war." - (Psalms 69:30).

Let the world ponder - what does history show that the white man can call his own outside of Europe? However, they spread out and over into the homes of black mankind of the earth, taking by armed force, the black people's home and making slaves of them for many centuries.

The day has arrived and the TIME IS AT HAND. Every man to his own. It is the days of Allah (God), and the people of peace MUST HAVE PEACE. The troublemakers must be punished and brought to an end so they will never be able to give trouble anymore.

Many shall suffer because of the corruption that this world has brought and is bringing upon innocent people.

LET NOT YOUR FLIGHT BE IN THE WINTER. War throws people out of homes; it is a grievous thing. A HOLY WAR IS TO BE DREADED.

Oh, my people, fly to Allah and the TRUE RELIGION, ISLAM. Get out of the names and religion of this wicked troublemaking people for Allah (God) will destroy them with their own hands. I am very much concerned over my people in America for they know not that this is the TIME OF TROUBLE. Join and send in your names to the following address: Muhammad's Temple No. 2, Inc., 5335 Greenwood Ave., Chicago 15, Ill.

"KNOW THYSELF"

It is knowledge of self that the so-called Negroes lack that which keeps them from enjoying Freedom, Justice and Equality, and this belongs to them divinely as much as it does to other nations of the earth.

It is Allah's (God) will and purpose that we shall know ourselves; therefore he came himself to teach us the knowledge of self. Who is better knowing of whom we are than God himself? He has declared that we are descendants of the Asian black nation and of the tribe of Shabazz.

You might ask, who is this tribe of Shabazz? Originally, they were the tribe that came with the earth (or this part), sixty trillion years ago when a great explosion on our planet divided it into two parts. One we call earth and the other moon.

This was done by one of our scientists, God, who wanted the people to speak one language, one dialect for all, but was unable to do so. He decided to kill us by destroying our planet, but still he failed. We were lucky to be on this part, earth, which didn't lose its water in the mighty blasting away of the part called moon.

We, the tribe of Shabazz, says Allah (God), were the first to discover the best part of our planet to live on. The rich Nile Valley of Egypt and the present seat of the Holy City, Mecca, Arabia.

The origin of our kinky hair, says Allah, came from one of our dissatisfied scientists, fifty thousand years ago, who wanted to make all of us tough and hard in order to endure the life of the jungles of East Asia (Africa) and to overcome the beasts there. But he failed to get the others to agree with him.

He took his family and moved into the jungle to prove to us that we could live there and conquer the wild beasts and we have.

So, being the first and the smartest scientist on the deportation of our moon and the one who suffered most of all, Allah (God), has decided to place us on the top, with a thorough knowledge of self and his guidance.

We are the mighty, the wise, the best, but don't know it. And being without that knowledge we disgrace ourselves, subjecting ourselves to suffering and shame. We could not get the knowledge of self until the coming of Allah. To know thyself is to know all men, who, from us came all, and to us all return.

I must keep warning you that you should give up the white race's names and religion in order to gain success. Their days of success are over; their rule will last only as long as you remain asleep to the knowledge of self.

Awake and know that Allah has revealed the TRUTH. Stop believing in something coming to you after you are physically dead. That is untrue and no one can show any proof of such belief.

Again, know that Jesus was only a prophet and cannot hear you pray any more than Moses or any other dead prophet. Know too, that this white race was created to be the enemy of black mankind for six thousand years, which makes their number to be six. That is not yours or my number; we don't have a number; because, we have no birth record. Don't let anyone fool you. This is the separation and the War of Armageddon. KNOW THYSELF. Write and join up with your own kind and religion before it is too late.

December 8, 1956

ISLAM IS FOR THE BLACK MAN

The religion of Islam makes one think in terms of self and one's own kind. Thus, this kind of thinking produces an industrial people who are self-independent. Christianity does just the opposite; makes the so-called Negroes lazy, careless and dependent people.

Think over such slavery teaching as this: "That a rich man can't see the hereafter," while Allah (God), in the same breath; is offering the righteous Heaven (riches) while they live. I must continue to warn you that you can't depend on the white race to care for you forever. There is an end to your dependence on them. So, why not start in time seeking something for self?

This is the fall and end of power on the earth. Know this, the white race as a dominant so-called American Negroes (Tribe of Shabazz), that the loss of Asia to the white race means the end of their luxury. It must come to pass, believe it or not. As it is written - "Blessed is he who understands." You need a country to yourself. You will never be able to live as you desire until you are in your own (Islam). Hold unity meetings among yourselves to better your understanding of each other.

Whatever profession or trade you may have, do something for yourself and your kind and choose for yourselves the one religion, Islam. Islam will secure for you, favor and protection of Allah (God), also universal brotherhood. The nation of Islam will be the winner, especially the lost-found with Allah.

Stop looking for anything after death - Heaven or hell. These are in this life. Death settles it all.

Stop eating yourself to death by eating three meals a day. Eat once a day and eat the best food, which, when eaten correctly, keeps you in the best of health. Stay away from the HOG meat. Don't eat stale beef, chicken or fish. Eat fresh products.

Don't eat field peas such as brown or black-eyed peas, lima beans. Don't eat collard greens, cabbage sprouts, cornbread. Eat brown bread (whole wheat), butter, if not overweight and a little cheese. Drink milk. Cook your food well done. Pray five times a day with your face towards the east. Love your black brother as thyself. Do good to all.

Write and join your own. Write to Muhammad's Temple No. 2, Inc., 5335 Greenwood Ave., Chicago 15, Ill.

December 15, 1956

"IF GOD WAS YOUR FATHER, YOU WOULD LOVE ME" - (JOHN 8:42)

READ and study the above chapter of John 8:42-44, all of you, who are Christians, believers in the Bible and Jesus, as you say. If you understand it right, you will agree with me that the whole Caucasian race is a race of devils. They have proved to be devils in the Garden of Paradise and were condemned 4,000 years later by Jesus.

Likewise, they are condemned today, by the Great Mahdi Muhammad, as being nothing but devils in the plainest language. The so-called American Negroes have been deceived and blinded by their unlikeness, soft, smooth, buttered words, eye-winking, back-patting, a false show of friendship and handshaking.

The above-mentioned acts, with the exception of handshaking by men is a disgrace to any decent, intelligent person. Know the truth and be free of such disgrace to you.

Surely, if the Father of the two people (black and white) was the same, the two would love each other. In a family where the children are of one father, they love each other because they are of the same flesh and blood.

It is natural then for them to love each other. Again, it is not unnatural then for a member or members of a different race or nation not to love the non-member of their race or nation as their own.

The nature in which we are created just won't allow us to be like that and it works the same in all things living that have a bit of intelligence, including the birds, animals and beasts.

The argument here between Jesus and the Jews is, the Jews claim they all were the same people (children) of one God or Father, but this Jesus disagreed with and proved they were not from the same Father (God).

He, having a knowledge of both Fathers, knew their Father (Devil) before his fall, and before he had produced his children (the white race) of whom the Jews are members. Here, in this chapter (John 8), it shows there was no love in the Jews for Jesus.

THE COMING OF ALLAH (GOD)

THE REALITY of God. I have been and am still trying, to make clear to you how important it is. This knowledge of the True God, the reality of God, has been and is even now a mystery to the world of mankind, with a few exceptions. The day has come that all mankind MUST know the reality of Allah (God).

Previously, I said: "There can be no judgment of the people until this knowledge has been given to the people."

How can we serve a God without knowledge of Him? My people, the so-called Negroes (the Tribe of Shabazz), are the worst off when it comes to the reality of God.

THE WHOLE WORLD has been and is looking for the coming of God. Several places in both the Bible and Holy Quran refer to the coming of Allah (God) . . . "The Coming of the Son of Man." Referring to God as the Son of Man should remove all doubts as to him being anything other than a man.

The Bible mentions him as the Son of Man and also mentions him as not being a man, but a spirit.

On one side he is made clear and on the other he is made a mystery. Representation such as this causes confusion in understanding. We are blind to the knowledge of God when we make him a mystery and unreal.

ANYONE SO BLIND to the reality of God is the servant of the devil, until he or she sees God as a reality.

Thousands of years the devil has been blinding man to God's reality and that is why, or the reason God had to come in person (and he has), to clear us of such ignorance and blindness to the knowledge of him.

Therefore, we have the "Coming of Allah (God)." He is referred to as the Son of Man because (first) - He is the Son of Man and gotten for a special purpose which is to return the lost back to their own; to punish and destroy the wicked for their destruction of the righteous; that the righteous may live in peace and do the will of the God of righteousness, free of trouble and interference.

(Second): He must be a man to deal with a man and we can't receive nor respect other than man.

SINCE HIS WORK is to destroy the wicked, he must remain hidden from the eyes of the world until the time is ripe (the end), for neither of the two (God and devil) can rule together.

The Son of Man (Allah) must wait until his TIME, after the works of the devil.

(II Thessalonians 2:8-9) - (Holy Quran 7:14-18) and in another place, the Holy Quran describes them as the people with the blue eyes (Holy Quran 20:102).

Third: The reality of God is as clear as the reality of the devil, but we didn't know it until His coming to judge the world. For instance, if we take God for something other than a man (not the man devil), we can't prove it.

If we believe that he is a spirit and not a man, then we can never expect to have any knowledge of him except by the sense of feel.

WE CANNOT SEE a spirit, therefore, the teachings of His coming would be false. The spirit of life is and has been with us all of our lives.

God is in person among us today.

HE'S A MAN, HE IS IN HIS TIME. God sees, hears, knows, wills, acts and is a person (man). The evil workings of the devil MUST come to an end. Join your own kind.

I AM ALLAH THE BEST KNOWER
(HOLY QURAN SHARRIEFF 32:1)

THERE are many other chapters of the Holy Quran Sharrieff that opens with the above words, "ALLAH IS THE BEST KNOWER." The beautiful teachings of the Holy Qur-an has no equal in other scriptures.

All so-called Negro preachers should have one, but be sure it is one translated by Yusuf Ali, or Maulvi Muhammad Ali. Any other translation of the Holy Qur-an by Christian authors is as poisonous to the reader as a rattlesnake.

What I am trying to make clear in this column is that, white people don't believe in Allah and Islam, nor the prophets of Allah. Why then, should you seek the truth of it from them? You will soon come to know that you should not seek any truth from them. They have you following in the wrong direction, and hope to keep you like that; but by my Allah's Power and Wisdom, and my life's blood, you shall know the TRUTH even against your own will.

They (white people) have nearly all of the poor black preachers on their side to oppose Allah, myself and Islam, the true religion of the righteous. They will fail and be brought to disgrace as Pharaoh's magicians and himself were by Allah and Moses, His servant. You must come face to face with Allah (God) for you have not known Him, nor His religion, as Israel had not known God by His name **JEHOVAH** (Exodus 6:3).

They felt that they shouldn't believe Moses' representation of God by any other name than God Almighty, regardless to Moses' stress upon **JEHOVAH** as being the God of their Fathers. Pharaoh had not used that name (**JEHOVAH**), so Israel wouldn't accept it until a showdown between Jehovah and Pharaoh. I would not like to have you wait until a showdown between Allah and the modern Pharaoh's people, therefore I come to you with the truth verifying that which is before it, and giving good news to the believers that, they most certainly shall have Heaven in this life. I also come to you with a warning to you who disbelieve that you most certainly shall have a hell in this life, and in the hereafter you most certainly will be among the losers, or do they say, "He has forged it?" Nay, it is the truth from your Lord, that you may warn a people to whom no warning has come before, that they may follow the right direction (Holy Quran 32:3).

You say, "Who is this Allah, and this religion Islam?" Know my people the Divine Supreme Being has 99 attributes that makeup His name and Allah is the 100th. Surely His are the most Beautiful Names. He will make Himself known to the world that He is God and besides Him there is no God, and that I am His Messenger, that Islam is a religion backed by the Power of Allah (God) to free you from the hands of your merciless enemies (the slave masters) once and forever.

You are living under the very shadow of death, murdered daily, and the white murderers are never killed for doing so. They shoot our women down as well as our boys and men, with nothing done about it but talk. AWAKE! my people, unite with me and Allah, your God, and believe in His true religion Islam. Allah will grant you power to overcome your enemies though their power may look as endurable as the mountains.

FEAR NOT! Allah is the BEST KNOWER. Armageddon has started, and after it there will be no Christian religion, nor churches. Jesus was a MUSLIM, not a Christian as you believe.

You may secure a Holy Qur-an and other Islamic teachings from Saikh Muhammad Ashraf, Lahore, Pakistan. Go back to your religion, Islam and Allah your God.

1957

ANSWER TO MR. R. R. DEROUGEMENT

REGARDLESS to the black man's mass suffering the rule of the Caucasian race, there is always someone who would like to justify their treatment of the black man and many times it comes from the mouth of the sufferer.

The above-mentioned Mr. DeRougement's letter was given plenty space in the editorial section of this paper recently to tell his dislike for Mr. Malcolm X's "Truth of Our Slavemasters." Mr. Malcolm X is one of my ministers and followers.

Mr. DeRougement desires to defend the white slavemakers of our people by mentioning their medical treatment to some blacks of Africa, which was done to enslave them, and not for any love of them.

He asks Minister Malcolm to prove that Islam is the original religion of the native African. I say, yes, and all the people who are members of the black nation, according to the meaning of Islam and what the Holy Qur-an Sharrieff teaches us of Islam. Islam means peace and entire submission to the will of Allah (God), who is the author of Islam.

The name Islam was not invented as in the case of other religions. It is the religion of (peace) all the prophets according to the Holy Qur-an, Noah, Abraham, Moses and Jesus and Muhammad the last.

Entire submission to the will of Allah (God), brings us into the peace of Allah and that is the religion of Islam.

"Yea, whoever submits himself entirely to Allah and he is the doer of good to others, he has his reward from his Lord and there is no fear for him, nor shall he grieve" (2:112). "And then set your face upright for religion in the right state, the nature made by Allah in which he has made men."

Do we not all love peace for self if not for others? Further in another place: "Surely the true religion with Allah is Islam (3:18). Peace with God implies complete submission that is Islam, and it is as old as God himself.

"They shall not hear therein vain or sinful discourse, except the word, peace, peace" (56:23).

Could we imagine Allah (God) giving mankind any other religion - but one of peace? "He is, who sent his Apostles with the guidance and the true religion that he may make it overcome the religions, all of them, though the Polytheists may be averse" (6:19).

We can't believe that Allah (God) ever had but one religion for mankind. According to the Holy Qur-an, Islam was the religion of all the prophets of God so could we imagine a prophet of God bringing us a religion other than peace? Islam is the religion of peace that God offers us in the Bible (Num. 6:26), (Psalms 29:11, 85:8), (Isaiah 26:3, 32:17). There are many other places in the Bible that prove that Islam, the religion of peace, is mentioned as being the religion of Allah (God).

It is the last of the three great religions, Buddhism and Christianity. Christianity is the youngest of the three. The father of the black African tribe went there 50,000 years ago from the tribe of Shabazz and his religion and the whole tribe of Shabazz was none other than Islam.

The religion of the father of the white race (Yakub) before his fall was none other than Islam. According to the word of Allah (God): "This day I have perfected for your religion and completed my favor on you and chose for you Islam as a religion" (5:3).

January 12, 1957

ANSWER TO MR. R. R. DEROUGEMENT (Continued)

NO ONE knows the age of Islam; it has no birth record. It will dominate mankind after the destruction of the devil, who is the sole troublemaker and disturber of the black man's peace.

Islam ceased to dominate mankind after the making of devil; 6,000 years ago to rule mankind. People began to divide themselves into families and tribes and set up their own religions and objects of worship all over the earth. Allah (God) and His religion, Islam could not or would not interfere with the rule of the devils and their false religion.

If we had, there wouldn't have been any devils or false religion. The proof: When Muhammad started teaching it (Islam) in Arabia over 1300 years ago, just 600 years after the death of Jesus, he and his followers and successors almost converted the whole world back into Islam in a few hundred years.

IT (ISLAM) WAS slowed down to allow the devils to rule their time out. Now, time is out and Islam again is on the march to never relax until all is under her or off the planet earth.

Not to mention the people of the Gold Coast of West Africa only, but all black Africans are now turning Islam. Go make an inspection for yourself. Islam is now in America for the first time since the Red Indian came here 16,000 years ago. Islam is now for the acceptance of the so-called Negroes whose fathers were once Muslims in Islam and who now, are the last members of that chosen people to hear Islam, the religion of Allah (God).

It is a known fact that the whites did not and will not teach the so-called Negroes Islam. We can't expect to find the truth of God, his religion, nor the black nation, in what the white race writes as history.

THEY DON'T HAVE that knowledge, as their knowledge is limited to 6,000 years. Some Arab Muslims think Islam's birth is from Muhammad, though their Holy Qur-an does not teach them to believe Islam had its birth from the teachings of Muhammad.

Mr. DeRougement thinks that Jews or Hebrews' religion is the oldest. He says it is more than 5,700 years old. The white race, including the Jews, is only 6,000 years and they spent 2,000 years of that time in the hills and caves of Europe without any religion or civilization.

Only a few of them escaped that punishment and they remained there until the birth of Moses, who was their first prophet or guide to lead them back to civilization, and the knowledge of Islam.

THE RELIGION which Moses taught them, according to the Holy Qur-an, the name Hebrew, also according to the Biblical dictionary was given to Abraham by the Canaanites (Gen. 14:13). Just how true it is, I am not the judge. I do know that all the white race received their first teachings from Moses, and he lived 4,000 years ago. The age of Buddhism is 35,000 years as taught to me from the mouth of God, not that Buddha was that old, but that type of religion.

Now, as for the Arabs having slaves, no Muslim will enslave a Muslim. The Arabs will answer for themselves, but I do know that all Muslims are the brothers of a Muslim.

Any so-called Negro Muslim can go and live among the Muslims of Arabia or anywhere on the planet and will be accepted as a brother and citizen of that government. Try it for yourself, brother. All are equal in Islam, not like your proud white Christians. Join your kind.

January 19, 1957

"CHALLENGE ELDER MCCOY TO PROVE HIS CHARGE OF FALSITY OF MY ARTICLES AND THE REVELATION OF GOD TO MUHAMMAD."

ELDER McCOY, point out with truth that which is false doctrine that I am putting out, and the false revelations that you charged Muhammad with receiving from the Angel Gabriel.

If Muhammad received false revelations, how could the false take away the evils of his people, made them obedient to the Divine Laws, made them pray five times a day and saw his victory over his enemies in his lifetime? Further, his revelation has and still is making the best people on earth after nearly fourteen centuries.

He has nearly a billion followers, and that number is now being increased day and night, all over the earth. He is recognized by the wise of this world as being the most successful of all the prophets. Neither Moses nor Jesus was able to unite their people into one brotherhood, or even break the evil habits of the people.

Muhammad was not born and put in a basket or placed in a river like Moses, nor born in a stall like Jesus. His birth was not visited by angels saying, "Peace and goodwill to all mankind." Yet, his revelations have succeeded in bringing about more peace among his followers than any prophet before or after him.

We can't have peace and goodwill, kingdom of heaven on earth until Allah removes the devils and their followers from the earth. This, Jesus nor the angels did 2,000 years ago, but you may expect it real soon from the Mahdi (God in Person), the One whom Jesus called the Son of Man.

Secondly - Minister Malcolm is right and you are wrong about the rising from the dead (mentally dead). The "We" that he referred to are the believers like himself, who believe in the Truth (Allah and his Messenger, Muhammad) and the religion of Islam. Most surely, the slavemasters killed us mentally to the knowledge of self, God and the devil for 400 years. I wish that you would accept the truth so that you could rise from the dead. When one knows himself and the God of Heaven and Earth, the devil (enemy of Allah) and the righteous, he is called the Living. This is the life Minister Malcolm and thousands of others are receiving from my column in this newspaper.

Those who know not self and the true God and their enemy, the devil in reality, are called "dead."

Thirdly, Elder McCoy, if the so-called Negroes and their slavemasters are not the answer to Jesus' parable of the rich man and poor Lazarus, then where is the answer to such parable?

Again, parables such as the Prodigal Son and the Lost Sheep, the ass speaking with man's voice to his rider Balaam and most all the other parables are referring to "We," who have been lost from our own people and country by following our enemies. You admit that once we had the worst of everything; you are still a long way from being treated right.

January 26, 1957

MY work or teachings won't help anyone by the Believers. You boast about your having some of the finest schools and mention a few well-known men by names. Is it not true that your schools, colleges and universities are from your slave masters? Who then is benefitted by your schools' graduates;, the white man or the so-called Negroes?

Regardless to how much education your slave masters give you, if they never teach you a true knowledge of self, you are only a free slave to serve them or others than your own.

Is your educational system that you boast of getting you independence from the slave masters' children? Is it or has it put the idea in your head to seek some of this good earth for you and your people, who number over 17 million in America, a place to call you own? NO!

Who appoints your men of degrees and scientists to high government posts? Is it not his white masters whom they are going to serve? You will seek white men's jobs, but not a country for your people.

I want to see you and them in a country that you can call your own and where your highly trained and educated men and women can be benefitted. May Allah and Islam give it to them. There is no hope for such under the slave masters' children and their flag.

We know and acknowledge that you have made great progress with the unequal chance that you have.

Fourth - You admit that the trouble is that you have too many Gods. Then why not believe in One God (Allah) and we all will be trouble-free.

Fifth - I don't think Minister Malcolm had reference to me and my work to Malachi 1:5, but rather Malachi 4:5. Was John the Messenger of the Covenant whom the people delighted in and that must be sent to prepare the way before the Lord in the (Mal. 3:1)? Then who should we look for to come and unite the hearts of the American so-called Negroes to their Fathers?

Are they not to have a Messenger of God to warn and righten them? I think, Elder, that you are a little off in understanding the Scriptures. Continue to read my articles after you digest this.

February 2, 1957

"THOSE WHO LIVE IN GLASS HOUSES SHOULDN'T THROW STONES"

THE old Christian missionaries, writers, on the life and teachings of Muhammad, were his enemies. They were so grieved over the great success of Muhammad and Islam that they have written falsely against the man of God by attributing His success to the use of the sword instead of to Allah (God) from whom it actually came.

All who hate Islam (The Truth) use those same false charges against Muhammad and Islam. As I have said before in this column, "Muhammad was a member of the Black Nation, and the white race, by nature, is against black man leadership, regardless, whether spiritual or political." They have so educated and trained the leadership of the so-called Negroes that they are their best weapons against all mankind.

ELDER McCOY, a follower of his slavemasters' faith and beliefs, says that "Muhammad's big mistake was in warfare." According to history, there was no mistake. He and His followers were the most successful in war against their enemies than any before them. Why? Because Muhammad and His followers obeyed Allah, and Allah (God) was with them. Who started the war? Was it Muhammad and His followers? No! It was his powerful enemies who cared not for the Truth and made war against the poor man, Muhammad and His followers who were far from being equally armed with their enemies.

He accomplished His aim in converting Arabia by obedience to Allah, the one God, and they still remain unto this day.

Is it the sword that's spreading Islam over the world today - even here in America?

THE HOLY Qur-an, "Muhammad's Revelations," forbids compulsory converts. It teaches the Muslims against being the aggressor, but fight with those who fight against you - but never to be the aggressor. "Fight in the way of Allah with those who fight with you." (Chapter 2:190.)

It is a divine law for us to defend ourselves if attacked. Maybe if Jesus had let Peter and the other Disciples use the sword on the Jews He would have been more successful, for it was the sword that put Him

[CORRECTION Because my people (the so-called Negroes) know so little about themselves and know so little of the treachery of the many other racial groups, we suffer untold human indignities, in order to obtain so-called equality of opportunity of public accommodations, schools, churches, sports, etc. We seek to be accepted as members of the white slavemaster family.

Regardless of the savage treatment we receive, we pour out our life blood like water to be near our enemies. Allah opened my people's eyes that they may see and know the truth, if they only knew the truth they would prefer sitting as far removed from their enemies as the East is from the West. My people, return to your God, Allah, and His religion, Islam, that I may protect you and save you. Elder McCoy, point out, with truth that which is false doctrine that I am pointing out.

to death, and the Jews remained disbelievers.

According to the Bible (Matthew 10:34), Jesus didn't come for peace but to bring the sword. Neither did he come to unite. (Matthew 10:35.) It stands true today that Christianity, as we see it in practice in America, certainly does not unite, but rather divides the people against the other. According to the history of it, she has caused more bloodshed than any other combination of religion; her sword is never sheathed. If Jesus was a peacemaker, then the Christians are not His followers.

ELDER McCOY - you ask: "What have I done?" I am doing that for thousands which Christianity failed to do, and that is uniting the so-called Negroes and making them to know God and the Devil, and making them to leave off evil habits that the preachers of Christianity haven't been able to do for a hundred years. We are that in Islam what Christianity offers beyond the grave.

February 9, 1957

"ISLAM FOR THE AMERICAN SO-CALLED NEGROES"

WE WERE taken from servitude slavery nearly one hundred years ago, and put under the teachings of white-controlled Christianity - a mental slavery. The poor, so-called Negroes never tried to understand his slave-master's religion (Christianity) by questioning its teachings; they don't understand and won't listen to understandings. Why should they believe in Christianity prepared for them by the slavemasters, which has no saving power on this side nor the other side of the grave?

It has never defended them against their slavemaster's whip, gun, lynch, limb and fire.

THE BLACK CHRISTIAN, preachers' homes and churches are now being bombed by the white Christians in the South because the black Christians want to be recognized and treated as brother Christians with their slavemasters. This is enough to teach the black man that there is no salvation in Christianity for them. Yet, regardless of such evils performed against them they refuse to turn to Allah and His religion for protection. They fear the devil as they should fear Allah. TRUTH hurts falsehood.

The so-called Negroes are getting excited and fear for their jobs as they read of the Government offering their European white brothers a home in America. Why should you fear for your future? Why not turn toward your people for a place and a job? Four hundred years slaving and shedding your blood like water for your slavemasters only now to be denied equal justice. But you seem to like it.

I WARN YOU of the day that is near, not distant, when Allah will force them to give you up. CONSIDER the TIME; most surely you are ignorant of it. But your slavemasters are not; they are wide-awake and are watching every move made to help you. They know that your God ALLAH has come for you.

No religion but Islam will take away your evils. There is no fear nor grief for you in Islam. Why not Islam? There are plenty false things said about Islam and its half-billion believers, but you must REMEMBER - anything that is good for the black man will be spoken of as evil by his enemies.

I am sorry that a few mistakes have been made by the printers in my articles for the past two or three issues that made the articles to read other than their true meanings.

February 16, 1957

ISLAM THE TRUE RELIGION - HOLY QUR'AN 61:9

THE TRUE religion of Allah (God) and His prophets, Noah, Abraham, Moses and Jesus, was Islam, and not what you called Christianity. Islam is the last of the religions; it is to overcome all religions. "He, it is who sent His apostle with the guidance and the true religion, that he may make it overcome all other religions, though the Polytheists may be adverse." (Holy Qur-an 61:9). The truth, the white race and the Indian Hindu have always been and are now the enemies of Islam and the Muslims.

Today, Islam is being offered to the so-called Negroes of America for the sole purpose of bringing them into the knowledge of Truth that they would not get otherwise.

SECOND, TO give them divine protection. Third, to set them on top of civilization (this is in the Bible if you can understand). Otherwise, they would never become a free independent people under the very people that enslaved them. It is Allah's (God) doing, and we can't hinder.

Some people think that they should be left alone to believe in whatever they want to. They say let them be free to serve God in their own way. We have been warned that one day all people will have to serve and worship the One God (Allah), and one religion or be destroyed from among the people. You and I now live in that time.

God would not be just to Himself and the law of justice to allow us to continue to do as we please about serving and obeying Him and His laws, while all of his Creation bowing in obedience to Him. We can't convert the devils to Allah and His religion, Islam, because nature did not give them any righteousness. Therefore, Allah limited their rule (six thousand years).

You say, be tolerant with you and I, too, do as we please about serving Him and his true religion, Islam. Regardless to who dislikes Allah and Islam, they will be the losers today, for the TIME has come that righteousness must rule, to bring about love, peace and universal brotherhood.

Islam changes the believer in every respect, into a better person and makes evil hateful to him. It manifests that which is in us whether good or evil (even that which we didn't know was in us). It is not hard for us to understand the TRUTH if we only know the TIME that we are living in. The life of this world as the Holy Qur-an teaches us, is nothing but sport and play.

Such world has and is attracting the members of the righteous to take part in such life; good is not wanted by this world. Turn to Allah, your God, and He will turn to you, for there is no God but Allah. The so-called

Negroes think of God in terms of something without form (spirit or spook) and that his throne is somewhere in the sky.

This is due to their ignorance of just what spirit means. The teachings of Christianity has put God out of Man into nothing (spirit). Can you imagine God without form, but yet interested in our affairs who are human beings? What glory would an immaterial God get out of a material world? We learn that spirit is not self-independent; it is dependent upon air, water and food. Without it, there is no life. You had better wake up.

ISLAM FOR AMERICAN SO-CALLED NEGROES

"Say, O people, if you are in doubt as to my religion, (know that) I serve not those whom you serve besides Allah, but I serve Allah, Who causes you to die; and I am commanded to be of the believers." (Holy Qur-an, 10:104).

According to the past histories of prophets and reformers, the very people to whom they were sent with the light of TRUTH were their rejecters and even their enemies. When it comes the time for a change in the life of a people, there are those who will not appreciate a change. They are suspicious, in doubt to that which is other than what they have been believing all their lives.

The people of Noah, Abraham, Moses and Jesus were in doubt as to what those Prophets brought to them from Allah (God), until Allah brought about a showdown between the two.

THE SO-CALLED American Negroes are so gravely deceived by the white man's Christianity and Bible that they doubt everything that has not the white man's approval. Again the time has arrived for a change; this time it is universal and the so-called American Negroes are now the great problem to awaken.

They are made to believe that all other than the Christian religion is false and idol worship, while the Christians worship idol gods in their churches and religious literature. They have statues of wood, metal and imaginary pictures of God, angels, prophets and disciples that they bow and revere them as if they could speak.

The worst of all, the pictures and statues are not of God, His Angels, Prophets and Disciples of Jesus. Therefore they are false worshippers and ignorant enough to love the falsehood. Isaiah and Ezekiel have well described them. The Christian believers claim to believe in ONE GOD. Should not the Divine Supreme Being destroy those who serve and worship gods other than He? Allah (God) does not approve you and I worshipping His angels and prophets as His equal. It is a disgrace.

The religion of Islam teaches that ALLAH in ONE GOD; again the Holy Qur-an teaches that what you worship besides Allah is the firewood of hell. You doubt the truth of Islam while it is the religion of Allah (God) and the Prophets whom you claim to believe.

The principles of belief in Islam are: One God, His Prophets, His Scriptures, His Judgement, His Resurrection of the mental dead. The main principles of action: The keeping up of prayer, spending in the cause of truth, speak the truth regardless to whom or what, be clean internal and external, love your brother-believers as yourself, do good to all, kill no one whom Allah has not ordered to be killed, set at liberty the captured believer, worship no God but Allah, and fear no one but Allah. The above are the teachings of the Prophets.

Why should you doubt Islam and you know that it is the truth? There is no fear for you nor shall you grieve today. If you will accept Allah and His religion - Islam. It is unlike your Christianity which has really put fear in you, and your promise of help or defense comes only after death. I am commanded that I should serve Allah and to His, I submit.

I hope to see you here on the 26th of this month for our convention.

March 2, 1957

ISLAM FOR THE SO-CALLED NEGRO

1. Say: I seek refuge in the Lord of the dawn, 2. From the evil of that which he (Yakub) has created, 3. And from the evil of intense darkness,

when it comes, 4. And from the evil of those who cast (evil suggestions) in firm resolutions, And from the evil of the envier when he envies. Holy Qur-an 113).

THE dawn of a new day has arrived to seek our place in that which is new. We must have a guide. Allah (God) has always provided guides for those who seek to walk in His path.

We should hasten ourselves to the light of truth as we hasten to get ourselves into the light of the day (the Sun). The light of Allah (God) is even greater than the light of our day (the Sun). We must learn to be intelligent enough to distinguish truth from falsehood and seek refuge in the God of truth.

IF WE shall know the truth (John 8:32), and that TRUTH will make us free, we can truthfully say that we already have long since known the truth that Jesus was referring to was yet to come, not in his days (John 16:8, 13). If that truth had been revealed 2,000 years ago there would not be any falsehood in the world. However, Jesus being a Prophet foresaw the future and the end of the devil's rule. "Seek refuge from the evil of that which He (Yakub) created."

The Father (Yakub) of this world created a world of evil, discord and hate. If you do not agree with their evil doings, your goodness is then called hate or infidel and peace-breaker.

This world of Christianity has gone mad and they think that every cry is against them. They are like robbers who have robbed and are afraid that they will be recognized by their victims. Thieves know that light makes them manifest.

Since Christianity has falsely accused Jesus as being her founder, she is now being plagued with spiritual darkness and confusion. Under such darkness the Prophet and His followers (the Muslims) are warned to seek refuge in the light of Allah (God) for under such spiritual darkness the wicked seek to persecute and kill the Prophet of Islam and His followers.

THEY ARE mad and cannot see, nor hear the truth, so they call the truth false, and the false they call truth. The Truth (Islam) has angered them (Christianity), "And the nations (Christianity) were angry, Thy wrath is come, the time of the dead, the time that the mental dead black nation, especially the so-called Negro must come into the knowledge of the truth, of their enemies and the enemies' false religion that was used to deceive them. Thy shall give reward unto Thy Servants, the Prophets and the saints, and will destroy them which destroy the earth." (Bible, Rev. 11:18)

THE WHITE Christians and Jews are the guilty race. They have persecuted and killed the Prophets of Islam and their followers (the Muslims or black people in general). Now should not they be destroyed or get what they put out?

Christianity is so afraid of the true religion (Islam), awakening the mental dead so-called Negroes to the knowledge of truth that in nearly every Negro church you will see a white Christian sitting in on the meeting, to watch and see that the dead do not rise. They try to prevent it (the awakening of the so-called Negro) as they know the so-called Negroes think that is an honor to have them present. However, if the so-called Negroes' only understood his Bible II Thessalonians (2:4-8). They are trying to make the so-called Negroes believe they too are the beloved of God, then why not believe in Allah?

(**SEEK REFUGE** in Allah from the envier when he envies.) The success of the Messenger and his followers of Islam are envied by the enemies and they are not leaving a stone unturned in trying to stop the light (Truth) of Allah (God) with their mouths. "Allah (God) will perfect His light though the Polytheists be adverse" (Holy Qur-an 61:).

They (Christians) are mad and so afraid of being manifested by the light of Allah (God) in His true religion, Islam. They fulfill that which is written of them, "Why do the heathen rage and the people imagine a vain thing? The Kings of the earth and the rulers take counsel together against the Lord (Allah and His Messenger) and against His anointed" (Psalms 2:1).

You must remember that the above said is not referring to the Jesus time of 2,000 years ago. Jesus was not made the ruler or king of the Jews, nor can he ever be made such. The devil is working many tricks on the so-called Negro today to deceive them for they (the devils) know that their time is up. They know that the so-called Negroes still believe in them as divine guides. **"Heaven"** is offered to the so-called Negro and "hell" to his enemies. Which one will they (so-called Negroes) "believe"?

"AND MIX NOT UP THE TRUTH WITH FALSEHOOD, NOR HIDE THE TRUTH WHILE YOU KNOW." (HOLY QUR-AN 2:42)

The Holy Qur-an is a great book when it is understood. The above verse warns against mixing TRUTH with falsehood, as it is the policy of the devils. But, nearly all the religious leaders of Christianity are guilty of mixing up the DIVINE TRUTH with falsehood. Now they don't know which is TRUTH and which is falsehood. They are really confused, thinking and planning against the TRUTH, trying to teach--- falsehood. They mixed up the TRUTH of the Bible so much that today they admit someone has tampered with the book. The Bible now teaches against evil and for evil. For instance, it says that we should not drink strong drinks, wine is prohibited in some places and in others it says that it is good for us.

The TRUTH must triumph over falsehood, as day triumphs over night. When we deny the truth it shows that we love falsehood more than truth. If we fear to speak the truth for the sake of falsehood, this is not only hiding the truth, but is actually showing fear and distrust in the Divine Supreme Being, His Wisdom and His Power.

The hiding and mixing the truth with falsehood because of fear of the enemy (devils) is taking a great number of our people to hell with the devils.

IT IS NATURAL for one to fear that of which he has no knowledge. However, when TRUTH and Knowledge are made clear to you as you find is being done today in this column, you have no cloak for your fear. Your mixing up TRUTH with falsehood is only because you fear your enemy (the devils).

Allah (God) doesn't care for us when our fear is greater for our enemies than for Him. Allah says: "Me, and me alone should you fear. Believe in that which I have revealed, verifying that which is with you and be not the first to deny it; neither take a mean price for my message; and keep your duty to Me, and Me alone." (Holy Qur-an 2:40-41.)

Once the so-called Negroes drop slavery (Christianity) and accept Allah for their God and His religion (Islam) Allah will remove their fear and grief and they will not fear nor grieve any more.

IT IS A shame to see our people in such fearful condition. "The fearful and the unbelieving shall have their part in the lake which burns with fire and brimstone which is the second death" (Rev. 21:8).

The devil whom they fear more than Allah (God) was not able to protect himself against Allah; therefore, his followers shared with him the fire of hell. Though they had suffered one death (mental-death), and by fearing the devils and rejecting the TRUTH they suffered a physical death, which was the final death.

The devils know that they have deceived the world with their false religion (Christianity). The devils are so afraid that ISLAM is going to give life and light to the so-called Negroes that they sit and watch over them (the so-called Negroes) day and night.

March 16, 1957

"ISLAM FOR THE SO-CALLED NEGROES OF AMERICA"

"And the Jews and the Christians say: 'We are the Sons of Allah and his beloved ones.' Say: "Why does He chastise you for your faults'?" – (Holy Qur-an 5:18.)

THE ABOVE sayings of the white race have deceived the so-called Negroes in America 100 per cent, and many black people throughout the earth. Christian whites claiming nearness to Allah (God) and making Jesus a member of their wicked race and even ascribe Sonship.

How have they been so successful in deceiving the whole world of dark mankind? Why did they kill the prophets of Allah? They even seek to take my life because I teach the truth of Allah which gives life to my people whom they have killed mentally.

MY PEOPLE, because of the prosperity the Christians have enjoyed, think that the white race is the beloved people of Allah; therefore they think their religion, Christianity, is right. This is due to their lack of knowledge. They are given a great time of prosperity as never before witnessed by that race.

But this doesn't mean that they are the beloved of Allah. Their prosperity will be followed by destruction. My poor black people were blinded and dumb and think they have no place in the Divine Family, but this is a sad mistake. Wake up! Today, you have been chosen to be placed on top.

Islam is the religion of peace and security. You should accept it by the thousands. If the white people are the beloved of Allah, why aren't they good people? Why aren't they living the life of Jesus, whom they claim to be following?

They say Jesus taught them love; where is their love? Allah says: "We excited among them enmity and hatred to the day of resurrection: And Allah will inform them of what they did." (Holy Qur-an 5:14.)

This is a manifest truth. They are being informed of what they did. The white race is not at peace with each other. Can we seek peace among such evil, hateful and bloodthirsty people? They hate you so much that they dislike seeing you live in peace in their midst.

ISLAM IS the religion of peace and security. Why not Islam? Come down off the cross and get under the Crescent of Islam which will give you freedom, justice and equality. We are a nation in a nation. Do we want respect as others? First, respect self and other will you.

Protect your women as other nations do. Take your women at any price, out of the arms of the slavemasters' children and all men. Put a stop to this freedom of your women mixing with whom they please, regardless of the cost. Why do your women want their enemies? Give back to them everything you have received and accept your own and be yourself.

I am sorry that you did not visit our convention on the 24th through the 26th of last month. We enjoyed a wonderful time; the greatest and best of all. Converts began to pour into the Temples of Islam since the public learned in those three days of our convention. That will never be forgotten by those who visited it.

BETWEEN TWO and three thousand people attended throughout the convention, including two thousand Muslim delegates of my followers from every state in the Union. There was no smoking, drinking, weapons or disputes among them. A true example of brotherhood and peace as never witnessed before among persons who have been said to be the worse of mankind. It was a wonderful sight of unity to behold and which was due to Allah and Islam, the religion of peace.

Let the white race think well: if they would leave us to go to our God and religion of Islam and stop trying to hinder us by their threats of persecution, they would be doing themselves and their country a great favor, if they but knew.

M a r c h   2 3 ,   1 9 5 7

ISLAM FOR THE SO-CALLED NEGROES

Behold I, (Allah), make all things new, and He said unto Me, write: For these words are true and faithful. Bible (Rev. 21:5).

IT IS NECESSARY for me to consult or refer to the Bible for this subject. It can be found in the Holy Qur-an, but not in the exact words as they are found in the Bible. So, due to the truth of it, and, that my people know no Scripture nor ever read any Scripture other than the Bible (which they don't understand), I thought it best to make them understand the book that they read and believe in, since the Bible is their graveyard, and they must be awakened from it. There are many Muslims who don't care to read anything in the Bible. But, those Muslims have not been given my job.

Therefore, I ignore what they say and write! By all means, we must get the "Truth" to our people (the so-called Negroes) for the time is limited The coming of a "New World," or a new order of things, is very hard for the people of the Old World to believe. Therefore, THEY are opposed to the New World.

IT DOES NOT take a wise man to see the necessity of a new order or a new world, since the old has fulfilled its purpose. Let the Christians' preachers and scientists ponder over the above prophecy of his Bible. If the time comes when Allah (God) will make all things NEW, will the

Christians as we see it today, be in that which Allah (God) will make NEW? When should we expect Allah (God) to make all things NEW? After the destruction of the wicked and their king and world. Just when should the end of the old world be? The exact day is known only to Allah, but many think that they know the year. But we all know that 1914 was the end of the 6,000 years that was given to the old world of the devils to rule. A religion used by the devils to convert people can't be accepted by Allah. Especially when it didn't come from Him.

We all know that Christianity is from the white race. Should we be surprised at this late day to see it come to pass? Think over the saying of your own Bible: "The great deceiver of the nations?" (Rev. 20:3,8). Of course, he deceived them (the Negroes) that had received his mark (the mark of Christianity, the cross).

MORE THAN anyone else and those who worship his image, (the so-called Negroes) are guilty of loving the white race and all that that race goes for. Even one can find the pictures of white people on the walls, mantle shelves, the dressers and tables of their homes. Some carry them on their person. The so-called Negroes go to church, bow down to their statues under the name of Jesus and Mary, and some under the name of Jesus' disciples, of which are only the images of the white race, their arch deceiver.

They even worship the white race's names of that which will not exist among the people of the new world for they are not the names of God.

The so-called Negroes would greatly benefit themselves if they would seek their places in "that" which Allah, (God) makes new by giving back to the great deceiver, his religion, Christianity, churches and names, and accept the religion of their righteous nation, Islam, a name of their God, which is unlimited in the eyes of any white person.

THERE IS NO end to the black nation, that nation will live forever, but the so-called Negroes don't know it, and their slavemasters know that they don't know; therefore, have the so-called Negroes deceived 100 per cent. The poor black preachers are really pitiful, to see how they are blinded and chained by the slavemasters hand and foot, can't speak nor agree with truth even if they wanted to. Come to me, brother preachers, and believe in Allah, the true God and the true religion, Islam! And free yourselves from such chained slavery.

I AM VERY insignificant in your eyes, but I have the keys of God to your problems, and you should not fear; for the DAY has come that you will have to seek refuge in (the new world) something better and more enduring than the white race's Christianity, as it is not your religion. It is a joy to us to see our people in Ghana, Africa, get their independence, as you ought to be seeking yours instead of integrating. Since your number is three times the population of Ghana. Look at your brothers in the Sudan, you outnumbered them all. Where is your independence in these 48 states? But you don't love to be independent, unless your white man is the boss.

March 30, 1957

ISLAM FOR THE SO-CALLED NEGROES
(CONTINUED)

"Behold, I make all things new." Rev. 21:5

"Will the Old World accept the New? No, the Old World will not accept the New. Therefore, the Old must be destroyed. And the nations were angry, and Thy wrath is come, and the time of the dead, and (Thou) shouldest destroy them which destroy the earth (black people)." - Rev. 11:18

NEVER was this scripture so plainly being fulfilled. The nations are angry, and warring against each other, over who shall rule the other, and over what part of the earth they shall possess. Yet, it is the TIME of the DEAD (the mental dead - or so-called Negroes), that they should be judged (be given justice). For, it is this world that killed them, and did them injustice. The "old" must be destroyed. She is the great trouble-maker, and will not accept the "new." She prepares to go to war against the "new," and against the righteous Ruler. And the dragon,(the devil) stood before the woman - the messenger of Allah (God), which is pregnant with the life-giving truth - for to devour her child - (to hinder the truth from being believed by the people of the messenger) - as soon as it was born." (Rev. 12:4)

THE PRESENT world is using everything within its power to prevent the TRUTH from reaching the hearts of the so-called Negroes. Allah has chosen the so-called Negroes to build a new world. A world of truth, freedom, justice and equality. A people that was no people - the rejected and despised - shall soon come to birth. Out of nothing was the present universe created and out of the weak of the BLACK NATION, the present Caucasian race was created. They have built a world of evil and bloodshed, and have destroyed the peace of the black nation - the real owners of the earth.

But that which was to be, must be. So today, the Old World of sin will be replaced with a New World of righteousness. The religion of Islam will be the New World's religion, and there will be no other religion in the world to oppose it.

THERE ARE many - other than the devils - who are actually ignorant of the fact that though Islam being the religion of the New World, will also be new Islam. For there are some practices of it that won't be necessary in the New World. Even both the Bible and Holy Qur-an teachings take us up to the door of the New World, and there, stops with us, as qualified members to be received on the inside. On the inside of the door of the New World is that which no eye has seen nor ear has heard. Nor has it entered the heart of man to know what Allah has prepared for those who serve Him. The people of Allah will also become a new people.

All prophets and their knowledge stop at the door of that which Allah will make "NEW."

THE SO-CALLED Negroes will be the beneficiaries for they will be made to take on a new growth of both the spiritual and physical. And will become the most beautiful, the most wise, the most powerful, and, the most progressive people that ever lived. For Allah has declared it, and will do it.

The white Christians think that they and their religion will be the rulers in the New World. Many other religions and their followers think the same. But, they will be greatly surprised, and disappointed. For, Allah has rejected the Christian race and their religion, and this generation will live to witness this change.

Lift up your heads, my people! Shake off the Old World of evil, and put on the new garments of the New World's righteousness!

I have warned you. Write to me and join with your own. Sit yourselves in heaven, at once! Not after death, but while you live!

"SALVATION FOR THE SO-CALLED NEGROES IN ISLAM"

I DON'T have to say to the so-called Negroes that hell is for them in the white man's Christianity! They know it, and have experienced it, in this Christian's hell. The white Christians and their religion, whom they falsely say, and teach is from Jesus, and is - in reality, from the Pope of Rome who is the head of the church, and not Jesus. Therefore, the blinded, deaf and dumb of my people can never hope to be successful with their white enemies, as their religious heads and guides.

J.B. Stoner, archleader of the Christian party, Atlanta, Ga., told the truth in his letter last week in this paper, when he said that "Christianity has only been successful in white nations, among white people, but does not appear to have roots in any colored (black) nation." I thank him for bearing witness with me, that the false white Christian religion was for them (white race), and not for the black nation, and that Islam is our (black nation) religion, and Allah is our God and author of Islam, and not the Pope of Rome. No black nation can be successful trying to play the white race's (the devil's) game of civilization; they will only be trapped as slaves for them.

ISLAM IS a religion of divine power, and will give power to the helpless so-called Negroes, to overcome the devils and their false religion, Christianity. It has never helped the Negroes against the white Christian's brutality.

Black Africa should have learned her lesson from it, and driven it back to Europe and America, where it belongs.

The white Christians preach that Jesus, who they killed 2,000 years ago, will hear and save the Negroes. Let them prove that lie! How can a dead man hear and save people? You are not taught to pray to be heard by Moses and other prophets, not even Elijah, whom they say, went to Heaven whole soul and body. If Elijah cannot hear a prayer, and he was not killed as Jesus was, then how can Jesus hear a prayer? We must not pray to dead prophets. They can't hear our prayers.

WE, MUSLIMS, love all of Allah's prophets, but we will not pray for life to come to us from a dead prophet. Not even Muhammad, who lived nearly 1,400 years ago. We pray in the name of Allah, and mention the name of His last prophet, in our prayer, as an honor and thanks to Allah, for His last guide to us.

The **DAY** of **RESURRECTION** of the dead so-called Negroes has arrived. They have lived overtime in bondage to the white Christians. The white Christians will not accept Islam, for Islam is a religion of the truth, freedom, justice and equality. And this is something nature just did not put in white people. They have lost the power of attraction and rule over the black of Asia, and in their frenzied effort to restore it, are now running all over the world trying to deceive the black nation, so as to allow them time to continue their wicked rule of injustice.

YES, SIR, Mr. Stoner, we Muslims will do our utmost to keep our nation pure, by keeping you away from our women. We're proud of our black skin, and our kinky wool, for this kinky woolly hair will be the future ruler. Look into your poison book, Dan. 7:9, Rev. 1:14. Mr. Stoner boasts of America being a white man's country, but why did they bring us here? If the white race is such a super race, why don't they live alone, and - leave us to live alone in our own country. Why are they fighting to stay in Asia? Why not be satisfied with Europe and America? We didn't ask your people to bring us here.

He says that we can't live without the white race to rule us (smile). I am sorry for the so-called Negroes who would believe anything so false.

MR. STONER, tell us who brought you and your race into civilization when you were walking on all-fours, climbing trees, living in hills and caves sides of Europe, just 4,000 years ago? Was it one of you, super whites or one of our blacks? Who put you there, was it yourself or did we put you there? Where did your race first see the black man, in the jungles of Africa, or across the border east of Europe, in beautiful cities and homes? Who did you find in the Western Hemisphere, your people or our people? Who created the heavens and the earth, my fathers or yours? Who created your race, yourself or one of my nations? Can you claim this earth or any other planet to be that which your fathers created or my fathers?

WHO STARTED the dust storms in your country? Who is quaking your country, your kind or Allah? Drive us out and see how long you will remain. But if we drive you out, we will live forever without you, as we did before you. Let the white race keep silent about who shall live on this planet, for they haven't anything. This is OUR earth! Be happy, white folks, that you have the so-called Negroes in your midst, and especially those who are Muslims, for if they were not, you wouldn't last very long. But they shall be taken from you, it is binding upon Allah, to fulfill His promise to Abraham, that He would return them again to their people.

April 13, 1957

AMERICA IS FALLING - HER DOOM IS SEALED

I COMPARE the fall of America with the fall of ancient Babylon. Her wickedness (sins) is the same as the history shows of ancient Babylon. "Babylon" is suddenly fallen and the destroyed howl for her; take balm for her pains, if, so she may be healed." (Jer. 51:8) What were the sins of ancient Babylon? According to history she was rich, she was proud and her riches increased her corruption. She had every merchandise that the nations wanted or demanded; her ships carried her merchandise to the ports of every nation.

She was a drunkard; wine and strong drinks were in her daily practice. She was filled with adultery and murder; she persecuted and killed the people of God. She killed the saints and prophets of Allah (God). Hate and filthiness, gambling -sports of every evil as you practice in America, were practiced in Babylon. Only America is modern and much worse. Ancient Babylon was destroyed by her neighboring nations.

MY SPACE in this paper is limited; therefore I can't quote this ancient history here I only warn you to let their destruction serve as a warning for America. This people has gone to the limit in doing evil; as God dealt with ancient people - so will He deal with the modern Babylon (America). As God says: "Son of man, when the land sinneth against me by trespassing grievously, then will I stretch out mine hand upon it, and will break the staff of the bread thereof, and will send famine upon it, and will cut off man and beast from it (Ezekiel 14:13)

We see with our own eyes - but, the wicked Americans are too proud to confess that they see the bread of America gradually being cut off. Take a look into the Southwest, and Middle West, see the hand of Allah (God) at work against modern Babylon - to break the whole staff of her bread for her evils done against His people, the (so-called Negroes).

TEXAS AND Kansas were once two of the nation's most proud states. Kansas - known for its wheat and Texas for its cattle, cotton, corn and many other vegetables and fruits. They are today in the grip of a drought, continuous raging dust storms; their river beds lay bare, their fish stinking on the banks in dry parched mud. When the rain comes, it brings very little relief and does more damage than good. Snow comes - it brings not joy but death and destruction. After the snow comes more dust storms. With the rain comes hail stones, very large stones. America has not seen the large hail stones; she will see hail stones the size of small blocks of ice breaking down crops, trees, the roofs of homes, killing cattle and fowls. Behind this terrific earthquakes, the people frightened, killed, much sickness and death will be widespread. You are getting a token of it now. On the outside, a threat of an atomic war between the nations of the earth. Yet, you have your eyes closed at the manifest judgment of Allah (God), going on in your midst to bring this country to nought.

ALLAH (God) has found His people (the so-called Negroes), and is angry with the slave-masters for the evil done by them to His people (the so-called Negroes). Allah (God) is going to repay them according to their doings.

My poor people who have turned to their own God and religion (Allah and Islam), are being tracked down and watched as though they are about to stick up a bank. This is done to try and put fear in them - so that they might stay away from their God Allah and His true religion Islam (as the devil knows) their salvation and defense.

They (the devils) watch the steps of the righteous (the Negroes), and seek to slay them (Psalms 37:32). The so-called Negroes live under the very shadow of death in America. There is no justice for them in the courts of their slave-masters. Why should not America be chastised for her evils, done to the so-called Negroes? If God destroyed ancient Babylon for the mockery made of the sacred vessels taken from the Temple of Jerusalem, what do you think Allah (God) should do for America's mockery of the so-called Negroes, that she took from their native land and people and filled them with wine and whiskey.

NOW SHE (America) puts on a show of temptation with their women (white women) in newspapers, magazines, in streets half-nude, and posing in the so-called Negroes' faces in the most indecent manner that is known to mankind - to trick them (the so-called Negroes) to death and hell with them. Be wise my people and shut your eyes at them - do not look at them in such an indecent way. Clean your homes of white people's pictures - put your own on the walls. The only so-called Negroes' pictures you will see in their homes is one they have lynched, one they want to kill or one who has betrayed his own people for them.

AMERICA IS falling; she is a habitation of devils and every uncleanness and hateful people of the righteous. Forsake her and fly to your own before it is too late. You that believe, write me and get your name on the Book of Life. Help me to get the message to our people with whatever cash that you are able to give, for it takes a lot of it to put this work over. But, remember you will get from two to ten for one. The whole earth will be given to you to rule forever. So help yourselves to escape out of her. She is falling - falling.

SALVATION FOR THE SO-CALLED NEGROES IN ISLAM

WILL they accept or reject it? Allah (God) is self-independent - having infinite knowledge and power over all - yet is the most loving, the most merciful. We are dependent upon Him, but yet the foolish disbelievers think and feel that they are self-independent of Allah.

The so-called Negroes will believe in Islam when they learn the **Truth** of it and a **chastisement** from Allah. According to the prophecies of the Bible and Holy Qur-an Sharrieff, they will accept Islam, the true religion of Allah and the prophets. They are mentioned under many types in the Bible - in Ezekiel, the 37th chapter, as dry bones that only needed the word of **TRUTH** of Allah - to be able to live again (that is become divinely civilized and self-independent). The symbolic dry bones in the vision of Ezekiel, who had lost hopes of ever being anything like independent - as other people (37:11 Ezekiel), refused to listen at the word of TRUTH and had to be whipped into submission by the winds (wars) blowing from all parts of the earth. It is not the right understanding of the 37th chapter of Ezekiel to say that it is referring to Israel or any of the white race. The Holy Qur-an teaches that it is incumbent upon Him to give life (the truth) to the dead.

THE SO-CALLED Negroes are hindered by the old false believers (the Christians) with their ever-preaching the same old false, singing, mourning over the air, calling on a dead Jesus and a mystery God that doesn't exist. They (the so-called Negroes) were born in such falsehood and made to fear it by the slavemasters - lest they would not be fed, clothed or sheltered. This fear in the so-called Negroes has now increased to the fearing of not being given work to make an honest living. The slavemaster is practicing this scheme of fear on the so-called Negroes (who accept Islam) on certain Government jobs to frighten the so-called Negroes from accepting Islam.

IT IS ONE of their main tricks (the slavemasters) to keep them away from their (the so-called Negroes) salvation in Islam. The so-called Negroes should be **wise** to this old-time trick. The clergy and the educated class have the fear of losing their present positions and false respect of the slavemaster. But such people are mentioned as going to hell with beasts (Rev. 19:20), they must and will be made to acknowledge the **TRUTH** - for the slavemaster will soon be forced to give them up (Rev. 20:13).

When Pharaoh had enough of divine chastisement, he gave up the slaves so that they could go out with Moses and Aaron to the land that God would have for them. So will America give up the blind, deaf and dumb so-called Negros - whom she (America) made blind, deaf and dumb when they were babies - and will help them to leave her as Egypt did her slaves, whether the so-called Negroes want to leave her or not. (Read Isaiah 14) Ninety-eight per cent of the so-called Negroes at the present time are in doubt about Islam being the true religion. The other 2 per cent are with me - but they all will be with me soon as they see and feel a little of the chastisement from Allah.

AMERICA IS the place where Allah will make Himself known and felt. I know Him and I am with Him. You say that you know God and only lie, for those who know Allah love, fear and obey Him. But, you love, fear and obey the devils - your open enemies - not Allah - the God of Truth, Freedom and Justice.

The **TRUE** religion must overcome all other religions, though the polytheists may be against it (Holy Qur-an 61:9). Christianity does not care for the true religion (Islam), because her nature is against truth and justice, and secondly, she fears her slaves (the so-called Negroes). Today, they are watching all the so-called Negroes to see which one shows signs that he or she believes in the Truth (Islam), that Allah (God) has given to me to give to my people (the so-called Negroes).

ALL OF THEM will wish that they were Muslims before it is over. They (the Christians) desire to put out the light of Allah with their (lying) mouths, but Allah will perfect His light though the disbelievers may be averse. (Holy Qur-an 61:8).

Join onto your God (Allah) and religion, Islam, my people - the time is limited!

"THE SO-CALLED NEGROES' SALVATION IS IN ISLAM, THE ONLY TRUE RELIGION OF GOD"

THE NUMBER ONE PRINCIPLE OF BELIEF

"Say: He, Allah is one. Allah is he on whom all depend. He begets not, nor is he begotten, and none is like him."

(HOLY QUR-AN 112:1-4)

A MUSLIM is one who believes in ONE God. It is forbidden of Allah (God) for us to believe or serve anyone, other than Himself as a god. He warns us not to set-up an equal with Him, as He was One in the beginning from whom everything had its beginning, and will be the ONE God from which everything will end. He is self-independent, having no need of anyone's help; but on the other hand, upon HIM we all depend. It is the highest of ignorance for us to choose a God or attempt to make something as an equal to Him. Foolish people, all over the earth, for the past 6,000 years, have been, and are still at it, trying to make an equal to Allah (God). He has no beginning nor is there any end of Him. How, O foolish man, can you make an equal for such ONE? How foolish we make ourselves serving and worshipping gods other than the ONE God Allah.

The foolish become rich, highly educated in their way and not in the way of Allah, and then begin their making and worshipping gods of their own; the work of their own hands - then comes the end of them as it is of today.

IT IS THE fundamental principle of the religion of Islam to believe in Allah, the ONE God. According to the belief, the teaching and preaching of the prophets of Allah is of One God. Noah, Abraham, Moses and Jesus - all believed in ONE God (Allah). The Christians claim a belief in the above said prophets - then how do they make Jesus the equal of Allah (God)? The Bible says: and God spoke all these words saying- "I am the lord thy God, thou shalt have no other gods before me. Thou shalt not make unto thee any graven image, or any likeness of anything that is in the heavens above, or that is in the earth beneath, or that is in the water, under the earth; thou shalt not bow down thyself to them, nor serve them, for I the Lord Thy God am a jealous God."

Both Jews and Christians are guilty of setting up rivals to Allah (God). Adam and Eve accepted the guidance of the serpent other than Allah (Gen. 3:6). They make and took a golden calf for their god and bowed down to it (Ex. 32:4). This was the work of their own hand to guide them and fight their wars. The Christians have made imaginary pictures and statues of wood, silver and gold - calling them pictures and statutes of God. They bow down to Jesus, His mother and disciples, as though they can see and hear them. They (the Christians) claim sonship to Allah (God), and take the Son to be the equal of the Father - though they say: "That they killed the Son." Today they take the weapons of war for their gods and put their trust in the work of their own hands.

MUHAMMAD (may the peace and blessings of Allah be upon Him) took hold of the best, the belief in One God (Allah) and was successful. Fourteen hundred years after him, we are successful, that is, we, who will not set up another god with Allah. The fools who refuse to believe in Allah alone as the One God if asked: Who made the heavens and earth? They most surely would say God and would not say God the Son and the Holy Ghost. Then why do they not serve and obey Allah (God)?

It is a perfect insult to Allah (God) who made heaven and earth and makes the earth to produce everything for our service and even the sun, moon and stars - they serve our needs - for us to bow down and worship anything other than Allah as a god. THE GREAT MAHDI, Allah, in person, who is in our midst today will put a stop once and forever to the serving and worshipping of other gods besides Himself.

IT IS THE devil's way of bringing the people (so-called Negroes) of Allah (God) in opposition to Him by teaching the people to believe and do just the thing that God forbids. Muhammad (may the peace and blessings of Allah be upon Him) did not try making a likeness of God, nor have his followers. He and his followers obey and do the law of (the One God) Allah while the Jews and the Christians preach it and do otherwise. We are now being brought face to face with Allah (God) for a showdown between Him and that which we have served as God beside Him. The lost and found members of the Asiatic nation are especially warned in the 112th chapter of the Holy Qur-an against the worship of any other God

than Allah, for it is Allah in person who has found them among the worshippers of gods other than Allah. So-called Negroes should read carefully the five principles of Islam which I will be writing in this paper from
now on.

"THE SO-CALLED NEGROES' SALVATION IS IN ISLAM - THE TRUE AND ONLY RELIGION OF GOD"

(Continued From Last Week)

THE NUMBER ONE Principle of belief is that your God is ONE God,
and beside Him you have no other God that can help you. I shall begin
with this, the most important of all principles of belief:

How many non-Muslims will we find who do not believe in God as
being ONE God? Regardless of the trinity belief preached by the Chris-
tians, they (the Christians) claim and agree that Allah (God) is ONE God.
Though they make fools of themselves when they reject Islam and the
Muslim's five principles of belief: One God, His Prophets, His Books, the
Resurrection, the Judgment. Then how did they (the Christians) go astray
believing in three Gods? Nevertheless, they make one of the three, the
Father of the other two - and these remaining two the equal of the Father.

THE SO-CALLED Negroes have been led into the gravest errors in the
knowledge of God (Allah) and the true religion (Islam), by their white
slavemasters. They (the so-called Negroes) have been robbed more than
any people on the Planet Earth. If they will only read and listen to the
simplest of truths that I write and teach, they would not remain in error
any longer. That which, I write and speak has three essentials in it: Power,
Light and Life.

To you who are writing to me and asking questions - continue to read
my columns and you will find your answer. If Allah (God) is the Author
of the Word - then be aware of how you treat it.

"I AM A MORTAL like you - it is revealed to me that your God is One God" (18:110). Will you not bear witness with Muhammad in the above said chapter and verse of the Holy Qur-an?

I have made it clear in this column on many occasions - why white people will not agree with Muhammad and the true religion of God (Allah) - which is Islam. They do not agree because of the nature that they were created in - as the opposers of Allah and the TRUTH. They (white people) know that the so-called Negroes believe in them, but with the help of my God (Allah) - who came in the Person of Master W. F. Muhammad-we will show up the false with the truth in its plainest and simplest form.

IT IS FOOLISH to believe in three gods - foolish to make Jesus the Son and the equal of His Father (the one of two thousand years ago). If Jesus said in His suffering - "My God, my God, why hast thou forsaken me?" (Matthew 27:46), then most surely he did not recognize himself as being the equal of God and no other scripture shows Jesus as the equal of God.

If Jesus said that he was sent (Matthew 15:24 and John 4:34), then he cannot claim to be the equal of His sender. God is not sent by anyone; He is a self-sender. He says in Isaiah (44:81-45:22): "Is there a God besides Me? I know not any." In another place He states: (Isaiah 46:9) "I am God, there is none else." Also in Mark 12:32 - "One God and none other."

May 18, 1957

THE AMERICAN SO-CALLED NEGROES' SALVATION IS IN ISLAM, THE ONLY TRUE RELIGION OF GOD

THE POOR people called Negroes, who are not Negroes but descendants of the Tribe of Shabazz, are the victims of every known cruelty and evil treatment known to mankind. Through being ignorant of the knowledge of self and others, they bring a lot of it upon themselves. The One and Powerful God is now seeking them to believe in Him alone - that

He alone will defend and deliver them once and forever from the cruel hands of those that hate and kill them daily.

Their fear and belief are not in God nor Jesus, but in the white race, their slavemasters. Were we to put all of our faith and fear in the One God, Allah, we will not suffer. The so-called Negroes are home-born slaves and they think that they should be recognized as equals in everything with their slavemasters. They boast in calling themselves after the names of the slavemasters and citizens of America, and at the same time begging their masters for civil rights - and their so-called spiritual leaders disgracing themselves, preaching and offering up prayers to a dead prophet (Jesus) and an unknown God that they imagine is living somewhere in the skies. When one enemy mistreats them, they seek refuge in the enemy's brother that they may punish their brother for the wrongs done to them. This shows how blind and ignorant the poor so-called Negroes' spiritual leaders are.

THEY SELL themselves to be the friends of the enemies of their own people to oppose their own salvation; thus becoming agents of the slavemasters against their own people. They are leading themselves and their poor, blind, deaf and dumb people to destruction. May Allah help me to open their eyes before it is too late.

They need the help of the One God Allah who is now with outstretched arms willing and able to help us all. The slavemasters gladly put them on the air to preach, shout out their ignorance to the public - any government that has respect for its religion wouldn't allow any ignorant (one that doesn't know the true meanings) person to represent it to the public.

The black nations' religion, Islam, is a true and upright religion of a True and Up-right God of whom the so-called Negroes are members; who are blinded, robbed and spoiled by the slavemasters. They really feel and think that they are the same as their masters. They seek their masters' friendship above Allah (God) and feel secure in doing it. May Allah have mercy on my people in America.

OF ALL the histories on people being enslaved by others, never have you read where the slaves loved and worshiped their slavemasters; but the so-called Negroes who live under death from the enemy, beaten and killed in the public like wild animals and they never are recognized in the slavemaster' so-called courts of justice as an equal citizen of the land. The smart enemies keep their eyes and ears open on the so-called Negroes night and day seeking an excuse to kill them.

The lack of love, unity and self-respect among us is one of our greatest enemies. Love your black, brown, yellow and red brothers as thyself; do good by each other; never think of shedding the blood of your own kind; treat all human beings right as you are the righteous - then do righteous by all; but if we do good only to self and evil to others, we can't be called the righteous.

THE ABOVE said must not be taken to mean that we should love the devils, but do righteous and justice according to the law of justice. God does not love the devils, but His work of righteousness and justice extends over all. Say: "Do you bid me serve others than Allah, O ye ignorant ones? And certainly it has been revealed to thee and to those before thee: If thou associate with Allah (God) their work would certainly come to nought and thou wouldst be a loser. Nay, but serve along and be of the thankful. The whole earth will be in His grip on the day of resurrection (at the present time) and the heavens rolled up in His right hand."

Hurry and join on to your own. Just write me and say I believe, write me down on the book of life.

June 1, 1957

UNITY

ISLAM - A UNIFYING RELIGION - THE SALVATION FOR EVERY SO-CALLED NEGRO OF AMERICA.

FOR THE past three weeks, I have been teaching on the No. 1 principle of belief in Islam (the belief in One God) not three. This principle (No. 1) includes all the 99 attributes that make up the One Divine Supreme Being (Allah). I hope that you - who read and have been reading my article - will agree with me on this point - that it is both ignorant and foolish to believe in anything as being the equal of Allah (God).

No prophets - from the first to the last - are to be worshipped as the equal of His Sender (God). It is purely infidel to claim sonship to Allah

(God) - and it is also a sin. To do so would be charging Him (Allah) with an act of adultery since God is married to no woman. The teaching of sonship (the Trinity) came only from the devils, who have not lost one minute in trying to prevent people from believing in Allah, the One God.

TODAY, I will take up with you another principle of the religion of Islam and its believers who are called Muslims.

UNITY: This principle (unity), when understood and carried into practice, is the real purpose of Allah (God) and His religion - Islam. God (Allah) created everything for a purpose. Unity is the purpose of the coming of Allah (God) and the judgment of the world - to unite that which is disunited; to destroy that which has destroyed the unity and peace of His people (the American so-called Negroes). Dis-unity is worse among the so-called Negro than any of the other people on earth. There is none to equal my poor people (the so-called Negro) in America.

If the so-called American Negroes would unite, regardless to their faiths and beliefs as a Nation of Brotherhood (the love and help of each other), the greater part of their problems would be solved. "Unity" among us is a greater weapon for us than all the atomic bombs that the West can manufacture. The devil slavemasters have mistreated and bred fear into the so-called Negroes to the extent that the so-called Negroes' belief and love of their slavemasters is so great that they will kill one another to satisfy their open enemies (the devil slavemasters). The unity of Allah (God) is the greatest teachings of the Holy Qur-an and the prophets of old.

HERE IN AMERICA, everything is opposed to the unity and brotherhood of the so-called Negroes. They are a people of whom all other people seem to dislike and shun, delight themselves in spoiling and further ruining of the already spoiled and ruined (the so-called Negroes).

Who is with me to unite my people in America - that are not afraid? I am sure on One - that is Allah (God) - who came in the person of the Most Honorable, Master W. F. Muhammad, The Great Mahdi, the Restorer, the Saviour and only Friend of we, the lost-found members of the Tribe of Shabazz. Certainly, He is with me and the Powers of Heaven and Earth to bring you into unity and knowledge of your God and self. Fear none but He (Allah). Certainly, the slavemasters - you and God's open enemy - hate black man's unity. Will you remain dis-united to please your open enemies - to your hurt?

Let us take a look at the work of the slavemasters' black friends, (the preachers). They are united with the slavemasters - your open enemies - they are against the Truth (Islam) because their white slavemasters are against it; as it is written of them, they fear only the white God. They openly oppose me and my followers to their own ruin and damnation for God is with me and not with the enemies and blinded preachers. You shall soon come to know. Unite and follow me to Allah - Unity and Power.

THE POOR things headed for a March to Washington on the 17th of this month to pray to "Balaam" to have mercy on them and grant to them a place near to them (the slavemasters). Will "Balaam" hear them and grant this plea? The President and Congress, who make the laws and choose agents to enforce it on those whom it pleases, are so hard of hearing that the preachers and their followers must go to his house to beg him for justice. He and Congress have ignored you for 400 years with a full knowledge of their Constitution, and you have been reminding them for 100 years of what is written in the Constitution. Will they listen to you today? Who is at fault - you or they? It is you and your blind leaders. Why not unite onto a God Who will answer your prayers? Come and follow me to power. STOP begging white people to accept you as one of them, or even to give you justice. Unity will get it. There is not, unity, in Christianity.

I am your brother who loves you. I have the key to your salvation. Thanks to you who are helping me, for you shall be helped also. Join up with

June 8, 1957

SOLUTION FOR THE NEGROES' PROBLEMS

WHITE man's Christianity has absolutely failed to get recognition and respect for us - even from those who taught it to us. It is a religion that teaches you to love your enemies and hate your friend, to seek your reward after death. It has produced more division and hate than all the other religions combined.

White Christianity has robbed and destroyed our peace and love for one another. It was white Christians who brought our fathers into slavery; it is white Christianity that is keeping you a subject people. They rape and murder your families, bomb your homes and churches if you demand equal rights and justice. They don't want you, nor do they like to see you go from them to your own. They fear your unity with your own.

So let us unite - and be one people under the crescent of our religion, Islam. Seek for our nation what others seek for their nation. A country to ourselves where we can live in peace away from our enemies.

Islam, the religion of peace, in believing it, brings about a peace of mind and contentment. It's a unifying religion, its author is God. It teaches against the doing of evil of every kind, great or small. The aim of Islam in America is:

1. **To teach our people the truth.**
2. **Clean them up and make them self-respecting and unite them on to their own kind.**
3. **Bring them face to face with our God, and teach them to know their enemies.**

The problem began 400 years ago, from the very first day that our fore-fathers set the sole of their feet on the soil here in the Western Hemisphere, in the days of John Hawkins. It was in the year 1555. He was an English slave trader. In the year 1555 when John Hawkins began bringing our people away from our own native land and away from our own people, to sell us to his white brothers here in the West, for the slave markets here to become merchandise, little did John Hawkins realize at that time that by bringing us here as slaves, he was sentencing his white brothers here to their doom. For the evil that they have, and are still doing to our people here cannot be forgiven.

But was all for a Divine purpose: that Almighty God Allah might make Himself known, through us, to our enemies. And second: To the world that He alone is God. But our poor black mothers and fathers who were deceived by this devil John Hawkins' lies and empty promises, didn't have the slightest idea that their coming here to be sold into slavery would create a problem that would take Almighty God Allah himself, and the righteous nation of Islam to solve . . . and that this problem, would be solved at the end of the time of their arch-deceiving enemies (the devils). That time has arrived. 1914 was it. But as long as you stay asleep from lack of knowledge about yourself, you are extending the life of them. They can continue to live only as long as you remain mentally dead to the knowledge of yourself and the devils.

My followers and I have, and are still spending much time and money, and are suffering much persecution and ridicule to awaken our people to the knowledge of their own salvation. But, we must remember that this present suffering is nothing compared to the joy that awaits us.

Before we ever suffered ourselves, He, Master W. F. Muhammad, Our God and Savior, the Great Mahdi, Almighty God Allah, in Person, suffered persecution and rejection Himself. All for you and for me.

We are now living in the days of the judgment, and in the days of a great separation of peoples and nations. This problem of separating (the boundary line of many nations are now being removed), you and me from our enemies, and placing us in our own land back among our own people . . . to help raise the so-called Negroes of America up to our proper place in civilization.

Remember it was Muhammad's finding of the black stone out of its place and inviting the four chiefs from four divisions to come forward and take hold of each corner of the mantle and lift it into its place, and Muhammad with His own hands who guided it into its place. Was a sign of me and you here today. We need the help of our people who are living in the four major points of our compass to come and help raise us, their dead brothers, and put us back into our own place, in our own nation among our own people in our own native land.

June 15, 1957

ALLAH Himself has said that we can't return to our land until we have a thorough knowledge of our own selves . . . And this first step is the control and the protection of our own women. There is no nation on earth that has less respect for, and as little control of their women as we so-called Negroes here in America. Even animals and beasts, the fowl of the air, have more love and respect for their females than have the so-called Negroes of America.

Our women are allowed to walk or ride the streets all night long, with any strange men they desire. They are allowed to frequent any tavern or dance hall that they like, whenever they like. They are allowed to fill our homes with children other than our own . . . Children that are often fathered by the very devil himself . . . Then when the devil man decided to marry her, the so-called Negro press and magazines will make it front page news. The daily press will not print a so-called Negro man marrying into their race, but you seem to think it is an honor to your own nation when your daughter goes over to your enemies, the devils.

Our women have been and are still being used by the devil white race, ever since we were first brought here to there States as slaves. They can't go without being winked at, whistled at, yelled at, slapped, patted, kicked and driven around in the streets by your devil enemies right under your nose and in your eyesight, and yet you do nothing about it, nor do you even protest.

You can't control nor protect your women as long as you are in the white race's false religion called Christianity. This religion of theirs gives you no desire or power to resist them. The only way and place to solve this problem is: In the religion of Islam.

It is a pleasure to Allah to defend us from our enemies. In the religion of Christianity the white race has had us worshipping and praying to something that actually didn't even exist.

Islam will not only elevate your women, but will also give you the power to control and protect them. We protect ours from against all their enemies.

We protect our farms by pulling up our weeds and grass by the roots, by killing animals and birds, and by poisoning the insects that destroy our crops in order that we may produce a good crop. How much more valuable are our women, who are our fields through whom we produce our nation.

The white race doesn't want us to destroy their race by intermarrying with them, they will even kill you to protect their women. Can you blame them? No. Blame your foolish self for not having enough respect for your own self and your own nation to do likewise. Stop our women from trying to imitate that race, from trying to look like them. By bleaching, powdering, ironing and coloring their hair, painting their lips, cheeks, eyebrows, wearing shorts, going half-nude in public places, going swimming with them and on beaches with men.

Have private pools for your women and guard them from all men. Stop them from going into bars and taverns and sitting and drinking with men and strangers. Stop them from sitting in those places with anyone. Stop them from using unclean language in the public (and at home), from smoking and drug addiction habits.

Nothing but Islam will make you a respectable people. We, Muslims, are your example, living here in your midst.

There is no delinquency in Islam. Are you with us to put our people on top of the world? If so, register at once. For information write to:

June 22, 1957

SALVATION IS ISLAM

WHY SHOULD not we unite under one brotherhood? Are not white people united when it comes to black mankind? Are not all others than the white race united; e.g.: the brown and yellow races? Are not they our brothers belonging to the same nation (black mankind)? Are not we all brothers under the same burden of white slave-masters' injustices?

In the eyes of our white masters we are all Negroes, a people that no decent civilized nation should accept as their equals. In the eyes of our own black, brown, yellow and red brothers, we are the most ignorant, blind, deaf and dumb people on earth. In the eyes of Allah (God) we are mentally dead and His choice. Allah (God) has given to us (the so-called Negroes) - life and made us His special people - a people to be the head and not the tail . . . as it is written. When will you be convinced - that our unity is all that is necessary to become a strong and most dreaded and mightiest nation that ever lived.

If a small well twisted cord is hard to break, then how much harder is it to break 100 such twines or cords well twisted into ONE? We are well educated in the knowledge of what the slave-masters dislike of us. If they are afraid of our unity as ONE nation of brotherhood - then why shouldn't we unite? You know that they have deceived us in regards to the TRUTH of God, religion and our own selves. We have served them more obediently than we have the God of heaven and earth. In all our humblest submission to them, we received the most outright cruel injustice ever meted out to any human beings.

Our American black women are their prostitutes. They are free for them at all times and you look on helplessly, not being able to put a stop to it - because we are dis-united. **Why not unite?** You see and hear of my mighty work - the teaching of God's truth and power in your midst - how it is uniting those that believe and are following me.

Yet - you are afraid to join in unity with us, regardless of the plain truth that you hear coming from me. Allah (God) has revealed and taught this truth to me - to teach and warn you.

You see and hear your leaders and preachers pleading to the white Christians to accept them as brethren and at the same time the white Christians and their government in many places don't want even to look on your black faces. You see and hear that 50,000 of our people headed by their white-loving leaders - in Washington - the nation's capital - praying and singing to the President and his law-making Congress to give them civil rights which they think the slave-master granted to them in the constitution . . . only to be deceived.

If 50,000 so-called Negroes would turn to Allah (God) and accept Islam . . . follow me . . . they could remain at home and get what they desire. **Why not unite with us in Islam?** In Islam you will have the love, Power and help of Allah . . . the entire nation of black mankind is with you. This earth is ours and the God of it. **Why not unite with us?** You see and hear the talk of white mankind . . . Is there anything good in it for you and me? One of their preachers by the name of Herbert Armstrong (of Pasadena, Calif.) is on the radio 11:30 P.M. week days preaching both the destruction of white government and the salvation of his people after their destruction for their evil doing.

He takes the Bible's prophecies of the salvation of the lost-found members of the Tribe of Shabazz (so-called Negroes) to be a promised blessing for his people - whom God will destroy and give the kingdom to the slaves (so-called Negroes). No one but Allah (God) and myself are preaching love and salvation for the so-called Negroes.

No one can and is proving it from the same scriptures that Mr. Armstrong claims to be the salvation for his people (the enemies of Allah (God) and all black mankind, but Allah (God) and myself.

Why not unite with us? I am your brother and I suffer along with you.

<hr>

June 29, 1957

"THE BLOOD SHEDDER" (REV. 16:6)

ACCORDING to the word of Allah (God) and the history of the world, since the grafting of the Caucasian race 6,000 years ago, they have caused more bloodshed than any people known to the black nation. Born murderers, their very nature is to murder; the Bible and Holy Qur-an Sharrieff are full of teachings of this bloody race of devils. They shed the life blood of all life, even their own, and are scientists at deceiving the black people.

They deceived the very people of Paradise (Bible Genesis 3:13). They killed their own brother (Genesis 4:8). The innocent earth's blood (Genesis 4:10), but revealed it to its Maker (thy brother's blood cryeth unto me from the ground). The very earth, the soil of America soaked with the innocent blood of the so-called Negroes shed by this race of devils, now cryeth out to its Maker for her burden of carrying the innocent blood of the righteous slain upon her. Let us take a look at the devil's creation from the teachings of the Holy Qur-an.

"And when your Lord said to the angels, I am going to place in the earth one who shall rule, the angels said: 'What will Thou place in it such as shall make mischief in it and shed blood, we celebrate Thy praise and extol Thy holiness.'" (Holy Qur-an Sharrieff 2:30).

This devil race has and still is doing just that - making mischief and shedding blood; and the black nation whom they were grafted from (when your Lord said to the angels): "Surely I am going to create a mortal of the essence of black mud fashioned into shape." (Holy Qur-an Sharrieff, 15:28).

The essence of black mud (the black nation) mentioned is only symbolic, which actually means the sperm of the black nation; and they refused to recognize the black nation as their equal though they were made from and by a black scientist (named Yakub). They can never see their way in submitting to Allah and the religion Islam and his prophets. You may have read in last week's issue of this paper's magazine section of a Southern devil's letter, whose name this paper withheld, making fun of you and especially our women, whom he classified as nothing, getting children from different men, which we know is the truth. He and his fathers are responsible for making their slaves such as they are, but the foolish slave should now awaken and fly with his family from his slave-masters and protect his woman from making love with his enemies even to his death. This same Southern devil criticized this paper for its news, and pointed out Mr. Jones and myself as trash - that this paper should get rid of us along with its love potion. As for the love potion, the so-called Negro press would make a wise step towards better respect if they would leave out of their papers and magazines this filthy love mess, which is ruining their younger generation to the extent that when our children get their hands on the papers or magazines they go first for such readings and pictures. To rid the paper of myself or article is the real thing that the devil desires out. Why? Because I am telling you the truth. The old bloodthirsty devil - I fear you won't get your desire of getting rid of Elijah Muhammad, not if it isn't the will of my God, Allah, who is ever with me to slay you for slaying His messengers of old and the so-called Negroes.

Their every cry is to beat - beat - kill - kill - the so-called Negroes. Maybe the day has arrived that Allah will return to you devils - that which you have been so anxious to pour on the poor innocent so-called Negroes, as you love to shed the poor innocent blood of your Negro slaves, and plan to kill me for teaching them the truth that they may have friendship with their God and people. Allah will give you your own blood to drink like water, and your arms and allies won't help you against Him. (Rev. 16:6).

The heads and bodies of the so-called Negroes are used to test the clubs and guns of the devils, and yet the poor, foolish so-called Negroes admire the devils regardless to how they are treated.

America is now under DIVINE PLAGUES. One will come after the other until she is destroyed. Allah has said it.

Join on to us at once!

J u l y   6 ,   1 9 5 7

THE DEVIL ("that man of sin is revealed, the son of perdition" Thessalonians 2:3). The true knowledge of the devil (the man of sin) is the base of the coming of God to judgment, for without the knowledge of the devil how can anyone be saved?

If you had believed in that which later you learned is not what you really thought it was, then your belief is changed by the true knowledge of that thing. Truth is then to be given credit for revealing the false.

The so-called Negroes, and even most of the black nation, including a great percentage of Muslims, have not the true knowledge of the devil in human form. Such Muslims and themselves in these days of the resurrection of the so-called Negroes, opposing Allah and the true religion of Islam to the joy of the devils along with the ignorant so-called Negroes, who are really afraid of the devils - who have been their evil gods and masters for 400 years and who have put fear of them in the so-called Negroes from the cradle to the grave. Therefore, one cannot blame the so-called Negroes for that fear the devils (white race) - that was put into them when they were babies. But if their God, Allah, reveals the devils - that they are really nothing but devils from the beginning - should then the so-called Negroes, be held blameless? Why, **NO!** Their love and fear of these devils (the man of sin) is the thing that will destroy them along with the devils.

Notice: The note that you read above this article by the editors of this paper shows how much **FEAR** the so-called Negroes have of white people (the devils), but should I stop telling Allah's (God's) revealed **truth** to please your fear?

I have offered my life to Allah to help Him get the truth to my people regardless to whom or what. How can Allah bring us to the judgment and destruction of the devils without making manifest the devil, His and our arch-deceiving enemies? That would be injustice. So then the above chapter (2 Thess. 2) teaches us that the judgment won't come until the devil (the man of sin) is revealed, for according to this chapter (2 Thess. 2) no one actually had the knowledge of the devil but Allah Himself. (See verse 8). For if He (Allah) will consume with the spirit of His mouth, on His coming proves without questioning that the true person of the devils was hidden from the knowledge of 90 per cent of the black nation until today. Therefore, allowing the devils to deceive the entire black nation that he could until they are revealed. Again, this chapter (Thess. 2:9, 10) makes it clear that when the devil (the man of sin) is revealed that is the end and judgment of the world's greatest deceiving evil race of people who ever lived on the earth and ever will.

Read (Rev. 20:8-10). Read Holy Qur-an Sharrieff 2:36, 7:20, 20:120, 7:17, 4:119, 17:62. The natural religion of man then disowns the responsibility for having misled them, threatens to mislead the whole of humanity (17:62), gives false promises (14:22), opposes the Prophets (22:52), makes evil deeds look attractive (16:63). He has no authority over you except those who befriend him (16:99, 100).

This is the description and characteristics of your devils whom you love and hate me for teaching the truth of them. Let them try disproving the above said. Take a look at chapter seven of the Holy Qur-an Sharrieff verse 16 and 21; here the devil swears that he will mislead the righteous.

Hurry and enter your name on the Book of Life.

July 13, 1957

ISLAM THE TRUE RELIGION, THE SO-CALLED NEGROES' SALVATION AND ETERNAL LIFE. ACCEPT IT AND LIVE.

ALLAH reveals the real devil in human form, that man of sin (the white race). (Thess. 2:3).

Why shouldn't the so-called Negroes and the whole of the black nation know the truth of the devil who has ruled us for 6,000 years? Now the end of that race of devils has arrived. Just how are we to reject them and accept Allah (God) if we have not a true knowledge of the devils? But Allah (God), the best knower, never destroyed a people without first revealing His truth and purpose through a messenger, whom He chooses of that people, according to the Bible and Holy Qur-an Sharrieff.

The wise tricks today being used by the devils (white race) on the American so-called Negroes to deceive them to share hell fire with the devils, could trap 99 per cent of them in going to their destruction, if the so-called Negroes are not taught the true knowledge of this universal, arch-deceiving race of devils, who have been their guides and teachers since the days of slavery.

Shall I, for the sake of your fear and ignorance of the devils, withhold from telling you the truth which Allah (God) has revealed to me that will free you of that fear and ignorance - that is now hindering you from being sat in heaven and power? No! I won't withhold the truth from you to be called a friend of the devils - even at the price of death - for this is that truth which Jesus prophesied that "you shall know that which shall make you free." (John 8:32).

Today it has come to you and me from the Lord of the worlds. A true knowledge of the person of God and the devil. I am not responsible for your rejection. Mine is only to teach and warn you. According to the Bible (John 8:42), Jesus told the devils that "if God were your father you would love Me." In the 44th verse of the same chapter eight, Jesus says: "You are of your father the devil." This proves beyond a shadow of a doubt that this race (white race) cannot believe the truth and especially Allah and Islam. Not being of Allah, they can't by nature love and obey Him nor the prophets of Allah, nor His people, the black nation. Just try teaching them of Allah and His religion, Islam. Some of them will claim they never heard of Islam, to see how much you know of it, though their Father (Yakub), sometimes referred to as Adam, was once in Islam.

This religion (Islam), the American white race doesn't like for the so-called Negroes to believe, but the poor lost, found members of the tribe of Shabazz are now learning very fast. Islam is truth - but what they (the whites) hate the most is the true knowledge of themselves - that is; that they themselves are the devils. But the Bible (John 8:44), (Thess. 2:3, 4, 8, 9), teaches that they are nothing else but devils, for II Thessalonians,

Chapter 2, makes it very clear to us, that the man of sin's (the devil's) time is limited, and that he must do a work of deceiving, lying, murdering and opposing the true God and His prophets, and that the truth of them will put a stop to their deceiving the people of Allah (the black nation) which will only come after the time of the man of sin (the devil) has been fulfilled. Though you may not agree with your own Bible, that is its true meaning. Allah comes after the time of this man of sin (the devil) and that is true. He has come and I am directly sent from Him, to make this truth known to my people, that they shouldn't love and follow the devils, for Allah (God) will destroy this enemy and His works. The country now is under the plagues of Allah (God). Join on to Islam my people, it is your salvation. This devil desires to frighten you away from accepting Islam. Don't let him do that, for Allah is well able to protect you and me from their evil planning.

July 20, 1957

ISLAM, THE TRUE RELIGION, THE SO-CALLED NEGROES' SALVATION

The History of Jesus' Birth and Death and What It Means to You and Me

I WON'T be able to give a complete knowledge in one article. It will take a series of articles to tell of all the Prophets of God who are recorded in the Bible and Holy Qur-an Sharrieff. None is more controversial than the history of Jesus and none is more misunderstood. This misunderstanding is nearly 100 per cent among the so-called Negroes in the U.S.A., due to their following and believing what their enemies (the devils) have taught and written concerning Jesus' birth and death.

I do believe that if my poor, blind, deaf and dumb people could be taught the true knowledge of the true history of Jesus, they would awaken at once. Some of the so-called Negroes' leaders (preachers) are dumber to the knowledge of Jesus' birth, life and death means than those who are following him, and for the sake of being called a leader (preacher) they are proud against the truth, and they will oppose it fearing the loss of their office. Thus - leading themselves and their followers to hell with the devils because of their blindness, love and fear of the devils.

I will teach you the truth as I have received it from Him - who is the Author of Truth - regardless to whom or what, for I speak not of myself - for I, too, was once blind, deaf and dumb, but I speak and write that which I have received of Him (Allah), and on Him do I rely.

There is no mentioning of Jesus in the history of Moses (Deut. 18:15-18). This cannot refer to the Jesus of 2,000 years ago, nor (Isaiah 9:6), nor even the 53rd chapter of Isaiah. For you disbelievers and blind guides who want me to prove what I teach, take a look at his history as recorded in the Holy Qur-an Sharrieff (3:41, 42, 44, 46), and try comparing it with the Bible's birth of Jesus.

When the angels said: "O Mary, surely Allah gives you good news with a word from Him (of one) whose name is the Messiah, Jesus, Son of Mary, worthy of regards in this world and the hereafter."

NOTE: In the verse above, Jesus is called according to Arabic transliteration "Al-Masih, Isa and Ibn-Maryam," meaning in English, the Messiah, Son of Mary. "Masih," says the commentator on the language, means either one who travels much or one wiped over with some such thing as oil, the same word as the Aramaic "Messiah," which is said to mean, the anointed. If the name means one who travels much, it could not refer to Jesus of two thousand years ago who spent his life in the small state called Palestine.

One of the main things that one must learn is to distinguish between the history of Jesus two thousand years ago and the prophecy of the Jesus who is expected to come at the end of the world. What we have as a history of the birth of Jesus 2,000 years ago often proves to be that of the Great Mahdi, the Restorer of the Kingdom of Peace on Earth who came to America in 1930 under the name of Mr. W. D. Fard. Later, he admitted that he was Mr. Wallace Fard Muhammad, the one whom the world had been looking for to come for the past 2,000 years. According to the Holy Qur-an chapter and verse we have under discussion, the name Messiah, the meaning fits that of the Mahdi more than any other man.

The Mahdi is a world traveler. He told me that he had traveled the world over and that he had visited North America for 20 years before making himself known to us, his people, whom he came for. He had visited the Isles of the Pacific, Japan and China, Canada, Alaska, the North Pole, India, Pakistan, all of the Near East and Africa. He had studied the wild life in the jungles of Africa and learned the language of the birds. He could speak 16 languages and could write 10 of them. He visited every inhabited place on the earth and had pictured and extracted the language of the people on Mars and had a knowledge of all life in the universe. He could recite by heart the histories of the world as far back as 150,000 years and knew the beginning and end of all things.

The names Christ, Jesus, Jehovah, God, Allah and many other good names, rightly are His names and He came to give divine names to the whole of the 17 million so-called Negroes, Jesus was made an example for the Jews (Holy Qur-an 43:59). Jesus and his mother were made as a sign (23:50).

July 27, 1957

THE HISTORY OF JESUS (CONTINUED)

AS WE have the Bible's version of Jesus' history, I bring to you some of the history as given in the Holy Qur-an Sharrieff, translated into English by Maulvi Muhammad Ali, which is given for the purpose of clearing Jesus of false charges made by his enemies, the devil's writers.

Since the so-called Negroes' knowledge of Jesus came solely from the Bible, translated into English by the enemies of Jesus they will not accept anything other than what the devils teach, "Jesus and His mother a sign." (Holy Qur-an 23:50) This is the best answer as yet given, for with such answer we have the key to this Man's birth, ministry and death - for that which serves as a sign is not the thing that it is a sign of, but only a sign of something to come or to be. As Moses birth, history and death as given in the Bible and Qur-an was a sign of that which was to come, and I may add to the dislike of many Muslims, Muhammad's life and history was also a sign of that which was to come at the end of the World of the Infidels, be it understood.

He, who is the last of the Prophets, was clearly seen and made known to those Prophets before Him, and their life work reflects for us the life and work of the last Prophet, who is not really a prophet in the sense of the word, but rather an apostle or messenger, for He is the Answer and End of the Prophets. His call is unlike the others before him, for all of the Prophets before the last one had their call and mission through inspirations and visions for they saw not the Person of Allah (God) in reality - only in visions - but the last one is Chosen and Missioned directly from the mouth of Allah (God) in person at the end of the world. He will also bring a Book for His people. A Book that the present world has not as yet seen and the devils (infidels) may not see it nor touch it. It is not the present Holy Qur-an nor Bible, but a Book containing the guidance for the people in the Hereafter. Not of this world, therefore, it is carefully guarded from the eyes and ears of this world.

The last Messenger of Allah (God), his position to Allah (God) is not only like that of the Moon to the Sun, which only reflects light in the absence of the Sun, but is like that of the Planet Mercury, which is all but lost in the light of the Sun, and no other planet is between mercury and the Sun. His message (the Truth) is like the Sun, which makes clear and distinct that which the Moon and Stars cannot. Can one say that of the present scriptures? The verse mentioned above (23:50) included Jesus' mother as also being a sign. Just what are the two a sign of? Look for the answer in this column.

It has been reported to me of the police brutality on my followers and my people who were listening to the Truth, preached by one of my followers on the streets of Detroit in the section dominated by our people, Sunday, July 7, 1957. These attacks made upon us by the city's lawless officers, who are supposed to be peace officers, are ignored by the mayors of these cities, bear witness to the Truth that Allah (God), in the person of Master W. F. Muhammad, said that they are nothing but a race of devils. Think over the attack made on us in New York by that brute force, and in Alabama, all within six months of this year. Not even waiting for any answer, they jump on an unarmed, innocent group of people with guns, nightclubs, blackjacks, pick handles, crushing their skulls, breaking legs and even swinging at little children and women who were standing by, in Detroit last Sunday, so I heard, and now claim that they were attacked first. No justice for us among these devils. Separate yourselves from among them. No one was teaching aggression, only the Truth of self, love and unity of our God, religion and people. A squad of brute officers parked around them to make a sudden attack, not caring to arrest them, but maim and kill them. They were not first asked to submit to arrest.

Join onto your own kind, the Nation of Islam, at once.

August 3, 1957

THE HISTORY OF JESUS (CONTINUED)

Jesus, a sign; His mother, a sign; Muhammad and his birth, ministry, persecution and death, was also a sign of another one yet to come. I hope the readers of this column won't jump to conclusions before I have finished this history of Jesus and have shown the proof. You don't have to tell me - I know that it is no easy thing to change your belief in something that you were born in, but readers, just be intelligent enough to admit and agree on the Truth.

The birth of Musa (Moses) under the government of Pharaoh, who along with his people were enemies of Musa (Moses) and his people and who enslaved and killed Musa's people without justice, and the hidings and fleeings of Musa (Moses) from Pharaoh, are all a sign of the last Messenger. Jesus' birth, ministry and persecution, hated by Herod and the spiritual teachers of the Jews, as Pharaoh and his magicians hated Musa (Moses) and his followers. These two prophets' histories show that they had no peace among the rulers and people to whom they were sent to guide and warn. The birth of Musa (Moses) meant the end of Pharaoh's power and the freedom of the Caucasian race. The birth and death of Jesus meant the end of the rule and independence of the Jews, who rejected him as being a Prophet of Allah (God), which serves as a sign of what we may expect in the days of the Last One whom these two prophets, Musa and

Isa (Moses and Jesus) prophesied would come in these last days or would be present with Allah (God) in person.

The Jews were expecting a prophet to be born in their midst (2,000 years) after the death of Musa (Moses) and know that one is to be raised up from the midst of their race just prior to the end (judgment) of their time.

They soon learned that Jesus was not **that** prophet. Muhammad, born in the Seventh Century after the death of Jesus, the last sign of that last one coming with Allah (God) in the judgment or end of the world of devil's rule. Muhammad turned on the light (Islam) in the ancient house (Arab nation) that had burned low since the time of Ibrahim (Abraham) and cleaned it up for the reception of a much brighter light of the Mahdi (Allah in Person) and His people, which will come from the West out of the house of the infidels.

That last Messenger is the One chosen by the Mahdi, Allah (God) in person, in the last days whom the Mahdi finds lost and enslaved by the infidels in the West, of whom Abraham made a sign with a small, unhewn black stone and set it in the Holy City of Mecca, and veiled it over with a black veil which will not be unveiled and destroyed or discarded until he whom the sign represents is returned (the last Messenger and his followers).

Jesus spoke of the future of that stone in these words, "The stone which the builders rejected is become the head of the corner." (Mark 12:10) Muhammad found the stone out of place and had it put back into its proper place. This act of Muhammad shows that he was not the fulfiller of the sign which the stone represents, but rather a prototype of that which the stone represents. Moreover, Muhammad's replacing and repairing the sign (the stone) was a sign of the work of the Mahdi, who would, in His day, raise and put into proper place that which the stone now serves as a sign of.

Oh, that you would only understand the Scriptures. The Christians think the stone was Jesus. The Muslims think that it represents Muhammad 1,370 years ago. The Prophets, for the saved people in the Hereafter, will love and praise Allah for him as this is the meaning of Muhammad, as the Muslim world respects and honors Muhammad today. There certainly is a surprise in store for both worlds (Islam and Christianity) in the revealing of this last One. Some of the religious scientists are already wise to it.

Hurry and join onto your own kind.

August 10, 1957

JESUS' HISTORY FROM THE
MOUTH OF ALLAH (GOD)

We know that most all white menfolk love to insult the black women; it is the nature of that race to destroy the black.

So he told his daughter (Mary) when she went out to care for the stock, to wear his clothes, and he made her a beard out of a goat's beard to wear so that the filthy thinking devils would think that it was he (the father of Mary).

After giving his daughter his instructions on how to protect herself against the insults of the devil, while he was visiting the new construction of a mosque, he took leave of the home for three days. After the father's departure, just at the time to feed the stock, there arose a great dust storm (dust cloud) which blotted out visibility. Under this darkness she became afraid to venture out, so while thinking of how the stock would be fed, she thought of Yusuf (Joseph), the only man that she could trust and the only one that she ever loved.

She called him to come and go with her to feed her father's stock. Joseph came in answer to her call. On his arrival at the home of Mary, she showed him the old man's clothing and the goat's beard that she was to wear in her father's absence; but Joseph suggested to Mary to allow him to wear her father's clothes and the goat beard, and that she wear her own clothes as usual so that the infidels would think that he (Joseph) was the old man (Mary's father). So Joseph and Mary went together from that day on until the return of the old man three days later.

Mary asked Joseph to return after the first day, and on the second day she asked Joseph: "What about your wife, and what will she think of your coming here?" Joseph said, "I will tell her that I am working, building an infidel a house," as he (Joseph) was a carpenter. Mary said, "What if your wife says to you, 'Where is the money?'" This question Joseph had no answer for, so Mary gave Joseph some money to carry home with him (just in case). On the third day the old man returned.

About three months later he began to notice his daughter taking on weight.

He asked her, "Mary, what have you been eating? You seem to be taking on weight."

She denied that there had been any change in her eating. The old man, her father, went on for a while and became very suspicious he kept noticing Mary's continued increase in weight. Again he said to Mary: "What has happened?" Mary denied not and said: "Father, do you remember when you left home to go to the building of the new mosque?" The father said, "Yes." She said: "Well on that day when you left a dust cloud arose and there was darkness; I was afraid to go out in such darkness to feed the stock, so I called Joseph to go with me, so he came and he did go with me that day and help feed the stock; and also the next day, until you came home."

Her father said: "Yes, it looks like he fed them plenty." And she said: "And this is why I am like this. I told you that I loved Joseph and while alone together, this is what happened. Now I have told you the truth. You may kill me or do as you please."

The father, listening to such confessions from his daughter felt real bad, for the law was the same then as it was in the time of Moses and the Jews and as it is today in the dominant Muslim world. If an unmarried girl is found to be pregnant out of wedlock, she must be killed and the killing falls to the lot of the parents.

As time passed he began to hate to look at Mary's pregnancy. He became sick over it and went to bed. He nearly pulled out all of his beard looking and worrying over what to do about his daughter.

So, at this time, an old prophetess (spiritual woman) met Joseph. **(To be continued).**

Write me at Muhammad's Temple No. 2, 5335 S. Greenwood Ave., Chicago 15, Ill., Elijah Muhammad, Messenger of Allah.

JESUS' HISTORY, BIRTH AND DEATH

WHEN THIS old, spiritual woman met Joseph, she said to him: "O, Yusuf (Joseph), you are the father of Maryam's (Mary's) baby." This was a surprise to Joseph, to learn that this old woman knew of his secret visit to Mary, his boyhood and manhood sweetheart, and he began to deny his guilt by saying:

"No! No! I am not the father of Mary's child!" The old prophetess woman reaffirmed her charge and said: "Oh, yes, you are the father. I have only come to help you. Don't deny the child. He is the one prophecied in the Holy Qur-an as being the last prophet to the Jews. He is going to be a great man, and as long as His name lives, yours, as being His father, will live.

"I have come to teach you how to save and protect him from the Jews' planning; for the Jews will kill the child. They are expecting a prophet from Allah (God) to be born at this time, and if the child is not carefully protected, they will kill it."

Remember the Bible's saying: "Then Joseph, her husband under the Jews' marital laws, being a just man and not willing to make her a public example, was minded to put her away privily. While he thought on these things, behold, the angel of the Lord appeared unto him in a dream, saying: "Joseph, thou son of David, fear not to take unto thee Mary, thy wife, for that which is conceived in her is of the Holy Ghost." (Matt. 1:12, 20). (The 18th verse of the above chapter of Matthew says, that Mary was espoused to Joseph before they came together).

THIS WORD "espoused," according to the English language, when referred to man and woman - means engaged to be married, or to give in marriage, or to take up and support. In the case of Joseph and Mary, this seems to fit very well; for they were engaged to marry from childhood, but were never married. The child was conceived out of wedlock, for Joseph was already married to another woman and had six children by her, and these children by his wife are mentioned in Mark (3:31, 32). Of course, you will have to be careful about the readings of what the Bible calls the Gospel of Jesus, because much of it is not authentic truth, and all Bible scholars will agree with me. Much of it is lost as that of the Torah (which they called Old Testament) or the books of Moses. Of course, we know that the original Torah was one book and the Injil (Gospel) given to Jesus, was only one book. Adding in and out of the truth, by the world writers, has caused so much misunderstanding of just what Allah (God) said and His prophets, that to correct it, Allah (God) has prepared a new book altogether, for the lost found brother (the so-called Negroes). All the present scriptures, even the Holy Qur-an, have been touched by the hand of the enemies of truth (the devils).

"**JOSEPH**, after hearing from the mouth of the old prophetess, that his son, by Mary, was going to be a great man, a prophet, and the last one to the House of Israel (or the white race in general), he confessed that he was the father, regardless of the cost; which by the law, meant death for both him and Mary. But they were for - a sign of something that was to come - and Allah (God) said that the old prophetess woman, told Joseph to go and confess to Mary's father, that you are the father of his daughter's un-born child. And, that the child is going to be the great and last prophet to the House of Israel (the Jews), and, that the Jews would try to kill the child - and, if you will allow me to take care of Mary, it won't happen. Now - I have told you the truth, so if you like, you can kill me. The old man (Mary's father) had the same thought as Joseph. Since the child is to be a prophet of Allah (God), as being the father of Mary, his name also would live; so he agreed to let Joseph look after Mary."

THEN JOSEPH asked the old man for the use of one of the stalls of his stock. Joseph took and filled the sides of the stall with straw and made a bed for Mary in the center. From the outside, it looked as though it were filled with straw. Joseph left a hole through which could feed Mary, and he was the nurse. In the dominant world of Islam, then and today, the parents teach both the boy and the girl, how to take care of the wife at childbirth. It is not like it is here in this world, where everything, along with yourself, is commercialized.

Write me and join onto your own kind.

JESUS' HISTORY BIRTH AND DEATH – FROM THE MOUTH OF ALLAH(GOD) MARY FLEES TO EGYPT

(Continued From Last Week)

JOSEPH RENTED one of those fast camels, put Mary and her baby on it, and said to the camel: "Take this woman to Cairo, Egypt. Hurry! Hurry!" The camel went directly to Cairo with Mary and her child, Jesus.

When Jesus was 4 years old, he began school, and at the age of 14 he graduated. Jesus was very fast in learning (as Allah taught me). Jesus and his mother were Aboriginal Egyptians. This may be the reason Joseph sent them to Egypt - so that she would be among her own people, away from the Jews, whose intentions were to kill her child. The Aboriginal Egyptians are people of the black nation, and even the modern people of Egypt – in fact, all original Asiatic people are of the black nation. But, the America so-called Negroes think that they do not have any people except those who are in the jungles of Africa. The only people who are not members of the black nation are the white race.

At the time of Mary's flight to Egypt, the Jews' every intention was on finding and killing the child Jesus. But, once in Egypt the child was safe. Between the ages of 12 and 14, an old prophet came looking for Isa(Jesus). This old prophet had a knowledge of Jesus' presence and future life. He wanted to get to Jesus and inform him of just what he may expect, and how to protect himself from the evil intentions of his enemies (the Jews). He began going to the school and the time of dismissal to get a chance to meet Isa (Jesus). When the boys started home, this old prophet would walk up and start looking among them for Jesus. On the third day, he pretended to be looking for a certain address and the address was next door to the house where Jesus lived. He asked one of the boys if he knew where it was. While the boys were trying to think just where the place was, another boy looked and said: "Here comes Isa(Jesus). He lives just next door to the number where you want to go. He will take you to it." The boy told Isa(Jesus) of the old man's desire of to find the number, so Jesus said to the old man: "Yes, come with me, I know where it is. It is next door to where I live." As Jesus and the old man walked on, alone, the old man asked Jesus what course he was studying. Jesus mentioned mathematics. The old man said to Jesus: "Yes, that is fine. I have a boy going to school taking the same course. Maybe you could help him." Jesus, who loved to teach someone, said: "Yes, I will teach your son." As they neared the address, the old man said to Jesus: "I am not looking for that address; it is you that I have been trying to get for three days. I had intended to get to talk to you, if I had to fall down in front of you and let you stumble over me." He then said to Jesus: "Do you know who you are?" Jesus answered and said; "I don't know, but I believe I am going to be a great man." The old man said: "Yes! You are the one who, the Holy Qu-ran says, will be the last prophet to the Jews. I have come to teach you how to protect yourself. You will finish school and after finishing school, you will return to the Jews' land and begin teaching them. If you don't know how to protect yourself, they will kill you. I will teach you how to tune in on them, so you can tell when they are planning to come and do you harm."

So, from that day, the old man began teaching Jesus in lessons, how to tune in on people and tell what they were thinking about. By Jesus already a righteous boy, he learned in three lessons. The old man tested him and asked Jesus to tune in on him and talk with him. (It is not near as hard to receive a message as it is to send one out to a certain person.) Jesus tuned in on the old man and greeted him. The old man returned the greeting and said: "You are fine. Now you are able to take care of yourself. This is what I wanted to teach you. Now, you may go."

Write me and join unto your own kind.

HISTORY OF JESUS' BIRTH AND DEATH

(Continued from last week)
JESUS finally made the trip walking from Cairo, Egypt to Jerusalem, Palestine. Just how long it took him, I don't know. By having to stop and

teach along the wayside, it must have taken quite some time. Nevertheless, on his arrival, he began teaching the Jews the religion of Islam. The Jews rejected him and what he taught, except for a few.

Jesus, according to Allah (God), never was able to get over 35, or around that figure, to listen to him at one time. They hated Jesus and would refer to him as a liar, and that Moses was their prophet. They would call Jesus names that were so terrible, they can't be described in writing. There are any number of scripture in both the Bible and Holy Qur-an that Jesus was a prophet, sent to the House of Israel alone. We have no scripture of him teaching anywhere else but among the Jews. He was not a universal prophet (not sent to the whole world). He made no attempt to teach the Arabs nor the blacks of Egypt or Africa. According to the history of his disciples, none of them carried Jesus' name and teachings into the countries of the black nation.

Paul, one of the greatest preachers and travelers of Jesus' followers, made no attempt to teach the black nation; nor travel into their countries. (I just can't see how the so-called Negroes think that he is their Saviour, when he didn't save the Jews to whom he was sent, and he has not saved the so-called Negroes from the slavery of white Americans). It is really a shame and a crime, worthy of death, for the devils to have tricked my people into the belief of Prophet Jesus being their God and Saviour - a hearer of their prayers, and at the same time, teaching them that they killed Jesus. It just doesn't make sense. May Allah burn such liars from the face of the earth, for deceiving my people whom they now kill and burn at will - because they know not their God - nor, even know themselves! It is sickness to listen to our poor people calling on Isa (Jesus) of 2,000 years ago, as though he were alive in their midst; and, they are really sincere. By my Allah (God), I will bring them into the knowledge of truth; and, to their God, Allah - or die in the effort.

Break the head of falsehood. Confuse and bring to naught his lying missionaries, who have deceived my people with their lies on Allah and His Prophet Isa's (Jesus) birth and death; and, the scriptures of the prophets. (The so-called Negroes want to know why white people hide the truth from them; the answer is that they are the devils and know that one cannot be enslaved who knows the truth).

The Death of Jesus. Allah, the best knower, to whom be praised forever, who came in the person of Master W. F. Muhammad, said: "That, Jesus, after teaching and running from the devils for 22 years, learned from reading and studying the scripture, that he couldn't reform the infidel race. And that they had 2,000 years more to live to do their devilment, and deceive the nations of earth. He decided to give his life for the truth (Islam) which he taught - and was rejected - for the 22 years of his life in Palestine.

One Saturday morning, between 9 and 10 o'clock, he came out on the streets of Jerusalem and saw a small group of people standing under an awning in front of a Jew's store, trying to shelter themselves from the rain. Jesus walked in under the awning with the people and began teaching them. As his teaching began to interest the people, the storeowner came out and told Jesus to leave for he was causing him the loss of sales. Jesus said to the Jew: "If you will allow me to continue to teach them here, while it is raining, I will make them buy something out of your store." The Jew agreed for a while. But as time passed on, the Jew saw that the people were not buying as he thought they would. The Jew warned Jesus again to leave his store front. Jesus refused, because he had about 35 people, who had gathered to hear him. The Jew told Jesus: "I know who you are and if you don't leave my store, I will call the authorities."

Write me and join onto your own kind:

September 7, 1957

JESUS IS KILLED

(Continued from last week)

AFTER the Jew called the authorities to come and take Jesus, they sent two officers to arrest him. There was a reward of $1,500 dollars if he were arrested and brought in alive - $2,500, in gold, if he were brought in dead. The two officers wanted this reward, so both ran to take Jesus and arrest him. They arrived almost at the same time. The two laid hands on Jesus and began quarreling over who was the first to lay his hands on Jesus.

While arguing over whose prisoner Jesus actually was, Jesus asked the two officers if they would allow him to tell who touched him first. The two officers agreed. Jesus said: "the one of the right touched me about three-tenths of a second before the one on the left." The officer on the left accepted the decision and left.

Then Jesus and the other officer started walking down the street to turn him over to the authorities. While going on, the officer said to Jesus: "Since you came here to give yourself up to be killed, why not let me kill you and you will not feel it. But if I take you to them (the infidel Jews), they will want to torture you – make you suffer. I will kill you in an instant and – you will never feel death. Furthermore, I will get more for taking you there dead than alive. I am a poor man with a large family. Why not let me get the larger reward since you came to die?" Jesus agreed and said to the officer: "Come do it." The officer took Jesus to an old deserted store front, which was boarded up to protect the store from possible stones, thrown by boys, that might break the glass. The officer said to Jesus: "Stand with your back against this store front and put your hands up." Jesus, being a brave man and ready to die, obeyed the officer and stretched forth his hands, like a cross (not on a cross, but made a cross of himself).

The officer drew a small sword-like knife from his side (which looks like the American hunting knife). Only this little sword is short, on both sides of the blade, to about two-thirds of its length. He plunged the sword through the heart of Jesus with such force that it went clear through and stuck itself into the boards that he was standing against (and left him as a crucifix). But Jesus having such strong nerves, his death was so instant that the blood stopped circulating at once. And Jesus was left stiff, with both arms outstretched in the same position as he put them when ordered by the officer. The authorities came and took him from the boards where the knife had pinned Jesus' body.

When Joseph heard of his son Jesus' death, he came and got the body from the authorities. He secured some Egyptian embalmers to embalm the body to last for 10,000 years. Joseph wanted the body embalmed to last as long as the earth (petrified) but was not able to pay for such embalm-ment. The Egyptian embalmers put the body into a glass tube filled with a certain chemical (known only to the Egyptian embalmers) that will keep one's body looking the same as when it died, that is if they get the body at a certain time, for many thousands of years - as long as no air is allowed to enter the tube that the body is in. They buried the body in the old city, Jerusalem.

His body lies in the tomb in such manner that it reflects in four different directions. This was done to keep the enemies from knowing in just what direction the real body is laying.

No Christian is allowed the see the body, unless they pay a price of $6,000 and must get a certificate from the Pope of Rome. The tomb is guarded be Muslims. When Christians are allowed to see Jesus' body, they are stripped of weapons, handcuffed behind their backs, and well-armed Muslim guards take them into the tomb. But, Muslims, the brothers of Jesus can go to see his body at any time without charge.

September 14, 1957

THE MAKING OF A RACE OF DEVILS

MR. YAKUB'S (God and Maker of the white race) charges to his laborers was very strict - death if one disobeyed. They didn't know what Yakub had in mind until they were given their labor to do. He made his laborers, from the chief to the least, liars. The doctor lied about the blood of the two black people who wanted to marry, that it did not mix. The brown and black could not be married (brown only). The doctors of today hold the same position over the people. You go to them to get a blood test to see if you two are fit to be married. Today, they say it is done to see if there are any contagious germs in the blood. I wish that they would enforce such a law today (keep the white from mixing with black - just the opposite). Perhaps we could remain black and not be disgraced by a mixture of all colors.

In the days of Yakub's grafting of the present white race, a new and unalike race among the black nation for 600 years. His law was that, they should not allow the birth of a black baby in their family, but the white (the devil) should mix their blood with the black nation, in order to help destroy black; but, they should not allow the black to mix with their blood.

His aim was to kill and destroy the black nation. He ordered the nurses to kill all black babies that came to birth among his people, by pricking the brains with a sharp needle as soon as the black child's head is out of his mother. If the mother is alert (watching the nurse), then the nurse would lie and fool the mother to get possession of her child to murder it, by saying that she (mother) gave birth to an "Angel Child." And that she (the nurse) would like to take the baby to Heaven, so when the mother dies, she would have a room with her child in Heaven, for her baby was an angel.

This is the beginning of the first lie or liar; and, it was so that the nurse would take the black baby away on this falsehood and claim that they were taking the poor black baby to Heaven. As Yakub had taught them, they would feed it to wild beasts, and if they did not find a wild beast to feed the black babies to, Yakub told the nurses to give it to the cremator to burn. Mr. Yakub warned the laborers, from the doctor down to the cremator, that if anyone of them failed to carry out his orders, off go their heads.

When there was a birth of a brown baby, the nurse would come and make much ado over it; and, would tell the mother that she had given birth to a holy child and that she would nurse it for the next six weeks for her child was going to be a great man (that is when it was a boy baby).

After the first 200 years, Mr. Yakub had done away with the black babies and all were brown. After another 200 years, he had all yellow or red, which was 400 years after being on "Pelan." Another 200 years, which brings us to the 600th year, Mr. Yakub had an all-pale white race of people on this isle. Of course, Mr. Yakub did not live but 150 years; but, his idea continued into practice. He gave his people his guidance in the form of literature. What they should do and how to do it (how to rule the black nation). He said to them: "When you become unalike (white), you may return to the Holy Land and people, from whom you were exiled."

The Yakub made devils were really pale white, with real blue eyes; which we think are the ugliest of colors for a human eye. They were called Caucasian - which means stale-faced and weak boned. Later called "Shaitan" which means, according to some of the Arab scholars, "One whose evil effect is not confined to one's self alone, but affects others." Good was not taught to them while on the island. By teaching the nurses to kill the black baby and save the brown baby: so as to graft the white out of it, by lying to the black mother of the baby, this lie was born into the very nature of the white baby, and, murder for the black people was also born in them - or made by nature a liar and murderer.

Hurry and lose no time in joining onto your own kind.

JESUS' BIRTH AND DEATH

MY PEOPLE, who believe in Jesus as God and the Bible as the True Word of God on face value, have gone to the extreme in their belief, without the least knowledge of the true meanings of what they read and believe. You have been reading the history of Jesus in this article as it was revealed to me by Allah (God) in person, whom you can't believe to have been God, because of your total blindness to the reality of God. (The truth hurts the guilty.)

Now that you believe that Jesus was a man of flesh and blood, born of a woman as you and I were; and, that flesh was wounded by a knife that brought death to Jesus (and, the same wounded flesh came to life again and was seen going up in the sky of its own accord, until the view was shut out by clouds) that is the wrong way to believe, and understand that Bible story of Jesus. Nearly 75 per cent is referring to a future Jesus, coming at the end of the white races' time, to resurrect the mentally dead, lost members (so-called Negroes) of the Tribe of Shabazz. This Jesus is now in the world.

Jesus and his mother made a sign of something to come; and, we are the end or fulfillment of that sign. "And we made the Son of Mary and his mother a sign." (Holy Qur-an 23:50). There are some who think that the sign refers only to the Jews, in the sense that Jesus was the last of the prophets; not only to the Jews, but to the white race in general. We must not forget that Jesus was not a member of that race. Jesus belonged to the black nation.

In order to make the American so-called Negroes worship the devils, the American devils paint Jesus, God and the Angels white. Many of the so-called Negroes take these imaginary pictures as real; while there is not a real picture of Jesus, nor his disciples. The foolish American so-called Negroes have worshiped the devils (white race) all of their lives. Now, today, he will openly dispute with you that Jesus was a white man (a Jew); not taking the time to think, that if Jesus was a member of that race, he would have been a devil. Again, Jesus would not have declared that the Jews were devils (John 8:44). The above chapter (8th Chapter: John) should convince the so-called Negroes, that the white race can't love and do good by them. They are not from the God of goodness, mercy and truth. (John 8:42) Jesus also condemned them in claiming Abraham to be their father (John 8:39).

The white races' works; their open hatred of us; their murdering and killing of you and me, themselves and the righteous; proves beyond a shadow of a doubt, that they are the real devils. They actually love the making of war; persecuting and killing the so-called Negroes; and, worst of all - they make the frightened so-called Negroes help them war against whom they term to be their enemies; while they are the worst enemies of the Negroes, on earth. They openly tell the so-called Negroes that they will not give them equal justice with themselves. They will go to war against any few who attempt to give the Negroes justice.

The so-called Negroes see all of this going on against them; and, yet love and desire to destroy themselves with such enemies rather than follow me to their own God and people, with whom they will be given equal love and justice. They (so-called Negroes) even hate me for teaching the truth, due to their ignorance of the truth.

Jesus and his mother were a sign of the so-called Negroes' (the actual lost and found members of a chosen nation) history, among the devils, in the last days of the devils' time on earth. The birth of Jesus (out of wedlock) was a sign of the spiritual birth of the lost-found so-called Negroes in North America; who are out of their own people and country (out of the wedlock of unity) living and mixing their blood with their real enemies, the devils, without knowledge. Yusuf (Joseph) and Mary's childhood love of each other, at the age of six, and promises to marry each other when old enough, was a sign of the love of Allah (God) for the lost-found, so-called Negroes, at the end of the devils' time (6,000 years). The visiting of Mary by Joseph, for three days under the cover of darkness, and in the absence of the father, and under the disguise of Mary's father's clothes and Joseph's wearing a goat's beard, was a sign of how Allah (God), who is referred to in the name "Mahdi," would come under disguise Himself, in the flesh and clothes of the devils, for three days (three years), to get to the lost-found so-called Negroes and start them pregnating with the truth through one of them, as a messenger, under a spiritual darkness.

RELIGION OF ISLAM:
JESUS AND HIS MOTHER A SIGN

(Holy Qur-an 23:50)

My people (the so-called Negroes) should be real happy after reading the articles of truth in this paper that God has revealed to me, seeing that the salvation belongs to them and not to the Jews, as they have been made to believe.

It is a pity that they have been made so blind, deaf and dumb, to the extent that in order to make them believe the truth Allah (God) will have to whip them into submission. That is why I am teaching them night and day, for the chastisement of Allah is to be feared - even by the devils.

Beware, my people! Do not take what I am writing here in this paper as a joke or mockery. It is the divine truth, from the very mouth of God, and not a made-up story of myself. I have not the brains to think up such truth. I once was as dead as you are. Don't give men any credit for Allah's (God's) revelation of truth to me (even you who believe). Give praises to Allah, to whom it is due, for I am only your brother and a sufferer with you, under the same. But if you would believe in Allah (God) as I do, though under your burden, you would feel it not.

So many of you are writing and asking almost the same questions. If you continue to read my articles you will find the answers to all of your questions.

Isa's (Jesus') birth and death (history) of two thousand years ago, and his mother, are a direct sign of the history of the so-called Negroes here in America - the visit of Allah (God) and the raising of a Messenger from among them. Why can't you understand?

The fleeing to Egypt of Mary and her baby, to be schooled for His mission, is a sign of you (so-called Negroes). You will be schooled there for twenty years. You will be taught your language and many sciences of your people and your beautiful universe that have never before been taught. You will suffer here a little while longer but, the joy that awaits you will make you forget your suffering here overnight.

I see you on top and not on the bottom any more, for Allah (God) Himself is doing this. Not you, nor I, nor our kind - only by the orders of Allah. Fear not! Neither persecution or death will prevent your rise - those who believe. Allah has said it. It didn't work in the past, nor is it going to work today.

The Holy Qur-an and the Muslims have great respect for Jesus, but not as God. He was only a prophet. "He (Jesus) was naught but a servant, on whom we bestowed favor, and we made him an example for the children of Israel." (Holy Qur-an 43:59). Here he is mentioned as being an example for Israel; and he was, in the way of a true Muslim (righteous). An example of a doer of righteousness and obedient to the law of Allah, as Moses had given them.

Israel was never a doer of the law. The 57th verse of the same chapter refers to what the Christian-believing black people here (the so-called Negroes) will say to Muhammad. "And when the son of Mary is mentioned as an example, lo! The people (the so-called Negroes) raise a clamor (a loud outcry; uproar; vehement expression of the general feeling)."

This is true of the shameful way the so-called Negroes carry on over the name or mentioning of Jesus in churches and public places, as though Jesus is present and looking on. Poor people. I hope to bring you out of such ignorance of Jesus. He was only a prophet and is dead like Moses and the prophets of old. None can hear your prayers. You must pray to a living Jesus, or God, if you want your prayers answered.

Just be faithful and clamorous over the real Jesus of today; and you will surely go to Heaven with Him. The false doctrines of Jesus being God were introduced after His death.

And when Allah will say: "Oh, Jesus, Son of Mary, didst thou say to men: 'Take Me and My mother for two gods besides Allah?'" He will say: "Glory be to Thee; it was not for Me to say what I had no right to say. If I had said it, Thou wouldst indeed have known it. Thou knowest what is in my mind and I know not what is in Thy mind. Surely Thou art the great knower of the unseen. I said to them naught save as Thou didst command Me. Serve Allah, my Lord and your Lord; and, I was a witness of them so long as I was among them, but when Thou didst cause Me to die, Thou wast the watcher over them, and Thou art witness of all things.

"If Thou chastise them, surely Thou art the mighty, the wise (Holy Qur-an 5:116-118)."

Remember the Bible teaches that Jesus was dependent upon His Father (God) in these words: "I can of Mine own self do nothing: as I hear, I judge: and my judgment is just; because I seek not Mine own will, but the will of the Father which hath sent Me." (St. John 5:30.) God is not sent, nor does He depend on instructions from anyone. A prophet is sent with a message and is dependent on his sender for guidance. So Jesus was in every respect, even after His resurrection. He didn't claim to be God. "Touch me not: for I am not yet ascended to My Father." (John 20:17). "And now I am no more in the world, but these (His followers) are in the world, and I come to Thee, Holy Father, keep through Thine own name, those whom Thou hast given me, that they may be one, as we. While I was in the world, I kept them in Thy name." (John 17:11, 12.)

Compare the above with the 5:117 of the Holy Qur-an. Jesus declared that He is no more in the world and cannot be a witness of what His followers will do; nor be responsible for them after his death.

No other prophet is responsible for the people after he fulfills his mission to them or dies in the attempt. Study your book and understand the truth before you dispute with me. Jesus was only a prophet and is dead like Moses and the other old prophets. Pray to a living God and come follow me, and He will hear your prayers. (To be continued next week.)

THE SO-CALLED NEGROES' SALVATION IS THEIR OWN TRUE RELIGION, ISLAM, UNDER THE GUIDANCE OF ALLAH (GOD), TO WHOM BE PRAISE FOREVER

(Continued from last week)

THE HISTORY of Jesus and His mother is a sign of the history of the so-called Negroes, who have been lost from their people for 400 years - who now are found and must be returned to their own; or else every Western (Christian) government will be brought to an aught by the Great God, Allah, under the name of Mr. W. F. Muhammad, "The Mighty Mahdi, the Son of Man," Allah in person.

As I have said and shown in my articles on Jesus' history, most of Jesus' history 2,000 years ago in referring to an apostle in the last days, and not of the past. In several places, it is referring to the suffering of Allah (God) three and one-half years, trying to get to the so-called Negroes under disguise.

History repeats itself. The same race that hated Jesus 2,000 years ago hates Jesus' people (the so-called Negroes) today, and is casting them out. The limited knowledge that the so-called Negroes have of themselves and their enemies makes them think that the enemies' rejection of them is wrong. But it is not.

It is really their salvation to be rejected by the devils. The wrong that the enemies are doing to you is that they won't let you go free. Indeed, they won't allow even Allah (God) to do so without war. They won't teach you the truth of self, God, devil or the true religion.

They persecute and kill you without justice. They put fear into you, and that fear makes you harmless like sheep before a pack of hungry, merciless wolves, who stay in your family after the so-called Negro women.

THE POOR people (so-called Negroes) and their foolish leaders (preachers) should visit and join onto your own, Islam - from the cradle to the old man and woman leaning on a stick.

You shout and weep, pity poor Jesus' murder and death at the hands of His enemies 2,000 years ago, but it seems as though you should not cry nor weep over your own selves, being beaten and killed daily. Yet you say nothing nor do anything about it, but love the enemies.

The parable of us under the title "Lazarus Lay at the Rich Man's Gate" could not give a better type of the so-called American Negroes.

They just won't go for self, as long as the slave masters are rich and will allow you to be their servants and make rosy promises to you only to deceive you. But today is very serious for you and for them. Think well and wisely for your future.

Allah (God) and his religion, Islam, are your only friends. The white race is not able to help itself against Allah. So your believing and seeking a future in that race, today, is like one seeking shelter under a spider web from a storm of hailstones.

THE MOTHER of Jesus well represents a messenger from among you, pregnating with a new world out of you.

Almighty God, Allah, is the Father and must protect the infant "baby nation" (the so-called Negroes) whom he is carrying.

JESUS, MAKING a clay bird and breathing into it and it became a live bird by the permission of Allah, the healing of the sick, giving sight to the blind, raising the dead, teaching the people what they should eat and what they shouldn't eat (Holy Qur-an 3:48) means one and the same thing.

The work of the last apostle to the so-called Negroes, who are spiritually blind, deaf and dumb.

They are eating the wrong food and now being taught against the eating of poison foods by the Apostle of Allah. No such work was done among the devils 2,000 years ago. It was not necessary since the devils are not to be saved.

Hurry and lose no time. Join onto your own kind, for the Time of this World is at hand.

October 12, 1957

(Continued from last week)

LET ME make myself clear to you, in regards to last week's article. I am not trying to condemn the history of Jesus as being false; but, rather am trying to put the meanings and signs, or miracles where they belong.

That is, in the present so-called Negroes' history, and Jesus of today. Jesus and His parents were only a sign or prototype of that which was to come.

Of course, there are many student ministers in the theological seminary colleges, who probably know, or are learning, that most of what the Bible gives us of Jesus' history has got to be a future man and not one answering any such description of 2,000 years ago.

How could Jesus' birth and death 2,000 years ago serve as the price of sin and peace (reconciling God and the man of sin), of the world as the average Christian believe? The rejoicing angels at his birth; the mourning and directing angels at His tomb; the great earthquakes; the tense darkness; the seeing of resurrected saints; the going up to heaven in a cloud, as Matthew, Mark, Luke and John gives us in the gospel of Jesus?

It just can't be put in the past without disgracing the all-wise God's intelligent knowledge of the future. Let the poor so-called Negroes' minds relax for a few minutes, while reading this article, and use common sense. (1st) If Jesus were to have a flesh and blood body, He must be produced as we were, by the agency of man, who had flesh and blood. If God produces one, other than by man, He breaks His own law. And, we could not be held responsible for breaking the same law (getting children out of wedlock). (2nd) The world has never been without a righteous people on it. Could not God produce a son or prophet from a righteous couple as He had in the past? And, even as He did by Zacharias and his wife, to produce John, who was a little older than Jesus, according to the Bible (Luke 1:57).

Read the birth and death of Jesus as recorded in Matthew, Mark, Luke and John. Think it over. Would God have permitted such thing to happen 2,000 years ago with such evil results following afterward? If Jesus' birth was to bring peace and goodwill to all mankind (Luke 2:14), how could He have prophesied of "Wars and rumors of wars, nations rising against nations, and the hatred of one another?" (Matthew 24:7-10). There have been more wars and more evil, since the birth and death of Jesus than ever before. Jesus didn't bring peace to the world; according to the Bible (Matthew 10:34). Elijah comes to unite the family and put them on the path of God, to bring about a union between man and God (Malachi 4:5,6).

According to the Bible, Jesus taught to "hate every member of the family, even the father and mother," (Luke 14:26). Even God said: "He loved one brother and hated the other brother." (Romans 9:13). You, who preach that God is love and Jesus taught to love one another, should have consulted the translators of the Bile as to just why they charge God's and Jesus' teaching for a thing in one place and against it in another place.

Your Bible is poison, double-crossing itself. Be careful how you understand it. We know what it means and where it belongs; but, since you are disbeliever in the truth and disputers without knowledge, we challenge you to prove your sayings by your book - if you have understanding of it.

You have two Jesus' histories, as I have said time and again; and, even an apostle's history of the last days, all under the name of Jesus, 2,000 years ago.

Hurry and lose no time in joining onto your own kind. The time of this world is at hand.

JESUS, A SIGN AND EXAMPLE

(Continued from Last Week)

I AM so happy that Allah (God) has revealed to me the truth, believe it or not. Oh, you die-hard Christians, who are stubborn and proud against Allah (God) His word, and we who believe in Him and His word. My people are deaf, dumb, and blind; and gravely mislead by the enemy (devil). Use common sense, my people, and judge between the truth, which I am writing, and the false that was taught to you by the devils.

Jesus came as a sign of that which was to come. His birth, ministry, persecution and death as I have written, of the future of you (the so-called Negroes) his people, and the persecution and rejection of the Great Mahdi (God in person) who has appeared among us in these last days of this race of devils, and has suffered the same. Jesus was an example of righteousness, a doer of the law of the Jews, which was given to them by Musa (Moses).

The world, looking for that Jesus to return, is not only ignorant but foolish. No one but a fool would believe that Jesus, who was here 2,000 years ago, is sitting in heaven waiting until His time to return and execute judgment. Tell the world the truth, and stop fooling yourself, if you know it; and, if you don't know it, step aside and stop trying to hinder us, who are telling the truth.

The Bible makes it a little too hard for the average reader to believe in Jesus as a prophet, or a man born by the agency of man, like you and I; though, never did God intend otherwise. The Holy Qur-an makes Jesus only a prophet of Allah (God), and, that is all He was. It does not mention his father by name, though on many occasions prophets and their great works of the past are mentioned without their father's names. There are many Muslims who think that His birth was without the agency of man. Most commentators, on the life and death of Jesus, disagree with the saying that, "Jesus died on the cross, or was even murdered (killed)." They think that He traveled into India and died in Kashmir, but this is wrong. He did not go there, nor is that His tomb in Kashmir. It is only an old belief among those who actually did not know who the Nabi (prophet) was, who came to Kashmir and died and was buried there, whom old settlers claimed came from the West. No real proof is shown that it was Jesus' body.

The scholars on the Holy Qur-an go to the extreme with the word "spirit" as the Christians do, especially in the case of Allah. My work is to bring you face to face with God, and to do away with spooky beliefs. The revealing of the spiritual word of Allah (God) to Mary or anyone, does not mean for you and me to believe that Jesus was born without the agency of man. The spirit or word of Allah (God) came to Moses' mother, to inform her about the future of her son (that He was a prophet). (Exodus 2:2.) Both the Bible and Holy Qur-an seem to be very careful not to accuse Mary of fornication. Why? If she and her son were to be a sign for the nation, she should not be charged with fornication. (2nd) If the act was to serve as a lesson for us, that we should never allow two people who are in love with each other, to be alone together, in a place where there are no others, for nature has no self-control. That was the case of Mary and Joseph. They were childhood sweethearts, and wanted to be married when of age; but Mary's father objected to it. His objections could not destroy the love between the two. To this day, the Muslims keep boys and girls, men and women, from mixing freely together. Even the boy and girl courtships and marriages are controlled by their parents. There is no fornication, and very little or no divorce cases in the dominant Muslim world. That is why Islam is hated by white Christian devils, because they are not allowed to mix with Muslim women; with their filthy, indecent hearts and winking blue eyes. "We breathed into her of our inspiration, and made her and her son a sign for the nations." (Holy Qur-an 21:91.)

Regardless to the carefulness and chaste language of their scripture, used on Mary, having a baby out of wedlock, we can see through it all; after knowledge from Allah (God) in the person of Master Fard Muhammad (to whom be praised forever). In another chapter it mentions the spirit sent to Mary in the form of a man. "So she screened herself from them. Then we sent to her, our spirit, and it appeared to her as a well-made man." (Holy Qur-an 19:17.)

Hurry and join onto your own kind. The time of this world is at hand.

Write to Muhammad's Temple No. 2, Ill., 5335 S. Greenwood Ave., Chicago 15, Ill.

October 26, 1957

CHARACTERISTICS OF A REAL DEVIL

[Next Week: "The Infidel and Anti-Christs preparing to go to war with God and His People"]

SINCE READING these articles for the past year you have learned how the devils were made, by being grafted from the Black Nation, 6,000 years ago, to try them at ruling the original nation of our Planet Earth. Through this process of grafting, out of that which was originally pure by nature, it made this grafted race weak physically and wicked mentally. Some so-called Negroes, who are in love with the devils, do not like to see nor hear them being made manifest.

We could lose them without ever missing them; for all who are found believing in, and in love with, the devils will be destroyed with the devils.

Now the world must know how to distinguish the real devils from the non-devils; for there are thousands of our people throughout the world who can hardly be distinguished by color from the real devil.

There are certain climates which seem to change the white race into a red or brown color. And where they mix freely with our kind, their skin and eyes show a difference in color. Their eyes are brown and grayish blue. By carefully watching their behavior, you can easily distinguish them from our people (dark, brown, yellow or red).

The characteristics of their children are easily distinguished from the Original children, regardless to how near in color they may be. The devil children, whenever they are around and among Original children, like to show off and love to make mockery of the Original children. They teach them evil; talk filth; sing filthy songs; filthy dancing and games and will not leave the Original children without starting a fight.

Their little mouths, like their parents before them, are filled with cursing and swearing. No intelligent so-called Negro parents should want their children mixing with devil children, in school or out. For they poison your children's minds wherever they are allowed to mix. Naturally, they are not like your children, and their unlikeness attracts your children and self.

Remember the Bible's teachings of this race of devils, and especially II Thessalonians, 2:3-12, and Revelation 12:9-17, 20:10. The treatment of the so-called Negroes by the devils is sufficient proof to the Negroes that they (the white race) are real devils, and if this teaching, along with what they are suffering from their beloved devils, does not awaken them to the knowledge of the devils, all I can say for them then is that they are just lost. They won't be accepted by God, nor the righteous Muslims, with even the name of the devils.

Why don't their preachers preach this "vital truth" to them or help me to do so when the Bible teaches it? Is it a fact that the preachers would rather see their people and themselves suffer at the hands and mouth of this race, and even go with them to their doom, rather than teach the Truth or help those who are teaching it?

The foolish call the Truth that I am teaching from the mouth go God "hatred." To tell the Truth cannot be classified as hatred only by those who dislike the Truth. It is a manifest truth that white Americans and Europeans hate the so-called Negroes and the whole of Black People the world over, even to the black religious teachers (prophets of the Black Nation).

Let us take a look at the run-down on the characteristics of the devils from the Holy Qur-an: "He is in human form" (not a spirit) 3:174 and footnote; 8:48. "As a leader in unbelief," 22:3, 2:6. "Standing for wicked opponents," 23:97. "Evil doers are forces of the devils" (he, devil, is referred to as "Foreign Tribes"), 38:37. "As a serpent" (he is referred to as "being created from fire"), 7:12. "See you from where you can't see them," 7:27. "Has no authority over the righteous except those who befriend him," 15:42, 17:65, 16:99. "He is one who loves to snoop on the Black Man, to steal a hearing," 15:16-18. "Mis-leads Adam," 2:36, 7:20, 20:120. "Leads man to evil," 36:63.

You will find all of the above said to be the characteristics of the white race and you will follow them. But the Black Man is not a real devil - only can be a follower of the real devil.

Write me and join onto your own kind

November 9, 1957

JESUS' HISTORY MISUNDERSTOOD
BY THE CHRISTIANS

THE GREAT misunderstanding over the Father and Sonship, birth and death of Jesus, is now being made understandable from the mouth of God in person; whose coming has brought light and truth to us who sit in darkness. The great arch-enemy of Allah and the righteous, the devil in person (Caucasian race), who has deceived us for 6,000 years, took us out of the light of truth into darkness, and now Allah (God), by His grace and power, dispels the darkness and is making manifest this great enemy (the devil). The poor black man of America should rejoice and be glad for this divine truth of Jesus' birth, life, and death, as the real truth of it has never before been told.

Who is this Christ, and His Father that Jesus questioned the Pharisees about? Was Jesus referring to Himself, or another one as Christ? Or does, the above question of Jesus prove that He was the Christ, or that His Father was other than a man? By no means, for according to Joseph's dream (Matthew 1:20-21) concerning the birth of his Son, his name was to be called Jesus. "And she shall bring forth a son, and thou shalt call His name Jesus, for He shall save his people from their sins." (Matthew 1:21). Did he save the Jews from their sins? They no doubt were not His people according to John (8:42-44). The Jews could not be saved from their sins if their father was the devil, for by nature they were sinners.

Joseph was the husband of Mary and the son of Jacob. In Joseph's dream, he was addressed by the angel as being the Son of David (Matthew 1:16-20). Jesus is called "Jesus Christ," and "Emmanuel." Did the people in those days ever call Jesus, "Emmanuel."

Today, he is called "Jesus, and Christ, the Son of God." Since we have learned that He did not save the Jews from their sins and that he denounced the Jews as being none other than the children of the devil; that He did not restore the independence of the Jews and did not bring peace to the world, nor even to his disciples; nor did He put a stop to death, nor did He destroy sickness from the people, but referred to the Son of Man (Matthew 9:6) as having power on earth to forgive sins. He could not have been referring to Himself as the Son of Man who had such power, for He prophesied of the coming of the Son of Man (Matthew 24:27, 30, 37, 39, 44).

The Bible is very questionable, but it can be, and is now being understood, for God has revealed her hidden secrets to me. Such things as "forgiving sins of a special people, nor even as much as healing them; giving spiritual light; resurrection of the dead; bringing peace and goodwill between man and man," could not have been in the days of Jesus 2,000 years ago. Think over it! "Angels coming from heaven to bear witness that he is the One to set up the Kingdom of Peace"; and yet, when He began His ministry, He was dependent on His Father for help, and prophesied of another: "the coming of the Son of Man, who would be self-independent, having power to restore the Kingdom of Peace on earth and to destroy those who had destroyed the peace and brotherhood of His people."

Learn, my dear readers, that the prophesied Son of Man, is Almighty God. And, the Christ, long looked for, has come in the person of Master W. D. Fard Muhammad, as it is written: "without observation," or "as a thief in the night." The work that I am doing in the midst of you bears witness of His presence; for by no means do I have power of myself to give life to the spiritually dead (so-called Negroes) except it be from Him. You have had and still have the wrong understanding of the Bible. According to the Bible, David in his psalms, prophesied that he heard the Lord say unto his lord, "Sit on my right hand until I make thine enemies thy footstool." This prophesy cannot refer to Jesus of 2,000 years ago, for the Jews have not been made Jesus' footstool; which means being brought into submission, and Jesus being made the victor or their conqueror. The "Lord" that David refers to is Almighty Allah (God), and "his lord" is none other than the Great Prophet, coming just prior to the end of the world, whom the wicked will attack to do to Him what they did to the prophets of old. But Allah (God) will come to his aid. David, also being a prophet, saw the last prophet to be much greater than himself and calls him "his Lord." Let the so-called Negroes rejoice for they are the ones whose sins will be forgiven and shall be saved.

November 16, 1957

THE COMING AND PRESENCE OF "THE SON OF MAN"

"For as the lightning cometh out of the East, and shineth even unto the West, so shall also the coming of the Son of Man be." (Matthew 24:27.)

My greatest and only desire is: to bring true understanding of the word of God, His prophets and the scriptures - which the prophets were sent with, pertaining to the lost-found people (the American so-called Negroes) of God, and the judgment of the world.

You must forget about ever seeing the return of Jesus, who was here two thousand years ago. Set your heart on seeing the One that He prophesied would come at the end of the present world's time (the white race's time).

He is called the "Son of Man." The "Christ," the "Comforter." You are really foolish to be looking to see the return of the Prophet Jesus. It is the same as looking for the return of Abraham, Moses and Muhammad. All of these prophets prophesied the coming of Allah; or, one with equal power, under many names. You must remember that Jesus could not have been referring to himself as returning to the people in the last days. He prophesied of another's coming who was much greater than he. Jesus even acknowledged that he did not know when the hour would come in these words:

"But of that day and hour knoweth no man, no, not the angels of heaven, but my Father only." (Matthew 24:36).

If He were the one to return at the end of the world, surely He would have known the time of His return - the knowledge of the hour. But He left Himself out of that knowledge and placed it where it belonged, as all the others - prophets - had done. No prophet has been able to tell us the hour of the judgment. None but He, the great, all wise God - Allah. He is called the "Son of Man," the "Mahdi," the "Christ." The prophets, Jesus included, could only foretell those things which would serve as signs - signs that would precede such a great one's coming to judge the world. The knowledge of the hour of judgment is with the Executor only.

The prophets teach us to let the past judgments of people, their cities and their warners serve as a lesson, or sign, of the last judgment and its warners. Noah did not know the hour of the flood. Lot did not know the hour of Sodom and Gomorrah until the Executors had arrived, and Jesus prophesied (Matthew 24:37-39) that: "It will be the same in the last judgment of the world of Satan." You have gone astray because of your misunderstanding of the scripture, the Prophet Jesus, and the coming of God to judge the world. My corrections are not accepted.

Your misunderstanding and misinterpretations of it are really the joy of the devils. For it is the devils' desire to keep the so-called Negroes ignorant to the truth of God until they see it with their eyes. The truth of

God is the salvation and freedom of the so-called Negroes, from the devils' power over them, and the universal destruction of the devils' power.

Can you blame them? No! Blame yourself for being so foolish as to allow the devils to fool you in not accepting the truth after it comes to you.

The devils have tried to deceive the people all over the earth with Christianity; that is God, the Father; Jesus the Son; the Holy Ghost - three Gods into One God; the resurrection of the Son and His return to judge the world, or, that the Son is in some place above the Earth, sitting on the right hand side of the Father, waiting until the Father makes His enemies His footstool.

The period of waiting is 2,000 years. Yet he died for the Father to save his enemies (the whole world of sinners).

My friends, use a bit of common sense. First: Could a wonderful flesh and blood body, made of the essence of our earth, last 2,000 years on the earth, or, off the earth, without being healed? Second: Where exists such a heaven, off the earth, that flesh and blood of the earth can exist - since the Bible teaches that flesh and blood cannot enter heaven? (Corinthians 15:50.)

Flesh and blood cannot survive without that of which it is made - the earth. Jesus' prophesy of the coming of the Son of Man is very clear, if you rightly understand. First: This removes all doubts in whom we should expect to execute judgment, for if man is to be judged and rewarded according to his actions, who could be justified in sitting as judge of man's doings but, another man? How could a spirit be our judge when we cannot see a spirit? And, ever since life was created, life has had spirit. For without life, there is not spirit. But the Bible teaches that God will be seen on the Day of Judgment. Not only the righteous will see Him, but even His enemies shall see Him.

November 23, 1957

THE COMING OF THE SON OF MAN -

THE GREAT MAHDI

"And then shall appear the **sign** of the Son of Man in Heaven: and then shall all the tribes of the earth **mourn**, and they shall see the Son of Man coming in the **clouds** of **Heaven** with **power** and **great glory**" (Matthew 24:30). The final battle between God and the devils will be decided in the skies. The devils see Him and His **power** in **Heaven** and **Earth**. The nations of the West are in great pain trying to form their defense. Now is a very serious time on our planet, and it will continue to be until the powers of this world are destroyed. The hour of this world has arrived. How will the Son of Man win the battle against this world's out-of-space weapons?

Read the answer in the next article.

As we now realize from my article of last week, Jesus' prophecy of a man (Son of Man) coming at the end of the white race's (Devil's or the Man of Sin's) time - which was up in 1914 - makes it so very clear as to what we should expect. It is a man, the son of another man, not a spirit, as we all are sons of men. On that day, a Son of a Man will sit to judge men according to their works. Who is the Father of this Son, coming to judge the world? (I will tell you soon, in this article). Is His Father of flesh and blood, or is He a "spirit"? Where is this Son coming from? Prophet Jesus said: "He will come from the East" (Matthew 24:27) - from the land and people of Islam, where all of the former prophets came from. Jesus compared His coming as "the lightning." Of course, lightning cannot be seen nor heard at a great distance.

The actual light (the Truth) which "shineth out of the East and shineth even unto the West," is our day sun. But the Son of Man's coming is like both the lightning and our day sun. His work of the resurrection of the mentally dead so-called Negroes, and judgment between Truth and Falsehood, is compared with lightning - on an instant. His swiftness in condemning the Falsehood is like the sudden flash of lightning in a dark place (America is that dark place), where the darkness has blinded the people so that they cannot find the "right way" out. The sudden "flash of lightning" enables them to see that they are off from the "right path." They walk a few steps towards the "right way," but soon have to stop and wait for another bright flash. What they actually need is the light of the Sun

(God in person), that they may clearly see their way. The lightning does more than flash a light. It is also destructive, striking whom Allah pleases, of property and lives. The brightness of its flashes almost blinds the eyes.

So it is with the coming of the Son of Man, with the Truth, to cast it against Falsehood - that it break the head. Just a little hint of it makes the Falsehood begin looking guilty and seeking cover from the brightness of the Truth. Sometimes lightning serves as a warning of an approaching storm. So does Allah (God) warn us by sending His messengers with the Truth, before the approaching destruction of a people to whom chastisement is justly due. They come flashing the Truth in the midst of the spiritually darkened people. Those who love spiritual darkness will close their eyes to the flash of Truth, like lightning, from pointing out to them the "right way," thus blinding themselves from the knowledge of the approaching destruction of the storm of Allah (God), and are destroyed. "As the lightning cometh out of the East so shall the coming of the Son of Man be."

Let us reflect on this prophecy from the direction in which this Son shall come, "out of the East." If He is to come from the East, to chastise or destroy that of the West, then He must be pleased with the East. The dominant religion of the East is Islam. The holy religious teachings of all the prophets, from Adam to Muhammad, was none other than Islam (Holy Qur-an 4:163). They all were of the East and came from that direction with the light of the Truth and shone toward the old wicked darkness of the West. But the West has ever closed its eyes and stopped up its ears against the Truth (Islam) and persecutes it, thus making it necessary for the coming of the Son of Man (the Great Mahdi) - God in person.

Being the end of the signs, in His person, He dispels Falsehood with the Truth - as the sun dispels night on its rising from the East. Why should the tribes of the earth mourn because of the coming of the Son of Man, instead of rejoicing?

Hurry and join onto your own kind. The time of this world is at hand.

THE COMING OF THE SON OF MAN: WILL YOU BE THE WINNER?

The non-Muslim world cannot win in a war against the Son of Man (God in Person), with outer space weapons or inner space. It does not matter for He has power over everything - the forces of nature and even our brains. He turns them to thinking and doing that which pleases Him. The great waste of money to build your defense against Him or the third world war is useless. You don't need navies, ground forces, air forces or standing armies to fight this last war.

What America needs to win with is: freedom and equal justice to her slaves (the so-called Negroes). This injustice to her slaves is the real cause of this final war. Give them up to return to their own, or divide with them the country that you took from their people (the Red Indians) which they have helped you to build up and maintain with their sweat and blood for 400 years. They even give all their brain power to you. They help you kill anyone that you say is your enemy, even if it is their own brother or your own brother. What have you given them for their labor and lives?

Is it just a job to labor for you? You hunt them and shoot them down like wild game; burn them; castrate them; they are counted as sheep for the slaughter - all who seek justice. You have continuously persecuted me and my poor followers for 25 years. Both fathers and sons are sent to prison. Just because we <u>believe</u> in justice and teach our brethen the same, we are imprisoned from three to five years and forced to eat the poison and divinely prohibited flesh of the filthy swine in our food to your joy.

You set your agents around and about our meeting places where we are trying to serve the God of our fathers, to frighten our poor, blind, deaf and dumb people away from hearing and believing in the truth. With 48 states, which equal approximately three million square miles; with billions of dollars in gold buried and resting which we helped to get for you, yet none is ours; not the tiniest nor the most worthless state of yours have you offered your loyal slaves. Nor even to one square mile for their 400 years of labor.

Shall you be the winner in a third world war? The God of Justice (the Son of Man, the Great Mahdi) shall be the winner. He is on the side of the so-called Negroes, to free them from you, their killers. As it is written, "Shall the prey be taken from the mighty or the lawful captives delivered? But thus saith the Lord, even the captives of the mighty shall be taken away and the prey of the terrible shall be delivered: for I will contend with him that contendeth with thee. I will feed them that oppress thee with their own flesh; and they shall be drunken with their own blood. As with sweet wine, and all flesh shall know that I the Lord am thy Saviour, and they Redeemer." (Isaiah 49:24-26.)

We the so-called Negroes are the prey. Thou are the mighty, the terrible one. Thanks to Allah, the Greatest, who is with us, to save and deliver us. His people - 17 million members of the Tribe of Shabazz - who must have some of this earth that they can call their own. Their God will give it to them. But woe unto you, for the Son of Man shall destroy thee and give the kingdom to the slave. He is not to come. He is here! Believe it or not. I seek refuge in Him, from your evil plannings.

White Christian America has been so busy trying to keep her slaves (the so-called Negroes) under her foot; sitting, watching, spying on them to prevent them from knowing the truth of this day of our salvation; she has failed to see and learn the strength and power of her enemies. She has boasted that she could police the world and has come pretty near doing so, but failed to see the "bear" behind the tree and the "lion" in the thicket. The sky over her is being filled with her enemies' arms which can be seen with the naked eye. Her scientists are troubled and at their wits end to find time to make ready, as it is written: "I have set the point of the sword against all their gates, that their heart may faint, and their ruins be multiplied! Ah! It is made bright. It is wrapped up for the slaughter." (Ezekiel 21:15.)

Answer: "For the tidings: because it cometh, and every heart shall melt and all hands shall be feeble and every spirit shall faint and all knees shall be weak as water." (Ezekiel 21:7.)

Hurry and join onto your own kind. The time of this world is at hand.

THE COMING OF THE SON OF MAN - THE INFIDELS (ANTI-CHRISTS) ARE ANGRY

Who is His father if God is not His father? God is His father, but the Father is also a man. You have heard of old that God prepared a body, or the expected Son of Man; Jesus is a special prepared man to do a work of redeeming the lost sheep (the so-called Negroes). He had to have a body that would be part of each side (black and white), half and half. Therefore, being born or made from both people, He is able to go among both black and white without being discovered or recognized. This He has done in the person of Master W. F. Muhammad, the man who was made by His Father to go and search for the lost members of the Tribe of Shabazz (though you find them among the infidels, return them to their own). Master W. F. Muhammad is that Son of Man that the world has been looking for to come for 2,000 years, seeking to save that which was lost. There are no historical records that there was ever a people lost from each other for 400 years other than we, the so-called Negroes. We have been so long separated from each other that we have lost the knowledge of each other. Even today the white American slavemasters are ever on the watch to keep out any Asiatic influence that might come among the so-called Negroes to teach them the truth. They are our real open enemies. This is no secret. The Son of Man is after the so-called Negroes to sit them in Heaven and His enemies in Hell. After His conquest of the black nation's enemies, the world will know and recognize Him (Allah) to be God alone. There is no problem today that is as hard to solve as the problem of uniting the American so-called Negroes. They are like a dead man totally without life. They have lost all love of self and kind and have gone all out in loving their enemies (the devils). They do not seem to want any God to do anything like blessing them unless that God blesses their enemies, too. FEAR of their enemies is the real cause. The time is now ripe that they should have no fear, only the fear of Allah, who is in person among them to save them from their enemies. By all means, they must be separated from the white race (the devils), in order that the scripture might be fulfilled. "For

I will take you from among the heathen and gather you out of all countries and will bring you into your own land" (Ezekiel 36:24).

The so-called Negroes have no home (country) that they can call their own. They have helped the white race (the devils) to own a free country, but they have nothing for themselves. This is the purpose of His coming: to give everyone that which is rightfully theirs. The Son of Man (the Great Mahdi, God in person) has power over all things. You cannot find a defense against Him in a war. Your weapons mean nothing. The powers of Heaven and earth today will be ordered to fight on the side of the Mahdi (Son of Man) against His enemies. He is the friend of the so-called Negroes and not of white people. His purpose is to take the so-called Negroes and kill their enemies, although many of us will suffer from persecution and hunger. But the good end is for those of you who will hold fast to Allah and His religion, Islam. They (the devils) are now planning many tricks to keep the Negroes here with them to suffer the fire of hell which they (the devils) cannot escape. Fly to Allah! Come, follow me. Although I may look insignificant to you, you will find salvation with us. The white race is excited and cannot think rightly for themselves. The so-called Negroes, Muslims, in their midst are a shelter but little do they know it.

Hurry and join onto your own kind. The time of this world is at hand.

December 14, 1957

THE COMING OF THE SON OF MAN (THE GREAT MAHDI) AND THE GREAT DECISIVE BATTLE IN THE SKY

(Continued from last week)

The final war between Allah (God) and the devils is dangerously close. The very least friction can bring it into action within minutes. There is no such thing as getting ready for this most terrible and dreadful war; they are ready! Preparation for battles between man and man or nations have been made and carried out on land and water for the past six thousand years. But, man now has become very wise and knows many secret elements of power from the nature world which make the old battles with swords and bows and arrows look like child play.

Since 1914, which was the end of the time given for the devils (white race) to rule the original people (black nation), man has been preparing for a final show-down in the skies. He has made a remarkable advancement in everything pertaining to a deadly destructive war in the sky. But Allah, the best of planners, having a perfect knowledge of His enemies, prepared for their destruction long ago, even - before they were created. Thanks to Allah, to whom be praised forever, who came in the flesh and the blood for more than seventy years making Himself ready for the final war.

Allah, to whom be praised, came in the person of Master W. F. Muhammad, the Great Mahdi expected by the Muslims and the anti-Christs (the devils) under the names: Jesus Christ, Messiah, God, Lord, Jehovah, the last (Jehovah) and the Christ. These meanings are good and befitting as titles, but the meaning of His name "Mahdi," as mentioned in the Holy Qur-an Sharieff 22:54, is better. All of these names refer to Him. His name, FARD MUHAMMAD, is beautiful in its meaning. He must bring an end to war, and the only way to end war between man and man is to destroy the war-maker (the trouble-maker).

According to the history of the white race (devils), they are guilty of making trouble; causing war among the people and themselves ever since they have been on our planet Earth. So the God of righteous has found them disagreeable to live with in peace and has decided to remove them from the face of the earth. God does not have to tell us that they are disagreeable to live with in peace; we already know it, for we are the victims of these trouble-makers. Allah will fight this war for the sake of His people (the black people), and especially for the American so-called Negroes. As I have said time and again, we, the so-called American Negroes, will be the lucky ones. We are Allah's choice to give life and we will be put on top of civilization.

Read your "poison book" (the Bible). What does your book say concerning the preparation of God against the devil? Take a look at Ezekiel's vision of it, 595 B.C. "Now it came to pass in the thirtieth year, in the fourth month, in the fifth day of the month, as I was among the captives by the river of Chebar, that the heavens were open and I saw visions of God. Now as I beheld the living creatures, behold one wheel upon the earth by the living creatures, with his four faces. As for their rings, they were so high that they were dreadful; and their rings were full of eyes around about them four." (Chapter 1:1, 2, 15, 18.)

It was on the fourth of July 1930, when the Great Mahdi, Allah, in person, made His appearance among us.

Hurry and join onto your own kind. The time of this world is at hand.

THE GREAT DECISIVE BATTLE IN THE SKY
THE SON OF MAN (GOD IN PERSON) AND THE DEVILS

(Continued From Last Week)

THE vision of Ezekiel's wheel in a wheel is true, if understood. There is a similar wheel in the sky today which well answers the description of Ezekiel's vision. This wheel corresponds in a way with the spheres of spheres called the universe. The Maker of the universe is Allah (God), the Father of the black nation which includes the brown, yellow and red people.

The great wheel which many of us see in the sky today is not so much of a wheel, but rather a plane made like a wheel. This wheel-like plane was never before seen. You cannot build one like it and get the same results. Your brains are limited. If you would build one to look like it, you could not get it up off the earth into outer space.

MAYBE I SHOULD not say the wheel is similar to Ezekiel's vision of a wheel, but that Ezekiel's vision has become a reality. His vision of the wheel included hints on the great wisdom of Almighty God, Allah; that really He is the Maker of the universe, and reveals just where and how the decisive battle would take place (in the sky).

When guns and shells took the place of the sword, man's best defense against such weapons was a trench, poison gas and liquid fire to bring him out. Today, he has left the surface for the sky to destroy his enemy by dropping bombs. All this was known in the days of Ezekiel, and God revealed to him through Ezekiel we may know what to expect at the end of this world.

The originator and his people (the original black people) are supremely wise. Today we see the white race preparing for the sky battle to determine who shall remain on this earth, black or white. In the battle between God and the disbelievers in the days of Noah, the victor's weapon was water. He used fire in the case of Sodom and Gomorrah. In the battle against Pharaoh, He used 10 different weapons, which included fire and water, hailstones, great armies of the insect world and droughts.

The Holy Qur-an says: "The chastisement of Pharoah was like that which God would use against His enemies in the last days." Throughout the Bible and Holy Qur-an teachings on the judgment and destruction of the enemies, fire will be used as the last weapon. The earth's greatest arms are fire and water. The whole of its atmosphere is made up of fire and water and gases. It serves as a protected coat of arms against any falling fragments from her neighbors. Ezekiel saw wheels in the middle of a wheel. This is true; there are wheels in the wheel.

THE PRESENT wheel-shaped plane known as the mother of planes, is one-half mile by a half mile and is the largest man-made object in the sky; a small human planet made for the purpose to destroy the present world of the enemies of Allah. The cost to build such a plane is staggering! The finest brains were used to build it. She is capable of staying in outer space six to 12 months at a time without coming into earth's gravity. It carries 1,500 bombing planes and the deadliest explosives; the type used in bringing up mountains on the earth. The very same method is to be used in the destruction of this world.

THE GREAT DECISIVE BATTLE IN THE

SKY BETWEEN GOD AND THE DEVILS

(Continued from Last Week)

"And there shall be signs in the sun and in the moon and in the stars, and upon the earth distress of nations, with perplexity; the sea and the waves roaring; men's hearts failing them for fear; and for looking after those things which are coming on the earth; for the powers of heaven shall be shaken. They see the Son of Man coming in a cloud with power and great glory" (St. Luke 21:25-27).

You will bear me witness that we are living in such time as mentioned in the above prophecy - signs in the sun and in the moon. The phenomenon going on in the sun and its family of planets testifies to the truth that something of the greatest magnitude is about to take place. The final war or battle between God and the devils in the sky.

Allah (God) who has power over all things, is bringing the powers of the sun, moon and stars into display against His enemies. The fire of the sun to scorch and burn men and the vegetation and dry up the waters. The moon will eclipse her light to bring darkness upon man and upon all living, to disrupt with her waves all air communications. The magnetic powers of the moon will bring about such tidal waves of seas and oceans as man has never witnessed before: the sea and the waves roaring.

As men's heart fail them with fear at sea looking upon great tidal waves coming toward them like mountains, they also shall see such a "great" display of power from Allah (God) in the sky that their hearts will fail. Great earthquakes never felt before since man was upon the earth will take place, say the Bible and the Holy Qur-an. The Holy Qur-an says: "There will not be one city left that will not be leveled to the ground." Using this force against the enemies of Allah will make it impossible for them to survive.

This is all known to this world, but why are they trying to build up a defense against God. It is useless. America has it coming. Look how she has and still is mistreating her freed slaves (so-called Negroes). In the South, they are beating and killing the so-called Negro boys about their own so-called Negro girls. Neither the Negro girl nor the Negro boy can walk free at night in certain parts without being attacked, according to a certain worker's paper. Yet the foolish Negro preachers and leaders want social equality with these, their enemies. The great distress of nations spoke or prophesied of coming in the above chapter and verses is now going on. Confusion, confusion all over the Western world today.

Should not it make you think that there is something of a very great importance going on among the nations of earth just to see the President leave his own country to visit another country during his tenure of office? They see the end of their world and they see the signs of the Son of Man coming in the sky with power and great glory (the great Ezekiel's wheel and the unity of the Muslim world and the distress of nations).

The nations are so well armed today that one nation fears the attacking of the other, lest he set off the whole third world war. The so-called Negroes must awaken before it is too late. They think the white man's Christianity will save them regardless to what, and they are gravely mistaken. They must know that the white man's religion is not from God nor from Jesus or any other of the prophets. It is controlled by the white race and not by Almighty Allah (God).

"The near event draws nigh, there shall none besides Allah to remove it. Do you wonder at this announcement? And will you laugh and not weep? While you sport and play, so make obeisance to Allah and serve Him" (Holy Qur-an 53:57, 58, 59, 60). Let us remember another Qur-an saying: "None disputes concerning the communications of Allah (God) but those who disbelieve, therefore let not their going to and fro in the cities deceive you. The people of Noah and the parties after them rejected (prophets) before them, and every nation purposed against their Apostle to destroy him, and they disputed by means of the falsehood that they might thereby render null the truth. Therefore I destroyed them: how was then my retribution and thus did the word of your Lord prove true against those who disbelieved that they are the inmates of the fire" (Holy Qur-an 40:4-6).

Hurry and join onto your own kind. The time of this world is at hand.

1958

ISLAM SUBMISSION TO ALLAH (GOD)
TO DO HIS WILL

WHAT RELIGION is greater than Islam in the sight of Allah (God)? Can we find one among the people of earth? The religion of Islam demands the believer to submit entirely to the Will of Allah, the Supreme Being, who created -the heavens and the earth and has power over all things, great or small; a religion whose Author is Allah (God). The same religion Allah gave to everyone of His Prophets from Adam to Muhammad, the last. (May the peace and blessings of Allah be upon him).

Adam and his race refused to submit (accept Islam) and for his rejection, he was punished with exile and a death sentence placed upon his race. Today, they still refuse to submit to Allah and His Prophets and seek to kill the Prophets and their followers, and have killed them. What better religion does the servant of God want than Islam?

Islam, the religion that brings peace and contentment to his or her heart after one submits; this great religion of entire submission to Allah (God) that brings about peace has come to you and me, after the false religions of the devils which have destroyed our peace, and unity, and caused men of all colors to war against each other.

These people (white race) who rejected the religion of Allah (God) (Islam), are too proud to do good or serve the God of righteousness. They hate good, and love evil, and have filled the earth with bloodshed. Now every nation must go to war on account of them. They delight in warring against each other. They never cease to make ready for war. Their day of making trouble, killing and persecuting these poor people of mine, in this part of our planet earth, is coming to an end. They shall not be able to protect themselves, as God has said to me. The people that will not submit to Allah will be removed from our planet.

Islam is now being preached in your midst. My dear people, join onto a religion that will bring peace to you. Islam could not have dominated the people before today because of the time (6,000 years) that was given to the devils to destroy the peace of the righteous, to fill the earth with trouble and bloodshed. But we have lived to see the dawn of the religion of entire submission to the Will of Allah (God) and that eternal peace of God that He promised to you and me if we submit to Him.

The proud Christians, woe to them! They are too proud to serve the God that feeds and clothes them. My people who have been deceived by these devils are also too proud to submit to Allah, because of their following and believing in the devils, and their false religion called Christianity.

A religion that turns one into lying and charging God with getting children out of wedlock which is contrary to the law of nature, and setting up equals with Him (a Son and a Holy Ghost), worshipping His Prophets as His equals, is also against the very teachings of the Prophets.

The proud Christians, the world deceivers, the world's divisions of faiths and divisions of people, turns the brother against brother, children against their parents, and parents against their children. This is all caused by the religion called Christianity, which was organized by them after the death of Jesus. They have lied by calling it the religion of Jesus, a prophet of Allah, when the world knows that His religion was Islam. (Submission to the Will of Allah.) Jesus never heard of this religion (Christianity).

Trace the histories and teachings of Allah's (God's) Prophets in your Bible, and see if you can find one teaching the people to believe in three gods, or saying that He is the son of God, or even teaching against the teachings of the divine prophets who were before him. Islam demands us to believe in one God, whose proper name is Allah. Say: He Allah is one.

Continued in next article, Islam and Christianity.

Hurry and join onto your own kind. The time of this world is at hand.

January 11, 1958

ISLAM VERSUS CHRISTIANITY

THE TRUTH has arrived for us, the lost-found members of the darker people of earth here in America, to stop playing the "fool" among ourselves and the world of mankind and make up our minds whether we are going to hold on to that religion which the white race teaches us, or believe in the religion of the God of our people, which is taught by our people.

We make fools of ourselves to please our enemies (the white race). The average so-called Negro in America is not concerned about love and unity among their own kind, but are really interested in trying to get love and unity among other than their own kind (the white race).

Of all the histories of people upon our planet earth, past and present, we can find no people who have loved heir enemies and hated themselves but the American so-called Negroes. They love and admire their enemies and all that goes for their enemies. They are ready in an instant to dispute, oppose and kill you if you are not likewise.

I AM a lover of my own people and a hater, like God, of all our enemies, and fear only God who has risen me up from among my people to bring them out of the darkness of falsehood into His light of truth so that they may enjoy heaven while they live. There are but a very few so-called Negroes who have spent any time examining the truth of the Bible and the white man's Christianity.

Therefore, they are without the real truth of the Bible and Christianity. I know the consequence of trying to bring truth to our people who are in love with those who have taken their fathers out of truth into falsehood. But my life and my death are for this cause (to bring truth to the American so-called Negroes).

If we are to accept a religion that is said to be from God, we should diligently examine the truth and the author of that religion, its people and the contents of its book or books before we bear witness that it is the truth from God and the right religion. Let the so-called Negroes take a second look at the Bible, which the white Christians want the black man to believe that every word of it is from God. There is no mention of a religion by the name of Christianity for God or the prophets. Again, we must remember that God does not represent Himself to us in the opening or closing of the Bible. He is represented by someone other than Himself.

THERE HIS creation is pointed out to us as a proof that there is a Supreme Being over all this universe, and that it was made in six days (Genesis 1:1-31). God does not address Himself to us throughout the first chapter, nor His religion, nor even the name of the representative of God is mentioned there.

The reader is without authentic proof of just who the author is of this book called Genesis. You must remember that according to the preface of the Bible, under the authorized version of King James, it has been 346 years and you have only been permitted to read the Bible for the past 90 years. The white man, our slavemasters and enemies, had the Bible over 150 years before we were allowed to read the book.

Now you seem to know more about the purity of the Bible than those who translated it into their own language. Not only do you try defending the Bible as being the word of God, but you equally try to defend the white race and their wicked world.

YOU MUST remember, and never forget: that the white Christian race made slaves of our fathers and will not allow you now to rise above the status of a free slave! Why is the Pope, who lives in Rome, Italy, the head of the Christian churches, when Jesus was born in Palestine and did the greater portion of his teachings in and around Jerusalem? Why is not Jerusalem the capital and head of the Christian churches? We (the Muslims) took Jerusalem and the tomb of Jesus in 1187 A.D. and it is still in our possession and will remain in our possession.

Certainly there is a Jesus predicted for you, but not the one of two thousand years ago, but the one that Jesus prophesied would come after him, who will redeem us from the hands of our enemies.

He came in 1930 under the name of Mr. Wallace Fard Muhammad (to whom be praised forever). He suffered here for three and one-half years to pay for our redemption. (You shall soon come to know.)

Hurry and join onto your own kind.

January 18, 1958

ISLAM - SUBMIT TO ALLAH

AND ENTER INTO PEACE

"Yea, whoever submits himself entirely to Allah, and he is the doer of good to others, he has his reward from his Lord, and there is no fear for him nor shall he grieve." (Holy Qur-an 2:112).

One never knows how stubborn or how proud one (yourself) can be until he or she is invited to submit to Allah (God). It has been very hard throughout the past, under a proud ruler (the devils), to submit to Allah. The white race thinks that they are better than we (the black nation). They were made like that: "And when your Lord said to the angels: 'Surely I am going to create a mortal of the essence of black mud fashioned in shape. So when I have made him complete and breathed into him of my inspiration fall down making obeisance to Him.' He said: 'I am not such that I should make obeisance to a mortal whom Thou has created of the essence of black mud fashioned in shape.'" (Holy Qur-an 15:29, 33).

The white race will not accept the black man as their equal.

What we really are to learn from the above verses of the Holy Qur-an is: Just who are the proud rejectors of the ones whom Allah (God) created from black mud fashioned in shape? The Adamic race (the white race) was created from the black man. It is now becoming universally known from the revelation of Allah, which was revealed to us, of the history of the white race which I and my followers are now preaching to the world of our kind.

The Maker (God) of the white race demanded respect for his devil, mischief-making race, and got it; but not from the angels, who cannot be said to have worshipped the devils and their evils doings. What we are to learn from the Adamic creation is this: As they were made a ruling power of evil, for a limited time (6,000 years); Allah, the God of righteousness, will create one from the same soil (black) who shall rule the people with "justice and righteousness." This one is referred to in the Bible as the "second Adam," in whom all will live. It is not the Jesus of 2,000 years ago, but rather one from among the so-called American Negroes, whom the white race (Iblis, the devils) will reject and also the intellectual class of the Negroes.

Both of these classes (the proud white race and the educated Negroes) will reject the black ruler raised up from among the so-called Negroes in America, for God's choice fell upon an uneducated one; therefore, making it hard for the proud educated ones to accept Him. This is done to make the proud submit, and to prove the power and wisdom of God over the power and wisdom of the world (the white race, who are the first Adam). If he (the one whom God chose) were educated by this world (the white race), they would have a claim in His preparedness. That is the reason why God's choice is an uneducated person of this world; for His will bring in a complete new world. Nothing of this world (white race) will be used in the new. This is why the so-called Negroes are warned to give up the white race's religion called Christianity, which they have been deceived by, because of the name (Christ Jesus) attached to it.

They (angels) will accept and recognize the second Adam (ruler of justice and righteousness) from the black nation (not the white race). As the Holy Qur-an says: "So the angels made obeisance, all of them together. But Iblis(the devils), He refused. He said: 'I am not going to make obeisance to a mortal, whom Thou has created of black mud (the black man) fashioned in shape.'" (15:31, 33). Search the history of the Prophets of Allah (God). The white race has never accepted a black prophet, of whom all were black. Even Abraham, Moses, and Jesus belong to the black nation, not to mention Muhammad whom the white race knows was black. They (the white race) rejected him and his revelations from Allah (God) as recorded in the Holy Qur-an.

If the so-called Negroes wait until the white man approves a leader for them, he will either be white or one who believes in the white race and hates black mankind.

Hurry and join onto your own kind. The time of this world is at hand.

CHRISTIANITY VERSUS ISLAM

EXAMINING the truth of the two religions, the basic beliefs in Christianity are:

1. God is the Father;
2. Jesus is His son, and
3. The Holy Ghost, and, that these Three are one God.

Note: Adam is supposed to have been the First Man that God created, but he is never referred to as the Son, or as a begotten or only Son.

There is one thing I hope to make clear to my people, and that is: the Christian religion, as taught and misunderstood by them, is not what they have thought it was. Jesus' history refers more to a future Jesus than the past. There is a prophecy of a Son being prepared to redeem man (the so-called Negroes). This Jesus made His appearance 27 years ago, and His work is now in effect.

Jesus (Isa) of 2,000 years ago, cannot do us any good, nor harm. It is outright ignorance to believe that he can. We should be intelligent enough to believe in that which can or has been proven true. Making the Son, and the Holy Ghost the equal with the Father is absolutely sin. There is no such thing as proof that there was or ever shall be a time when people will return to life after they are physically dead. There is no proof that God was the father of Mary's son, nor is there proof that he is alive some place waiting for the judgment to return.

THE HOLY QUR-AN says: "And they say: The Beneficent God has taken to Himself a son. Certainly you have made an abominable assertion: The heavens may almost be rent thereat, and the earth cleave asunder, and the mountains fall down in pieces, that they ascribe a son to the beneficent God. And it is not worthy of the beneficent God that He should take to Himself a son." (Holy Qur-an 19:88-92). God is self-sufficient. He does not need a son to help Him with the people. "What do then those who disbelieve (the Christians) think that they can take My Servants to be Guardians besides Me? Surely we have prepared hell for the entertainment of the unbelievers." (18:102).

The Christians who are guilty of disbelieving in Allah and His religion Islam, and who charge God with getting a son by Mary, are here warned that Allah has prepared hell for them. You should question the teachers and their teachings of any religion. Take no religion without the knowledge of its truth, lest you be made a fool.

JESUS DID not make himself the equal of God. The Qur-an says: Jesus said: "Surely I am a servant of Allah; He has given to me the Book and me a prophet (not His son) and He has made me blessed wherever I may be, and He has enjoined on me prayer and poor-rate so long as I live!" (19:30-31). We cannot find anything to give to Jesus as a title but a "prophet," and He did prophesy. But as the Holy Qur-an further says: "But parties from among them (the Christians) disagreed with each other, so woe to those who disbelieve, because of presence on a great day." (19:37) There just is no defense for such false teachings as the religion of Christianity. Who can say, with truth, that they have seen the Jesus in flesh and blood after his death? Who can say, with truth, that the Holy Ghost or spirit is the equal to its producer? The very emblem of Christianity is disgraceful to the righteous; a cross and the image of a man nailed thereon with a crown of thorns on his head and a wound in his heart. Such signs, the so-called Negroes should never look at, and should hate and abominate the one who offers them such ghastly and shameful emblems. Most times the crucifix is nude except for a strip of cloth over his private parts.

THIS IS the very way that they lynch so-called Negroes, mutilating their bodies, and then offering you a piece of the rope that the man was hung with as a warning to you that you will be next. They burn the cross as warnings to you even though the cross they claim is sacred among their religious believers.

I say with almost tears in my eyes: Brothers and sisters, give up believing in such a religion, and join on to the religion (Islam) of our fathers, Abraham and take for yourself the crescent for your emblem which is universally recognized.

Hurry and join onto your own kind. The time of this world is at hand.

ISLAM - SUBMIT TO ALLAH
AND ENTER INTO PEACE

"Yea, whoever submits himself entirely to Allah, and he is the doer of good to others, he has his reward from his Lord, and there is no fear for him nor shall he grieve." (Holy Qur-an 2:112).

THE AMERICAN so-called Negroes have been chosen by Allah (God) that He may make them the greatest and most successful people who ever lived on the earth.

But, they have been made so blind, deaf and dumb by the white race, our open enemies (the devils), that they even fear to submit to their Allah (God), and His religion of Islam (Peace) - their salvation.

The white race (devils) are the disbelievers and opposers of Allah (God), and the setting up of His government of Peace, Justice and Righteousness.

To fear the devil above the fear of Allah (God), your god and my God, is the highest of ignorance. Your doom is written in your Bible (Rev. 19:20), which you read, for fearing them above the fear of Allah (God).

OF ALL THE black, brown, yellow and red faces, as they are called, none fear the white race, but the so-called Negroes whom the white man reared up his slaves.

They (white race) put fear into them when they were babies 400 years ago.

Today, they keep that fear in the so-called Negroes by beating and killing them without a cause. Their court decisions are always made in their favor.

In many places in this unjust America, the so-called Negroes' own people are put into authority by the white man over them.

These fall upon their own race beating and killing them to the pleasure of the enemy of both. Many so-called Negro officers are guilty of the above said treatment of **their own kind**.

The white man has put Negroes against Negroes, and being made such, there is no love in the so-called Negroes for their own until they accept **Islam**.

As long as they remain in the white man's religion called Christianity, they will never have sincere love for each other. Therefore, they never will be able to unite and enjoy peace and contentment. They will bear me witness that the above said is true.

UNITY ON THE side of their God, Allah, and His religion, Islam, will put a stop to all their suffering at the hands of their enemies.

Come, follow me to your God. It is the desire of God to repay your enemies for their evils done to you, and He is doing it. As it is written, you shall know that He is your God and only Saviour when He has brought to aught your enemies. Submit to Him!

Think over the sins of these so-called Christian people. They are even their own enemies!

They are the greatest **swine eaters** on earth, although their Bible forbids it; the **greatest drunkards** on earth, yet the Bible forbids it; the "**greatest liars** on earth, yet the Bible forbids it; the **greatest gamblers** on earth, yet the Bible forbids it; the **greatest murderers** on earth, yet the Bible forbids it; the **greatest peace-breakers** on earth, yet the Bible forbids it; the **greatest adulterers** on earth, and yet the Bible forbids it; the **greatest robbers** on earth, yet the Bible forbids it; the **greatest deceivers** on earth, yet the Bible forbids it; the **greatest troublemakers** on earth, yet the Bible forbids it.

You will agree with me on the above charges that they are true. Then, how can you claim yourselves to be like Jesus and lovers of God?

Can Christianity be the choice religion of God? **NO!** "Allah, has sent His Apostle with the True guidance and the True religion, that He may make it overcome the religions, all of them, though the Polytheists may be adverse." (Holy Qur-an 61:9.)

OF ALL the religions, none is hated and feared by the white race more than Islam. Why?

Because it is the **Truth** and the Religion of God and His people (the black nation). Thousands of our people (the so-called Negroes) of America are now entering Islam from the truth that Allah (God) has revealed to me.

The devils and our own disbelievers would not like that our people accept Islam, for they know what it means to be the black man.

Next Week: The Prayer Service of Islam.

Hurry and join onto your own kind. The time of this world is at hand.

February 8, 1958

This prayer service is taken from the Holy Qu-ran and translated into English by Maulvi Muhammad Ali.

THE PRAYER SERVICE OF ISLAM

This is something that I have been trying to get around to writing for a long time. This prayer service performed by the believers (Muslims) is one of the most beautiful services ever performed. Of all the prayer services of non-Muslims I have never seen nor read of one to equal the prayer service of the Muslims. I hope the non-Muslim readers of my articles will pass their criticism of it when I have completed it.

I thought it to be most important to teach my people - the lost members of the great nation of Islam, found in the most evil and wicked part of our planet earth - this prayer service. We were never taught the proper way to serve and worship Allah (God), the most merciful God of the universe. The way the American so-called Negroes are taught to pray and worship God is wrong, and is even an insult to God and the righteous. They say their prayers, on most occasions, unclean - of which they never give a thought - and many times the prayer is said in an unclean place.

The Islamic prayer service **demands** the prayer to be clean **internally** and **externally** as well when doing service to Allah (God). The Muslims, in one of their prayers, declare to Allah that they worship Him in the best manner in these words:

"O Allah, we beseech Thy help and ask Thy protection and believe in Thee and trust in Thee, and we laud Thee in the best manner, and we thank Thee, and we are not ungrateful to Thee, and we cast off and forsake him who disobeys Thee. O Allah, Thee do we serve, and to Thee do we pray and make obeisance, and to Thee do we flee, and we are quick, and we hope for Thy mercy and we fear Thy chastisement; for surely Thy chastisement overtakes the disbelievers."

I just had to write the whole of this prayer because I greatly admire those words that make it. Anyone will be touched, whether a believer or a disbeliever, to see or be in the Muslims' congregational prayer service, to see their sincere devotion to our Maker.

Prayer is an out-pouring of the heart's sentiments. A devout supplication to Allah (God) and a reverential expression of the soul's sincerest desires before its Maker. Prayer, according to the Holy Qur-an, is the true means of that purification of the heart which is the only way to commune with Allah (God). The Holy Qur-an says: "Recite that which has been revealed to you of the book and keep up prayer; surely prayer keeps (one) away from indecency and evil, and certainly the remembrance of Allah is the greatest" (29:45).

Prayer is a means of moral elevation of man. Prayer degenerating into a mere ritual, into a lifeless and vapid ceremony performed with insincerity of heart, is not the prayer enjoined by Islam. Such prayer is expressly denounced by the Holy Qur-an:

"Woe to the praying ones who are unmindful of their prayers" (107:4,5). With a Muslim, his prayer is his spiritual diet of which he partakes five times a day. (A couple of times during the night.) Says Muhammad Ali.

I do not believe in Maulvi Muhammad Ali as being the promised Mahdi. But, along with others, his scholarly work is admired as given to us in the translation of the Holy Qur-an into English, with the beautiful outline of the Muslim's prayer service in his preface of the book.

PREPARATION FOR PRAYER

Before saying prayers, it is necessary to wash those exposed parts of the body: (1) The hands are cleaned up to the wrists. (2) The mouth is cleansed by means of a toothbrush or simply with water. (3) The nose is cleansed with water. (4) The face is washed. (5) The right arm is washed, and then the left arm; both are washed up to the elbows. (6) The head is then wiped over with wet hands. (7) The feet are then washed up to the ankles; the right foot first and the left foot after; that is, if the feet have been exposed, if not, then pass your wet hands over your socks. The feet should be washed at least once every 24 hours, regardless to their being inside of shoes or boots. A fresh washing of the hands should be given whenever a man has answered a call of nature or has been asleep. In cases of husband and wife, a total bath of the whole body is necessary.

TIMES FOR PRAYER

(Continued from Last Week)

THE SAYING of prayer is obligatory upon every Muslim, male or female, who has attained the age of discretion. It is said five times a day as follows:

(1) The morning prayer is said after dawn and before sunrise. (2) The early afternoon prayer is said when the sun begins to decline, and its time extends until the next prayer. (3) The late afternoon prayer is said when the sun is about mid-way on its course to setting and its time extends to a little before it actually sets. (4) The sunset prayer is said immediately after the sun sets. (5) The early night prayer is said when the red glow of the sun in the west disappears, and its time extends to midnight. But this prayer must be said before going to bed.

Note 1: When a person is sick or on a journey (or in case of rain when the prayer is said in a congregation in a mosque), the early afternoon and the late afternoon prayers may be said in conjunction, also the sunset and early night prayers.

Note 2: Besides these five obligatory prayers, there are two optional prayers which are said after midnight, after being refreshed with sleep, and before dawn. This prayer is specially recommended in the Holy Quran. There is a breakfast-time prayer, but since my followers do not have breakfast it is not necessary to mention the description of this prayer to you.

SERVICE

The service consists ordinarily of two parts. One part is called the **Fard**, to be said in congregation, preferably in a mosque, with an Imam leading the service. The second part is called Sunnah, to be said alone, preferably in one's house. However, when a man is unable to say his prayers in congregation, (the Fard) may be said alone.

To begin prayer service, we must always be sure that we are clean. Some of this service I will have to omit, but the important part of this service is a follows:

The chief features of the Muslim congregational service are that the services may be led by anyone. The only condition being that he should know the Holy Qur-an better than the others and should excel the others in righteousness and in performance of his duties towards Allah and His creatures. The second, there should not be the least distinction of caste, rank or wealth to be met with in a Muslim congregation. Even the King stands shoulder to shoulder with the least of his subjects.

Every congregational service must be preceded by an Azan (a call to prayer said in a sufficiently loud voice) to be heard by the congregation, and those assembled for the congregational service to stand up in line, or in several lines if necessary.

The caller to prayer stands with his face toward the Holy City Mecca (toward sunrise), which is the center of the Muslim world and, in fact, the spiritual center of the whole world, with both hands raised to his ears - but not holding nor touching the ears - with the palms of each hand open towards Mecca (the east). Standing upright (not sluggish), with the feet close together and the head erect, not downcast nor holding it backward, and repeat the following four times:

(1) Allah-u Akbar (i.e. Allah is the greatest). (Repeat four times.)

(2) As-hadu-an-la-ilaha-ill-Allah (i.e., I bear witness that nothing deserves to be worshipped but Allah). (Repeated twice.)

(3) Ash-hadu-anna-Muhammadar-rasul-ullah (i.e., I bear witness that Muhammad is the Apostle of Allah). (Repeated twice.)

(4) Hayya 'alas-salah (i.e., Come to prayer). (Repeated twice, turning the face to the right.)

(5) Hayya-ala-falah (i.e., Come to success). (Repeated twice, turning the face to the left.)

(6) Allah-u Akbar (i.e., Allah is the greatest). (Repeated twice.)

(7) La ilaha ill-Allah (i.e., There is no God but Allah).

Study the preparation of the Muslims for their prayer service, the direction in which they turn, the positions made by them, and the words used in honor and praise to God and try finding another religion equal to theirs.

Prayer service will be continued next week.

Hurry and join onto your own kind. The time of this world is at hand.

February 22, 1958

PRAYER SERVICE

"O you who believe, enter into submission one and all, and do not follow the footsteps of the devil. Surely he is your open enemy." (Holy Qur-an, 2:108.)

HERE THE MUSLIM is about to begin his prayer. He has cleaned all the exposed parts of his body, washed out his mouth, nose and ears. Standing upright, with his face towards his Holy City (Mecca), which is in the direction of sunrise, he lifts his cleansed hands up beside his head with the thumbs towards the lobes of his ears, and declares that: "Allah is the Greatest" (four times), and that: "Nothing deserves to be worshipped but Allah."

What better preparation could have been made for the service of our God? With due honor and great respect, he is turned in the direction (of sunrise) in which our planet is carrying him at a speed of 1,037 1/3 miles per hour. Physically, he has turned his face in the direction in which he is traveling, and in which he looks forward to the light of day. In the same direction (sunrise) came all the spiritual light - the holy prophets, the holy land and the holy cities of the earth.

WITH HIS cleansed hands open, with the palms towards the holy land and cities, he signifies an open confession of his internal purity and entire submission to the will of Allah (God). Whatever evils that he has committed with his hands, by washing them with the water of life is to show forth his heart's repentances for the evils that his hands have committed.

Now as the open cleansed hands, showing forth a sincere surrender to its Maker without concealing or hiding anything in his hands, so it is with the heart that only Allah (God) can see into is clear of the evils and desires forgiveness, for such evils have been washed from the heart, the ears from hearing them, and the eyes are closed to keep from seeing them (evils).

He now declares in unity with the prophets and the righteous that: "Allah (God) is the Greatest and that there is no God who deserves to be worshipped but Allah (God) and that Muhammad is His Apostle." He turns his face to the right after declaring, "Allah is the Greatest" (four times) which equals the four major points of the compass - east, west, north and south - and invites the whole of humanity to "come to prayer," repeating it twice, in the same direction (to the right). If the call is made in the early morning at the mosque, it is followed with the words, "Prayer is better than sleep" (repeated twice). He then turns his face to the left (to the disbelievers) and says: "Come to success" (repeated twice). Surely prayer to the right Allah (God) will bring us success.

THE ABOVE position is called "rakat" in the Arabic language. It is the same standing position with hands raised to the ears. The right hand is placed upon the left on the breast, and the following prayer, or part of it, should be recited; or, if the hands are held open with the elbows slightly resting against the front of each side, this position is also accepted. The prayer (not to be yelled out real loud or in too low a voice) is as follows:

"Surely I have turned myself, being upright, to Him who originated the heavens and the earth, and I am not of the polytheist. Surely my prayer and my sacrifice and my life and my death are all for Allah, the Lord of the Worlds: No associate has He, and this am I commanded, and I am of those who submit.

"O Allah, Thou art the King, there is no God but Thee; Thou art my Lord and I am Thy servant; I have been unjust to myself and I confess my faults. So grant me protection against all my faults, for none grants protection against faults but Thou, and guide me to the best of morals, for none guides to the best of morals but Thou, and turn away from me the evil morals, for none can turn away from me the evil morals but Thou."

THE ABOVE prayer is preferred as the morning prayer, but can be said by the individual any time that he likes. Here the prayer declares that he is strictly a believer in one God who originated the universe (the heavens and earth) and not in three, and further declares "that his sacrifice, life, and death are all for Allah (God), and to Him does he submit." He acknowledges his sins and asks protection against them, or rather against a future sin.

Hurry and join onto your own kind. The time of this world is at hand.

March 1, 1958

THE SIGNIFICANCE OF PRAYER

"O you who believe, remember Allah, remembering (Him) frequently and glorify Him morning and evening. He it is who sends His blessings on you, and (so do) His angels, that He may bring you forth out of utter darkness into the light and He is merciful to the believers. (Prayer is better than sleep.)" Holy Qur-an (33:41-43)

This alone is salvation just to be brought out of the darkness of ignorance into the light of the **truth**. Who is in more need of the **truth** than the American so-called Negroes who do not have the knowledge of self nor anyone else, and who love those who hate them and spitefully use them?

"O Prophet, surely we have sent you as a witness and as a bearer of good news and as a warner and as one inviting to Allah by His permission, and as a light-giving torch." Holy Qur-an (33:45, 46). Come to success; prayer and obedience to Allah will bring you success. The prayer is recited standing erect with face towards the east with hands raised and declaring to the one God, Allah, that he has turned himself to Allah (God), the originator of the heavens and earth. This prayer and positions made are especially designed and worded for those lost sheep (the Negroes) who have been lost from the knowledge of their God and people and now declare that they are turned again to their God, Allah, and are upright to Him.

IMAGINE A native Muslim who never was lost from Allah and his people in the Holy Land or Holy City, reciting the above prayer. The prayer has been turned into the wrong direction. He is in the west, looking again due East, confessing his faults for going astray from his God and people and declares that he has been unjust to himself, and confesses his faults, and declares that none can grant him a protection against his faults but Allah (God). He further asks that evil morals be turned away from him and to be guided to the best of morals. He is now leaving the infidels of the west who brought him into darkness, and pleading to be guided to better morals. Surely we, the so-called Negroes, lost all of our good morals among the enemies of the west. The type of the so-called Negroes is given in many parables of the Bible. In fact, if the Bible is rightly understood, it is referring to none other than the so-called Negroes and their enemies; the chosen people of God whom the God gave the first born (convert) and even the (Mahdi) Christ offered His life to restore the Negroes again to their own kind.

BUT THE NEGROES are blinded with a picture of the Jews' salvation and cannot see their own selves in prophecy. They should shout with joy over the understanding that God has and is causing me to give them of the Book.

It is with prayer of forgiveness, that Solomon advised you and me to make to Allah if we be lost from our own under the name of Israel (II Chronicles 6:36-39). Solomon was a Muslim prophet and king. He and his father, David, were of the black nation. He advised us to pray toward our own land and toward the Holy City (Mecca) which He has chosen.

The parable of the prodigal son (which is one of the most beautiful) and the lost sheep are, or should be, easier for the so-called Negroes to see that they are the ones referred to. It is with the turning to prayer toward his home and father's house that the sins of the prodigal son were forgiven, and he is accepted by his father and restored to his rightful place among his brethren. It is the turning against of the lost-found so-called Negroes - the tribe of Shabazz - in prayer to Allah, their true God, and His true religion, Islam, that they will be seated in heaven overnight (at once). The enemy knows this as well as I. They (the white race) cannot regain paradise because they are not members of that family. But, on the other hand, the lost-found so-called Negroes are really, by nature, members of the original family of paradise. It was by prayer and the turning in the right direction (toward the Holy Temple Mecca) that delivered Jonah from the belly of the fish (Jonah 2:2-4) which is only a type of us here in America (the anti-typical fish) who has swallowed us.

Our prayers will be speedily heard and Allah will fight out battles against our enemies and bring them to disgrace.

Hurry and join onto your own kind. The time of this world is at hand.

"Allah is the greatest; come to prayer, come to success. Prayer is better than sleep."

MUSLIM PRAYER SERVICE AND ITS MEANINGS

We must study the words and the different positions taken by the Muslim in his daily prayer. This helps us to better understand the true way to worship Allah (God). The following short prayer should be said by all darker people in America, as it fits us so well:

"Our Lord, do not punish us if we forget or make a mistake; our Lord, do not lay on us a burden as Thou didst lay on those before us; our Lord, do not impose upon us that which we have not the strength to bear; and pardon us and grant us protection and have mercy on us. Thou art our protector, so help us against the unbelieving people."

Our prayer in the past was made to Jesus, the last prophet God sent to the Jews, according to the way we were taught. It is wrong to take Jesus or any prophet of God as His equal. We may pray to God in their names, but not pray to the prophet. The Sender (God) is greater than the sent.

We have been away from our own people and native land so long that we no longer turn in the direction of home to pray. You follow the way of your enemies who are against Allah (God) and His religion (Islam) and all black mankind. You will be acting wise to begin turning and traveling eastward, to the God of our fathers, otherwise your prayers are hopelessly made to Jesus and to a God which you nor your teachers know anything of.

According to the teachers of Christianity, no man has ever seen Him nor can see Him unless he dies. That is infidelic teachings. Why are you representing something that no man has ever seen nor will see (a mystery God; unknown)? Why are you praying to a dead prophet who the infidel teachers claim is now alive in heaven, sitting on the right side of His Father, who is called a spirit, but yet the Son is not for He has flesh and bones. And this flesh of the Son, wounded 2,000 years ago, does not heal nor does it decay, according to the Christians' religion?

This is the greatest falsehood ever told, or the greatest mistake ever made. Such doctrine cannot be proven true. Most of such believers will try to contend that the spirit, which they feel is the proof. Then it is the God of feel that the Christians worship, and still there is no proof that God is something other than man; for a spirit must have a base. Let us recite another prayer of the Muslim:

"Glory to Thee, O Allah, and Thine is the praise. Blessed is Thy name and exalted is Thy majesty, and there is none to be served besides Thee. I betake me for refuge to Allah against the accursed devil."

Study the words of the Muslims' prayers and try finding anything to equal them in any other religion. The Christians have no intelligent prayer service set forth in the Bible. There is no mention of God teaching Adam to pray. Jesus set forth only one prayer to His disciples and did not appoint any certain time to recite it. That prayer will be discussed in this column in the near future.

The following is the oft-repeated prayer of the Muslims:

"In the name of Allah, the Beneficent, the Merciful; all praise is due to Allah, the Lord of the worlds; the Beneficent, the Merciful, Master of the day of requital. Thee do we serve and Thee do we beseech for help. Guide us on the right path of those upon whom Thou hast bestowed favors, not of those upon whom Thy wrath is brought down, nor of those who go astray." Amen.

What a good prayer for one who is lost from the right direction to pray as the so-called Negroes are.

Hurry and join onto your own kind. The time of this world is at hand.

"Surely prayer keeps (one) away from indecency and evil; and certainly the remembrance of Allah is the greatest (force) and Allah knows what you do."- Holy Qur-an 29:45

PRAYER IN ISLAM

Surely the best way to strive to be upright in a sinful world is to continuously pray to the One True God, whose proper name is Allah, for guidance.

As we are generally sinful and easily yielding to temptations, it is only fitting to keep up prayer.

Allah, the One True God, has blessed us with the universe. A sun to shine and brighten up the heavens, giving light for us to see: warmth to enable us to live and cause vegetation to grow and all life to exist. We reside on the planet through His will, so why should we not pray and continuously thank him for this privilege?

He it is who created the atmosphere for us to breathe air. He it is who created every good vegetation for us to eat, plus the fowl and other animals which we partake of daily. He it is who created the beautiful atmosphere in which we live, and with our own hands mutilate and destroy for lack of proper guidance.

We cannot improve upon the nature in which Allah (God) has created all beautiful things, yet we try. We cannot substitute the original beauty with artificial creations, but yet we try. So, let us realize the power of Allah, that without Him we cannot exist, and make obeisance to Allah through our prayers to Him.

AS YOU have been reading in this article, prayer is obligatory in Islam (the true religion). "And remember Allah's favor upon you and the covenant which He made with you, when you said, 'We hear and we obey.' And fear Allah. Surely Allah knows well what is in the minds.

O ye who believe! Be steadfast in the cause of Allah, bearing witness in equity; and let not a people's enmity incite you to act otherwise than with justice," says the Holy Qur-an. Be always just, that is nearer righteousness. And fear Allah. Surely Allah is aware of what you do.

Allah has promised those who believe and do good deeds that they shall have forgiveness and a great reward.

We owe our very lives to Allah, the Lord of all the worlds. Why should we not thank him? Our every good thought we owe to Allah, the beneficent, the merciful. Surely as often as we sin, we turn to Him in prayer. He is most merciful and grants us pardon and often times we generally drift back again to some other flaw for which we must turn to Him again, asking to be forgiven. Surely Allah knows what is in our hearts, and what is yet more, is oft-forgiving.

He it is who is the All Perfect One, who knows our imperfection and pardons most through His messenger. Remember: And the best way for remembrance of Allah (God) is through prayer.

IT IS an encumbrance upon the Muslims to keep up prayer at least five times a day, as previously illustrated in this article.

The five prayers of the day are his spiritual refreshments and he who cleanses himself in and out leaves no filthiness. It would be an insult to invite his Lord's holy spirit in a house that the outside was filthy.

Why should we not pray five times a day to our Maker since we feed our bodies three times a day? What is so important that would keep us away from prayer to the Originator of the heavens and the earth?

Let us give praises to our God and submit ourselves to the Lord of the worlds and learn how to pray the right prayers in the right manner. Let us serve the One True God whose proper name is Allah in the right state.

"My Lord, make me to keep up prayer and my offspring too; Our Lord, accept the prayer; Our Lord, grant Thy protection to me and to my parents and to the faithful on the day when the reckon will be taken." (The prayer of the Muslims will get you an answer!)

Hurry and join onto your own kind. The time of this world is at hand.

March 22, 1958

"O Allah, we beseech Thy help and ask Thy protection and believe in Thee, and trust in Thee, and we laud Thee in the best manner, and we thank Thee, and we are not ungrateful to Thee, and we cast off and forsake him who disobeys Thee."

PRAYER IN ISLAM

In the above prayer we learn that the whole of the Muslim prayer, as Maulvi Muhammad Ali says, "is only a declaration of divine majesty and glory, divine holiness and perfection, and of the entire dependence of man on his Maker." (Preface of the Holy Qur-an.)

If you would only adopt the saying of the Muslims' prayer, you would be helped. Of all the praying people on earth, the Muslims' worship to God is in the best manner. The words used in their prayers are the best and most humble. They cast off and forsake those who disobey Allah (God).

The Christians teach love for the enemy due to the fact that they are really the enemy and desire to mingle with you for the purpose of misleading you. It is nothing but right to sever friendly relations with those who do not care to serve and obey Allah (God).

THERE ARE many Muslims and black Christians who, for the sake of certain privileges, do not carry into practice the casting off of those who disobey Allah (God) and think it is a sin for the true righteous Muslims to do so. Today I am often asked, "Can white people attend your service?"

When told that white people are not Muslims, some of the ignorant Muslims falsely charge me in their writings and sayings as not teaching Islam. They also falsely charge that my teachings not only do not represent Islam, but that it is not recognized by the Muslim world. This is just what the enemies of Islam and the so-called Negroes of America desire that the Negroes believe. They sow such lies in the hearts of the weak Muslims and the Negroes in general. You are going to be greatly surprised. I have Allah (God) on my side to bring my people out of the darkness and power of our enemies, is not He (God) sufficient? And most surely He is with me, and I with Him. You most certainly will be the losers if you are not on our side.

THE LORD'S PRAYER, as it is called, contains some words that should not have been written there, such as: "Lead us not into temptation" - God will not lead us into temptation. It is the devils that tempt us to sin. The above words show a lack of confidence in God to lead us aright; that He must be reminded just how to lead us.

Another is: "Give us this day our daily bread." Here again, the words "this day" could lead one to believe that on **that** day the prayer was given, there was a shortage of bread, or that the Christians' prayers seek their physical bread first and spiritual bread last, even though the Bible says (Luke 12:31): "You first seek the Kingdom of Heaven, and all these things shall be added unto you." And, in another place (Matthew 4:4): "Man shall not live by bread alone, but by every word that proceedeth out of the mouth of God."

These scriptures are contrary to the prayer, although it stands true of the Christians who seek bread, swine's flesh (the poison), whiskey, wine and beer first, and the prayer for spiritual food last.

THE BIBLE shows (Exodus 16:2, 3, 8) that it was the want of bread and meat first of all that they gave Moses and Aaron much trouble trying to lead them into the spiritual knowledge of Jehovah and self-independence. They even said when they were hungry: "Would to God we had died by the hand of the Lord in the land of Egypt" (Exodus 16:3).

Oft-times, they angered Moses and Aaron by their longing for the food of their slavemasters even while on their way to freedom and self-independence.

The Muslims pray in their oft-repeated prayer to seek Allah's help in guiding them on the right path, the path of those whom God has favored, and not on the path of those who have caused His anger to descend upon (the Jews and Christians). This want of the slavemasters' bread, meat and luxuries is depriving the so-called Negroes today of their independence.

Hurry and join onto your own kind. The time of this world is at hand.

March 29, 1958

THE SO-CALLED NEGROES' SALVATION IS IN THE TRUE

RELIGION, ISLAM

"As for those who disbelieve and turn away from Allah's way, He shall render their words ineffective. And as for those who believe and do good, and believe in what has been revealed to Muhammad, and it is the very truth from their Lord, He will remove their evil from them and improve their condition. Those who disbelieve follow falsehood." (Holy Qur-an 47:1, 2.)

Why should not we believe in what God has revealed to Muhammad when it is the truth? It is no one but a fool or a devil who would disbelieve it! I am also named Muhammad and have a much worse job of getting the so-called Negroes to believe in Allah and His religion (Islam), than Muhammad had in getting the Arabs to believe. The Arabs did not have to be taught who they were, nor were they enslaved to a people other than their own. They were in power.

The poor so-called Negroes never had a teacher of their own nation for the past 400 years. Their teachers are their enemies (the slavemasters' children), who killed them mentally when they were babies. Now they are DEAD and cannot be resurrected by those who put them to death. The resurrector must come from our own kind (God).

THIS ALSO is strange to the mentally dead, so-called Negroes, for they think the God of the devils is the same as their God. NOT SO! The God of the righteous is not the God of the wicked (the white race). Ask the white race why they do not believe in Allah and His religion, Islam, which was revealed to Muhammad, and the prophets before Muhammad. They will say, "We follow Jesus and his religion, Christianity." Tell them that: Jesus' religion was also Islam and he was a prophet of Allah. They hate Muhammad, Allah and the Holy Qur-an. Why? Because it is the TRUTH (righteousness), and there is no such thing as truth and righteousness in that race. Nature did not give righteousness to them. But, you are welcome to believe God is a liar and that you already have the truth, and follow them to HELL if you please; for I will not lose time arguing with you over the matter.

You have had 400 years of experience here among them, you should know. You fear to serve Allah and pray to Him. Why? Because the white race has not taught you to believe in Allah. Why is it that they do not teach you to serve and pray to Allah? Because they know that Allah will answer your prayers and defend you against them.

DID YOU SAY I am a liar! I will stake my one life against everyone of you and your followers, that what you are calling on, other than Allah, cannot answer you! Turn to Allah, your own God, and He will hear you.

Remember how Pharoah and his people had fooled and deceived the Hebrews concerning Jehovah? Remember how Jehovah tried and proved Pharoah and his ministers to be liars with Moses' rod (Exodus 7:12), and by asking Pharoah to allow the Hebrews to go for three days journey into the wilderness to serve Jehovah, only to be deceived by Pharoah (Exodus 8:27-32). It took ten beatings from Allah to bring Pharoah into submission; all because he did not want the Hebrews to serve Jehovah, their own God. For 400 years the Hebrews had served other than their own God. They served and worshipped the God and religion of their slavemasters. The same problem exists here between the so-called Negroes and whites.

TODAY IS the day of our separation from our slavemasters and NOTHING will stop it; for it is TIME. Allah will bring it to pass, regardless to the efforts being made against it. There are a very few instances in the past histories of the destruction of people and their kingdoms that it all was due to interferences with the true servants and the worship of Allah (God). He will always intervene when His purpose is opposed.

For 6,000 years Allah (God and His Purpose, His prophets and His religion) have been opposed. The Hindus and Christians have been our worst enemies with their persecuting and killing of the Muslims and their prophets who were sent among them. In the days of the highest reign of King Nebuchadnezzer and Bellshazzar, it was their objections of the true God, Allah, and His servants' prayers to Him that Allah (God) destroyed them. The Jews received a curse and they lost their independence because of their objection to Jesus and His disciples.

Hurry and join onto your own kind. The time of this world is at hand.

TIME

IF YOU WHO DISBELIEVE in the Truth would only consider the time in which we now live, you would bear witness that it is the **very truth** from your God that I am teaching. Just when should we expect Truth to be triumphant? The answer is: After the removal of falsehood.

The **Time** referred to in this article is the time of the present world as Allah (God) has revealed it. This time covers a period of six thousand years. It began from the day that the first white person was made, which was in the year nine thousand (9,000) of our calendar history. This date is taken from the beginning of the present cycle of World History writings by 25 black scientists of which only 24 actually do the writing, and the 25th one acts as the judge of the writings of the other 24. This takes place once every 25 thousand years. In this history is written everything that will come to pass for the next 25 thousand years.

The original scriptures of the Bible and Holy Qur-an were taken from it, and revealed by word of mouth and inspiration to prophets. We are now in the 16th thousand year of this cycle and have nine thousand, nine hundred and fifty-six years to be finished before the next cycle. But we are not concerned with the 9,956 years from now; we are only concerned with that which the present time holds for us. A thorough knowledge of the time and changes to be made is the important factor for, you and me.

THE TIME GIVEN to the White Race (Yacob's grafted people) to rule the world is between the ninth and 15th thousandth year of our cycle of 25 thousand years, which is six thousand years. This time expired in 1914. A few years of grace have been given to complete the resurrection of the Black Man, and especially the so-called Negroes whom Allah has chosen for the change (a new nation and world). They (so-called Negroes) have been made so completely, mentally dead by the enemy (White Race) that the extra time is allowed.

The time (six thousand years) ruled by the White Race has been the worst of our known history; a time of complete trouble-making, war, bloodshed and death of both the righteous and the wicked as never before.

Therefore, the Black Nation and our God, Who is the Originator of the Universe, have decided to remove the trouble-makers from our planet Earth, as there is no way of the Black Nations getting along in peace with this wicked, grafted race known as the White Race. They have flooded the nations with deceit and divisions.

The time now has arrived for plain truth, wherein you shudder, and will call the Truth a lie and call falsehood the truth. This is due to your being reared and taught by "the deceiver!" But your disbelief in the truth will not hinder its progress for it is the **Time of Truth**, and this Truth is in our favor.

THE WHITE RACE progressed under falsehood for the past four thousand years because it was given to them. Now, that time has expired and the time of truth and righteousness again will rule. The interval of six thousand years of evil and falsehood makes the average person think that the Original Black Nation was never anything worthwhile. **Consider the time!** Most surely man is in loss except those who believe and do good, and enjoin on each other truth (Holy Qur-an 103:1-3). The time of the White Race is divided into three periods of two thousand years each.

The first two thousand years was the period between Yakub, the father and grafter of the White Race, to the birth of Musa (Moses) to the birth of Isa (Jesus), the last Great Prophet to the White Race. The third two thousand year period is from the birth of Isa (Jesus) to the coming of Allah, often referred to by the Christians as: "The coming of God, the Christ, the Messiah, the Son of Man," or the "Second coming of Jesus." In Islam, He is referred to as the "Coming of the Great Mahdi, the coming of Allah," to the birth of Muhammad.

April 12, 1958

TRUTH TO BE PROCLAIMED AT ALL COSTS

"O Apostle, deliver what has been revealed to you from your Lord; and if you do it not, then you have not delivered His message, and Allah will protect you from the people; surely Allah will not guide the unbelieving people." (Holy Qur-an, 5:67.)

When God decides to reveal His truth and bring an end to falsehood, that truth must be delivered regardless of the cost! The messenger of the truth should not fear to deliver it, for if that truth is from Allah (God), He will be the protector of it as well as the protector of the messenger who delivers it. A true messenger of Allah (God) never fears to deliver the message of Allah nor does he ever fail to deliver it. Even though most of them and their followers suffered severe persecutions and even death, yet the message of Allah was delivered.

The awakening of the Arabs nearly fourteen hundred years ago to the ancient truth (Islam) (not a new truth) of Allah by Muhammad and His work was typical of what will be done today. He was opposed by the Arabs for a while. Yet, since the Arab nation and their country are the birthplace of the great prophets and scriptures, and from there they are sent throughout the world from the time of Adam until today, they cannot be compared with the so-called Negroes who have not had a divine prophet nor scripture before.

ACCORDING TO the past histories of the major prophets, one comes every 2,000 years until the end of the world of sin. Jesus came 2,000 years after Moses, and the last one is to come 2,000 years after Jesus, bearing the names and titles of them all - Jesus and Muhammad, as well as bearing the title of David.

This man God raises up from among the American so-called Negroes in the West, and he will lead his people eastward by the guidance of Allah with a book of scripture for his people prepared and written by the finger of Allah. His teachings will be called a "New Islam" and will be opposed by many who would not like a change from the old to a higher knowledge of the divine.

The present Holy Qur-an Sharieff leads us right up to the door of that final book for our future, though not admitting us in, yet we are able to get a glance at some things.

Therefore, the so-called Negroes should try studying the Holy Qur-an Sharieff. The so-called Negroes fear accepting the plain truth because it shows up their enemies and their enemies are aware of this fear of them.

Some of the so-called Negro preachers recognize the truth of Islam, but the fear of the white man prevents them from preaching it. No Mason should reject it and especially the Shriners. They should believe and follow Islam for it will be made a MUST or ELSE! Why should we fear to believe in what Allah (God) has revealed to Muhammad when we know it is the truth? Are you afraid of it just because it has made manifest the devils and their false teachings? Is not their treatment of us alone sufficient proof? They never have and never will do justice by us.

Could we ever forget their beating, killing, lynching and burning of our people? (Not to mention their destruction of our women.) Yes, you may forget, but Allah will not. Know this: we do not grieve over the consequences of the disbelievers, though they may be our near kin. "And recite to them the news of Him whom we give our communications, but He withdraws Himself from them, so the devil overtakes him, so he is of those who perish" (7:175).

THE DEVIL watches the believers and when he finds one showing weakness, he helps him to become weaker in the faith. Islam is the greatest unifying force on the planet earth. Islam is a religion that is backed by the power of its Author, Allah, to whom be praised forever. Islam could save the world from its destructive fall, but the world has practiced evil for so long that she would rather go to her doom than to turn and do righteousness. Look at the silly things the world is doing, working "like mad" to destroy each other. For what? Is not there enough earth for everyone of us? Yes, there is enough if we would be satisfied with just that enough and not seek to rob the other man of his share.

Hurry and join onto your own kind. The time of this world is at hand.

April 19, 1958

WE ARE THE SEED OF ABRAHAM REFERRED TO

IN THE BIBLE, AND NOT THE ISRAELITES.

The Kingdom of Heaven is promised to the so-called Negroes and not to the white race (the Jews and Christians). If only the so-called Negroes could open their eyes to look for their own salvation and stop seeking the white race's salvation, they would soon be a happy people. You, in your blind way of understanding the Bible, even make the word of God and His prophets false. You want to show the slavemasters that you are their best and most loyal friends, even at the cost of your own lives! This is due to fear, and fear is our worst enemy.

Abraham was not a Jew nor a Christian; so how could Abraham's seed be Jews or Christians? Also, how could the covenant made with Abraham refer to the Israelite people? Jesus declared that they (the Jews) **were not the seed of Abraham!** "They answered and said unto Him, 'Abraham is our father.' Jesus saith unto them, 'If ye were Abraham's children, ye would do the works of Abraham, but now ye seek to kill Me, a man that hath told you the truth'" (St. John 8:39, 40). (Likewise, they seek to kill me too.)

THEY COULD not do the works of Abraham, which were the works of righteousness. The seed or children of Abraham must spring from a righteous Father, and the so-called Negroes' very nature proves that they are the answer. But the white race, as Jesus referred to them: "Ye are of your father the devil, and the lusts of your father ye will do. He was a murderer from the beginning (Yakub was the father of lies and murder), and abode not in the truth, because there is no truth in him. He that is of God's words; ye therefore hear them not, because ye are not of God" (John 8:44, 47).

The father of the white race Allah (God) taught me was none other than Yakub, who was a scientist of the black nation (the founder of "unalike attracts"), who lived 6,600 years ago. He was born 20 miles from the holy city Mecca, and was exiled after he was found entertaining the idea of making an enemy of us.

THE WHITE race is not the people referred to as Abraham's seed, which God promised Abraham that He would bless with the kingdom of heaven (Gen. 12:7; 13:15; 17:8). The Bible is so much misunderstood by the so-called Negroes and their preachers that it is real hard to teach them anything like the truth, although the truth is in their favor. They cannot, or rather do not, want to believe that God and the devils are human beings! They really think and look upon the white race as God's chosen people, when actually they are God's enemies, and are doomed to total destruction!

They (the fools of our people) call me a teacher of race hatred because of their love and fear of the devils and disbelief in Allah; while knowing the white race to be their worse haters! If they had lived in the days of Jesus and heard Jesus denouncing these evil people, would they have believed him? NO! They would have helped crucify Jesus just as the Jews did. Jesus did not love these people, nor their world. No righteous people love unrighteousness. This you call hatred. You are made to believe that you should love all human beings, including the devils that in so doing God would love you.

That is wrong, and the wise devils know that you are wrong for loving them and their way of life.

FOR NEARLY two years in this column I have told you the truth of these people as God has revealed and taught it to me. But, because of your fear of the devils, you have disbelieved me. You hold fast to them and in what they have misled you with as though the devils have power over Allah and His servants. **You shall soon come to know who has the Supreme Power!**

Allah wants to give **you** the kingdom and bless you forever because of your suffering under this heartless evil race of devils for 400 years. You are rejecting Allah for the sake of their friendship, which are only empty promises. They are our open enemies, and take them for enemies and not friends!

You are silly who believe that Jesus died two thousand years ago for the sins of the Caucasian world, to bring that race of sinners (the devils) - who had killed the prophets of God and the righteous - into the kingdom of heaven.

Hurry and join unto your kind. The time of this world is at hand.

"YOU MUST ACCEPT ALLAH AND THE TRUE RELIGION OF ISLAM OR SUFFER THE CHASTISEMENT OF ALMIGHTY GOD ALLAH."

To the readers of my articles, I wish to correct the number of scientists which appeared in article dated April 5, 1958. The number of scientists should have read 24, and 23 of them actually do the writing of the history. The 24th acts as the judge of the writing.

Time and again I have warned you in these articles of the consequences of rejecting Allah and the true religion of God and His prophets, Noah, Abraham, Moses and Jesus.

Believe it or not, America is falling. She is under divine chastisement just as Egypt was in the days of Pharoah and Moses, the servant of Allah. The same thing is being repeated here in America! Woe to the disbelievers in Allah! Egypt was made unfit for the Hebrews by divine plagues. Like-wise, America will soon be unfit for you. The Bible does not give us any knowledge of the previous condition of the slaves under Pharaoh until the birth of Moses. Only a prophecy of Abraham is given that they would sojourn in a land that was not theirs for 400 years.

IT SEEMS as if their treatment under slavery by the Egyptians was kept a secret from the outside world. Just as the so-called Negroes' en-slavement in America for 300 years, and the true knowledge of our condition was known only to Allah (God) until about 70 years ago, now all of Asia knows where the lost-found members of their nation are. For 300 years no outside teachers of our kind were allowed to contact us. Even now their movements among us are limited because the Negroes were born blind, deaf and dumb to the knowledge of self, not to mention other than themselves.

Therefore, the so-called Negroes (who are actually members of the Tribe of Shabazz) were reared and schooled by their enemies (their slave-masters). They do not have the true knowledge of self and kind, nor the true knowledge of God, nor His true religion of Islam.

Also the reason why it is so hard to get the so-called Negroes to believe in Allah and Islam is because the white race has spread their religion called Christianity all over the black man's world and have deceived millions of black people other than the so-called Negroes - the lost-found members of the Tribe of Shabazz - as mentioned in the Bible (Rev. 12:9; 20:10). It is now only a matter of time before the so-called Negroes' eyes will be opened and will believe and confess the truth of Allah and His religion, Islam.

THERE ARE many false charges made against me and my followers to keep you from believing in the truth of God and His religion. But you shall soon come to know who is speaking the truth and who are the liars! The government makes every Negro who opens his or her mouth in favor of their "own kind" a promoter of sedition and labels their teachings as being subversive or un-American. The "real divine truth" is un-American if it is on the side of the poor Negroes (and it is). But do not fear what you will be called by accepting Islam (the truth); rather fear Allah of losing your lives for not accepting the truth. America is falling! She is a real habitation of devils and every evil and unclean and hateful person. There is no future for her. One destruction after the other shall come upon her until she has been laid low, even to the ground. The only thing that can check her fall is that she accepts Islam - and that she will not do.

America has many of her own teachers warning her, but she will not believe. Fly to Allah, my people, and save yourselves and your children from her destruction!

Hurry and join unto your own kind. The time of this world is at hand.

May 3, 1958

THE TRUTH (ISLAM) IS REJECTED BY THE BLACK PREACHERS OF CHRISTIANITY

LIKEWISE, so did those before you reject the truth (Islam), and was brought to shame and disgrace by Him (Allah), who had sent His Messengers with the truth so that you may be successful.

Never before has there come to you a man with clearer truth and warnings than I have. For I bring to you that which I have received from the Lord of the Worlds. This truth which you have never heard or known before is now being preached to you and you are the first to reject it! You, who call yourselves God's ministers of the truth, but actually know not God nor the truth, for the favor and false friendship of our enemies (the devils) have rejected it, and by so doing, you are rejecting your own, as well as your followers' salvation. Also, you are fully aware that my followers and I have not been able to establish a decent place to even teach our people the truth. Therefore, you close your doors (the churches) against us, and in many instances will not allow us to even mention this Divine Truth of God in your midst.

IF ONLY YOU could see and understand; you would remove the cross from your churches and replace them with the crescent, the emblem of truth, justice and equality. The cross is the emblem of slavery, suffering, shame and death. It is a disgrace to God and His prophets for you to glorify yourselves in wearing such a sign. This very sign is burned by the devils when they are preparing to murder one of you. You would be wise to collect all such signs and pictures of white people who falsely represent the God, His angels and prophets that are kept in your homes and places of worship and burn them into ashes! You then should ask Allah to forgive you for being such fools to have been worshippers of devils. Bring them to me. I will burn them and show you there is no divine power of protection for them.

ISLAM is the true religion of God, and whatever you worship other than Islam is the false religion of the devils. You love to laugh and make a mockery of Islam and its Messengers, who are actually your real friends. You claim to be followers of one of our prophets (Jesus), but you do not even know Him. You have made Him, in your misunderstanding, the equal of God, and you are believing that He is alive somewhere in some place that you have no knowledge of. The devils shall be sent against you, and they shall make themselves manifest to you that they are not your friends. They will remind you of your rejection of Allah, and His true religion, Islam. I have warned you!

MUHAMMAD (may peace and blessings of Allah be upon him) was at first rejected because of being uneducated, according to the Holy Qur-an 43:30-35. He and Moses both were criticized for their inability to speak well. The disbelievers always think that they have an excuse for not believing the Messengers of Allah (God), but when the "showdown" comes to pass; they will find that they will have no excuse. Because of Pharoah's mockery of Moses, he and his people were brought to disgrace. "And Pharoah proclaimed amongst his people: 'O my people, is not the Kingdom of Egypt mine? And these rivers flow beneath me; do you not see? Nay, I am better than this fellow (Moses) who is contemptible and who can hardly speak distinctly!" (Holy Qur-an 43:51-52). But was Pharoah able to protect Egypt and her rivers whom he claimed were his from divine plagues?

Hurry and join onto your own kind. The time of this world is at hand.

May 10, 1958

Since 1914, the Nations have become more and more confused than ever before. What is the cause of this confusion? There have been many answers to this question, but very few have been correct. The root cause is that the time of the end of our enemies' (the devils) power to rule and deceive our Nation has arrived. We have been living under the rule of Satan (the devil) for the past 6,000 years. Now, that ruling power is being interfered with by a Superior Power and Force, which will create a "New World," a New People, a New Order and a New Government. In order to make way for a "New World," the old one must be removed. The builder of that "New World" is present even in our midst, Almighty God, Allah, in person. Not a return of Jesus of 2,000 years ago, but God in person is present; uprooting and overturning the kingdoms of the world.

THE PEOPLE are confused and destroying themselves. Truth and righteousness causeth much upstir among falsehood and unrighteousness. The world needs to pray the prayer of Daniel, the Prophet. "We have sinned and have committed iniquity, and have done wickedly, and have rebelled, even by departing from Thy precepts and Thy judgments: Neither have we hearkened unto Thy servants the prophets, which speak in Thy name to our kings, our princes, and our fathers, and to all the people

of the land. O Lord, righteousness belongeth unto Thee, but unto us confusion of faces, as at this day; to our kings, to our princes and to our fathers, because we have sinned against Thee." (Dan. 9:5-8).

The people have departed from God of Righteousness and accepted the
God of evil (the devil). They have covered themselves with sin as a gar-
ment, and shoes of iniquity, that they may tread the path of the wicked
without deviation. The white race rejected all of the Prophets of Allah,
and persecuted, beat, and even killed some, as they beat and kill America
so-called Negroes. They have robbed, spoiled, and deprived the so-called
Negroes of the knowledge of "self," and their God, Allah, and His true
religion, Islam. Now they all are confused. Rulers against rulers, and ever
conflicts between them. The work of their own hands shall destroy them.
We live in a world of sport and play, filthiness and shamelessness!

LET US REPEAT with Prophet Isaiah: "Open ye the gates, that the
righteous nation which keepeth the truth may enter in." (Isa. 26:2). The
devils have deceived the nations of earth with a false God and false religion under good names. Now, what the world needs to do is to open her
doors to Allah. His true religion, Islam, and the Muslims, (the Righteous
Nation). By doing so, they probably would save themselves for a long
time.

Hurry and join onto your own kind. The time of this world is at hand.

May 17, 1958

FOR THOUSANDS of years the people that did not have the
knowledge of the person, or reality of God, worshipped their own ideas
of God, and He has been made like many things other than what He really
is. The Christians refer to God as a "Mystery" and a "Spirit," and divide
Him into three. One part they call the Father, and another part, the Son,
and the third part, the Holy Ghost - and makes the three, one. This is contrary to both nature and mathematics. The law of mathematics will not
allow us to put three into one. Our nature rebels against such belief of a
God being a mystery and yet be the father of a son and a Holy Ghost
without a wife, or without being something in reality. We wonder how
can the son be human, and the father a mystery (unknown), or a spirit?

Who is this Holy Ghost that is classified, as being the equal of the father and the son?

THE CHRISTIANS do not believe in God as being a human being, yet they believe in Him as being the Father of all human beings. They also refer to God as He, Him, Man, King and the Ruler. They teach that God sees, hears, talks, walks, stands, sits, rides, and flies. Also, that He grieves or sorrows, and that He is interested in the affairs of human beings. They also teach that once upon a time He made the first man like Himself, in the image and likeness of Himself, but yet they believe that He, Himself, is not a man or human. They preach and prophesy of His coming, and that He will be seen on the Judgment Day - but is not man. They cannot tell us what He looks like, yet man is made like Him, and in the image of God, and yet they still say that He is a mystery (unknown).

How can one teach the people to know God if he, himself, does not know God? If you try teaching the Christians that God is also a human being, they say that you are crazy and that you do not believe in God, and you are called an infidel. In the meantime, while they admit that He is a Mystery God (unknown), they teach not to make any likeness of Him, yet they adorn their walls and churches with pictures, images and statues like human beings.

CAN GOD be a Mystery God and yet send prophets to represent Himself? Have the prophets been representing a God that is not known? (Mystery). They tell us that they heard God's voice speaking to them in their own language. Can a spirit speak a language while being an immaterial something? If God is not material, what pleasure would He get out of material beings, and of the material universe? What is the base of spirit? Is the spirit independent of material?

All of these questions will be answered by me in this article.

Hurry and join onto your own kind. The time of this world is at hand.

M a y   2 4 ,   1 9 5 8

Did God say that He was a Mystery God, or did some one say it of Him?

Did God say that He was only a Spirit, or did some one say it of Him?

THE MOST important question of all questions that one could ask is: "Who is God?" It is like a child who does not know his father, asking his mother to tell him the name of his father; wanting to know what his father looks like, and does he favor his father. Can we not ask the same questions, who are seeking the knowledge of Our Father, God? Should we be called disbelievers or infidels just because we seek the truth or knowledge of Our Father, God? The mother may, in some cases, think it best to keep the name of her child a secret, as it was in the case of Mary and Joseph 2,000 years ago. But, in the case of God, one would say that we all should know Him, but at the proper time.

It has been for the past 6,000 years that we had to wait for the proper time to learn just who is Our Father, for the false god (the devil) would not dare tell us lest he lose his followers. Naturally the child will leave a foster father for his real father, especially when he is a good father. The real father by nature loves his own flesh and blood regardless of how it looks or acts, for it is his own child.

SO IT is with us - the so-called Negroes, "Lost-found members of the Asiatic nation." He who has found us in Our Father, the God of love, light, life, freedom, justice and equality. He has found His own, though His own does not know Him. They (the so-called Negroes) are following and loving a foster father (the devil) who has no love for them nor their real father, but seeks to persecute and kill them daily. He (the devil) makes the lost and found children (the American so-called Negroes) think that their real father (God), is a mystery (unknown), or is some invisible spook somewhere in space. The only chance that the children have to know their real father is that he must come and make Himself known by overpowering and freeing them from him whom they fear.

The devils reared the poor so-called Negroes for 400 years, and put fear in them when they were babies. They (the devils) kept them apart from their own kind coming in from abroad; so as to deprive them of any knowledge other than what he (the devil) has taught them. As soon as they hear of a so-called Negro learning and teaching his own people that which they (the devils) would not teach them, the devils then seek to kill that one, or trail him wherever he goes, threatening those who would listen to him, believe, and follow him. Knowing that their very presence and inquiries might frighten or scare Negroes they ask: "What is this you are listening to and believing in?" This will frighten most of them away from accepting his or her own salvation, and keep them from returning to their own God, religion and people.

MY PEOPLE, if you only knew the time and presence of your God, Allah, there should be no fear for you nor grief. But, you are deceived in the knowledge of your God. If your God was a mystery, you and I would be a mystery people. If He was a Spirit and not a man, we would all be spirits, and not human beings! If He was a mystery or only a Spirit, the prophets could not have predicted the coming of that which no one has knowledge of, or of a spirit which cannot be seen - only felt.

Because of the false teaching of our enemies (the devils) God has made Himself known; for I teach not the coming of God, but the presence of God, in person. This kind of teaching hurts the false teachings of the devils, for they knew that God would come in person after you. They (the devils) also are aware that God is present among us, but those of you who are asleep, they desire to keep asleep.

The enemies of God today are the same as they were thousands of years ago - thinking that they will be the winner against Him. America, for her evil done to me and my people shall be isolated and deceived by her friends. The heavens shall withhold her blessing until America is brought to a disgraceful ruin.

Hurry and join onto your own kind. The time of this world is at hand.

May 31, 1958

WHAT SHALL WE EXPECT TO SEE?
A SPIRIT OR A MAN?

THE NATIONS of the earth expect the coming of a God who will overcome and destroy all idol gods and set Himself up as the Supreme God over all; for all nations have made their own gods, according to the Bible (Kings 17:29).

Many people have been saying for a long time that God is already with us. Most of the people believe God to be a "Spirit." If He is only a spirit, it is not necessary for us to ever look to see Him; only to feel Him, for a spirit cannot be seen; and, this has been the only God that we have had in the past.

LET US SEARCH the Bible and see if it teaches us to believe in the coming of God to be a spirit and not a man. The Bible teaches us of the spirit of God in many places, but only once do I find where it mentions God as being only a spirit (John 4:24). And this came from a Prophet (Jesus), not from the mouth of God. If one reads the previous verse (John 4:23), he or she will see that even Jesus could not have believed God to be only a spirit in these words: "But the hour cometh and now is, when the true worshipers shall worship the the Father in spirit and in truth: for the Father seeketh such to worship Him." (Here a Father is mentioned that we are to worship in Spirit, and not a God of Spirit, but worship God in spirit).

Here it is made clear that the "**hour cometh**." This "hour" cannot be referring to anything other than the **doom** or **end** of the devil's wicked world of false worshipers, who claim that they are true worshipers of the true God but are not. "For the Father (God) seeketh true worshipers." The devils and those who follow them deceive the people are not true worshipers, no Jesus could have only been referring to the time of the presence of God in person **(this is the time)**. The world of satan, the devil, did not convert people to God, according to the parable of the wicked husbands, whom the Lord let His vineyard out to (Matthew 21:33-41). In the 42nd verse of the same chapter, Jesus makes another parable of the true worshipers under the "stone that the builders rejected"; that it became the "head stone."

It is the so-called Negroes who have been rejected by the builders of Governments (civilizations), who are now destined to become the head in the new world (or government) under the Divine Supreme Being in Person. It is natural to say that God is the Spirit of Truth, of Life. It is natural to say such and such one is a liar, but where there is no one to tell a lie, there is no liar.

So it is with truth for the spirit of truth. If there is nothing to produce the spirit there is no spirit; nor can we know the truth without someone to teach the truth. Where there is man, there is the spirit. Where there is no man, there is no spirit, for the spirit cannot produce itself.

Hurry and join onto your own kind. The time of this world is at hand.

J u n e 7 , 1 9 5 8

GOD CAME FROM TEMAN, AND THE HOLY ONE FROM MT. PARAN (HABAKKUK 3:3). IS HE A MAN OR A SPIRIT?

ACCORDING to the Dictionary of the Bible, Teman was the son of Eliphaz, son of Esau by Adah (Gen. 36:11, 15, 42 and 1 Chron. 1:36). Now if Habakkuk saw God come or coming from the sons of Esau (Eliphaz), then God must be a man and not a spook. If Habakkuk's prophecy refers to some country, town or city, if there be any truth at all in this prophecy, then we can say that this prophet saw God as a material being belonging to the human family of the earth - and not a spirit (ghost). In the same chapter and verse, Habakkuk saw the Holy One from Mt. Paran. This is also earthly, somewhere in Arabia. Here the Bible makes a difference between God and another person who is called the Holy One. Which one should we take for our God? For one is called God while another one is called Holy One. This Holy One, glory covered the heavens and the earth, and the earth was full of His praise.

IT HAS BEEN a long time since the earth was full of praise for a Holy One. (Even to this hour, the people do not care for holy people and will persecute and kill the Holy One if God does not intervene.) In the fourth verse of the above chapter, it says: "He had horns coming out of his hand; and there was the hiding of his power." Such science used to represent that God's power could confuse the ignorant masses of the world. Two Gods are here represented at the same time. (It is good that God makes Himself manifest to the ignorant world today.)

"The burning coals went forth at His feet" has a meaning, but what is the meaning? The ignorant do not know. The "burning coals" could refer to the anger and war among the people where his foot trod within the borders of the wicked. (Here God has feet - spirits do not have feet and hands.) This Holy One does not refer to anyone of the past - not Moses, Jesus nor Muhammad of the past 1300 years. "For this Holy One measured the earth, drove asunder the nations; scattered the mountains, the perpetual hills did bow, Cushan in affliction; the curtains of the land of Midian did tremble." (What is meant by the curtains trembling? Who is Cushan?) "The mountains saw thee, they trembled." (Whom does this mean?) "The sun and moon stood still in their habitation." (What does this mean?) The answers to the above questions are easy when we understand who this God called the Holy One coming from Mt. Paran is.

THE 13th VERSE should clear the way for such understanding; for it tells us why all these great things took place on the coming of the Holy One from Mt. Paran. It says: "Thou wentest forth for the salvation of thy people (not for all people) for the salvation with thine anointed (His Apostle). He wounded the Head out of the house of the wicked, by discovering the foundation unto the neck (by exposing the truth and the ruling powers of the wicked race of devils.) "Cush" or "Cushan" represents the black nation which is afflicted by the white race. "The curtains of the land of Midian" could mean the falsehood spread over the people by the white race, and their leaders trembling from being exposed by the truth. "The mountains" represent the great, rich and powerful political men of the wicked; and they also are trembling and being divided and scattered over the earth. **"The Holy One" is God in person, and not a spirit!**

Hurry and join onto your own kind. The time of this world is at hand.

June 14, 1958

GOD CAME FROM TEMAN AND THE HOLY ONE FROM

MT. PARAN (HABAKKUK 3:3)

IS GOD A SPIRIT OR A MAN?

God is a man and we just cannot make Him other than man, lest we make Him an inferior one; for man's intelligence has no equal in other than man. His wisdom is infinite; capable of accomplishing anything that His brain can conceive. A spirit cannot think, for a spirit has no brain to think with. The spirit is subjected to us and not we to the spirit.

Habakkuk uses the pronoun "He" in referring to God. This pronoun "He" is only used in the case when we refer to a man or boy or something of the male sex.

Are we living in a material universe or a "spirit" universe? We are material beings and live in a material universe. Would not we be making ourselves fools to be looking forward to see that which cannot be seen, only felt? Where is our proof for such a God (spirit) to teach that God is other than man? It is due to your ignorance of God, or you are one deceived by the devil, whose nature is to mislead you in the knowledge of God. You originally came from the God of Righteousness, and have the opportunity to return; while the devils are from the man devil (Yakub) who has ruled the world for the past 6,000 years under falsehood, labeled under the name of God and His prophets.

THE WORST thing to ever happen to the devils is: The truth of them made manifest that they are really the devils whom the righteous (all members of the Black Nation) should shun, and never accept them as truthful Guides to God! This is why the devils have always persecuted and killed the righteous. But the time has at last arrived that Allah (God) will put an end to their persecuting and killing the righteous (the Black Nation).

I and my followers have been suffering cruel persecution - police brutality - for the past 25 years; but have patience, my dear followers, for release is insight. Even those who made mockery of you shall be paid fully for his or her mockery; for the prophecy of Habakkuk is true if understood, wherein he says: "Thou wentest forth for the salvation of Thy people" (the so-called Negroes), (3:13).

Never before this time did anyone come for the salvation of the so-called Negroes in America, whose rights have been ignored by their enemies (the White Race) for 400 years. Now it is incumbent upon Allah to defend the rights of His lost-found, helpless people called Negroes by their enemies.

THE WHOLE of the third chapter of Habakkuk is devoted to the coming and work of God against our enemies and our deliverance. We must not take our enemies for our spiritual guides lest we regret it. You are already deceived by them. Why seek to follow them and their evil doings. If I would say that God is not man, I would be a liar before Him and stand to be condemned. Remember! You look forward to seeing God or the coming of the "Son of Man" (a man from a man) and not the coming of a "spirit." Let that one among you who believes God is other than man, prove it! (Continued next week: "The Origin of God Being a Spirit and Not a Man.")

Hurry and join onto your own kind. The time of this world is at hand

June 21, 1958

THE ORIGIN OF GOD BEING
A SPIRIT AND NOT MAN.

"Take heed to yourselves that your hearts be not deceived, and you turn aside, and serve other gods; worship them." (Deut. 11:16)

THE AMERICAN so-called Negroes are gravely deceived by their slavemasters' teaching of God and the true religion of God. They do not know that they are deceived, and do earnestly believe that they are taught right, regardless of how evil the white race may be. Not knowing "self" or anyone else, they are a prey in the hands of the white race, the world's arch-deceivers (the real devils in person). You are made to believe that you worship the true God, but you do not! God is unknown to you in that which the white race teaches you (a Mystery God).

The great arch-deceivers (the white race) were taught by their father, Yakub, 6,000 years ago, how to teach that God is a spirit (spook), and not a man. In the grafting of his people (the white race), Mr. Yakub taught his people to contend with us over the reality of God by asking us of the whereabouts of that first (God); one who created the heavens and the earth, and that, Yakub said, we cannot do. Well, we all know that there was a God in the beginning that created all these things, and do know that He does not exist today. But, we know again that from that God, the person of God continued until today in His people, and today a Supreme One (God) has appeared among us with the same infinite wisdom to bring about a complete change.

THIS IS HE whom I preach and teach you to believe and obey. The devils call Him a Mystery God, but yet claim that He begot a son by Mary. They call on you and me to take this son of Mary for a God, who was a man before and after his death; yet they deny the coming of God to be a man. If Jesus was a son of God, what about Moses and the other prophets? Were they not His sons since they were His prophets? The belief in a God other than man (a spirit), Allah has taught me, goes back into the million of years - long before Yakub (the father of the devils) - because the knowledge of God was kept as a secret from the public. This is the first time that it has ever been revealed, and we, the poor rejected and despised people, are blessed to be the first of all the people of earth to receive this secret knowledge of God. If this people (the white race) would teach you truth which has been revealed to me, they would be hastening their own doom - for they were not created to teach us the truth, but rather to teach us falsehood (just the contrary to truth).

It stands true that they are enemies of the truth by their ever warring against the truth. They know that Islam is the truth; they know that the history of them that God has revealed to me is the truth, but do not like for you to know such truth of them. Therefore, they seek every means to oppose this teaching. They try everyone of you that say that you believe it and are my follower. They are watching you and me seeking a chance to do us harm. They are so upset and afraid that they visit you at your homes to question you of your sincerity of Islam.

AS DAVID SAYS in his Psalms (37:32): "The wicked watcheth the righteous and seeketh to slay him." Also, Psalms (37:30): "The mouth of the righteous speaketh wisdom, and his tongue talketh of judgment." And, in another place, Psalms (94:16): "Who will rise up for me against the evil-doers? Who will stand up for me against the workers of iniquity?" I have answered Him and said, "Here I am, take me." For the evil done against my people (the so-called Negroes), I will not keep silent until He executes judgment and defends my cause. Fear not my life, for He is well able to defend it. Know that God is a Man and not a spook!

Hurry and join onto your own kind. The time of this world is at hand.

WILL AMERICA REPENT?

This is a great question. America knows her evil doings against us, but to repent of it, I doubt it much. She feels that if she tries to make up with us for her evil doing to us, she would be inviting her disgrace among the nations of the earth. Her determination is to try and keep the so-called Negroes from believing in the true God, Allah, and the true religion of Islam, which is our **salvation**. They are using many tricks, now, to deceive the so-called Negroes. The foolish so-called Negroes are falling for them.

False friendship is not able to stand up for very long; an enemy is just not able to put over false friendship for long. You should be able to know them and their tricks as long as they have been putting them over on you.

According to the Holy Qur-an (60:1), friendly relations with enemies of Islam is forbidden. "O, you who believe do not take my enemy and your enemy for friends: Would you offer them love while they deny what has come to you of the truth, driving out the Apostle ad yourselves because you believe in Allah, your Lord?"

IN THIS KIND of doings, the foolish so-called Negroes will be trapped. There are even some weak Muslims who ignore this warning. Some even go as far as to marry the enemies of Islam, and even hate me for teaching the truth of the enemies. But, Allah is with me, and I have no right to worry about the doings of the people after knowledge. The enemy does not love either you or me. As the next verse teaches "If they find you, they will be your enemies, and will stretch forth towards you their hands and their tongues with evil, and they ardently desire that you may disbelieve. They would slay you with their hands, and speak evil to and of you with their tongues."

You must remember that you do not like one who befriends your enemy. How much God dislikes you for making love with his enemies? The enemy does not have to be the real devil; he could be your father, mother, brother, husband, wife or children. Many times they're of your own household near of kin. Today is the great time of the separation of the righteous Muslims and the wicked white race.

THE WICKED ARE not by any means asleep to the knowledge of the time. They are really on the job of trying to keep all those who are blind, deaf and dumb to what is going on in that condition. They watch every step of the righteous (Muslims), seeking to harm them and their work of spreading forth the truth. You must know the truth whether you accept it or reject it! Ask yourself these questions:

(1) If Christianity is the religion of Jesus, why is it that the wicked (white race) represents it, instead of the righteous or holy people of the East (Islam)? (2) Why has not the Holy City Mecca allowed it to be taught within her? (3) Why is not Jerusalem the capital of Christianity instead of Rome, Italy? (4) If Christianity was the religion of Jesus and the white race is Jesus' beloved people, why did he preach the "doom" of the white race and the coming of a new world?

This people will most certainly carry to their doom many of our people because of our peoples' fear and love of them. Look out of your door or window; see the black woman sitting in the car close in the arms of your and her enemy. The enemy does not love her. He only wants to disgrace her and you, and keep her from seeing the hereafter. You cannot have any such freedom with his women, and especially not in front of his door. Love of them will get you the hell.

Hurry and join onto your own kind. The time of this world is at hand.

THE BIBLE AND HOLY QUR-AN

THE BIBLE is my poor people's graveyard. The Holy Qur-an will resurrect them if they would make a study of its teachings, along with someone to teach its meanings. It is fatal to read either Book without understanding. It would have been better that you played with rattlesnakes and been bitten by them than to have read the Bible without understanding! It is a "fixed Book" that has been added in and taken out of the truth by the devils - slave makers of my people. It is revised every few years, and some of the filthy readings in it cannot be read in public by any decent person without feeling ashamed.

The Book was prepared for you and me (the black man), not for the white race. Is there any truth in the Bible? Yes, there is plenty of it if you understand it, and where to place it. The Bible is dedicated to King James and not to God! The Book is made up of many Books or histories, prophecies, and poems. The first five Books are called the Books of Moses. There in the first Book (called Genesis), is an attempt made to tell us how God made the universe. But nothing is given to us of the knowledge of the Maker, which should have been the first of the Bible's teachings.

IF THE BIBLE is the word of God, He should be the One speaking, addressing Himself to us, and not a Prophet of His. Moses does not tell us where he received his knowledge of the history of the creation here in Genesis - of the histories of Adam and his sons, Noah and his sons, Abraham and his sons. Genesis does not begin with: "Thus saith the Lord," nor does it read: "Moses said unto the people that God taught him these histories mentioned in the First Book called Genesis." I wonder how did you get your knowledge that it is the word of God.

Moses' birth took place in the Second Book called Exodus (2:2), and according to his history there, he was commissioned by God to go to Pharaoh. In the Chapter 3:2, it reads that "an angel of the Lord appeared unto him in a flame of fire out of the midst of a bush." And, in the 4th verse it says: "And when the Lord saw that Moses turned aside to see, God called unto him out of the midst of the bush." While the second verse says: "It was an angel of the Lord in the bush." From the 4th verse on, it is the Lord or God addressing Himself to Moses as being the God of Moses fathers and people. What became of the Angel? According to the 6th Verse: "Moses hid his face for he was afraid to look upon God." Since he had not seen God, why should he now be afraid to see that which he had never seen before, and being the God of his fathers? Should not one be glad to see the God of his father? Was this a vision that Moses had of a burning bush and of an angel and God? It seems that he had already seen the angel in a flame of fire out of the midst of a bush. The angel was seen but said nothing. The angel was replaced by the voice of God. Why did not the angel speak, or was the angel God?

ACCORDING TO the 2nd verse, the bush was real, and the fire unreal; and that the voice was real, but the angel was unreal. But if this was Moses' first experience with God, how about the angel? Could Moses have known the angel to be of the Lord, since he had not seen or met either one before?

Allah (God) addressed Himself to Muhammad in the Holy Qur-an (2:1). The Holy Qur-an is the word of Allah (God), and not the Prophet. The whole of the Book is Allah (God) talking, and not the Prophet Muhammad.

Hurry and join onto your own kind. The time of this world is at hand.

July 12, 1958

THE BIBLE AND HOLY QUR-AN

IF THE Bible and Holy Qur-an are all the exact word of Allah (God), then the books are holy. But if not, we should not call them holy. The exact word or words of Allah (God) are holy wherever they are found. The so-called Negroes (most of them) have not the knowledge of the books and are misled by the wrong interpretation; and especially the Bible. The Holy Qur-an is universally recognized as being the true words of Allah (God) communicated to Muhammad in the seventh century.

Due to the pureness of the Holy Qur-an, the Muslims for many centuries would not allow it to get into the hands of the infidels (the white race)
because it teaches us that none shall touch it but the purified ones (or a
believer). The Muslims learned from the reading of the Holy Qur-an that
the infidel (white race) had altered the Torah and the Gospel that Allah
(God) gave Moses and Jesus. Therefore, the Muslims did not intend that
the infidels should alter the holy words of Allah (God) as given in that
sacred book. But, finally, the Qur-an got into the infidels' hands. If you do
not believe that they (the white race) are guilty of altering the words of
Allah (God), go to the public libraries and read some of their copies of the
Holy Qur-an translated into English by their scholars and missionaries of
Christianity - William Muir, Stanley Lane Poole, Sales, and many other
European writers and haters of the truth (Holy Qur-an, Allah and his serv-
ant Muhammad).

IF THEY WILL alter the truth of the Holy Qur-an, how much more
would they alter the truth of the Bible that was given to them by Moses
and Jesus? The Twelve Imams of Islam do not consider anything as pure
that the hands of the infidels (white race) have touched - and they are
right!

Why the so-called Negroes believe in the infidel (white race) is because
they were reared by the white race. Therefore, they love and hate all that
the white race loves and hates - even to themselves! This is why it is so
hard to teach the truth to the so-called Negroes, which would unite them.
You must know that the Bible and the religion Christianity are to be removed and destroyed from among the people to make way for the "pure
truth" and religion of Allah (God). The truth that I teach you, which is
direct from the mouth of Allah (God), is true and will remove it.

"Surely this is a reminder, so whoever will, let him take a way to his
Lord; and you will not, unless Allah (God) please. Surely Allah (God) is
ever knowing, wise" (Holy Qur-an 76:29, 30). The Holy Qur-an requires
a belief not only in its own truth, but also in the truth of previous scriptures
delivered to the prophets of different nations of the world (Maulana Muhammad Ali's preface of the Holy Qur-an translated by him into English)
- "And those who believe in that which has been revealed to thee (Muhammad) and that which was revealed before thee" (2:4). "And we have

revealed to thee the book (Holy Qur-an) with the truth, verifying that which is before it of the book and a guardian over it." (5:48).

WHAT OTHER scripture or book claims such justice for the truth which was revealed, regardless to whom or when? The Holy Qur-an acts as a guardian over the truth and as a judge to decide the differences between the various religions. The Christians make bias the Bible and their religion, and seek to condemn others as false, inferior and godless. The Holy Qur-an is a manifestor. There is no book that has thrown a clearer light on the Divine Supreme Being, His attributes, the requital of good and evil, the life after death, the paradise and hell.

Surely before the revelation of the Holy Qur-an, the world was in darkness to the true knowledge of the above said. It is a perfect revelation of the Divine Will: "This day have I perfected for you your religion and completed my favor to you, and chosen for you Islam as a religion" (5:3).

Hurry and join onto your own kind. The time of this world is at hand.

July 19, 1958

THE BIBLE AND HOLY QUR-AN

BOTH BOOKS are called holy. The word of Allah (God) is holy, and His word is true. Therefore, all truth is holy; for Allah (God) is holy and is the author of truth, without the shadow of a doubt! Allah is the representative of the Holy Qur-an (not a prophet) in these words: "This book, there is no doubt in it, is a guide to those who guard against evil" (2:2), translated by Maulvi Muhammad Ali. Abdullah Yusuf Ali's translation of the same verse reads near the same: "This is the book; in it is guidance, sure, without doubt, to those who fear Allah (God)" (2:2).

The Bible does not claim God to be its author. Jehovah calls Moses out of the burning bush to go to Pharaoh (Ex. 3:9). There is no mention of a book or Bible that is found that Jehovah gave to Moses in the first five books of the Bible, which are claimed to be Moses' books. Moses' rod is the only thing used against Pharaoh and the land of Egypt; and tables of stones in the mountains of Sinai. The miraculous rod of Moses, and not a book, brought Pharaoh and his people to their doom. The Ten Commandments served as a guide for the Jews in the promised land. Where do we find in the Bible that it was given to Moses by Jehovah under such name as Bible or the book?

BUT, ON the other hand, Allah (God) tells that He gave the book, "the Holy Qur-an to Muhammad." I am Allah, the best knower, the revelation of the book there is no doubt in it, is from the Lord of the worlds" (Sura 32:1, 2). Allah says to Muhammad in the same above Sura (32:23): "And We indeed gave Moses the Book — so doubt not the meeting with Him — and We made it a guide for the Children of Israel. (If Moses' rod and book were given as a guide for Israel, and the gospel God gave to Jesus as a guide and warning to the Christians, and the Holy Qur-an to Muhammad for the Arab world, will God give us (the so-called Negroes) a book as a guide for us? Will He bring it or send it? For those books were for other people and not for us.)

IF WE are in the change of the two worlds (Christianity and Islam), then surely we need a "new book" for our guidance; for those books have served the people to whom they were given. But all or both books are guidance for us all. Yet we must have a new book for the "new change"; that which no eye has seen nor ear has heard, nor has entered into our hearts what it is like. We know these books; they have been seen and handled by both the good and no good. Certainly the Holy Qur-an is from the Lord of the worlds, there can be no doubt in the word of Allah (God). But if the book or books have the words of someone else other than Allah's words in it or them, there is no doubt in our hearts concerning the receivings of such book or books!

Hurry and join onto your own kind. The time of this world is at hand.

July 26, 1958

THE BIBLE AND HOLY QUR-AN

THE ORIGINAL scripture called "the Torah" revealed to Musa (Moses) was holy until the Jews and Christian scholars started tampering with it. Today, the Bible has become a "commercialized book" and, therefore, many are allowed to rewrite or revise it. I think when it comes to the word of Allah (God) or a book revealed by Him, that word or book is sacred and should be protected from corruption by the hands of people who care nothing for its sacredness. I will ever repeat; it is like a "rattlesnake" in the hands of my people; for they (most of them) do not understand it.

Some believe in that story of the Bible that the black people are from a curse of Noah on one of his sons (Ham) because this son laughed at his father's nakedness while being drunk from some wine (Genesis 9:21-25) The black nation has no birth record. There were as many or more black people on our planet in the days of Noah as there are today. The Bible's record of the flood is 2,348 years before Christ, and if the records are true, we are nearly 4,500 years from Noah's flood. If there were no black people before Noah, then that wicked people who were destroyed in the flood were white people before Noah, then those of that race, the warning of the destruction of the wicked world by fire the next time is made clearer to whom that fire will destroy.

THE BLACK PEOPLE, and especially the so-called Negroes, are now in the very area where God has said to me that the fire (often referred to as the "fire of hell or hell fire") will begin first which will destroy the present wicked white race of America first. The sins of the white race are far worse and more pungent to the nostril of God than the sins of Sodom and Gomorrah! The fire of hell is not intended for the so-called Negroes; only those who, after hearing this teaching of the truth which I am giving to you and the warnings of Allah (God), will willfully hold on to the white race and its religion, Christianity.

The so-called Negroes are made so poisoned by this wicked race of devils that they even love them more than they love their own people. And, really, it is because of the evil done to them by the American white race that Allah (God) has put them on His list as the first to be destroyed. The others will be given a little longer to live, as the prophet Daniel says (Daniel 7:11, 19 and Rev. 19:20). Believe it or let it alone, the above prophecy refers to America. She is the only white government out of the European race that answers the description of the symbolic Fourth Beast. The so-called Negroes are warned to come out of her (America) (Rev.

18:4), though the truth of Daniel and the Revelation could not be told until the time of the end of this prophecy.

As I have said again and again in these articles, the Bible means good if you can rightly understand it. My interpretation of it is given to me from the Lord of the Worlds. Yours are of your own and from the enemies of the truth. The so-called Negroes will be the lucky ones, that is, if they stop following and practicing the evils and indecent doings of this wicked and doomed race of devils (whose true self has been a secret for 6,000 years).

Negroes, accept your own God, religion and people so that you may be successful in escaping the fire!

Hurry and join onto your own kind. The time of this world is at hand.

August 2, 1958

WE NEED a home that we can call our own! We have no more time to waste on our problem. We know our problem and we know the solution to our problem. Now let us solve it! We have wasted too much time arguing with each other over that which keeps us slaves to the same slave master. There may be one party trying to defend the slave master's evil and deceitful doings to us, while the other party (the Muslims) is trying to defend our cause for the whole entire so-called Negro population in America. This means that we need some of this earth. This is the only solution to our problem in this country claimed and owned by our enemies (the white slave masters).

Study our problem for yourself, and if you arrive at a better solution than God and myself, write it and send it to me. Why should not we who number seventeen million in America have some of this earth that we can call our own and for our children's as other nations have for themselves? After spending 300 years as servitude slaves and nearly 100 years as free slaves (to make you feel better you are called "Second Class Citizens"), you still get about as much justice as a herd of sheep among a pack of hungry wolves!

THE HATRED of the white race for us, the so-called Negroes, is easily seen in their eyes and actions. There is no hope for sincere friendship with our slave masters and especially after God has given to us the knowledge of them to be the real devils! Even if we would take them for friends, could we have friendship with God and the devils at the same time? **NO**, and that you and I know Allah (God) has made known to me the truth and His purpose. It is up to you and me to believe it, or go on believing as we always have until we meet with that which is certain!

Since being free slaves in the land of our enemies, there is no future for us and our children in this people, nor hope of ever owning any of this good earth here as a home. The white race, as we know them, will never agree to divide America with us, though our blood is spilled on this soil and on foreign soil for the freedom of white Americans and their European friends.

Yet we are born here but not wanted as residents in their neighborhood. To show how much they hate and dislike us, the so-called Negroes, as soon as we move in, they move out (that is, if their law enforcement agents will not let them brickbat and shoot us out!) Yet we fight and die and kill whoever they call their enemies in order that they may live and be free to kill us here in America, while we continue to live in trouble and in fear of being killed by them day and night.

We are kicked around, "dogged" at, called all kinds of evil, nasty, disgraceful names (even after calling us by their own names). They run around with our women and break up our homes (at least the place where we are temporarily stopping until they say: "Move out, n----r.") even though they killed our people (the Indians) in order to possess the country for themselves.

SINCE OUR status in it is that of a free slave, why should we longer remain among them receiving headaches and heart aches trying to get along with them in peace, with no future for our ever-increasing population upon a land that is not our own? Do we not as men love a future for our own children, as they (the enemies) love for their children? If so, let we stop wasting our time disagreeing with each other over the white man's Christianity which has brought us into their hands as helpless sheep to hungry wolves! Such has caused us to be unrecognized, and unwanted by even our own kind. They have made us to hate our own selves and kind, and love them and their kind, our open enemies.

How long will we be the world's fools? How much longer shall we go from city to city and state to state in America (the land of our enemies) seeking to slave for them instead of seeking a permanent piece of this earth that we can call our own, and where we can live in peace and not in fear of being evicted?

Follow me and your God and my God. Allah will give us such a place as He has promised; and believe me, Allah fulfills His promises - unlike the devils who make promises only to deceive you. I desperately plead with you for your own sake and the sake of the future for yourself and your children.

Hurry and join onto your own kind. The time of this world is at hand.

August 9, 1958

WE MUST HAVE SOME OF THIS GOOD EARTH THAT WE CAN CALL OUR OWN!

WE ARE 17,000,000 so-called Negroes a hundred years up from slavery without a home that we can call our own; fighting everyone all over the earth whom the white man calls his enemy to keep the white man's home secure (for him and his white European brothers). Many of the so-called Negroes are out of jobs and out-of-doors. They are without security whatsoever and yet are satisfied to be called an American Negro. Our women work in the homes and offices of the slave masters - subject to the will of our enemies who have spotted us like a leopard - and, our foolish women, because of their lack of knowledge like it.

It is time for us to secure a home and put our women who are disgracing us with these devils, into it; and keep her there for yourself, if it costs her and your lives to do so. You are begging and licking the white man's "boots" for them to smile and pat you on the back. It is said that we are foolish enough to spend an average of $16,000,000,000 annually with these people who keep us from freedom, justice, and equality. We are a race of bums walking and hitch hiking from city to city and state to state seeking a job, love, and friendship of the murderers and disgracers of our nation.

PUT YOUR BRAINS to thinking for self; your feet to walking in the direction of self; your hands to working for self and your children; and fight like "hell" with those who fight like "hell" against you and the world of mankind will respect us as their equals! Stop begging for what others have and help yourself to some of this good earth where you can produce something for self like other nations. Actually, there are no jobs that the white man has for you that he, his people, and machines cannot do. That is why you and I should start trying to make jobs for ourselves.

If our leaders do not like to go along with us, then leave them and see which one will suffer the most - you or the leaders. We have been too good a servant for 400 years for these white slave masters of ours. We have, among us, men and women who can do almost anything that we want done; but at present, they are doing it for our slave masters. Why should we not utilize our brains for self? This all can be done overnight if we stop putting frightened leaders into office to lead a race (the so-called Negroes) who were born with fear of the slave masters?

The God of heaven and earth is on our side. Why should we be anyone's free slaves? The preachers like you like that, for they too can get more money out of a fool than out of the wise. Do not "sweetheart" with white people, your open enemies, for their "sweet hearting" with you is not sincere today any more than it was in the days of George Washington. We must go for ourselves for a home. This calls for the unity of us all to accomplish it!

God is with us to do it. Why not unite and do it? It is impossible to do it in the white man's church and religion. Come and follow me! Allah will give it to you.

Our friendship with self and kind today is number one important regardless to what the white race thinks of us. (That is the way they are doing). Fear no one but Allah, and come follow me and live in heaven here!

Hurry and join onto your own kind. The time of this world is at hand.

WE MUST HAVE SOME OF THIS GOOD EARTH
THAT WE CAN CALL OUR OWN

STOP WASTING your money! Your money was not given to you, so why should you give it away for that which you can do without? If you and I would do just that, we could save millions of dollars which we could put into education, the purchasing of land, machines, poultry, milk, cows, beef cattle, sheep, machines to cultivate the land, to cut and saw timber to build homes for yourselves, dig for mud to mould and burn into bricks for your own homes and factories, and make your own cotton and wool clothes which you wear. Feed your own stomach and hire your own scientists from among yourselves. Produce and make that which we need to save our people from want before it is too late!

HOW CAN we begin? Stop spending money for tobacco, dope, cigarettes, whiskey, wine, beer, fine clothes, fine automobiles, fine furniture, expensive rugs and carpets, gambling, prostitution, idleness, sport and play, games of chance and horse racing.

Stop careless spending of money, living on credit loans at a high interest (which means selling yourselves to slave for the loan sharks). Stop going into stores seeking the highest priced merchandise to purchase. Buy according to your means (your income). If you income is only $75 or $100 per week, and your rent is about the same every month, and food about the same price, and you have clothes, transportation and other little bills to pay, can you then afford a high-priced car note of a $100 or $145 per month? If you must have a car, buy the low-priced car, or a rich man's used car, and not his used Cadillacs and Rolls Royces. I hope that you will begin leaving off the use of these things which you do not need to buy.

And, for your health's sake, stop eating the swine's flesh (the animal that was grafted from cat, rat and dog for medical purposes, and said to be 999 per cent poison!). Live like a civilized person and we will soon be able to say that we are living like civilized people along with love and unity in the name of your God and religion, Islam.

IF YOU will write to the public relations department, Muhammad's Temple 2, Illinois, we will send you information on how we can help build a great future for the so-called Negroes in America, by just sacrificing the money that we throw away to destroy our health in cigarettes, beer, wine, hog and whiskey for one week out of each month!

God does not like for us to break His law by eating the swine's flesh, drinking intoxicating drinks, and the using of the poison tobacco weed. We must have a better future for ourselves and our children. Stop wasting and spending your money with the rich and spend it with the poor of our kind. Stop walking past your own black brother's business to buy the merchandise of the rich just because the rich can sell at a lower price than your poor brother. Trade with your own kind until you can grow up equal with other than your kind.

Hurry and join onto your own kind. The time of this world is at hand.

August 23, 1958

WILL THE WHITE CHRISTIANS ACCEPT ISLAM?

WE HAVE thousands of the darker people joining Islam all over the earth, but a very few whites accept Islam. The door of Islam has never been open to everyone who desired to accept it, but today it is different. The door of this religion is now being closed against the white race who has repeatedly rejected Islam, makes mockery of it, persecuted and killed the Prophets and the Believers (the followers), hid and concealed the truth of it, and its God, Allah, who is the God of the Universe, and Islam, His only religion. They follow the poor teacher of Islam seeking a way or an excuse to kill him. They put spies (stool pigeons) on him to try to find a way to charge him with something other than the truth in order to do him evil for he truth's sake that he teaches.

As David says in his Psalms 94:20, "Shall the throne of iniquity have fellowship with thee, which frameth mischief by a law?" The poor lost-found members of the Tribe of Shabazz (nicknamed "Negroes" by their slave masters) can well understand that they are the victims of such frame up against them throughout America when they seek truth, love and unity among themselves. The white race does not want to see the poor Black People of America unite in Islam, a religion that is of Allah (God) backed by the spirit and power of God to unite all of its believers into one Nation of Brotherhood. It is the only unifying religion known and tried by the Races and Nations of Earth. This the white race knows.

THEY WERE offered Islam by Musa (Moses), Jesus, Muhammad and many other Prophets, but they rejected it period. "And certainly we raised in every Nation an Apostle saying serve Allah and shun the devil. So there were some Allah guided and there were others against whom error was due; therefore, travel in the land, then see what was the end of the rejecters." (Holy Qur-an 16:36). The prophets had delivered to them the message of truth and shown them the right way; they choose to remain in error (evil doings). This stands true of this people today. They know the truth, and right from wrong, but they like wrong or evil better than right; therefore, they are against Islam and its truth. The Holy Qur-an says:

"Surely we have revealed to you as we revealed to Noah and the Prophets after him and we revealed to Abraham and Ishmael and the Tribes, and Jesus, Job and Jonah, Aaron, Solomon and we gave to David a scripture. We sent Apostles as the givers of good news and as warners, so that people should not have a plea against Allah after the coming of the Apostles." (Holy Qur-an 4:163, 165.) The Messengers of Allah (God) bring good news to the people, but if that good news is rejected, therefore, they are warned that bad news will come.

The Christian White World, whose leader and teacher is the Pope of Rome (the Father of the Church) claims that Jesus brought a new religion to them. But the scripture of both Bible and Holy Qur-an denies such false charge and makes Jesus' religion the same as the Prophets who were before him. Muhammad was also given the same religion of Jesus and the Prophets before him.

The Holy Qur-an further says: "Surely those who believe and those who are Jews, and the Christians, and the Sabians, whoever believes in Allah and the last day and goes, they shall have their reward from their Lord, and there is no fear for them, nor shall they grieve." (2:62) The religion of Islam is everything that we need for salvation. The poor black man is waking up to this truth and is coming into Islam by the thousands, against the wishes of the whites, because of the love and unity and universal friendship which Islam brings to the believers. This is what the poor black man of America needs more of all - TRUE FRIENDS! He gets them in Islam! The white race has and still is trying to keep us from having true friends among our own kind or even among ourselves here in America. Because of the truth of Islam, their now charging that it fans hate against them (smile).

Hurry and join onto your own kind. The time of this world is at hand.

August 30, 1958

ADAM AND EVE (the father and mother of the white race - Yakub is the real name) refused the religion of Islam (peace) because of the nature in which they were made. This makes it impossible for the white race to submit to Allah and obey His Law of Righteousness. This, the lost-found members of the Asiatic Nation from the Tribe of Shabazz must learn of the white race - that it is a waste of time to seek mercy and justice from a people who by nature do not have it for each other. They talk and preach the goodness of God and His Prophets only to deceive you, who by nature are of the God of Righteousness, into following them away from our God to a God who does not exist.

Our future is at stake, and 99 per cent of us do not know it. With ever-evil snoopers around you seeking an excuse to do their worst to you makes it hard for the 99 per cent ignorant to ever know the truth. Their greatest desire is to prevent you from ever accepting the truth. They claim the truth to be subversive and hate teachings. They seek any kind of charge to place against us to get revenge for our preaching the truth. They tap our telephones, eavesdrop, and follow us around from place to place; use tape recording machines and the hypocrites and stool pigeons from among us to keep them up to date on what we say and do. They are bold enough to even ask your own relative to help them to do you evil; and due to fear and ignorance on the part of my poor people, the enemies hire them to destroy themselves. Truth hurts the guilty. Will persecuting and murdering the truth-bearer help the evildoers in this late hour of the day (the end of their time)?

OUR PROBLEM must be solved, saith Allah, the God of Righteousness, Who is with you and me to raise up us, the poor lost and found members of the Original Owners of the Planet Earth (the Tribe of Shabazz). A good solution is as follows:

1. Stop opposing the spread of Islam (Peace) among us. Leave us to go back to our God, Allah, and our religion of Islam (Peace). Since you will not give us (the so-called Negroes) equal justice, and do not want social mixing with your free slaves because of degrading and lowering your own status in the eyes of the world, help us to go for ourselves, either out or in your country.

For 400 years we have served you with our labor, sweat and blood, the lash of your whip, your killings, lynching and burning of our innocent black flesh, without even a hearing in a Court of Justice, nor even our murderers being punished. Although we are marched before your enemies and there we pour out our lives for the freedom of your lives, children and your country, we return home to meet an even worst enemy. We are hated and kicked out in certain places like an "unwanted dog" who has caught the game, but was not given a taste of it (only that which the hunter could not and should not eat himself). The dog being too ignorant to recognize the injustice done to him by his master will jump to his feet again at the call of his master to offer his life for his master's life. This we have and still are doing for you.

WE ARE NOT wanted in your better neighborhoods, in many places we have to be guarded and protected by your armed forces in order to live in a house which one of your kind has sold to us. Yet, we are the most peaceful and humblest of the population. We are taxed equally, and perhaps more than those of your own kind, who are the real citizens and owners of this country, America, though our labor and the labor of our fathers made and built it for you.

Think it over - millions of us working, fighting and dying at your hand and others for 400 years without a home which we can still call our own - not being allowed to worship our God, religion, nor have unity among self and our kind without being charged with the worst of crimes: Subversiveness, sedition, treason and seeking to overthrow the Government by force (though we have no arms to do such) just to have an excuse for your persecuting and seeking to kill the same poor 400 year old slave.

Continued next week - "We must have a peaceful home to live in on this earth, here or there."

Hurry and join onto your own kind. The time of this world is at hand.

S e p t e m b e r   6 ,   1 9 5 8

SEPARATION SOLVES THE PROBLEM

THERE is no doubt that we are living in the time of universal separation of black and white. You probably would not like to hear or talk about it. This is due to your ignorance of the time, people and the divine plans of Allah (God). The wise and alert people of yours have knowledge of it, but do not like to talk of it because of the love they have for the present world. The poor ignorant have no knowledge of it, and care less as long as he or she is given the crumbs. It is not your will or power which is bringing it about, but it is the will and power of Allah (God) as foretold by His prophets from Moses to Muhammad.

How many of my own people, the lost-found members of the Asiatic nation (the so-called Negroes), know that this is the Bible's judgment of this world and that the divine truth of Allah (God) is that which separates the righteous from the wicked? You may ask, "Who are the wicked." The wicked are the people who were created wicked by nature (the Caucasian race), whose limited time and number are 6,000 years. They have many followers of all the races of earth - black, brown, yellow and red - but this does not mean that the black nation's family (races) is wicked by nature. They are the righteous by nature who are the real original people and owners of the earth.

THE WHITE of Caucasian (European) race is known to God and His prophets as Satan, the devil, the great enemy of Good, God, and His people (the original nation). It was given to them the power to rule (over-lord the earth) the darker nation under evil and falsehood for 6,000 years. This they have done and are now 44 years over time. (This they know.) It will take a few years to complete the separation but, nevertheless, the work is going on now at a very good rate of speed.

Search the history of these people. The two have never been able to live in peace together. The white race is, as the Bible says of them, under the symbol of a troubled sea (Isa. 57:20), never at peace, and are haters of truth and right doings. The so-called Negroes know them and their evil doings better than any people, but being without a teacher of their own kind for the past 400 years, they have become such lovers and great admirers of the devils and their evil doings that they do not want to be separated. That is why the problem is so hard to solve (though the work will be done, regardless of whom or what).

WE NOW NUMBER seventeen million here in America without a home of our own, and a true friend, unless it be Allah. The wicked must be punished for their wickedness poured upon us without ever being hindered. This country is large enough to separate the two (black and white) and they both live here, but that would not be successful. The best solution is for everyone to go to his own people and country. We, the so-called Negroes, have both a great nation to go to and a great country. Allah (God) has come to start us all to going. The native home of the white race is Europe. It is up to you and me to obey the word of Allah (God) or obey your own desire.

For the sake of saving your own blood and flesh from the destruction of this evil, murderous race of devils, who are ever seeking an excuse to take your innocent lives, and cut you off from good; ever around and in your homes after your girls and women to make you like a spotted leopard among your nation, you must join onto your own kind. You may hate me now, but one day you will love me.

Think it over. Why should we believe in their religion? Why should we be called by our enemies' names who enslaved our parents and will not give us equal justice in the courts, since we are free to choose our own people's names? Why should we continue to make fools of ourselves and our children begging them to accept us as their people when we have a great nation to turn to?

Hurry and join onto you own kind. The time of this world is at hand.

ROBBED AND SPOILED (ISAIAH 42:22)

SEVENTEEN million so-called American Negroes - the lost-found members of the Tribe of Shabazz, the original black nation of the earth - have been so successfully robbed and spoiled that today they do not know that they have been robbed, and now do not recognize their loss even when it is offered to them. They even prey upon each other. They are ever ready to help someone who should be helping them. They will open their purses to all of the independent of earth while dependent slaves, themselves, and will give without even asking for a receipt.

Just say, "Africa needs help" and you will see their dollars poured into the hands of a collector without even questioning the sincerity of the collector nor demanding to see a receipt from Africa showing the amount of money or charity given. This makes it so easy for the robbers of our people to rob you.

MILLIONS OF pennies are given in churches every week throughout the so-called Negroes' churches for foreign mission work in Africa. How do you know that these pennies are going for foreign mission work in Africa? There are some now giving their money to help Ghana's independence. Is the Government of Ghana sending you a receipt by the secretary of that state saying "Thanks" to you, that they received your gift; or do those whom you give it to here receive one from over there? Has Africa ever sent you any help for the past 400 years? The Prime Minister of Ghana was here visiting a few days ago, and we have not heard him asking private people for anything.

It would be a shame on the part of any independent nation's government to come here begging for help from the so-called Negroes whose status is that of free slaves - the most foolish of all people on earth. No one gives you nor seeks you. As Isaiah says of you (42:22): "They are for a prey, and none delivered; for a spoil, and none saith restore." But yet you are willing to help restore all except your own self here in America. Why not awaken to the knowledge of the robbers? If you have extra money to send abroad, why not use it on SELF and your people here in

America, for a good home on this good earth where they can live in peace without being afraid that someone will say, "Move over, this is a white man's country."

YOU ARE PICKED up off the streets in the South, beaten or shot by a mob of devils without even making any attempt for justice. None pity you, nor do you pity yourself. Nevertheless, you are foolish enough to have pity for those who beat and kill you. Have you any sense at all? First, help yourself and then if you are able, help others if you want to.

It is written and is proven that God helps those who help themselves. Let us first help ourselves to be free and independent with the help of Almighty God Allah, who has come to free us from our tormentors. Accept Him and the good religion Islam that makes true friendship with God and the righteous. Do not be satisfied with empty promises. Let us have some earth and PEACE on it.

The day has arrived that you will have to help yourself or suffer the worst! Unite and get some of this earth for a home like other nations.

Hurry and join onto your own kind. The time of this world is at hand.

September 20, 1958

ROBBED AND SPOILED (Isaiah 42:22)

(Continued from last week)

"THEY are all of them snared in holes, and they are hid in prison houses: they are for a prey, and none delivereth for a spoil, and none saith restore."

If my people's condition, or rather history, in America is not the answer to the above saying of Isaiah, then try to find the answer to it elsewhere. Our fathers were brought here as merchandise to be sold on the slave market. Some, according to the white man's own written history of that account, were brought in physical chains to be chained again mentally for 400 years and they are still mentally chained. They are still being beaten and killed out of any law of justice for them.

The white murderer's word is heard and believed by his brother murderer in the office and sent of justice. The poor black man - his master's most loyal and faithful slave - his word is not heard. They are afraid of an arresting officer taking them under arrest for fear of being mercilessly beaten; skull and face bashed in or shot outright, and the white brother says: "What is it to kill a d--- Negro." They are outright murderers clothed with authority to mistreat and kill my poor black people whom they have been murdering all of their lives for the past 400 years. Even when their own people (black) are put in authority and arrive on the scene with a gun and club, they will in many cases prove to be even worse and more quick to beat and kill their own people than the white officer. This, they do, to be befriended by the white.

"ROBBED AND SPOILED": They are pitiful - robbed by all - no not even spared by their priests (church preachers) Luke 10:32. The same robbers rob them of their own women; disgrace and corrupt them with all kinds of diseases besides spotting up her children like the animal family. They are robbed so completely that now, after 400 years, they love the robbers of themselves and their kind. After being completely robbed of the knowledge of their God, religion and people, they now are a prey in the hands of all first-rate robbers of all races and people.

Our open enemies, the devils, are now using every trick-knowledge on my people after hearing of the Truth (Islam) among us to take them (black people) to hell with them. There never was and never will be true friendship between white and black people regardless to what you try doing to bring it about. Nothing will bring peace between the two but SEPARATION of them.

America has and still is inflicting the worst kind of evil on the darker people of this country; and, she is and will continue to pay a dear price for it. Any so-called Negro who attempts to try to help his people, America seeks some way to hinder him or have him murdered outright. They are now playing clever tricks on all whom they do not like, such as investigations of income taxes or making a law that will declare that man a seditionist.

NO NEGRO WANTS to be trapped in the evil clutches of the devils' tricks, therefore the poor Negroes are a prey: "And none delivereth for a spoil and none saith restore." They are without a home that they can call their own. If they would believe in Allah (God) and His religion of Islam and come follow me, Allah (God) would give them the whole Planet Earth to rule forever; but, they believe not in Allah, the Great God of the Universe, and will surely suffer loss of life for their rejection.

REMEMBER: God is not to come, but has already come; and He will not be mocked. He came forth for the deliverance of His people (the so-called Negroes). He will whip you into submission and cause evil to continue to come upon the land and people until you are all destroyed. Do not look for Peace as long as there is no JUSTICE for the poor so-called Negroes. I plead with you, my people, to separate yourselves from a people whose doom is now at their door.

Hurry and join onto your own kind. The time of this world is at hand.

DISAGREEABLE TO LIVE WITH IN PEACE

ALLAH (God) is making manifest the real devil (the Caucasian race) and that we, the black nation (which includes in color - black, brown, yellow and red) cannot get along with them in peace. Let the students of history study the history of the Caucasian race from the time that they came into power up to the present time, and you will agree with God that you cannot get along with them in peace, for they are not at peace with themselves. How can a peace-breaker set up peace for others?

The only time in their history showing that they were not warring among themselves and making trouble among our people (the darker nation) is the 2,000 years before the birth of Moses when they were living in the caves and hillsides on the continent which is now called Europe. The only reason why they did not make trouble with us then was due to the fact that they had been deprived of civilization and were living like wild beasts - which was a curse put upon them for their troublemaking among us in the same area (the near East) where they are now making trouble.

THE POOR so-called Negroes have 400 years of experience living under and with the America white race and I may add that these so-called Negroes are owned by the white race until they have been redeemed by Allah (God) and united again onto their own nation and country. Until they are given up to let go to their own people and country, the entire World of Mankind will never have peace. Believe it or not, even the Kingdom of Heaven cannot come to the righteous until the so-called Negroes have been separated from their slave masters and given a home on this earth, which rightly belongs to them and their kind. They need a home where they can live in peace without the fear of their enemies beating and killing them night and day, without any justice whatsoever.

We are hated and despised by these same slave masters' children today as their fathers did in the past. The poor blind, deaf and dumb slaves still seek their hateful murderous slave masters to have mercy on them and accept them as their brothers and sisters. It is really a shame to see my poor people so dumb, kicked and beaten like dogs by the white race all of their lives, and still begging them to treat them like a brother treats a brother.

THE WHITE race has proved to you all of their lives that they do not want you as their equal. Why not be intelligent enough to seek freedom, justice and equality among your own kind which by far outnumbers the white race on our planet earth - (Though we have seven more inhabited planets, but there is not one of this race on them and there will never be one on them!) The white race of America charges me with teaching hatred of them (of course, I would like to know who taught them to hate us) but my teaching is making a far better people to live here than they have been able to make with the gun, whip and their Christianity and worship of a dead God that cannot answer his own call.

If you (the so-called Negroes) were trying as hard to get the white slave master to see that you need to be separated and given some of this earth for a home for yourself and your children to live alone to yourselves, or asking them to help you to return to your own native land and people, I am sure that they would listen to you and probably would help you to accomplish such desire - instead of wasting the taxpayers' money on an Army to keep their brothers from killing you for trying to force them to recognize you as they do their own kind.

ALTHOUGH THE time of the white race now is up, by acting wisely, they can and might get more extension of time, for they are now 44 years over their time. You cannot live with them in peace, so let us have some of this good earth for our hated and despised people that they can call their own, and let the white man have his own! This will end the disagreement between the two races and hatred of each other forever.

Hurry and join onto your own kind. The time of this world is at hand.

CHRISTIANS' DEVIATION FROM THE TRUTH

"O MESSENGER, deliver that which has been revealed to thee from thy Lord. If thou do it not, then thou hast not delivered His message, and Allah will protect thee from men. Surely Allah guides not the disbelieving." (Holy Qur-an 5:67)

The past histories of Prophets and their followers, their enemies and disbelievers, as well as deadly hypocrites mixed with true believers, is a sufficient answer to the above teachings of the Holy Qur-an. When the Divine Truth is sent to a people who believe in falsehood and love evil and evildoers, that truth and the truth bearer (the Messenger) is always rejected, mocked, and opposed. The disbelievers of today are the same as those who lived 6,000 years ago. They do not change. That is why they are so easy to be distinguished from a true believer. They would like for the Divine Messenger to deliver their message in part - that is, leave out that part which condemns them of being the enemies of God and the truth, of which God is the Author.

IT IS INCUMBENT upon a Divine Messenger of God to deliver the Message that God gives him to deliver, regardless to what the Message may be; otherwise, he would not be the Messenger of God, he would be the people's messenger. The **FEAR** of the American white race (devils) by our people (which was put into them while slaves when they were babies) will probably cause them to lose their lives in the divine destruction of the devils (Hosea 4:6). I have been continually delivering to you for many years that which Allah (God) has revealed to me of the truth - that you are in love with the devils, bowing, worshipping and fearing them. You should fear Allah, and Him only should you serve.

Because of your fear of them and your desire for worldly honor and certain privileges, you keep yourselves and your blinded, deaf and dumb leaders suffering from the lack of knowledge of self, God, and the devils. Regardless to your love and belief in the devils, they still prove to you that they are devils and have no love for you but to beat, kill and disgrace you. What the so-called Negroes need to do is to unite and accept Allah and the true religion of God and our people. There you will have millions of friends who are not afraid of world's devils; though Allah alone is sufficient for us. As the Holy Qur-an teaches you: "Only Allah is your friend and His Messenger and those who believe (the Muslims)." (5:55).

THE DIVINE MESSENGERS love their people and work and try and save them after God has revealed to them His intention to destroy them for their evil and unbelief. The devils have deceived not only you concerning the true God Allah, and the true religion, Islam, but they have deceived the whole world (nine-tenths). There are some who want to be called Jews, and others Christians, and you are not either one. All of these religions belong to the Caucasian race. "O you, who believe, take not the Jews and Christians for friends; they are friends of each other. And whoever amongst you, take them for friends, he is indeed one of them. Surely Allah guides not the unjust people." (Holy Qur-an 5:51).

You feel that friendship with them (the devils) is exalting you to high degree of respect and protection, but there is no protection against Allah. "O, people of the Book (the Bible) do you find fault with us for aught, except that we believe in Allah and in that which has been revealed before while most of you are transgressors?" (Holy Qur-an 5:59). Christians of America are surely guilty of speaking evil and making mockery of the Muslims. They will soon regret it and wish that they were Muslims!

We need some of this earth that we can live on in peace away and out of the midst of our enemies who have robbed spoiled, and disgraced us for 400 years. We are 17 million helpless, free slaves without justice, surrounded night and day by the devils who are seeking an excuse to do us harm. Let us forsake them and their religion and return to our God, His religion, and our people.

Hurry and join unto your own kind. The time of this world is at hand.

WE MUST HAVE A HOME

SEVENTEEN million so-called American Negroes must have a home that they can call their own. That home must not be a graveyard, nor in the open space (the Sky). No, it must be on this earth and while we live! Our 400 years as a slave for the white slave masters of America are sufficient for the price of a home for each and every one of the Black Slaves and their Children in America. You really need it and I am your brother to help get it for you at any price.

We are tired of being frowned upon, kicked out of the homes and societies of the Nations because of being (Black Negroes): ignorance, indecency, drunkards, dope addicts, and great fool lovers for our enemies (the white race) who enslaved us, disgraced us, made us drunkards, gamblers, and murderers of our own kind. They made us thieves and robbers of each other as they are haters, and dislikers of being members of the darker nation, and haters of our own God Allah and His religion of Islam (Peace). We fear them as we should fear Almighty God Allah.

THEY POURED into our hearts a belief in a God that does not even exist and prayer to a dead prophet (Jesus) who cannot help us against the slave masters' children, ever robbing, beating, killing, raping, disgracing us and our women. All of this we suffer at the hands of these devils daily. Should not we have a home of our own on this earth that our father created for you and me to live happy on? But for the fear of them (the Slave Masters) you even now think that you are all right. How can we be satisfied as free Slaves without a Country of our own, and without Justice in our white slave masters' courts, in a large country where our fathers' and selves' labor has been given free to build one of the richest and most powerful governments that the white race ever had and ever will have on this earth? Yet, after one hundred years of the so-called freedom, you are still without a home and the slave masters have not offered you one; not even in the worst part of this country, though our labor and our poor fathers' labor before us helped make America what it is.

WE HAVE NOT been given anything but hell in return for 400 years of hard labor, sweat and blood, without Justice. We are not wanted in their Society and are hunted like rabbits all over the Country to do us harm. They seek to kill off all our leaders if they attempt to teach and lead us into our Own. They have poisoned the so-called Negro preachers' minds under Christianity to help them against any Negro leader whom they do not like. The poor black preachers, full of fear of the white Slave Masters, have become the worst and the Cheapest Class of leaders for their people on earth. All so-called Negroes should refuse to follow and support such false and cowardly leadership which obeys and follows our enemies and not our God and His prophets. They all are satisfied if they can get just enough followers and a Church to keep them from working; and if they try helping the masses, it will only be in the way of making you a more permanent slave to the devils.

They are so afraid of bringing the white man's dislike against them if they dare come near to us (Muslims) and Allah's (God) only true religion Islam, that if they rent you their Church to teach Islam in, they themselves will not come into the meeting but a few, and will warn their followers to stay out. Poor things turning down their own Salvation for the friendship of our open enemies.

Hurry and join onto your own kind. The time of this world is at hand.

October 18, 1958

THE SO-CALLED NEGRO PREACHERS, WILL THEY ACCEPT ISLAM?

THE ABOVE question is asked daily by the new converts to Islam. The answer is "Yes." But when? There are a few of them who already have accepted Islam and are proving to be worthy and sincere believers.

Some formerly were pastoring churches and now are preaching the religion of Islam and making many converts. It is my greatest desire that they continue to preach, but preach the religion of Islam, which is the True Religion of God, His prophets, and His people. Islam is the religion that is in the right state, the nature in which He has made us; therefore, surely by nature, (what) we find in the religion of Islam (is) over all other religions when once we know what Islam is.

Most preachers have not even heard of any religion by such name (Islam) and, therefore, cannot be called disbelievers when they have no knowledge of that which they disbelieve. But to disbelieve after knowledge of the truth, God holds us responsible for our disbelief, or if we willfully and knowingly reject the truth for friendship or certain privileges among disbelievers and infidels, we bring upon ourselves the chastisement of God, the Author of Truth.

Of course, naturally, a disbeliever never believes that which he disbelieves in to have any power against him for his disbelief. This is the mistake that they make. I would say at the present time, there is not more than one so-called Negro preacher out of a hundred who has any knowledge of the religion of Islam. They never have studied any religion other than Christianity, and have not learned Christianity. Since they are taught, trained and licensed by their slave master's children (the open enemy of Black Man), naturally they believe only that which they have been taught.

PHAROAH'S magicians once believed in him and in whatever he believed in, but after a showdown with Moses, the servant of God, they became believers in the God of Moses. So will the present Christian preachers believe after they have seen a little more of the power of Allah. They are a little too wise to have a show-down with Allah and Elijah, His servant, because they are not too sure of the truth of that which they are trying to uphold.

There are two things which hold the preachers back from accepting Islam. They are: 1. FEAR of the white man. 2. Ignorance of Islam. Therefore, the above-mentioned makes them enemies of Allah (God), his Messengers, and His religion, Islam, and they will seek to do much harm to the cause of Islam, the true religion, and the Muslims (believers). But they, too, will accept Islam one of these days when they are convinced that their efforts to oppose Islam are useless.

THEY SHOULD read those scriptures which prophesy of their opposition to the truth in these days. As Jesus said of them (Matt. 23:13) they stay away from Islam, their salvation and hinder others who are trying to enter from entering. At the present time, they are one hundred per cent the friends of our enemies and are open opposers of the truth, Islam, the religion of God and His Prophets. So beware of them!

Let us ask the preachers a few questions:

1. - Who was Adam? Who are the Adamic people? If Adam is the father of the white race, who is our father?

2. - Did God give Adam a religion or religious guides and rules how to serve and obey Him?

3. - When and by whom did Adam receive religious teachings? What was it called?

4. - Surely if Adam was white, should not all of his descendants be white?

5. - If the Adamic people are doomed for total destruction, what people and religion will rule after them?

6. - Who is the second Adam and people that the Bible makes mention of that shall live?

7. - Do you believe that we are the Bible's (symbolic) lost and found sheep?

8. - Will you discuss Christianity and Islam with me in an open or private meeting?

Hurry and join onto your own kind. The time of this world is at hand.

October 25, 1958

THE FINAL WAR

THE CHRISTIAN world cannot win a war against the Son of Man (God in person), with outer space weapons or inner space. It does not matter, for He has power over everything - the forces of nature and even over our brains. He turns them to thinking and doing that which pleases Him. The great waste of money to build your defense against Him or the

World War III is useless. You do not need navies, ground forces, air forces, or standing armies to fight this last war. What America needs to win with is: Freedom and equal justice to her slaves (the so-called Negroes). This injustice to her slaves is the real cause of this final war. Give them up to return to their own, or divide the country that you took from their people (the Red Indians) which they have helped you to build up and maintain with their sweat and blood for 400 years. They even give all of their brain power to you. They help you kill anyone that you say is your enemy; even if it is their own brother or your own brother. What have you given us for 400 years of labor and lives?

IS IT JUST a job to labor for you? You hunt us and shoot us down like wild game; burn us, castrate us, and we are counted as sheep for the slaughter - (all who seek justice). You have continuously persecuted me and my poor followers for 25 years. Both fathers and sons are sent to prison. Just because we believe in justice and equality, and teach our brethren the same, we are imprisoned from one to five years, and forced to eat the essence of the poison and divinely prohibited flesh of the filthy swine in our food, to your joy.

You set your agents around our meeting places where we are trying to serve our God, the God of our Fathers, to frighten our poor, blind, deaf and dumb people away from hearing and believing the truth. With 48 states, which equal approximately six million square miles; with billions of dollars in gold buried and rusting - (which we helped to get for you, yet none is ours) not the tiniest nor the most worthless state of yours have you offered your loyal slaves. Not even to one square mile for their 400 years of labor and lives. And today, we still are without justice even in your Supreme Court.

SHALL YOU be the winner in a third world war? The god of justice forbid! The great Mahdi shall be the winner. He is on our side (the so-called Negroes) to free us from you, our killers. As it is written: "Shall the prey (the Negroes) be taken from the mighty or the lawful captives delivered? But thus, saith the Lord, even the captives of the mighty shall be taken away and the prey of the terrible shall be delivered; for I will contend with him that contendeth with thee. I will feed them that oppress thee with their own flesh; and they shall be drunken with their own blood. As with sweet wine, and all flesh shall know that I, the Lord, am thy Saviour and thy Redeemer" (Isaiah 9:24-26).

We, the so-called Negroes, are the prey. Thou are the Mighty, the Terrible One. Thanks to Allah, the Greatest, who is with us to save and deliver us. His people - seventeen million members of the tribe of Shabazz - who must have some of this earth that we can call our own. Our God will give it to us. But woe unto you, for the Son of Man shall destroy thee and give the kingdom to slave. He is not to come. He is here! Believe it or not. I seek refuge in Him from your evil plannings.

WHITE CHRISTIAN America has been so busy trying to keep her slaves (the so-called Negroes) under her foot from knowing the truth by sitting, watching and spying on them to prevent them from knowing the truth of this day of our salvation, until she has failed to see and learn the strength and power of her enemies. She has boasted that she could police the world and has come pretty near doing so, but failed to see the "Bear" behind the tree and the "Lion" in the thicket. The sky over her is being filled with her enemies' arms which can be seen with the naked eye. Her scientists are troubled and at their wits' end to find time to make ready, as it is written: (Ezekiel 21:15) "I have set the point of the sword against all their gates; that their hearts may faint, and their ruins be multiplied; ah! It is made bright. It is wrapped up for the slaughter." **Answer:** "For the tidings: because it cometh; and every heart shall melt, and all hands shall be feeble, and every spirit shall faint, and all knees shall be weak as water" (Ezekiel 21:7).

The Holy Qur-an: (45:28, 29) - "And you shall see every nation kneeling down. Every nation shall be called to its book: today, you shall be rewarded for what you did. This is our book that speaks against you with justice. Surely we wrote what you did."

Hurry and join onto your own kind. The time of this world is at hand.

November 1, 1958

WITHOUT a clear understanding of this final war between right and wrong, my people (the so-called Negroes) will be lost, that the scripture might be fulfilled (destroyed for the lack of knowledge, Hosea 4:6). If

Allah be with me, I do not want to see or hear that you were destroyed in the final war for the lack of knowledge; for Almighty God, Allah, has given to me the truth, and I shall give the same to you. You will believe if you are made to understand the scripture. The devils are the cause of this most dreadful and frightful war, ever to be forced upon the nations of earth, since it was created more than 70 trillion years ago.

I am so interested in the safety of my poor people here in America that I cannot hold my peace. I have seen, I have heard it from His mouth, and He has made me to understand the words of His prophets of old how it began and how it will end. There is no defense for anyone in this final war between Allah (God) and the devils; only in Allah (God) alone will there be a place of refuge.

EVEN THE EARTH itself will shake and tremble and seem as though she is frightened and desire to run away from the heart of the smelting elements that make up the atmosphere over North America. All life and water clouds above shall disappear and will not again appear for 1,000 years; and South America will not escape the effect of that awful and dreadful destruction of her sister, North America. The white race is exceedingly wise; but not wise enough to behave themselves as they should and be satisfied with the great blessings of God. In a large country, and untold wealth, that her peace may be secure. But, how can she cease from making mischief and causing bloodshed when her father was a liar and a murderer (John 8:44)?

My poor people must know these things: That there is no love or mercy for them in this people; and that they stop allowing themselves to be deceived by this arch-deceiver of the world - who is the chief trouble of all people of earth.

It is the purpose of this final war to rid the people of Allah (God) of these troublemakers who delight themselves in making war. These troublemakers beat and slay the innocent so-called Negroes without justice. As it is written concerning them: "Ye have lived in pleasure on the earth, and have wanton; ye have nourished your hearts as in a day of slaughter. Ye have condemned and killed the just; and he doth not resist you" (James 5:5-6). The above prophecy is fulfilled here between the slave master and his slaves (the so-called Negroes).

REGARDLESS of how the devils slaughter and kill the poor so-called Negroes they, like sheep, resist not their murderer for fear of being murdered. If they would come to Allah and submit and believe in Him and His true religion, Islam, they would not fear anymore and would have a "Mighty One" on their side against this blood-thirsty enemy. A God who will answer their prayers when they pray.

This devil has deceived us about the true God. There is nothing to what he has taught us to believe in as God. It naturally does not exist - a spook for a god, and a dead prophet of two thousand years ago, whom they want you to believe is somewhere in heaven, alive. Nothing could be worse, and the people believe it without any proof.

I WOULD LIKE to force and make you prove such false doctrine or suffer the consequence. There is no such thing as a heaven nor hell for one to go to after death. This is one of the first lies Yakub taught his **made devils** to teach to the people (you and me) even to this day. There are millions of people believing such lie. There are two conditions in our life (hell and heaven) not beyond the grave. Death settles it all!

Heaven in the hereafter is real - it is a heaven of peace and plenty of everything of good. The people will always be happy for there will be no devils to make them unhappy; and even that alone will lengthen their lives. **No more war**; for those devils who delight in war will not be there, for there is no discharge in that war (Eccl. 8:8). Never worry over the state of your condition beyond the grave. Worry over it on this side of the grave. Make heaven for it or hell.

Hurry and join onto your own kind. The time of this world is at hand.

November 8, 1958

"WHO IS LIKE UNTO THE BEAST?

WHO IS ABLE TO MAKE WAR WITH HIM?" (REV. 13:4).

This beast that is spoken of in the prophesy of the last Book of the Bible called Revelations has and still is being much misunderstood by my people. But one thing is certain, the name (beast) is believed by most of all readers of the Book to refer to a person or persons, which is right. But who is the person or persons? Note: There is mentioned in the same chapter and verse a dragon which gave power to the beast. Who can this dragon be? Is he also a person? Then how are the two related?

The 18th verse of the same chapter reads: "Here's wisdom, let him that hath understanding count the number of the beast: for it is the number of a man." Here we are told that the number of the beast is that of a man. Then beyond a shadow of doubt, the beast referred to here is a man or people. Now the only way of knowing just what man or people, is to watch and see what man or people's doings or works compare with the doings and works of the symbolic beast of the Revelations.

THIS NAME "beast" when given to a person, refers to that person's characteristics, not an actual beast. Study the history of how America treats the so-called Negroes who were her servitude slaves, and the present denial of freedom, justice and equality which is supposed to be given to all citizens of America (of course, the Negroes are not citizens of America). A citizen cannot and will not allow his people and government to treat him in such way as America treats her so-called Negroes.

To call a person a "beast" is simply to say, according to the English language: - n. violent person, berserk or berserker, demon, fiend, Shaitan or Sheitan or Satan, the dragon, the evil spirits, Satanas, devil, diable, Iblis, azazel, abaddon, apollyon, the prince of the devils, the prince of darkness, the prince of this world, the prince of the power of air, the wicked one, the evil one, the demon, the fiend, the foul, fiend, the temper, the adversary, the evil spirit, the archenemy, the arch-fiend, the devil incarnate, the father of lies, the author and father of evil, the serpent, the common enemy, the angel of the bottomless pit. Adj.: Satanic, devilish, diabolic (al), hell-born, demonic, etc., savage, brute, brutish, fierce, vicious, wild, untamed, tameless, ungentle, barbarous, unmitigated, unsoftened, ungovernable, uncontrollable, (obstinate), brute force, forcibly, by mainly with might and mainly by force of arms, at the point of the sword or bayonet (the devil and Satan). The above is the explanation of "Beast" when applied to a human being or people in general according to Roget's International Thesaurus. The so-called American Negroes, have and still suffer under such brutish treatment from the American Christian white race, who call themselves followers of Jesus and his God. Could a beast have done worse in the Till boy's murder? Could a beast be more brutish, to beat, lynch, torture, burn, castrate, rob and steal your life unaware, to persecute, and those if found seeking truth and justice?

THE REVELATOR could not have better described the white race's way of dealing with the black nation. They (white race) are the people described as "beast" in the Revelation of the Bible. Study them and their history and dealings with people, and you will without hesitation agree with me 100 per cent that these are the people meant by the Revelator, who foresaw their future and end, and wrote it while he and his followers were in exile from the Holy Land 6,600 years ago on the Island of Pelan in the Aegean Sea, where he grafted the present white race.

The revelation is claimed by the Christians to have been granted to a Saint John Divine who was a follower of Jesus, but this is erroneous and wrong. It is by the father of the white race (Mr. Yakub or Jacob). The people other than the beast are mentioned as worshipers of the beast: "And they (the people of the darker nation) worshiped the dragon which gave power unto the beast." The power given by the dragon to the beast refers to a higher wisdom and knowledge of the time and wise preparedness. The chief head and spiritual guidance of the white race is the **Pope of Rome** in Italy.

Hurry and join onto your own kind. The time of this world is at hand.

November 15, 1958

LAST week's article gave a slight summary of the meanings of the name "beast" when applied to a person or persons. This week, we seek further knowledge of this symbolic beast and what he will do from other prophecies of the Bible. The book (Bible) makes it clear that the beast referred to, according to his number, is a man or people (Rev. 13:18). It is further made clear in verses 3 and 14 that the beast is a man or people, and that man or people refers to the man and people of America, by that which America has done and still is doing.

A real animal beast cannot work miracles, nor bring fire down from heaven; but we do know that it was a man or men of America who brought fire down (atomic explosion) on Hiroshima, Japan, in 1945. It was the first such act in warfare known to mankind, and all did wonder and say: "Who is able to make war with him (America)?"

There is no nation that is so rich, so well-armed with carnal weapons of war, unless it is Russia. But I doubt it, because America is the richest. Therefore, with her wealth she can build greater arms. However, the Revelator or Revelation refers to America. She may repent for a while and get a few years' extension of time but I doubt it, due to her anger of the truth coming to her once slaves, the so-called Negroes. They have the history of the past of those who opposed the plans and messengers of God. Whether that will serve as a reminder to America, it remains to be seen.

Let us understand that which is written in prophecies concerning America and her so-called Negroes. We read in Daniel 7:7, "After this I saw in the night vision, and behold a fourth beast, dreadful and terrible, and strong exceedingly; and it have great iron teeth; it devoured and break into pieces, and stamped the residue with the feet of it: and it was diverse from all the beasts that were before it; and it had ten horns." The beast of Revelation 13:1 seems to be the same beast that Daniel 7:7 refers to. The symbolic horns represent the **power** of the beast.

Let one check (count) the small independent governments of Central and South America. There you may find the answer to the beast's ten horns. His seven heads (or brains) could well be, as many others believe, the seven hills that Rome is said to be built upon, which is the **spiritual head** of the Christian Church; for it is with the spiritual power of Christianity, used first by the white race, that captivated the black peoples of earth. This fourth beast is dreadful and terrible, says Daniel the prophet. It is the power and might of America that the nations fear and wonder: "Who is able to make war with him?"

There are many who can make war with America, but who is able to win in a war against him? All worship him whose names are not in the Book of Life (the Nation of Righteousness).

These four beasts that came up from the sea, of which the fourth one was the most powerful one of them all, could well represent, at the present time, England, Russia, France and America. America being the youngest of the other three is yet the most powerful. All four have sea power. If the sea represents the people, then it still stands true of the four. They all have had, and still have, power and great authority over the darker nations, from where their rise to wealth and power came or comes from. Take away this power and authority or exploitation of the black man's world and there will be no dreadful beast. America is diverse from the other three great powers of the European race.

The Kingdom of Islam (the religion of peace) shall be forever, and all darker people shall believe in it. It has no end as other religions such as Hinduism and Christianity. There is much more detailed knowledge that shall be given to you of the prophecy of this fourth beast to be continued in this article, which will greatly enlighten the spiritually blind, deaf, and dumb people of mine in America and throughout the world.

Hurry and join onto your own kind. The time of this world is at hand.

November 22, 1958

THE DREADFUL AND TERRIBLE BEAST WHO IS ABLE TO MAKE WAR WITH THE BEAST? (DAN. 7:7, REV. 13:4)

"AND ALL that dwell upon the earth shall worship him whose names are not written in the Book of Life of the lamb slain from the foundation of the world." (Rev. 13:8)

Those who refused to believe in Allah (God) and His religion, Islam, and follow and obey His Messenger (the Lamb) will worship the beast. (How true this is today). The symbolic name given to the last Apostle or Messenger of Allah (God) has been wrongfully applied to Jesus of two thousand years ago by Bible students; for Jesus' life and ministry were only a prototype of the antitypical last Messenger of Allah (God), who also would be born in the midst of the infidels, as Jesus was. The Lamb

(Apostle) could not have been physically slain. The words refer to his physical and mental conditions as he was seen in the midst of the beasts.

As we read of this symbolic Lamb in Rev. 5:6, "As if it had been slain" (not slain, only looked as if it were slain) as one looks at a lamb among beasts of prey; bruised and torn by the savage beasts. The choice of Allah's Messenger, in the vision of the Revelator (Yakub) looked as if he had been slain; which means that the blood of the Lamb was mixed with the blood of the beasts, was made blind, deaf and dumb to the knowledge of the beast and kind.

THE OUTSTANDING and most amazing thing about the slain Lamb is that he has seven horns and seven eyes," Rev. 5:6, which made him spiritually able to see and recognize God and His power over the beast, and gained the knowledge of the seven wisdoms of Allah (God), which served as horns of power to oppose the beast (see verse 12) that had seven heads and ten horns Rev. 13:1). The beast was angry with the Lamb and the righteous, and he sought to kill all that would not worship him (Rev. 12:17; 13:15).

The beast was full of eyes before and behind. (They had a knowledge of the past histories and this gave them knowledge of what to expect.) The eyes also refer to the secret agents of the beast.

"If any man hath an ear, let him hear" (verse 9). It is the refusal to use the organ of hearing to learn and recognize the truth which will send many thousands to hell in these days of the manifestation of the symbolic beast, the real human devil, as spoken of and written by the hand and mouth of the prophets of Allah (God). The rejecters of the truth of the Revelator's symbolic beast are thoroughly warned of the consequences of worshiping him in (Rev. 14:9, 10, 11). The believers are consoled by a hint of how they will be relieved of the suffering of persecution and killings by the beast in (Rev. 13:10) the following words: "He that leadeth into captivity shall go into captivity. He that killeth with the sword must be killed with the sword." He will reap that which he has sown. As thou hast done, so shall it be done unto thee.

AMERICA BROUGHT our fathers into slavery and has continued to keep their children in slavery by not teaching us the truth, and continuing to call us after their own names, and caused us to worship them and their religion by not teaching us the true knowledge of our own God and religion. Therefore, this has caused us to bow down to their images (little crucifixes of a dead prophet (Jesus), the imaginary status of Mary and the disciples, marks and doings of evil in our heads, and practicing it with the hands as they do).

The white American knows fully well that we, the so-called Negroes, can never be FREE and worthwhile in the sight of Allah and our nation as long as we are called by their names and do as they do; bowing to what they represent as god and religion. They have made us to believe in a dead god that cannot help you nor harm you (a mystery god and a dead Jesus), and we are ever bleeding at their hands (both physically and mentally). We are ignorant enough after 400 years to love them seemingly for nothing but the evils done to us by them. Forsake such teachings of the beast and come out of them or burn, says Allah to me.

Hurry and join onto your own kind. The time of this world is at hand.

November 29, 1958

"THE BEAST"

"Who is able to make war with him? (Rev. 13:4) dreadful and terrible (Dan. 7:7)"

THE REVELATION'S symbolic beast is referred to under other symbolic names, such as, "the Serpent," (Gen. 3:1, 4, 14; Isaiah 27:1, 65:25; Rev. 12:9, 20:2), even though they all refer to the one and same people (the white race). In Genesis 3:1 it reads like this: "Now the serpent was more subtle than any beast of the field which the Lord God had made." This word or name "serpent" has many meanings, but it is commonly known throughout the English-speaking world when someone refers to another as a serpent or snake. In other words, it means to call the person the following:

(n) cunning, sly, artfulness, craftiness, etc. Adj. craft, "the ape of wisdom," satanic cunning, the cunning of the serpent; finesse, subtlety, deceitful cunning, fraudulent skill or dexterity, guile, sharp practice, knavery, pellifoggery, dodgery, trickery, intriguing, etc. (v) intrigue, wire pulling, backstairs influence, temporization, cleverness (skill) duplicity, etc.; stealth (concealment) sagacity. (n) cunning person, person of cunning, sly boot, fox, Reynard, sly dog, sly old fish, dodger, file, smooth or slick citizen, slicker, schemer, plays tricks with, stoop to conquer, introduce the thin end of the wedge, undermine, waylay, throw off one's guard, temporize; be too much for, get the better of, snatch a thing from under one's nose, snatch a verdict; scheme, conspire (plot) deceive, steal a march upon, overreach, slick, slippery, wily, cunning as a fox or serpent, too clever by half, slippery as an eel, schemeful, designing.

THERE ARE many other names which mean the same or refer to the same (the Serpent). God and His Prophets could not have given the white race a better name (serpent), according to the characteristics of that race. The serpent of Genesis 3:1 was none other than the devil (white race). He deceived Adam and his wife causing them to disobey Allah (God), which was the plan of the serpent (devil), according to the history of the devils. Their greatest desire is to make the righteous disobey the law of righteousness.

They are referred to by this name "serpent" in the Holy Qur-an (37:65) translated by Maulvi Muhammad Ali: "To a tree that grows in the bottom of hell, its produce is as the heads of serpents which the disbelievers shall eat from." In this footnote (2112) he says, "that the Arabs apply the name Shaitan to a sort of serpent having a mane, ugly or foul in the head and face." In Mr. Abdullah Yusuf Ali's translation of the Holy Qur-an in English, in the same chapter and verse (37:65) it reads: "The shoots of its fruit stalks are like the heads of devils."

The Bible's forbidden tree (Gen. 2:17) was a tree of the knowledge of good and evil. This also tells us that the tree was a person, for trees know nothing! This tree of knowledge was forbidden to Adam and Eve. The only one whom this tree could be is the devil. After deceiving Adam and his wife, he has been called a serpent due to his keen knowledge of tricks and his acts of slyness, who made his acquaintance with Adam and his wife in the absence of the presence of God. Since this is the nature of a liar, he can best lie to the people when truth is absent.

WE KNOW that there was never a time when an actual serpent (or snake) could talk and deceive people in the knowledge of God's law. This same serpent is mentioned in Revelation 12:9, as a deceiver. There (12:9) it is made clear to us that the serpent is "the dragon, devil, and Satan, which deceiveth the whole world." In (Gen. 3:1) he appeared in the Garden of Paradise before the woman, and deceived her. (Rev. 12:4). He stood before the woman who was ready to be delivered to devour her child as soon as it is born.

The serpent, the devil, dragon, Satan, seems to have been seeking the weaker part of man (the woman) to bring to a naught the man - the Divine Man. It is his first and last trick to deceive the people of God through the woman, or with the woman. He is using his women to tempt the black man by parading her half nude before his eyes, ad with public love-making, indecent kissing and dancing over radio and television screens, and throughout their public papers and magazines. He is flooding the world with propaganda against the God and His true religion, Islam. He stands before the Negro woman to deceive her by feigning love and love-making with her, giving the Negro woman preference over her husband or brother in hiring.

IN SOME cities, the Negro woman receives a much higher salary than the Negro man. The devil takes the Negro woman on his job and uses her as he pleases, so I am being informed; he walks up to the so-called Negro woman and puts his hands and arms around her body. She may be married or single, but it makes no difference; ever making eyes at her whenever he catches her eye. This is an outright destruction of the moral principles of the black man.

In some cities, we convert five men to one woman. The so-called Negroes should unite and put a stop to the destruction of his women by the serpent. The woman in (Rev. 12:4) actually refers to the last Apostle of God, and her child refers to his followers, or the entire Negro race as they are called, who are now ready to be delivered (go to their own).

Hurry and join onto your own kind. The time of this world is at hand.

THAT OLD serpent, called the devil and Satan, which deceiveth the whole world (Rev. 12:9) - you are beginning to learn that the name "Serpent" is applied to a person or persons whose characteristics are like that of a serpent (snake). Serpents or snakes of the grafted type cannot be trusted, for they will strike you when you are not expecting a strike.

Let us return to Genesis. "Dan shall be a serpent by the way, an adder in the path that biteth the horse's heels so that his rider shall fall backward" (Gen. 39:17). Here Jacob on his deathbed foretelleth the future of his sons. (Moses calls Dan a lion's whelp; he shall leap from Bashan - Deut. 33:22.) That old serpent, devil and Satan, the old beast, the dragon which deceiveth the whole world of the poor, ignorant, darker nations and has caused them to fall off their mount of prosperity, success and independence by accepting advise, guidance and empty promises which he (the serpent-like Caucasian devil) never intended to fulfill.

HOW WELL the prophets have described the characteristics of this race of devils as corresponding with the nature of a snake (serpent). Most snakes wobble and make a crooked trail when and wherever they crawl; so it is with the white race which goes among the black nation leaving the marks of evil and crooked dealings and doings.

In spiritual dealings, there again you will find them like a snake (serpent), following on the heels of the truth bearers (prophets and messengers of God) to bite the believers with false teachings and fear in order that he may cause them to fall off from their mount of truth. Like a snake (serpent), he parks in and on the pathway of all the so-called Negroes who seek the way to truth, freedom, justice and equality (Allah and the true religion, Islam).

In many instances, they threaten you with imprisonment, the loss of your jobs, hunger, lack of shelter, and disrespect of human rights. On some occasions, they threaten to take away your very life! By speaking evil of the truth (Allah and His apostle and Islam), they cause fear to enter the hearts of the weak believers and they fall off the mount of the truth of God which would have saved them from fear, harm, hunger, and lack of shelter. As he caused the fall of Adam and his wife from the Garden of Paradise 6,000 years ago, so they are trying to cause the fall of you and me from entering Paradise by not believing in Allah and His religion, Islam.

ALLAH (GOD) drove out both Adam and Eve and cursed the serpent and set a day of execution upon the (human) serpent (the devil and Satan), and enmity and hatred (discord, dislike, disapproval) between the apostles and prophets of God and the human serpent, "And God said unto the serpent: Because thou hast done this, thou art cursed above all cattle, and above every beast of the field; and I will put enmity between thee and the woman and between thy seed and her seed; it shall bruise thy head and thou shall bruise his heel" (Gen. 3:15).

Notice that the above verse refers to the woman's seed as "it," and in the last two words of the verse 15, "his heel" is used. The woman's seed and the serpent's seed are involved. Therefore, the seed of the two will settle the wrong between the woman and the serpent caused by the serpent in the Garden of Paradise 6,000 years ago. The woman's seed shall bruise the serpent's head.

WHAT IS THE head of this human serpent? It is the false religious leaders of the human beast serpent. "Come hither, I will show unto thee the judgment of the great whore that sitteth upon many waters; with whom kings of the earth have committed fornication, and the inhabitants of the earth have been made drunk." (They are silly drunk off the false religious teachings of the head of the serpent. Under this drunkenness, they war against the truth and persecute and kill the servants of truth, thinking that they are doing God's will; or they try to prevent the truth from making manifest falsehood.)

In the fourth verse, the woman is arrayed in purple and scarlet color and is filthy. In the first and 16th verses, she is called whore. The beast supports her.

Next week: "The Woman and the Beast."

Hurry and join onto your own kind. The time of this world is at hand.

'THE WOMAN AND THE BEAST' (REV. 17:4)

"SO HE CARRIED me away in the spirit into the wilderness; and I saw a woman sit upon a scarlet-colored beast, full of names of blasphemy, having seven heads and 10 horns."

The human beast - the serpent, the dragon, the devil, and Satan - all mean one and the same; the people or race known as the white or Caucasian race, sometimes called the European race. They are the great universal deceivers of non-white people; the greatest murderers (heartless) who ever lived or ever will live on our planet earth. We have been far too ignorant of this people, but thanks to Almighty God, Allah, Who came in the person of Master Fard Muhammad, the long-awaited Great Mahdi, (the Self-Guided One), the Light and Life giver, Savior and Deliverer of the lost and found members of the tribe of Shabazz (the so-called Negro race in America), the great and mighty God in person, who was to come and is come, has revealed our common enemy (the Caucasian race - the race of sin) . . . The snake of Paradise, the beast of the West (wilderness), the devil and Satan, the murderers of the prophets of God and the righteous, the spoiler, robber, and killer of us the American so-called Negroes. But let us rejoice and be glad; thankful to Allah for wisdom, knowledge and understanding of the symbolic beast, serpent, that bit Adam and Eve, that he should not deceive you and me and cause us to not see the hereafter, as he caused them to be cast out of Paradise.

THE REVELATOR says: "That he was carried away in the spirit (a spiritual vision) into the wilderness." The wilderness in the spiritual sense of the word means, a place or people of unrighteousness (wicked), a freelance wild life. That wilderness is your North America.

"The woman." Just why does the prophet use the woman to represent the wicked beast, the serpent-like people? The woman is the womb of the nations. Sometimes, spiritually speaking, a prophet is referred to as a woman, because he gives spiritual birth to a nation as in Rev. 12:4,13; 14:1, 4. The woman (Rev. 17:4) that sits on the scarlet colored beast means both physically and spiritually. There are many religious theologians who agree that the woman represents the Christian Church, or a filthy hypocritical, religious system or government. The best answer is the one that fits or corresponds with that of the symbolic picture given by the Revelator.

Take the physical side of the history of the European white race. There you have the answer. They use the woman to trap the man. She is the bait, and she catches the prey for her master. She beautifies herself with much painting of her eyes and lips, fine clothes and jewelry, parading before her lovers showing nudist parts of her body without the faintest sign of shame. "She sits upon a scarlet colored beast." She is supported by the wealth and power of the beast to deceive the darker nations of earth. According to the histories of the nations, there never was one that put on a show of temptation that equaled Christian America.

IN REVELATION 17:4, she holds a golden cup in her hand full of abomination and filthiness of her fornication, which means that her outer appearance is that of a good and religious people, but within her, she is full of hypocrisy and hate, the mother of harlots (fifth verse same chapter) and murderers of the righteous. She seeks to deceive the nations as Jezebel tried to tempt Jehu and was trampled under the feet of his horse (2 Kings 9:30) (See also Jeremiah 4:30). "And the 10 horns which thou sawest upon the beast, these shall hate the whore, and shall make her desolate and naked, and shall eat her flesh and burn her with fire." (Rev. 17:16). Has she not (Christian America) burned our poor innocent black brothers' flesh with joy and sport?

White Christianity has deceived the black nations of the earth, trapped and murdered them by the hundreds of thousands, divided, and put black against black, corrupted and committed fornication before your very eyes with your women, and even bold enough, after blinding you, to make you confess that you love them and do not hate them for all the evils, filth, and murder done to you and your flesh and blood. What foolish people I have. Have mercy on them, O God, and open their eyes that they may see and come to knowledge of this open enemy - this terrible beast, this crooked serpent, this dragon, this devil and Satan. Nine times out of 10, their law does not punish them for murdering you.

Fear not! A defender for us is in our midst; we are not forsaken any more.

Hurry and join onto your own kind. The time of this world is at hand.

GOD ATTACKS THE TERRIBLE BEAST

The first attack that Allah (God) made on the beast was in Paradise, although the beast always attacks first and God retaliates. Allah said to me that in the year 8400 of our calendar history, which was 600 years before the birth of the white race, a great scientist by the name of Yakub was born. This man was the father and maker of the Caucasian race. When his intention or idea to make an enemy of the original nation (the black nation) was discovered, the King (Allah) had Mr. Yakub and his followers separated and put into boats and shipped to a small island in the Aegean Sea, and they took care of Yakub and his followers for 20 years until they were able to go for themselves.

On that island Yakub grafted the Caucasian race, known as the white race, to be the enemies of us (the black nation) for six thousand years or until we produced one greater and wiser than he (Yakub). That One is now on scene, whose wisdom is infinite, having power over all things.

YAKUB MADE great promises to his followers. He was the first liar and murderer of the righteous and drew the title of being the "Father of Devils," who has assumed many other names. His wisdom has ruled black men for six thousand years. He was not permitted to make his devils in the holy land (heaven), for if so, he could not have been moved. We would have had them forever. "And the Lord said, behold, the man is become as one of us, to know good and evil, and now lest he put forth his hand and take of the tree of life, and eat, and live forever." (Genesis 3:22.)

With his superior knowledge of both (good and evil), if allowed to remain and mix with the holy people it would have made it impossible to remove him. Therefore, he and his followers were shipped to the above-mentioned island. There he became mighty and made a race of people with his idea born into their very nature, to deceive, divide and rule the black man for six thousand years. He was successful in accomplishing his work. Why? Because (1) his followers obeyed him. (2) There was no one at that time who equaled him in wisdom. (3) The 24 scientists had predicted his work and the beginning and end of his world 8,400 years before the birth of Mr. Yakub.

THIS IS the first attack of Allah (God) on the Devil. This attack deprived Yakub of a home in the holy land for his deceitful work and lying to the holy people: turning people against Allah and righteousness. His (Yakub's) sole aim was to fill the earth with wicked people, as it had been ever filled with the righteous. He has done just that, except for one-tenth of the population.

Ninety per cent of the total population of the earth has been affected by evil caused by the devil Yakub and his made devils (the white race). They are called by many names and every name serves as a description of the different characteristics of that race. They can imitate a real righteous person and under such acts the righteous are deceived.

Today, God attacks them with TRUTH, to make them manifest to the world of the black man, whom they have deceived under a false religion using good names to hide that which is not good: The great, crooked human serpent, who hates and opposes the prophets of God and their followers. The following is from the Holy Qur-an by Muhammad Ali: "leads you to evil and indecency (24:21), the great tempter (7:17) who changes (4:119) the natural religion of man, makes false promises (14:22), disowns the responsibility for having misled (59:16), descends upon the sinful (26:221), makes evil deeds look attractive (16:63), the chief wicked opponent (23:97), who steals a hearing" (15:16-18) (seeks to know your personal sayings and doings to do you evil).

Hurry and join onto your own kind. The time of this world is at hand.

GOD ATTACKS THE BEAST

The second attack on the beast took place 600 years from the first one, after their return from the island in the Aegean Sea, at that time called Pelan. Remember: Yakub was the father and maker of the devil; therefore, he is also called devil, although he did not live to see his race of devils comes to birth. He lived 150 years, but he knew what they would look like, and how long they would live and rule the world of black men. This is his revelation of them, called "John," the "Revelation," the last book of the Bible, as Allah (God) taught me.

After the devils were made, they made an unsuccessful attempt to gain control of Paradise by telling lies on the righteous. These lies caused trouble and war broke out among the righteous. The devils used the woman to bring about the trouble. She spread the lies. Remember: Those who came from Pelan was the symbolic serpent of Genesis and the beast of the Revelation. Those people whom their father (Yakub) deceived who lost their place in Paradise when Yakub was cast out after his intention to make a devil was discovered - those fifty-nine thousand, nine hundred and ninety-nine (59,999) men and women who went with Yakub were the real Adam of the Bible and Holy Qur-an who lost their places in Paradise (the holy land of Arabia). They were deceived by Yakub who had knowledge of both good and evil as he was born in Paradise. His followers (59,999) are the ones who were grafted into a race of devils.

They returned 600 years later and acted like snakes weaving themselves among us, causing trouble. They would tell lies to one, against the other, setting them at odds with each other, teaching them against Allah and his religion (Islam). After they continued to make trouble and caused bloodshed among the righteous, the king had them all rounded up and carried to the Arabian desert. There, the king had his army to drive them westward across that great burning desert into what is called today Europe. This name means a place where people are roped in: "Eu" means hillsides, "rope," means roped in. This was done to punish the devils for causing trouble in the Holy Land 6,000 years ago.

Isolated, they did not have any contact with the civilized world for 2,000 years. This 2,000 years was before the birth of Moses, according to the Bible and Holy Qur-an, raised the devils up to civilization. Read John 3:15 "And as Moses lifted up the serpent (the white race) in the wilderness (in Europe) even so must the Son of Man be lifted up."

The average reader thinks the lifting up in the above verse means the crucifixion and death of Jesus. That is by far the wrong meaning. Moses lifted the White race up into civilization and ruling power. The same must be done for the so-called American Negroes, who are only children in the knowledge of God, devil and self. Jesus' crucifixion and death are absent in Moses' history.

They are angry at the presence of truth among us, and threaten you with the loss of a job if you are found believing. But, this too will finally prove to be of no avail. A job is all that was ever offered to us. It is different today; it is more than a job that God wants for us - it is some of this earth and true friends that we can call our own. We have been despised, re-jected, robbed, made hungry and homeless long enough. We have been living under the "shadow of death," without justice and protection among people who kill us at will, and will charge their government with injustice if their freedom to kill Negroes is hindered. Shall not the God of justice defend us against this merciless human serpent, beast-like people? We shall no longer be satisfied with just the promise of a job (a slave). We are going to have some of this earth that we can call our own. Allah (God) will give it to us.

Hurry and join onto your own kind. The time of this world is at hand.

1959

THE THIRD ATTACK ON THE BEAST FOR HIS EVIL ATTACKS AGAINST THE RIGHTEOUS

THE THIRD attack on the devils, by Allah (God), was made by Muhammad in the Seventh Century with the spread of Islam and Holy Qur-an after the birth of Jesus, who failed to accomplish the work of breaking the devil's power against the Righteous. After Jesus had learned that he was two thousand years ahead of the time and the end of the Yakub-made devils, he gave up his life to death that his name may live to the day of their doom. Muhammad and his work was far more effective on the devils, than any other prophet of the past, for that which Islam and the Holy Qur-an did not accomplish, the sword did. Jesus made no effort to defend his teachings as Muhammad and his successors did.

THE SENDING of prophets serves as checks on the wild spread of evil by the devils. In fact, if these checks had not been made by the prophets, there would not have been a civilized white race today. That race of people, by nature, are great troublemakers. Actually, they love fighting and killing. They are proud and boastful, scientists at tricks, world snoopers and meddlers, thieves and robbers. They are well known to hate the black Negroes without a cause; and are doing them evil day and night without even being questioned, while the poor, blind, deaf and dumb Negroes love and adore them, their open enemies, and think that their love for them is the will of God, while the same Negroes hate themselves and will kill one another for the sake of the enemy.

From the Seventh Century, from Jesus to the twelfth Century, Islam and Christianity were at war with each other which cost the lives of many millions of people. Christianity received, by far, the greatest losses. She was conquered up to the very center of Europe. The fiery, brave warriors of Islam stopped at nothing less than victory. In 1187, A.D., they took Jerusalem and the Holy Sepulcher of Jesus from the Christians, and they (the Muslims) still are in charge of the Holy Sepulcher of Jesus.

AFTER Muhammad learned that he could not make righteous Muslims out of the white race, he forbade them to speak the Arabic language and wear the Muslim's costumes. This attack caused a set-back to the dev-ils for about one thousand years. They overcame it after the discovery of the Western hemisphere by Columbus. They have been here, now, over 400 years, killing off the original owners, pushing their mischief-making and causing bloodshed throughout the Western hemisphere into the Pa-cific Ocean, and now are into the Far East.

They have lived up to their name, and that which they were created for, I quote here a saying from the Holy Qur-an which concerns them: "And when your Lord said to the angels, 'I am going to place in the earth, one who shall rule in it, they said, what wilt Thou place in it such as shall make mischief in it and shed blood?'" (Holy Qur-an 2:30.) This is most surely the truth of the white race. They do not love Peace, they love war and delight in it. They love to take others' lives, like savage beasts, which roam the jungles seeking the life of the prey. They have reduced the Black Nation's population of our planet, earth, from 5,000,000,000 to 4,400,000,000 since they have been on our planet. This means a loss of 600,000,000 or an average of 100,000,000 every 1,000 years that they have been in authority. They call the truth of them, that I am teaching, "Hate" teachings. They hate truth and love falsehood for the so-called Ne-groes. But, you must know the truth of it all, for the time has arrived for truth, and falsehood must vanish.

Hurry, and join onto your own kind. The time of this world is at hand.

January 10, 1959

THE BLOOD SHEDDER (REV. 16:6)

ACCORDING TO the word of Allah (God) and the history of the world, since the grafting of the Caucasian race six thousand years ago, they have caused more bloodshed than any people known to the black nation. They are born murderers made by nature to murder. The Bible and Holy Qur-an Sharrieff are full of teachings of this race of murderers. They shed the life blood of all the living, even their own. They are scientists at deceiving the black people. They deceive the very people of Paradise (Bible: Genesis 3:13). They kill their own brother (Genesis 4:8). The earth testified against them (Genesis 4:10) and revealed their guilt to its Maker. (Thy brother's blood cried unto me from the ground.) Thy very soil of America is soaked with the innocent blood of my people, the so-called Negroes, shed by this race of murderers, also cried out to it Maker for the burden of the innocent blood of the righteous slain upon her. Let us take a look at the devil's creation from the teachings of the Holy Qur-an.

"**AND WHEN** your Lord said to the angels, I am going to place in the earth One who shall rule, the angels said: What will thou place in it such as shall make mischief in it and shed blood, we celebrate Thy praise and extol Thy holiness." (Holy Qur-an Sharrieff 2:30.)

This devil race has and still is doing just that - making mischief and shedding blood. As the Holy Qur-an says, "When your Lord said to the angels: Surely I am going to create a mortal of the essence of black mud fashioned in shape." (Holy Qur-an Sharrieff 15:28.) The essence of black mud (the black nation) mentioned is only symbolic, which actually means the sperm of the black nation, and they refused to recognize the black nation as their equal, though they were made from them by one of their black scientists (named Yakub). They can never see their way in submitting to Allah (God), His religion, Islam, and His prophets.

THEIR EVERY cry is - beat, kill, kill the so-called Negroes! The day has arrived that Allah will return to our murderers that which they have been so happy to pour on the poor, innocent so-called Negroes, as they love to shed the poor, innocent blood of their Negro slaves, and even plan to kill me for teaching the truth. Allah will give you your own flesh and your own blood to drink like water. Your arms and your allies will not help you against Allah (Rev. 16:6).

The heads and bodies of the so-called Negroes are used to test the power of your clubs and guns. Yet, the poor, foolish so-called Negroes admire the murderers regardless to how much they are murdered. The day is near, even at your door, when you shall receive fully what you have sown. Allah has said it!

Next week: "The Final War on Satan and His Wicked World."

Hurry and join onto your own kind. The time of this world is at hand.

THE FINAL JUDGMENT OF THE BEAST

WE HAVE been studying the history of the Caucasian race (devils) for a long time, from the history of their father (Yakub) in the Garden of Paradise to Europe and the United States of America. They have been written under symbolic names as given in the Bible and Holy Qur-an to disguise or cover them to keep the darker people from the knowledge of them until the end of their time; for surely they have been hidden from our eyes. According to the Book (II Thess. 2:3): "There will be no judgment until that man of sin is revealed who opposed and exalted himself above all that is called God, showing himself that he is God."

ALTHOUGH THIS stands true of the Caucasian race, it is equally true of any proud religious leader, especially one in the last days who is predicted to oppose Allah, Muhammad and his followers. Some say it is the Pope of Rome and the religion of Christianity which will be exposed to the world, for the truth of Allah does expose the guilty. The Caucasian race has ever been the chief opposers of Islam, the true religion of God. We have learned of their mischief- making in Paradise which caused war and bloodshed among the righteous and of their killing the prophets of Allah (God) to prevent them from teaching the people the truth. The prophets' missions among them cannot be harmful, but rather helpful, for their good doings in the midst of evil was like water to fire. We have seen the devils punished for their mischief-making.

THEY WERE cast out of Paradise and made to walk across the hot Arabian Desert into the continent called Europe (West Asia). Genesis of the Bible (3:1,14) gives them the name "serpent" and "beast." The last book of the Bible, called Revelation gives them the same name only with a little addition (Rev. 12:9). This punishment did not stop the devils from opposing God and His prophets, for after 2,000 years of their being roped into the caves and hillsides of Europe, God had mercy on them and sent Musa (Moses) as a guide for them.

Musa (Moses) brought them out of the caves and hillsides and put them on the road to the conquest of Asia. Bringing them out of the caves and their being blessed with right guidance were like picking up a frozen snake which was harmless under the cold, but as soon as he thawed out he began biting his liberator. They began making trouble and war among the people of Asia. Diseases and plagues of war among themselves did not change them. Muhammad (may the peace and blessings of Allah be upon him) gave them a setback from this teachings of Islam and by putting to death with the sword the disbelievers and troublemakers. This setback lasted until their finding of the Western Hemisphere.

AFTER BEING blessed with a great new world and almost unlimited wealth, they began seeking ways to strike back at Asia, her first trouble-making spot. The serpent is not satisfied with the fields and unlimited jungles and woods, but will crawl into your yards and into your houses to sting your cattle herds, poultry, children and self. They cannot be trusted. The Caucasians are great deceivers. Their nature is against friendship with black people, although they often fool the black people under such deception as claiming that they are sincere friends and well-wishers. There the black man is deceived. Allah has said that they have been found disagreeable to live with in peace and He has decided to remove them from the planet earth.

Continued next week: "Final War."

Hurry and join onto your own kind. The time of this world is at hand.

January 24, 1959

"And swear by Him that liveth forever and ever, Who created the heaven) and the things that therein are, and the sea and the things which are therein, that there should be time no longer." (Rev. 10:6)

THE FINAL JUDGMENT OF THE BEAST

He that liveth forever is the originator, the owner of the universe (that is the black nation from whom all the others had their beginning). The beast, the Devil or Satan, is warned throughout his history that there is an end to his rule. The devil has not lost any time since emerging from the caves and hillsides of Europe. Today his progress in science proves that there is no such thing that God is a mystery. He is a living proof that man can accomplish what he will without waiting and staring up in the sky for some mystery spirit to come down or send us word what to do. God is a human being, but is supremely intelligent with the secret knowledge of the powers of how to control them by His will, which make and uphold the entire creation, which includes all human beings and every object in the universe, whether movable or immovable.

This secret knowledge is hinted in several places in the scriptures of the Bible and Holy Qur-an. It will be revealed in due time. As we see today an attempt is being made to conquer space. It can be done. As the Holy Qur-an teaches in these words: "Do you not see that Allah has made subservient to you whatever is in the heavens and whatever is in the earth?" There is no such thing as God being unreal. He is as real as you and I, only far more our superior.

The evil ones by nature (devils) cannot ever equal the Supreme Original One, for the key to that knowledge will forever be kept by a certain one or by a group. Remember the warnings: "And the Lord God said, Behold, the man is become as one of us to know good and evil; and now lest he put forth his hand, and take also of the tree of life, and eat and live forever." (Gen. 3:22)

The man (devil) cannot live and rule the people forever under evil and bloodshed, for there could never be any peace or united love and brotherhood between man and man, for the devils were not created with the nature of love and peace. Therefore, the good man of love and peace cannot allow them to forever trouble his home.

The knowledge of how to live forever is not with the devil, and is withheld from all but a few. The Holy Qur-an makes mention of the devils as trying to listen in on that group of scientists who have the secret knowledge which the devils want to be able to steal a hearing, in these words:

"And certainly we have made strongholds in the heaven and we have made it fair seeming to the beholders, and we guard it against every accursed devil. But he who steals a hearing, so there follows him a visible flame." (Holy Qur-an 15:16, 17, 18.)

And in another place: "They cannot listen to the exalted assembly and they are approached from every side, being driven off, and for them is a perpetual chastisement, except him who snatches off but once, then there follows him a brightly shining flame." (Holy Qur-an 37:8, 9, 10.)

The devils are world snoopers and they hire people, especially the American so-called Negroes, to snoop on their own selves that they may keep up-to-date on whatever goes on among the Negroes. If the intelligent of our people would sacrifice a few heads of the informing stool pigeons and Toms among the white-scared Negroes, this would put a stop to it. We have many such rotten apples who must be picked off the tree for the good of the brotherhood of the race.

God hates a stool pigeon. He made the stool pigeon of Jesus to go hang himself for the betrayal of his friend. (Matt. 27:5). As it is written (Rev. 14:9, 10), "They that worship the beast shall be tormented night and day."

(Continued next week.)

Hurry and join onto your own kind. The time of this world is at hand.

January 31, 1959

FINAL WAR AGAINST THE BEAST

I COMPARE the coming fall of America with the fall of ancient Babylon. Her wickedness (sins) is the same as the history shows of ancient Babylon. "Babylon is suddenly fallen and destroyed, howl for her; take balm for her pains, if so she may be healed." (Jer. 51:81). What were the sins of ancient Babylon? According to the Bible, she was rich, she was proud - and her riches increased her corruption. She had every merchandise that the nations wanted or demanded at that time. Her ships carried her merchandise to the ports of every nation. She was a drunkard. Wine and strong drinks were in her daily practices. She was filled with adultery and murder; she persecuted and killed the people of God; she killed the saints and prophets of Allah (God). Hate and filthiness, gambling, sports of every evil as you practice in America were practiced in Babylon; only America is modern and much worse. Ancient Babylon was destroyed by her neighboring nations.

MY SPACE in this paper is limited: therefore, I cannot quote this ancient history here. I only warn you to let ancient Babylon's destruction serve as a warning for America (the modern Babylon). This people has gone to the limit in doing evil. As God dealt with the evils of ancient people - so will He deal with the modern evil people (America). As God says: "Son of man, when the land (people) sinned against Me by trespassing grievously, then will I stretch out mine hand upon it, and will break the staff of bread thereof, and will send famine upon it, and will cut off man and beast from it." (Ezekiel 14:13). We see with our own eyes; but the wicked Americans are too proud to confess that they see that the bread of America will gradually be cut off. See the hand of Allah (God) at work against modern Babylon - to break the whole staff of her bread for her evils done against His people, the so-called Negroes.

THERE ARE raging dust storms; their river beds lay bare, their fish stinking on the banks in dry, parched mud. When the rain comes, it brings very little relief and does more damage than good. Snow comes - it brings not joy, but death and destruction. After the snow comes more dust storms. With the rain some hailstones - very large stones. America has not seen the large hailstones; she will see hailstones the size of small blocks of ice breaking down crops, trees, the roofs of home, killing cattle and fowl. Behind this, terrific earthquakes; the people frightened, killed, much sickness and death will be widespread. You are getting a token of it now. On the outside, a threat of an atomic war between the nations of the earth. Yet, you have your eyes closed at the manifest judgment of Allah (God) now going on in your midst to bring the country to naught.

Allah (God) has found His people (the so-called Negroes) and is angry with the slave master for the evil done by them to His people (the so-called Negroes). Allah (God) is going to repay them according to their doings. My poor people who have turned to their own God and religion (Allah and Islam) are being tracked down and watched as though they are about to stick up a bank. "This is done to put fear in them so that they might stay away from their God, Allah, and His true religion, Islam – (as the devil knows, it is our salvation and defense).

They (the devils) watch the steps of the righteous (the Messenger of Allah) and seek to slay him (Psalms 37:32). The so-called Negroes live under the very shadow of death in America. (A little white girl kisses two little black boys in the state of Carolina, they are subject to be lynched while the little guilty white girl be freed.) There is no justice for them in the courts of their slave masters. Why should not America be chastised for her evils done to the so-called Negroes? If God destroyed ancient Babylon for the mockery made of the sacred vessels taken from the temple in Jerusalem - what do you think Allah (God) should do for America's mockery and murder of the so-called Negroes whom she took from their native land and people and filled them with wine and whiskey?

NOW SHE (America) puts on an indecent show of temptation with her women (white women) in newspapers magazines - in the streets, half nude and posing in the so-called Negroes' faces in the most indecent manner that is known to mankind, to trick them (the so-called Negroes) to death and hell with them. Be wise, my people, and shut your eyes at them - do not look at them in such an indecent way. Clean your homes of white people's pictures - put our own on the walls. The only so-called Negroes' picture that you will see in their homes is one they have lynched, one they want to kill, or one who has betrayed his own people for them.

America is falling; she is a habitation of devils and every uncleanness and hateful people of the righteous. Forsake her and fly to your own before it is too late. You who believe, write me and get your name on the Book of Life. Help me to get the message to our people with whatever cash that you are able to give, for it takes a lot of it to put this work over. But remember, you will get from two to 10 for one. The whole earth will be given to you to rule forever. So help yourselves to escape out of modern Babylon. She is falling - falling, the hater of good and lover of evil filth, sport and play.

Hurry and join onto your own kind. The time of this world is at hand.

February 7, 1959

THE FINAL WAR AGAINST THE BEAST, THAT OLD SERPENT, THE DEVIL

AND SATAN (REV. 18:4)

"Heaven called to rejoice at her judgment. And I heard another voice from heaven saying: Come out of her my people (the so-called Negroes) that ye be not partakers of her sins, and that ye receive not of her plagues. For her sins have reached unto heaven" (Rev. 18:4, 5).

THE CALL to the darker people of America is now being made to come out of the white man's religion, and stop following and practicing his evil doings. But, only a few will accept the call, for the others will be chastised and brought to their knees. The call is the preaching of the true religion of God (Islam); and for their refusal to accept the true religion and turn from the wicked doings of the white race will bring the chastisement of Allah upon them in the form of grief, worry, great fear, and excitement. Under this condition the rejecters of Islam will seek death (seek someone to kill them to put them out of their misery) but death will flee from them; for death would take them out of the chastisement.

There are many hundreds of thousands of our people who are rejecting the religion of Islam waiting on the white man to approve their acceptance of Islam. Even the preachers are holding back due to fear of the white race. When Allah (God) warns us to do a thing, regardless to the dislike of it by anyone for the safety of your life, it pays to obey Allah's (God's) call. Say as the Muslims say in their prayer: "O Allah, we beseech Thy help, and ask Thy protection and believe in Thee, and trust in Thee, and we laud Thee in the best manner, and we thank Thee, and we are not ungrateful to Thee, and we cast off and forsake him who disobeys Thee. O Allah, Thee do we serve, and to Thee do we pray and make obeisance, and to Thee do we flee, and we are quick, and we hope for Thy mercy, and fear Thy chastisement; for surely Thy chastisement overtakes the disbelievers."

We can never serve and obey Allah (God) until we fear His chastisement. As a child loves his parents and parents love the child, the disobedience of the child brings upon it the chastisement of the parents. Therefore, it is not the parents that the child is afraid of, for he loves them; but it is their chastisement that the child fears. Should not we be more afraid of the Supreme Being's chastisement than our parents? But we are not.

For ever since the so-called Negroes have been so-called freed, they have been more fearful of the white man's chastisement of them than Allah's (God's) chastisement.

The white man can hire them one against the other for just a few dollars or for a few pats on the shoulders, or even a smile. The Negroes must put a stop to the white man's stool pigeons among them, as all other nations are doing today, if the so-called Negroes are ever to become a nation recognized by the nation of the earth. I love my people as myself, but the stool pigeon is an enemy to self and all of his kind. It is a work that makes one look and feel guilty. The most evil thing we can do is to seek to deliver each other up to our enemies to be mistreated and given injustice. Such a one should go out and hang himself or herself.

America's sins (and especially her sins of murdering the Negroes) have reached God and heaven and the Nation of Righteousness (Islam). Allah (God) has not forgotten to punish America, and today will reward her according to her doings. She is now receiving much affliction from within and from the outside.

You may help yourself at doing all you can of evil against me, but who will help you against my Helper who is Almighty God Allah? Rain, hail, snow, earthquakes and confusion are predicted to bring America to her knees along with continuous conflicts and wars. Fly to Allah while you can.

Continued next week: Hurry and join onto your own kind. The time of this world is at hand.

February 14, 1959

BEAST, THAT OLD SERPENT, THE DEVIL AND SATAN (REVELATION 18:4)

"And I saw another angel fly in the midst of heaven, having the everlasting gospel to preach unto them that dwell on the earth and to every nation, and kindred, and tongue, and people, saying with a loud voice, fear

God and give glory to Him; for the hour of His judgment is come: and worship Him that made heaven, and earth, and the sea, and the fountains of water." - Rev. 14:6, 7.

The angel that the prophet saw fly in the midst of heaven is not to be taken as a spirit being; for Allah has taught me that this angel is a human being flying in an airplane, with a mission to give the people the last warnings which will be in small pamphlet form. These pamphlets will be written (or printed) in two languages - Arabic and English - and they will be dropped from a terrific height over America, the only country that the Revelation is directed to. "The everlasting gospel," which means the last true warning to the so-called Negroes and foreign Muslims, will take place between eight and ten days before the final day of destruction, so says the word of Allah to me. The "every nation, kindred, tongue and people" refers to the foreigners who are now in America, who, if they desire could return to their homes (Europe and Asia) since they will not be citizens of America.

The angel warns the people to get on to their own kind within eight or ten days, whereas the chapter and verse under discussion warn the people to fear Allah (God) and not to be heedless to His warnings as they had been. Give glory to Him. Give praises to Allah, who is bringing about a just judgment for the people who are under the government of the Beast, the Serpent, the Devil and Satan, for the hour (the doom) has come. Worship Allah, the maker of heaven and earth, and stop worshipping the Beast (the Devil) who did not have the power to create himself.

They think that God and His angels, and the Devil and his angels are all spirits (not flesh and blood). They even think that Jesus, after being born a flesh- and- blood man and who lived and died as a man, is something unreal. So much so that Jesus, according to the Bible, had to convince them that He was a real man and not spirit. He says:

"Why are ye troubled? And why do thoughts arise in your hearts? Behold my hands and my feet that it is myself: handle me and see: for a spirit hath not flesh and bones as ye see me have." - St. Luke 24:38, 39.

You must come into the knowledge of the truth. You must believe in reality and get away from that slavery thinking. God and the Devil are real, not spirits. Remember, the spirit is like electricity, but there is something real that produces it. It is not self-independent. The book called Revelation's prophecy is referring to people and is using symbols of things which will give the reader a general knowledge of the characteristics of the person or persons under discussion, regardless of how bad or good the symbols may look to us. The truth of the Revelation is referring to the present world, and most of it refers directly to the American slave masters, the so-called Negroes, and the God of truth and justice battling the slave masters (devils) for the liberation of the slaves (the so-called Negroes).

We all know that one day, sooner or later, these two must be separated (Negroes and whites) if one or the other is to survive. Two distinct nations just cannot live as one in peace with the other, if equally educated, for then both will want to be equally independent. That will never happen between the American whites and blacks. The white man is already on top in everything that goes for a nation (except good) while the black man must start from the bottom. Will they (whites) equal themselves with the bottom and help the bottom to climb? The only one who will do that for us is Allah (God), Himself, and God will do it for us if we will submit to Him. That is the purpose of his coming. (Continued next week.)

Hurry and join onto your own kind. The time of this world is at hand.

February 21, 1959

THE FINAL WAR AGAINST THE BEAST, THAT OLD SERPENT, THE DEVIL AND SATAN, THE ARCH-DECEIVER OF BLACK MAN

"And upon her forehead was a name written, MYSTERY, BABYLON THE GREAT, THE MOTHER OF HARLOTS AND ABOMINATIONS OF THE EARTH." Rev. 17:5

The beast is charged with being the mother of harlots. This stands true of the Caucasian race. They are living up to this charge today. Before this evil, bold, adulterous, filthy-doing and filthy-acting race of people was created, there were no such filthy and evil practices among the original black people. The Holy Qur-an (24:21) warns us against following into the footsteps of this people in these words:

"O you who believe, do not follow the footsteps of the devil and whoever follows the footsteps of the devil then surely he bids the doings of indecency and evil."

From the day that they were created, they have ever tried to tempt black man to commit evil and indecent acts. The mother of harlots (the first), is supported by the beast (Government of the Caucasians). This woman represents the Christian religion. Study the history and people of Christianity. You will learn that wherever they go, preaching that religion, prostitution, illegitimate children, drunkenness, gambling, divorce, murder, sport and play, and many other evils too numerous to mention are the result.

TAKE A look at them on your television or listen to your radio. They are the boldest and most shameless people on earth. Read their magazines and newspapers. They love to show off their nudist parts. Be aware of their temptation. She is the abomination (hateful) of the earth. They hate and despise the black man (Negroes) throughout the earth. They think that they are better than we. She is drunk with the blood of the righteous and the poor Negroes of America. The churches are full of evil and filthy practices. Her sins have now reached Heaven (Rev. 18:4).

This means that even those righteous people in the Holy Land have been affected by the evil and filthy doings of the Caucasian, or white race, and this is true. Something must be done to put a stop to her evil and evil practices. The Christian religion is responsible, for it is that religion that has deceived the nations of earth and caused them to do these evils. The churches and their pastors are fast becoming a mockery, shamed and disgraced.

The Christian religion even charges God with adultery by claiming he was the physical father of Jesus.

THE NUMBER of the beast (white race) is 666. To understand his number one must first know the history of the beast (white race). The number "6," or 600 means the six hundred years it took to graft that race from the original black people. The second "6" represents the moral or spiritual law of working six days and resting on the seventh, as a memorial, that when they have lived on the earth for six thousand years they would cease to rule.

Death of the race means it came to rest. The third "6" means six thousand years is the limited time for them to do their evil work upon the nations of earth. This all means the time and life of the white race. They recognize their time and preach of it. Their time was up in 1914, but an extension was given them because of the mentally dead Negroes who must be resurrected first before the end.

Hurry and join onto your own kind. The time of this world is at hand.

February 28, 1959

"MYSTERY BABYLON, THE GREAT" - (REV. 17:5)

LAST WEEK we took up the Mother of Harlots and the abominations of the earth (which only means America). This week we shall take up the first part of the fifth verse, "Mystery Babylon, the Great." According to the English interpretation, the word "mystery" means unknown, uncertain, obscure, concealed, a secret, keep to oneself, between you and me, lock up, something that has not been or cannot be explained. In theology: a supposed truth or fact, of great religious import, which is beyond human comprehension. In the time of the translation of the Bible in English, some or all of the scholars were either without spiritual understanding or downright crooks, who sought to hide that truth in the Book that they thought would reveal to the world their un true selves. The "Mystery Babylon" had not come into existence.

IN ANCIENT BABYLON under the Kings, Nebuchadnezzar and Belshazzar was the great city of idol worship and evil. She was the Queen of Evil, rich and well-fortified. But this "Mystery Babylon" must refer to a future city or people. No city or people answers the description better than the cities and people of America. This "Mystery Babylon" just could not be the ancient Babylon, as we know her history.

You must remember that I am interested in bringing the truth to my people - as clear as sunshine - so be not disturbed in seeing and hearing it the clear and simple way: for they are the blind, deaf and dumb of the nations of earth. They must be taught the truth by one who knows it and I am he, who knows the truth, and have been missioned from the Lord of the Worlds to tell the truth whether it is to your liking or disliking.

America (and her future) was not known in those days when the Bible was being translated into the English language. It was not until 1611 did the translators bring into existence what is known as the King James Authorized Version. According to history, there were several attempts made before to get the Bible to the people in the English language, but they were met with opposition.

AMERICA was discovered in 1492. These first translations of the Bible were far more near the truth than these later translations. The so-called Negro slaves were not given the King James Version to read until it was over three hundred years old, for the white slave masters were not interested in "Educated Religious Negroes" (and are not today). The Negroes now must understand that which was hidden from them by their slave masters.

The "Mystery Babylon, the Great," is none other than America. This "Mystery Babylon" is full of riches, hatred, filth, fornication, adultery, drunkenness, murder of the innocent and idol worship. "Mystery Babylon is full of names of blasphemy." America is full of various religious faiths of the most ignorant kind. - She was once the greatest slave buyer and seller. She has the greatest Merchant Marine service, the world's greatest export shippers in the merchandise of wheat, beasts sheep, horses, chariots, gold, silver, iron, brass, wood, slaves, fine flour, corn and many other merchandise.

You must know that all of the "Revelation," or at least 90 per cent, is directed to America. The 17th and 18th chapters should open the Negroes' eyes to the white race and white Christianity. There is no hereafter for the white race. Some few who are in Asia will stick around for a while.

Hurry and join onto your own kind. The time of this world is at hand.

"THE REVELATION'S BEAST" (Rev. 17:8)

"The beast that thou sawest was, and is not; and shall ascend out of the bottomless pit, and go into perdition; and they that dwell on the earth shall wonder, whose names were not written in the book of life from the foundation of the world, when they behold the beast that was, and is not, and yet is."

Last week we discussed the 5th verse of this chapter (17) (the Mystery Babylon) of the revelation of John (Yakub). I hope you will agree with me of the truth of the vision that John (Yakub) saw concerning the final war between his people (the white race) and the people of God (the black nation). The beast referred to in the eighth verse is the same beast mentioned in the third and seventh verse of the same chapter (17). This beast (a people) was already in existence before this, "one that shall ascend out of the bottomless pit," and is in power in Europe and Asia. This actually refers to all European white powers who are over the world of the black, brown, yellow and red nation.

WHEN SHE (America) was found, she was a place of woods and plains, with unintelligent people living and roaming over her four sides. Now, she has become a wilderness of sin - a place of disorder, complexity, perplexity, "the bottomless pit," abysmal, unfathomed, unfathomable, deep as the sea. The wickedness of America cannot be measured or weighted or sounded out. Her evil is ever on the increase. She used to think that the two oceans (Pacific and Atlantic) were her security against a foreign enemy attack until better navies and air power were built. It is a different story today. The beast is to rise out of the bottomless pit of evil to increase it and bring about her doom.

"The beast" that we have under discussion is the ruler (the Presidents) of a people. The first ruler of America permitted the evil enslavement of the African black people into the hands of his people. There they remained for 300 years and have not, as yet, given them up. "The woman," whom the beast carries, is the Christian Church or Christian religion. The so-called Negroes have not had justice under Christianity nor a single President or Congress since they have been in America. White America hates her Negroes so much that her rulers are afraid to chance their lives to attempt equal justice for her dark-skinned slaves. Theodore Roosevelt was shot for his attempt to do so. Abraham Lincoln was shot dead for his freeing the slaves to weaken the power of the South against him, in his fight to bring about a union of states under one President. But, it was not for his love for the freedom of the slaves, as many so-called Negroes think, and even love his name for this misunderstanding. McKinley got his. Franklin Delano Roosevelt and his successors fulfilled to the very letter the prophecy of the work of deceiving and forcing all to cast their allegiance (receive his mark) for America under the National Recovery Act in (chapter 13). Mr. Roosevelt was a Navy man. His power rose up in the sea. His Navy quickly healed the wound received at Pearl Harbor. His successor, Mr. Truman, a farmer, power rose up on land (was seen coming out of the earth) and was responsible for the dropping of the first atomic bomb on an Asiatic nation, and frightened the whole world; and the nations began to say: "Who is able to make war with him?" (Rev. 13:4). (Of course, as you know, the world is no more afraid.)

"The beast shall go into perdition," which means - destruction, defeat, loss, perish, deteriorate. This is now going on, God is against America for her evils against the so-called Negroes. He is causing her defeat. She has not been able to win anywhere since she dropped her first atomic bomb. She is no more feared today by the nations of the earth. She has always delighted herself in doing evil against her loyal slaves (the so-called Negroes).

Hurry and join onto your own kind. The time of this world is at hand.

March 14, 1959

THE REVELATIONS BEAST (REV. 17:8)

"The beast that thou sawest was, and is not; and shall ascend out of the bottomless pit, and go into perdition: and they that dwell on the earth shall wonder, whose names were not written in the book of life from the foundation of the world, when they behold the beast that was, and is not, and yet is.."

"They that wonder" are the disbelievers in Allah and His religion, Islam. The devils and the disbelieving black people shall wonder. They were too proud to believe in Allah and His religion, Islam. They wonder about the truth of the message and the apostle of Allah who was delivering the message in their midst; whether he was the true apostle of Allah or a liar. They could not see their way of accepting him as a true apostle, therefore, they disbelieved in the truth of his message. They now wonder since they have been deceived by the beast and are even being tormented by the beast.

WHY DID not they believe the apostle and the message of truth which he had brought from the Lord of the Worlds, and had their names written down on the book of life with those who believe and follow the messenger of Allah? They now hate themselves for their rejection and wish that their names had been written in the book of life from the foundation of the world (the world of the beast, the Caucasian race); for they had believed in the beast's power to be sufficient to protect them against the God of the messenger of truth.

But the madness of the beast and the chastisement of Allah made them to change their minds and they now wish that they were Muslims so that they too could enjoy a peace of mind and contentment, for peace is given to all true Muslims, and they are contented.

The "Book of Life" here means the book which has the names of the so-called Negroes (believers of Allah and Islam) recorded therein. Of course, the entire nation of the black man is in the book of life, for they will live forever, and even the disbelievers of the white race will then wish that they had been created Muslims from the beginning of their world.

THE PEOPLE whose names are in the book of life mean that they will live forever. The "Book," the original black nation of life, is the nation whose life is unlimited; whose God is the creator of the universe. The time of others is limited.

The beast is wise to all or most of the scriptures and is ever planning to keep the dead, dead. They are ever watching the spread of Islam among the black people to see if there is a way to stop the progress of Islam. They will have to stop Allah (God) to stop the progress of Islam.

"And they wonder that a warner from among themselves has come to them. The disbelievers say: 'This is an enchanter, a liar.' And the chief among them say: 'Go and steadily adhere to your God: surely this is a thing intended.' " (Holy Qur-an 38:4, 6)

Hurry and join onto your own kind. The time of this world is at hand.

March 21, 1959

THE FINAL JUDGEMENT OF THE BEAST, THAT OLD DRAGON, THE HUMAN SERPENT.

"Swear by Him that liveth forever, that there should be time no longer" (Rev. 10:6).

Black people of America, hear and believe the truth or suffer the chastisement of Allah (God)! Get out of the beast's religion and name, for his names are not the "Attributes" of God. The beast's names will not be accepted, and they will be cut off forever. The name of God, alone, will save you. The holy names of Allah (God) and His religion of peace (Islam) are now being offered to you, and you are rejecting them for the worthless names and religion of the "Beast." We now have come to the end of his time and you know it not.

In the vision of John (Yakub) the Revelator (5th verse of the same chapter), he saw and heard one of the "Seven Angels" - whose commission is to execute judgment on the Kingdom of the beast (the Caucasian World) - lift up his hand to heaven (all Muslims spread forth their hands when praying in the direction of the Holy City Mecca which is due east). You should know that this Angel is not of the Christian religion, but of Islam. The Angel swears that time should be no longer. The reader may ask: "What is to be understood by:" There should be time no longer?" What should not be given any more time?"

THE TIME refers to two people or nations. The two people are the black and white people of America. The time of the White race was up in 1914 but they were given an extension of time to allow time for the resurrection of the mentally dead so-called Negroes. That time between 1914 and the end of the present world is limited to a certain number of years which will not exceed 70 years. Over half of it has already passed.

The end could take place at any time, now, for it will not come on the day that you think it will come. It can be said at any time now that: "Time should be no longer given to the "Beast," since they have had 45 years to repent and do good.

Since 1930 the American so-called Negroes have been called upon to accept the religion of God and His name, but they continue to reject it, except for a few. Therefore, the two people have been given time - one to repent of their evil done to the other; and the other to return to their own God and peoples' names and religion. So now: "What must be done?" The seventh verse of the same chapter reads: "But in the days (years) of the voice of the seventh angel, when he shall begin to sound, the mystery (the truth) of God should be finished as He hath declared to His Servants, the Prophets." This means that the time cannot end until the dead (the Negroes) hear the truth, and the believers are taken out of the beast's names and given names of Allah (God) to permit them to be restored again and forever to their own Holy Nation of Islam (the Black People).

IN ORDER to bring the mentally dead to realization of the Truth of God, self and the devils, this will come in the way of plagues and wars. These, plagues and wars will continue to come upon the wicked (the Christian world) until they have been brought to nothing. The power of resistance of the wicked must be broken. They hate the truth, good, and unity of the darker people. They are the open enemies of Black Mankind.

Due to the lack of knowledge of the so-called Negroes, they are in so much love with the enemy that it takes the intervention of God to make them know their enemies, and Allah as their God and Saviour; for they know not God nor the devil. As it was with Pharaoh in the land of Egypt in the days of Moses trying to lead his people, so it is today. This is God's way of making people know Him as God over all. So, fly to Allah, so-called Negroes!

Continued next week.

Hurry and join onto your own kind. The time of this world is at hand.

COME OUT OF HER, MY PEOPLE, "THE BEAST, THAT OLD DRAGON, THE HUMAN SERPENT." (REV. 18:4-8)

"The dragon," the devil, drags you out of the light of truth, after it comes to you, into the same darkness of ignorance and evil that the truth took you out of; therefore, the name "dragon" is an appropriate name for the devil. The name "serpent" is also one of the devil's names which fits his deceitful ways, his teachings of false against the truth, his setting the person of God up as a mystery (unknown), the changing of the natural religion of man into a false religion, and his seeking to make God (and His word) a liar, and he and his lie the truth, make the effects of his teaching and deceitful acts upon the blind, deaf and dumb black man and woman equal to the poisonous bite of a serpent (snake).

"Come out of her." He does not love you nor me but only hopes that with his soft words, songs, false promises, indecency, evils, sports and play, music, dancing and games of chance will keep you from accepting your salvation in Allah and Islam in the last days of his wicked rule of the world. His tricks, which he is playing on the world today, are deceiving 99 percent of the Negroes. He knows that the so-called Negroes have not been educated, nor morally trained into the knowledge of self and the societies of others which makes them unwanted by national and international societies. Therefore, they are making a false attempt of integrating the so-called Negroes for the sole purpose of keeping the Negroes with them and to prevent their return and escape of the doom and total destruction of the white race of North America.

"Come out of her," for America's sins have reached all the nations of earth and especially the holy nation of Islam and the Almighty God, Allah - the author of truth and righteousness - whose coming is to reward her as she has rewarded you, "and double unto her double according to her works." Her works are evil, deceit, robbery, murder, indecency, gambling, sport and play. "How much she hath glorified herself and lived deliciously; so much torment and sorrow give her (America)." The slave labor of a whole nation (the Negroes) for 300 years, and nearly another 100 years of free slave labor, as the free slaves were too dumb to unite and economize their earnings to become self-supporting, has made America the richest government on the earth. She lives and enjoys every modern luxury known to the science of man. "In her heart (not openly) saying: I sit a queen and shall see no sorry." Ancient Babylon and other overthrown nations before you said the same. "Therefore shall her (America) plagues come in one day (one year), death and mourning, and famine, and she (America) shall be utterly burned with fire, for strong is the Lord God who judgeth her."

He who judgeth America is Allah in person, who has revealed Himself and His purpose to me. He came under disguise in the person of Master W. F. Muhammad, the long-awaited coming of the "Son of Man" or as some say, "the second coming of Jesus" (the restorer of the kingdom of peace on earth by destroying the devil, the peace-breaker of the righteous). "Come out of her!" Unite and return to your own God, people, and religion. Stop evil practices. Show love and kindness to each other. Stop drunkenness, drugs, filthy and indecent doings, games of chance, fighting and killing each other! Let the world know that we love our brother as we love our own selves.

Next week "The Beast" to be continued.

Hurry and join onto your own kind. The time of this world is at hand.

IF ANY MAN WORSHIP THE BEAST AND HIS IMAGE (REV. 11:9, 10)

WE ARE warned in the plainest words against the love and worship of the symbolic beast (the Caucasian race) and not even to receive his mark in our heads or hands. To do so will bring upon us the wrath of God without mercy, according to the 10th verse of the above Chapter 1. There are no darker people on earth who worship this race of people as the American so-called Negroes do. Due to the lack of knowledge of this race and

their fear of them, they ignorantly love and admire them, their open enemies, who are the enemies of God and His prophets. While you faithfully
pray to God that you may not be a follower of the devils, you even now
love and worship them. Come out of them and save yourselves from the
wrath of Almighty Allah (God).

INTEGRATION will not solve our problem in this late day and time
of the judgment of the white race. Your problem can only be solved by
your separation from the white race. This will be brought about by the
work of God. Your names are of the beasts' (white race's) names. Your
religion and God, language and everything, are of the white race. To escape their doom and the wrath of God, you are warned to come out of
them.

"The mark in the forehead or in his hand," refers to your face or hands.
It is the face which includes the eyes, mouth, nose and forefront. It is in
the face where one looks for a sign of what the person really is. If the sign
is not in his or her general expression, it is in the eyes or what comes out
of the mouth in words. The hand is marked by the work they do in favor
of the beast, which comes from the head of our bodies. Therefore, whatever is in us, the mark or sign is in our forehead or the work of our hands.
Those who love the devils (the beast) are known by their works, looks,
talk, actions, and guilt.

THE WORKS of the beast are evil and filth, sport and play, games of
chance, love songs and temptation, drunkenness, murder and robbery. Under the above, they captivate you (the so-called Negroes). You need plenty
of teaching along these lines of how to keep yourselves from being
marked by the devils as unbelievers in your God. Remember, you were
reared by the devils, and your flesh and blood are already marked by them.
Today, they (the devils) are like roaring lions among you after your girls
and women, and many of his women and girls are after you for the sole
purpose of marking you as unfit to see the hereafter. God allows the devils
to tempt you that you may receive the infidel mark of unbelief in God, but
He will surely punish you who receive such mark.

The poor Negro preachers who understand not the scripture, nor God
and the devil, preach that you should love everybody, which includes the

devils, while God forbids us to love His or our own enemies, not to mention the arch-enemy devil. I warn you to receive not the mark of the beast in your head or hand.

Hurry and join onto your own kind. The time of this world is at hand.

"DIVINE CHASTISEMENT FOR ANY MAN WHO WORSHIPS THE BEAST, THE HUMAN SERPENT" (REV. 14:9 - 10)

"FOR BEHOLD, I will send serpents, cockatrices among you, which will not be charmed, and they shall bite you, saith the Lord." (Jer. 8:17)

The above-said scripture is a warning to you and me against the love and worship of the devils, the human serpents. Here God promises the willful worshipers of his enemies that He will even send those whom you take for friends above Him against you, and make them bite you (do you evil). For believing and obeying the serpent (the devil) after knowledge of God and His religion, Adam and his wife were punished by the serpent (the devil): "And I will put enmity between thy seed and her seed. It shall bruise thy head and thou shalt bruise his heel" (Gen. 3:15). God is not to be mocked. He warns us against loving and taking the devils for friends. Allah, alone, is our friend, and most certainly is able to make us know it.

The black man has ever suffered from his mistake in taking the white race for his friends. From that incident in Eden, six thousand years ago to this day, there is enmity and hatred between the two people (black and white). This cannot be removed except by the removal of one of the other race. The two could never come to and live up to a just agreement to do justice between each other. It is the impossible, unless their nature is changed. Adam and his wife accepted the advice of the devil against their Lord, and the serpent (the devil) has misled and put to death the prophets and the righteous servants of God ever since the fall of Adam.

"THE SERPENT BITE" - To cause trouble, disappointment, imprisonment, the loss of a good friend, the loss of paradise (the hereafter), to cause sickness and death. They did bite the disobedient followers of Moses (Numbers 21:6). Regardless of your good intentions for the serpent, he will bite you just the same. Who is any more submissive and lovable to the white man than the Originals (so-called Negroes)? Yet they receive the worst treatment from the whites than all the others of his kind. A couple of weeks ago I was told a few devils in Texas lynched a black man right on the streets for just disputing the devil's word. I know of plenty of places in the South where you will be killed if you dispute a devil's word or even ask for justice. I was born in such a place, and his Northern brothers are not angels to you and me; so do not feel safe anywhere, unless you are a believer in Allah.

AS IT IS WRITTEN of us: "They lived their life long under the very shadow of death." The Originals (so-called Negroes) are now offered the sure friendship of Allah (God) but they prefer the friendship of the devils (the serpent) rather than God. They are being beaten and murdered daily by them and denied justice everywhere. There just is no justice for us under this kind of people. Allah (God) desires that we come to the knowledge of Him and His salvation which he holds for us; therefore, the Holy Qur-an teaches us that he will send the devils against the disbelievers. Since it is the devils whom you believe in, then, by the devils you should learn from their actions and treatment that they are the devils.

ALLAH IS WELL able to prove His word true. The serpent cannot bite true Muslims - they are forbidden to him. The cockatrice mentioned in the chapter is just another name of the devils, which means: a monster, reptile, evil eye, a deceiver. So fly to Allah and keep away from the bite of the serpent.

Hurry and join onto your own kind. The time of this world is at hand.

UNIVERSAL CORRUPTION

"Corruption has appeared in the land and the sea on account of that which men's hands have wrought, that He (Allah) may then taste a part of that which they have done" (Holy Qur-an 30:41).

We cannot deny the fact that the Christian West is responsible for this universal corruption in the land and sea. From the same corruptions that their own hands have wrought will come their doom. The Christians preach that which they that do not do and cannot do. Such as "Love thy neighbor." I have yet to meet one that loved his neighbor as he did himself. "Thou shall not kill." I have as yet to meet such a Christian. They even fight against each other, rob and kill each other, but yet represent themselves as would peacemakers, what?

The great deceiver of the world will reap what he has sown. Have they not corrupted many people and nations under the false disguise as good, peace-loving Christians? The Christian West is full of the worst crimes, practicing her evils and indecencies to the fullest, and they seek to practice them on other nations as well. Universal tempters, ever parading before the world their bold, half-nude girls and women – they are before your eyes in almost everything, regardless. Murder, gambling, robbery, drunkenness, drugs, adultery, lying – there is hardly any end to it!

Their Land and seas are filled with deadly weapons of war, her islands of the sea she has filled with her corruption. Now she is hated and despised by all nations of earth, for she is proud and boastful and desires to rule all people according to her wishes. Her religion (Christianity) is a curse to us (the black man) which is full of slavery teaching. They have poisoned the Bible with their adding in and out of the truth. Now, her doom is in sight. It is their own work.

They fill the sea with powerful, deadly ships, parking them off shore of the homes of other nations. They secure air bases on foreign soil to park deadly bomb-carrying planes within striking distance of those whom she thinks to be her enemies. Is not this the way to make enemies? Is this the act of a real Christian, the follower of Jesus who they preach came for the peace of mankind and to teach the sheathing of the sword and the turning of the other cheek? Where is a good Christian among this race?

They love meddling in other people's affairs, they are in every fight or war regardless of whom or where; but yet crying, "Peace, peace," with every deadly modern weapon of war, brandishing them before the nations as a dare. Shall not the God of Peace and Justice deal with such trouble-making people as He did to those before you of old.

I warn every one of you my people, fly to Allah and follow me!

Hurry and join onto your own kind. The time of this world is at hand.

April 25, 1959

COMMON SENSE APPEAL TO UNITE

WHY SHOULD not we unite into one brotherhood? Are not white people united when it comes to black mankind? Are not all other than the white race united; e.g., the brown and yellow races? Are not they our brothers, belonging to the same nation (black mankind)? Are not we all brothers under the same burden of white slave masters' injustices? If you agree with me that we all are slaves and subject to the same injustice, why should we not unite as one nation of brotherhood?

In the eyes of our white slave masters, we are all Negroes - a people that no decent civilized nation will accept as equals. In the eyes of our black, brown, yellow and red brothers, we are the most ignorant, blind, deaf and dumb people on earth. In the eyes of Allah (God), we are mentally dead and yet His choice. Allah (God) is giving to us (the so-called Negroes) life to make us His special people - a people to be the head and not the tail . . . as it is written. When will you be convinced that our unity is all that is necessary to become a strong and most powerful and mightiest nation that ever lived? We know our slave masters have and are still doing all that they can to keep us divided, one against the other - then why not you and I unite?

IF A SMALL, well-twisted cord is hard to break, then how much harder is it to break 100 such twisted cords well twisted into **ONE**? We are well educated in the knowledge of what the slave masters dislike of us. If they are afraid of our unity as **ONE** nation of brotherhood, then why should not we unite? You know that they have deceived us in regards to the **TRUTH** of God, His religion, and our own selves. We have served them more obediently than we have the God of heaven and earth. In all our humblest submission to them, we received the most outright cruel injustice ever meted out to any human beings.

They make prostitutes of our American black women. They are free for them at all times, and you look on helplessly - not being able to put a stop to it because of our disunity. Why not unite? You see and hear of my work and the teaching of God's truth and power in your midst - how it is uniting those that believe and are following me, yet you are afraid to join in unity with us, regardless of the plain truth that you hear. Allah (God) has revealed and taught this truth to me to teach and warn you.

I am sure that you have learned that the Christianity taught to you by the slave master has not and cannot unite nor defend us against the injustice and brutality of the white race. You see and hear your leaders and preachers pleading to the white Christians to accept them as brethren and at the same time, the white Christians and their government in many places do not even like to look on your black faces. In Islam, you will have love, power and help of Allah . . . the entire nation of black mankind with you. This earth is ours and the GOD of it. Why not unite with us? You see and hear the talk of white mankind . . . is there anything good in it for you and me? NO!

ONE OF THEIR preachers by the name of Herbert Armstrong (of Pasadena, Calif.) is on the radio at 1:30 P.M. weekdays, preaching both the destruction of white government and the salvation of his people after their destruction for their evil doings. He takes the Bible's prophecies of the salvation of us, the lost-found members of the Tribe of Shabazz (so-called Negroes) to be a promised blessing for his people whom God will destroy and give the kingdom to us, the slaves (so-called Negroes). No one but Allah (God) and myself are preaching love and salvation for the so-called Negroes. No one can and is proving it from the same scriptures that Mr. Armstrong claims to be the salvation for his people (the enemies of Allah (God) and all black mankind), but Allah (God) and myself.

Why not unite with us? Regardless of the white man's opposition, we will be the winners, for God, Himself, is with me and those who follow me. I am your brother and a sufferer along with you. Let us unite.

Hurry and join onto your own kind. The time of this world is at hand.

<hr />

May 2, 1959

THE TRUTH HAS COME

"Say: The truth has come and the falsehood shall vanish. It neither creates nor reproduces anything new, nor restores anything; it shall not come back." (Holy Qur-an 31:19.)

WHAT has falsehood created or produced in the heaven and earth? We are now living in the time of truth, and falsehood cannot survive in the light of truth any more than darkness can survive in the presence of light. Allah has revealed the truth to me, and I am teaching it to you, but you do not believe it because of your love and fear of the slave masters. They too will be made to lick the dust, by the power of Allah. There never has been an enemy of His that He lacked power to rid Himself of. Neither does Allah lack power to rid Himself and the nation of Islam of this enemy that you fear and love; though you are even disgraced, beaten and killed by them, from your ministers of their slavery religion (Christianity) down to the lowly, ignorant man in the mud.

YOU HAVE MADE yourselves the most foolish people on the earth by loving and following after the ways of slave masters, whom Allah has revealed to me to be none other than real devils, and that their so-called Christianity is not His religion, nor the religion of Jesus or any other Prophet of Allah (God). You are a hard-headed, stiff-necked, rebellious people who are proud of your enemies and their slavery religion.

Allah is now sending the devils against you, that you may learn that His word is true, that they are heartless. Although they may do me and my followers evil, but by my Allah, they will not be able to get away with it; for every harm done to or against us will be returned doubly and tripled. Allah (God) is with me in person to bless you and me with right guidance and protection if we believe and rely on Him; otherwise, He can do us evil.

ALLAH (God) has not come to bring about love and peace between us and the devils (our slave masters) but rather to separate and make manifest to you and me our open enemies, the enemies of God and His prophets. We are now living in the judgment of this evil world of the devils, and the separation of the Bible's symbolic goats and sheep is now in effect. How blind you are, unable to see the truth, though it is like sunshine.

Do you not see and hear how your people of Africa from whom you were taken 400 years ago are separating themselves from the same enemy and establishing themselves into a united Africa for the African? Do you think the spirit of unity was created by themselves? No, it is the work of Allah to fulfill all that is written of Him by His prophets that He would do in these last days of the devils' world, (It is in your Bible.) If you are afraid of the truth, then how can truth help you when you disbelieve and are afraid of it? For such, the truth becomes your enemy.

ALLAH HAS revealed the truth of Jesus and His religion - that he was only a prophet (and was not the equal of Moses and Muhammad), and His religion was Islam, and not the Christianity of the Pope of Rome. Allah also revealed that Jesus was sent to the Jews and the Jews rejected him; therefore, he was unable to lead or convert them to Allah's religion, Islam, and that he died for his failure to accomplish that which he desired to do.

The truth of Jesus' death and burial God has revealed, and has condemned the fancy story of your Bible, of Jesus' rising from death and is somewhere alive sitting on the right hand of His father waiting for the judgment of this world to return to earth again. No one after death has ever gone any place but where they were carried. There is no heaven or hell other than on the earth for you and me, and Jesus was no exception. His body is still embalmed in Palestine and will remain there. Truth has come and falsehood will vanish.

Hurry and join onto your kind. The time of this world is at hand.

BROTHERHOOD OF BLACK MANKIND

WE MUST unite as brothers to all black mankind if we are to survive as human beings on this earth. We, the darker people of America, are the most disunited of all of our kind due to the evil and fear of the slave masters of America. Most of my people desire unity with all the nations, but do not know how to unite. Why should you fear to unite with your own people when you are trying daily to unite with other than your own? It is the will of Allah (God) that we be united.

Islam is a unifying religion, a religion of brotherhood, and the only true religion of Allah (God). Islam will be the only religion that will survive the great universal war which is now ready to burst upon the world of mankind. It is needless for you to put your trust in Christianity.

God has said to me that He will destroy it from the face of the earth. It stands true that Christianity has not helped us to unite, nor has it defended us against our enemies. It seems to have always been in the favor of our enemies. It even does not help the black preachers when the enemy attacks them, though they may be praying in the name of Jesus. You will come to know to the kind of Christianity that you are believing in is none other than the white race's tool used to trap the black people into a state of helplessness to the white race. God nor Jesus seems to care for it.

WHEN WHITE Christians go after the so-called Negroes, the Alabama black preachers should never preach the white man's slavery Christianity any more. According to this paper, the April 18 edition, --- Rev. Charles Billups was beaten with a chain by a mob of devils and left on the highway. The poor black people are gravely deceived in their faith and belief in Christianity. There is no such thing as hell or heaven after death. Death is the end of everything, righteous or wicked. When we die that is the last of anyone.

All Muslims believe in the resurrection - a mental resurrection. Some call it a spiritual resurrection. This resurrection is now going on among you from the preaching of this religion (Islam). We cannot hope for a better religion than Islam to unite us with Allah (God) and the brotherhood of the righteous. We must remember that we cannot unite in the brotherhood of the white race. It is pure nonsense to seek them for brotherhood. They are our enemies and take them for enemies, not friends. While living under their law and order, obey it and those in authority. All the righteous will do it. Unjust and evil people do not make the righteous be unjust and evil. A Muslim is the righteous. The very name means one who has submitted himself or herself to the will of Allah (God).

TRUTH AND righteousness will be victors over this world; for the world of sin and doings of evil are now drawing to an end. It is the purpose of Allah's (God's) coming to you and me to unite us onto our own kind, the nation of righteousness.

Hurry and join onto your own kind. The time of this world is at hand.

May 16, 1959

THE DEVILS GOING RAMPANT

THE ADAM's (devil) children, the great troublemakers, the demon, the fiend, Shaitan, the Adam's human beasts, the hell-raisers, the open arch-enemies of God, and all black mankind, who in the beginning disobeyed the law of God and introduced evil, filth and disrespect for God and His law of justice and righteousness (the black, brown, yellow and red people) are now on their traditional rampage against us, the so-called Negroes (their good old 400 year old slaves).

They have been murdering and raping us throughout the centuries and yet you are foolish enough to love and adore them (the devils) after all of their evils poured upon you and me. It just does not make sense.

Do not be surprised at anything like evil that you see them do; only be surprised when you see them do an act of good in your favor. Evil is the nature of Adam's children. They even have you believing that you are from Adam which is absolutely false. Never say that you are from Adam. Adam was the father (devil) of sin and disobedience, the devil of you and me.

THE RECENT Parker lynching and the Florida rape of one of our girls who was gagged and tied by four devils taking turns one after the other on her last Saturday morning (May 2) outside of the capital city of Florida (Tallahassee), a savage beast could-not do worse. They swooped down upon two of our original girls like hungry wolves after lambs with drawn shot guns and knives to destroy the virginity of our daughters and kill their black boyfriends if they attempted to try to protect the girls.

Of course, the boys would have been given more credit if they had received death in trying to defend their women against the filthy devils' attack. What good is our lives to us to allow our enemies to come into our families and rape our wives and daughters and lynch our men at will? Unite on the side of Allah and He will help us to put a stop to it, or die trying in the name of Allah.

APPEALING FOR justice from the lynchers and rapists brothers will avail us nothing. Parker's Mississippi mob of devils, the law's excuse is that the murderers cannot be found. The sheriff knew that Parker was charged with rape. Why did not he try to protect his prisoner by keeping the jail well-guarded from an attempt by his lynchers? How did the lynchers know where the keys were? Why did the nurse wait until the outlaws (lynchers) had captured their prey and was out of the town before notifying the sheriff's office or his home of the cries that she heard coming from the mouth of the murdered prisoner in and out of the jail? If it had been Negroes trying to take a white man out to lynch him, it would have been known at once; even to the U.S. Army!

Florida will protect her four devil rapists. She is already preparing a defense for them now by claiming the four devils to have been drunk, which we all know will be false. There is no justice for you under the American flag from their Supreme Courts to the jailhouse kangaroo courts. You fear to accept Allah and His true religion, Islam (Peace), and you will continue to suffer disgrace, beatings and killings at the hands of these devils. Remember, we live in a lawless world.

Hurry and join onto your own kind. The time of this world is at hand.

THE DEVILS INCITE THE HYPOCRITES
AND DISBELIEVERS

A HYPOCRITE is one who speaks that from his or her mouth what the heart does not agree with, or what is not in the heart. As the Holy Qur-an (2:8, 10) says: "There are some people who say: We believe in Allah and the Last Day; and they are not at all believers. They desire to deceive Allah and those who believe, and they deceive only themselves; and realize it not." A hypocrite is far more dangerous than your open enemy (the devil), for the hypocrite seeks to learn that about you which will hurt you with your enemies. They always hope evil for you. They claim brotherhood and friendship with you only to hurt you. The true Muslims, my followers, are at the present time honeycombed with such rotten characters of whom the believers must be aware of.

They are now joined with the devils receiving bribes to destroy me and my followers and the truth which Allah has revealed. Do you think that you will be successful in putting over this small-time evil murderous plan on Allah and His Apostle, and the true Muslims? Such plans, and the planner, were not successful in the days of Prophet Muhammad (may the peace and blessings of Allah be upon him), and they will not be successful in putting it over my Allah today. He it is whom I put my trust in, though I am willing to give my life for the freedom of my people from this merciless devil, their real open enemy.

MY LIFE, and the lives of my true followers are in the hands of Allah. It belongs to Him, for He has bought it with a price of suffering. On Him we rely. We will not raise our hands to do you harm; we are brothers and sisters by nature (same flesh and blood), so think before raising yours against us for the joy of devils who are your enemies as well as ours. I quote another few verses of the same chapter when it is said to them: "Believe as the other (Muslims) they say: Shall we believe as the fools believe? Nay, of a surety they are the fools, but they do not know. But when they are alone with the evil ones (the devils) they say: We are really with you, we are only mocking: Allah shall pay them back their mockery. He leaves them alone in their mockery, blindly wandering on."

FOR THEIR hypocrisy, the light of truth and guidance from Allah is taken from them and they think that they are being guided right when they are actually stumbling in the darkness of evil and ignorance. In another place the disbelievers are warned of their evil and proud attitude toward the Messenger of Allah in these words: "He said: (the proud disbelievers in the mission of the Messenger of Allah) - Tell me, is this he whom Thou has honored above me? If Thou will but respite me to the Day of Judgment, I will surely bring his descendants under my sway, all but a few, and beguile whomsoever of them you can with your seductive voice, make assaults on them with cavalry and infantry; and mutually share with them wealth and children, and make promises to them. But Satan promises them nothing but to deceive" (Holy Qur-an 17:62, 64).

The devils are playing this tricknowledge on my people here today. You shall soon come to know that Allah is your best friend, and that the devils are your open enemies. They are sharing with you wealth and children only to make you sharers in hell fire with them and their doom.

Hurry and join onto your own kind. The time of this world at hand.

May 30, 1959

Universal Brotherhood

IT IS the aim of Allah with His religion called Islam (Peace) to unite the world of darker people into one single nation of brotherhood. The lost-found members of the darker people (so-called American Negroes) must first be resurrected into the knowledge of Self, God, and the devil before they can recognize the importance of this plan of Allah (God) to unite the darker people of earth. This Universal Brotherhood cannot be a success unless we all believe in one God and one religion; and that one God is Allah, and that one religion is Islam (the only unifying religion of the human family of earth, and the only true religion of God).

We cannot successfully unite under any other religion. Christianity and the Church, as we know it, after a hundred years of experience in it, is not a unifying religion for the darker people. Really, it has failed to unite the white race, for they are at war with each other. The power of the Divine Spirit of God in Islam makes such sincere love for the brother believer that war or fighting among them is made impossible. When the so-called Negroes in America learn more about this unifying brotherhood religion called Islam, they too will come into it by the thousands and millions. We have here in America today all groups, including my followers, a little over one-half of a million. All over the world, over a half of a billion Muslims.

THE POOR BLACK man of America cannot and should not hope to have a sincere brotherhood with the white race. The nature of the races is opposed to it. This is why Allah must resurrect the dark people of America and teach them a knowledge of Self and others. The truth of it all is now being made manifest. Do not be surprised on learning that you were deceived in that which you have been believing to be the truth. We want unity of love, respect and protection. That can only be assured and enjoyed in the Universal Brotherhood of Islam and no other.

You should know today that you are a free people according to the Constitution of America and should exercise this freedom to be free indeed of that which brought us into bondage to the white race. We must think for self, do for self, protect self by unity of self and kind in the Universal Brotherhood of Islam. We must be a people seeking and accepting that which has the power to unite us and give protection for our unity. That power and protection can only be had and enjoyed with your belief in Allah and the Universal Brotherhood of Islam - this the white race knows. But, do not wait for them to tell you, for that they may never do.

YOU ARE FREE to think and do for self. You will be disappointed in waiting on your slave masters to think and do for you after being made free. They are not responsible for our failure in uniting on to self and kind. Naturally, they will try you with threats and the loss of jobs, food, houses and prestige. This, God permits them to do that you may be tried, but fear not such threats and trials when your salvation and future are at stake. They have no future in the hereafter. Their future and peace ended in 1914, and because of the lack of knowledge on your part, they, today, live on borrowed time. Universal peace and protection await you on your acceptance of Allah in the Brotherhood of Islam.

Hurry and join onto your own kind. The time of this world is at hand.

THE DANGER OF TAKING ENEMIES FOR FRIENDS

"O, you who believe, do not take for intimate friends from among others than your own people; they do not fall short of inflicting loss upon you; they love what distresses you; vehement hatred has already appeared from out of their mouths, and what their hearts conceal is greater still. Indeed, we have made the communication clear to you if you will understand." (3:118).

WE, THE LOST and found members of the Tribe of Shabazz (so-called Negroes), have for 400 years sought the friendship of our enemies - the white race, "the devils" – to the destruction of our own nation. The white race does not desire sincere friendship with black people. They may pretend to be your friends if you have something that they want, such as your women. Through her, they corrupt your nation and bring it to disgrace before the nations of the earth, as they have done for the poor black people of America. Because of disunity among us and no control over our women, we stand by with folded arms, cowards to the core, and allow the human brute beast to take our women and little girls out of our arms, to beat, rape, and destroy the most priceless gift of a nation (its woman). We cannot produce a pure, chaste nation with a "free-for-all" woman. If we are too cowardly to protect her against the human beast's advances, we should kill ourselves and our women. This suicide of the race would get us more credit in the eyes of the civilized nations of the earth than for us to continue to allow our girls and women to be corrupted by this human beast.

WE DO NOT love our girls and women as we should. If we did, we would protect them as other nations do. We should compel all of our males under the oath of death, regardless of faith, to regain control and

protect our black girls and women from being corrupted by both our enemies and non-enemies. The white race has made us to respect him and his
women; now let us make them and all races respect us and our women.
First, by self-respect. Second, with the help of Allah and our lives.

We are friends to everyone but self and kind. Our enemies love what
distresses us; but we are like the next verse says that we are: "Lo, you are
they who will love them while they do not love you." (3:118). Allah, to
whom all praises are due, said that: "You love the devils because they
give you nothing." That is so true. They lynch, burn, rape, beat and kill
you; yet you love and want to be like them in every way. Their way of life
will get you and me hell fire, for they were created for hell fire and know
it. But, their greatest desires is to carry you with them.

MAN GOES TO hell or heaven in this life, and to the grave or earth
after death. To love the devils is to be one of them and an enemy of God.
There is a Bible teaching that: "God so loved the world (the Negroes) that
He gave His only begotten Son that through Him (the Son) that they may
have eternal life." This is misunderstood. Allah (God) has never and never
will give a prophet's (a son's) life to save the world of devils. That scripture refers to the so-called Negroes, who were born and reared up in the
devil's world who must now be redeemed by the God of Righteous (the
promised Mahdi) or one whom He will choose from among the so-called
Negroes to be His apostle (Messenger). This man is the one the scripture
refers to as the first begotten of the dead (mentally dead so-called Negroes). He is also the first born of God because his first birth and teaching
was of the devils, which is considered a dead race without eternal life, for
the life of the devil race was limited to 6,000 years. So, the scripture
makes a distinction between the races, or race and nation (black and
white) by calling one (the devils) the dead or wicked, and the other (the
original black nation) the people of eternal life; for the black nations have
no limitation of life on the earth.

Hurry and join onto your own kind. The time of this world is at hand.

JUSTICE

WE THANK Allah for last week-end's visit to the nation's capital. We were welcomed and greeted by some six or seven thousand at the Uline Arena. Thanks to the wise and well-trained police department of the nation's capital, who assigned a police motorcycle escort to meet me at the airport. For this I thank them, as it was a wise, worthy and well-done job. My followers and I want them to know that we appreciated this great service. Allah will ever reward those who do good to others.

Justice is right, or righteous, opposed to wrong or evil doing. Justice is the nature of God and the righteous. It is the law that judges between right and wrong. Justice is the weapon that will be used by Allah (God) to judge everyone according to their works in His day, which is called the day of judgment. It is the purpose of His coming. Justice is one of the greatest principles of righteousness and fair dealings.

If justice had prevailed in the world over injustice there would be no judgment. The judges of this world are unjust. Nature did not give them justice and righteousness. This is why they and their world must be destroyed, for the poor righteous SUFFER UNDER THEIR RULE.

ALLAH HAS COME to make manifest this great enemy of justice and righteousness, -it was incumbent upon Him, the god of justice (I use the past tense "was" because God has come) - and the long-guarded secret of God and the devil is now revealed.

The god of justice will judge the world with justice, for it would not be a just judgment if you never knew God and the devil. We have been pleading and begging for justice from that which by nature is not there. Do they judge justly among themselves?

Then if by nature they do injustice to themselves, can you and I expect justice from them? Was it an act of justice that their fathers enslaved our fathers?

After 300 years of servitude slavery, blinded, deaf and dumb, did the slave masters of our fathers offer our fathers anything like a home here that our fathers could call their own, such as some part of the country where they could be free to live their own way of life?

THEY STILL LIKE to call you after their names which makes you still their slaves. They call us citizens without giving equal justice. With all of your blood and lives given to help keep America for white Americans, you return to meet lawlessness and injustice. You are beaten, raped, lynched, burned, disgraced and rejected and denied justice by the government's bar of justice whom we defend with our life's blood. Our girls and women are beaten, disgraced and raped by them.

White lynchers and rapers of our people are judged innocent by their own unjust judges. Though all of this injustice is done to you, you continue like sheep among wolves to go on suffering, being away from our God and our people. Anyone who seeks justice for you is labeled as an enemy to the government OR IS BRANDED A RACE HATER. The government makes itself clear to you and me that it is no defense for us against injustice at the hands of their people.

The only alternative left is to unite as one on the side of Allah. Get justice from people who love justice and who love you and me, and they are Allah and the Nation of Islam. "Fight with those who fight against you" (Holy Qur-an). "An eye for an eye" (Bible), and fight every injustice, against us with every drop of blood that is in us.

YOU AND I, a nation of 20 million, must unite together and agree whether or not we shall continue to live and suffer the lawless human beasts to beat, lynch, rape and terrorize our homes, or wives and children in a government that will not punish them for what they do evil to us. If not, it is better that we go and kill our unprotected women and children and then commit suicide ourselves, than to be called 20 million cowardly fools.

We have been afflicted by this race of devils for 400 years and now we must have equal justice in any government that we live in, and if not, you and I cannot be called citizens of that government.

Hurry and join onto your own kind. The time of this world is at hand.

THE SO-CALLED NEGROES OF AMERICA

IN A SMALL monthly paper printed in Morris Plains, N.J., in the language of true Moslem Shriners, the following appeared in the January 1959 issue:

It says: "The greatest shame upon the escutcheon of America. Its treatment of Negroes. These Americans are here because their forefathers were ruthlessly kidnapped in Africa, herded into suffocating ships, chained, beaten and sold into slavery.

"Much white blood is in the veins of American Negroes. Southern aristocrats had children by Negro women (and are still getting them by the Negro woman). Union occupation armies fathered many children by Negro women. Those fierce racists opposing the inevitable dawn of justice for Negroes ironically are fighting their own flesh and blood.

"These persecuted descendants of slaves go right on (like fools) defending the democracies of (white) Americans. Ralph Bunche, Negro Nobel Prize winner, UN Under-Secretary, refused an invitation to become U.S. Assistant Secretary of State because Washington, D.C. had Jim-crow laws.

"American Negroes dress American, talk American, live American, die American. Over a million Negro soldiers took up arms for America in World War II (some 400,000 fought for America in 1917).

"Dead Negro Americans are buried with white soldiers on every Revolutionary War battle field only to be denied justice by the white soldiers of America (the Government). The first (fool) American patriot killed in the Boston Massacre was a Negro. The first (fool) woman to fight in the American Army was a Negro who disguised herself as a man to fight for America's independence.

"**NEGROES** paid the crimson cost of liberty at Antietam, Vicksburg, San Juan Hill, the Argonne, Chateau Thierry, Leyte Gulf, the Ardennes Bulge, Anzio Beachhead, Iwo Jima, Hungnam, the Yalu and Inchon Reservoir.

"Every other tie on the roadbed of the Union Pacific and the DL&W is the worked out, sweated-out body of a Negro. The fiery tongues of molten iron pouring out of American Negro workers.

"And without recrimination. They sang 'Swing Low Sweet Chariot' and 'Come Down Sweet Jesus' as they lifted and existed on next to nothing, lived in unsanitary firetraps, ghettoed, Jim-crowed.

'Negro Americans can be the deciding factor in world power. Today two-thirds of the world are 'people of color.' It further takes a snap at Masonry which the Negroes buy, seeking justice and respect as a man and as the brother of man in these words: "If Masonry is for light, then there can be no lampshade on its light. If the brotherhood of man is all-inclusive - not a cruel joke - then Masonry must be honest with itself or go down as history's great mockery."

THE SO-CALLED Negroes are tools in the hands of their enemies and were made blind, deaf and dumb by their enemies (the slave masters) when they were babies. Yet they think their devil enemies are their friends. They give their lives for their enemies to be free to keep them subjects, beaten, lynched, raped and killed. They help the white devils destroy their own women by giving her all the freedom she wants in their homes, stores, restaurants, hotels, offices, factories, farms and as baby-sitters. They strip her before the devils and ask the devils to accept her, and she foolishly accepts the devil to destroy her family's morals and to spot her children with the devil's blood, even after having knowledge that the same white man will not give her and her menfolk justice in any court.

Negro Masons, do not buy the white man's masonry. There is no brotherhood there for you. It is only a farce of justice. Come and accept the real Islam, the Muslim. I am the door. I will let you in. For our slavery, sweat, blood and life, one-half of America is not enough as pay.

Hurry and join onto your own kind. The time of this world is at hand.

THE WHITE RACE'S FALSE CLAIM OF DIVINITY

THERE are several false teachers sponsored by the devil to deceive the black people by misinterpreting the truth in their favor, especially the Bible's teachings. Most of the white teachers of the Bible make the white race God's divine people. (Adam's race, Israel). These white teachers (beware of them) would love to have you and me (that is, if they could) believe that they are the beloved people of God. Their false claim is easily disproved. But, since they are the deceivers of the black nation, naturally, the so-called Negroes who were reared and taught all they know by white slave masters are made easy victims to such false teachings and claims.

The Bible itself, being tempered with and poisoned by them is made to read as though the salvation in it is for the white race. The so-called Negroes who are the real chosen people of God today are not mentioned under their name. The name "Israel" is used to blind the black people especially the American so-called Negroes. For example: Mr. Herbert Armstrong of Pasadena, Calif., a radio and TV preacher, and Theodore Fitch of Council Bluff, Iowa., the author and writer of a small 56-page book titled: "Our Lord's Plan for the White Race," with a sub-title, "Who we are? Where we came from? Why He chose us? What our work is? Why our descendants must remain white?" These questions I will truthfully answer.

MR. FITCH is against the mixing of race (intermarriage) which he calls "an awful sin," of which I, or any sane lover of his or her own people, will agree. Mr. Fitch does not seem to know himself and race. Of course, the true knowledge of the white race was first revealed in 1930-1933 by Almighty God, in the person of W.F. Muhammad, the God and Saviour of the American so-called Negroes. To him I submit and give praise all the days of my life.

Mr. Fitch and others will agree that Adam and Jacob (Yakub) was the father of the white race. Adam, according to the Bible (Gen. 3-6) Holy Qur-an (2:30), was the first sinner and divine law-breaker, liar, mischief-maker, murderer and world deceiver. As for Jacob (Yakub) whose name was changed to Israel (Bible - Gen. 32:28) because he wrestled with the angel and did prevail, according to the word and teaching of Allah (God) to me, the only angel that Jacob (Yakub) wrestled with was the black man, to bring out of the black man the present white race - for the white race was and is in the germ of the black nation.

Mr. Yakub was the first to discover this germ in us and grafted this germ of the black man into an independent race of people. Mr. Yakub taught his people how to rule the black nation for 6,000 years. Their time expired in 1914, but they have been given an extension of time, until the black man could be awakened out of his 6,000 year sleep; so as to restore the American black people (the real lost-found members of their people) onto their own kind.

JACOB (YAKUB) the great deceiver who deceived his own father and brother (Gen. 27:19, 35, 36) robbed his father-in-law, Laban, of his cattle (Gen. 30:37-43, 31:1-2). This Mr. Fitch would like to deceive you in making you to believe that the white race is the chosen people of God and Jesus. This is not true and I will disprove it.

Herbert Armstrong would like that we believe that the white race, even after they are punished for their sins, will yet be chosen by God to be the rulers. If it pleases Allah, I will defend my people with His truth, and make the devils' falsehoods manifest to the world.

The white race is not a divine chosen race. It is the black nation. The so-called Negroes of America are really God's choice to build the kingdom of peace on earth. The Negroes are the lost sheep of the Bible and not Israel. The white race has built a world of evil and bloodshed. We could not build our world in the time given to them to rule. We had to wait until their time was up.

Hurry and join onto your own kind. The time of this world is at hand.

THE WHITE MAN'S CLAIM TO DIVINE SUPERIORITY

THE TRUTH that the world has been waiting to know is just the answers to the questions Mr. Fitch asked in his book titled "Our Lord's Plan for the White Race" (the God of righteousness never had a plan for you) with a sub-title, "Who We Are?" (the enemies of God and the righteous); "Where We Came From?" (from the black man); "Why He Chose Us?" (the God of righteousness did not choose you; if He had, He would not destroy you); "What Our Work Is?" (evil); "Why Our Descendants Must Remain White?" (certainly, you should remain white).

The average so-called Negroes would be misled by Mr. Fitch and his answers to such questions if it were not that Allah (God) had visited us and revealed the true knowledge of the white race. The best of it all, He is making the white race manifest to the world of the original black nation that they are our enemies, the devils, and that their father (Yakub) that created them is also classified as the father (Yakub) of the devil race because of his idea and making of the devils.

SINCE THE truth of the devils has been revealed, the devils are still trying to hide their true selves in order to fool the black man and woman, and especially the American so-called Negroes, whom the white man has fooled for 400 years - and mean to keep them fooled regardless to the truth.

But, as it is written: "The truth would be made so plain that a fool should not err."

"What I teach you that Allah has taught me is just that plain. You that read what I write, and you that listen to what you hear me say of the truth, cannot have an excuse for misunderstanding; for there is none. I leave nothing for you to be misled in. If you are blind to this, you will be blind in the hereafter.

"Who is the white race?" I have repeatedly answered that question in this article for nearly the past three years. "Why are they white skinned?" Answer: Allah (God) said this is due to being grafted from the original black nation, as the black man has two germs (two people) in him. One is black and the other brown. The brown germ is weaker than the black germ. The brown germ can be grafted into its last stage, and the last stage is white. A scientist by the name of Yakub discovered this knowledge (that white could be grafted out of black) 6,645 years ago and was successful in doing this job of grafting after 600 years of following a strict and rigid birth control law.

WHITE IS not a superior color by nature to black, but it is inferior. If you allow them to teach you the truth of themselves, you will never know the truth. Many white writers on the race and color issue today, which has become universal because of the whites' claim to divinity and superiority, claim that the color of the skin is due to certain climatic conditions, such as, hot Africa produces the black man; the cold, frigid zones above the equator produce the color white. This claim is as false as darkness is to light. Ask yourself these questions: If our colors are caused by certain climatic conditions of earth, why should not the white man become black in hot Africa, South and Central America? Also, why should not a black person turn white above the equator in the cold frigid zones of the north? If not, then beware of the devils' tricks on the truth of Allah (God). Does the climate of Japan and China make them brown and yellow? Did the climatic conditions of America make the Indians red? Then, why are we all not red?

To be continued next week.

Hurry and join onto your own kind. The time of this world is at hand.

THE WHITE RACE'S FALSE CLAIM TO BE DIVINE CHOSEN PEOPLE

ACCORDING to the Bible (Gen. 3:20-24), Adam and his wife were the first parents of all people (white race only) and the first sinners. According to the Word of Allah, he was driven from the Garden of Paradise into the hills and caves of West Asia, as they now call it, "Europe," to live his evil life in the West and not in the Holy Land of the East. Therefore, the Lord God sent him (Adam) forth from the Garden of Eden, to till the ground from whence he was taken. So he drove out the man; and He placed at the east of the Garden of Eden cherubims (Muslims guards) and a flaming sword which turned every way to keep (the devils out) the way of the tree of life (the nation of Islam)." The sword of Islam prevented the Adamic race from crossing the border of Europe and Asia to make trouble among the Muslims for 2,000 years after they were driven out of the Holy Land and people, for their mischief-making, lying and disturbing the peace of the righteous nation of Islam.

The Holy Qur-an says: "But the devil made them both fall from it, and caused them to depart from that (state) in which they were; and we said: Get forth, some of you being the enemies of others, and there is for you in the earth an abode and a provision for a time." (The time here refers to the limited time of the Adamic race. The time is 6,000 years.) According to the above verse (2:36), they were driven out because they were the enemies of the people of the Garden. In these words: "Get forth, some of you being the enemies of others." The "others" cannot refer to any others than the people of the Garden (the Muslims).

THE ADAMIC RACE is still the enemy of the Muslims (the black man). Nevertheless, Allah did not deprive the Adamic race of right guidance through His prophets, whom they persecuted and killed. The Adamic race's (the white race) history is a proof that they are the enemies of God and the righteous, for they never did sincerely accept a prophet of God. Can they now claim to be the chosen race of God? Where is their proof? Is it because they were allowed to rule us for 6,000 years? If they are the chosen race of God, why would God limit their time of rule? Why did God send His prophets to warn them that He was going to destroy them? The Holy Qu-ran 7:14 says "He said (the devil); respite me until the day when they are raised up." Those that are referred to as being "raised up" refer to the resurrection of the black man into the knowledge of the white race as being the devils', the enemies of Allah (God) and the black nation. "He said (the devil); as Thou hast caused me to remain disappointed, I will certainly lie in wait for them in Thy straight path."(Holy Qu-ran 7:166). What Allah disappointed the devils in was the limiting of their rule over the nations and making them manifest to the world of black men, that they are the enemies and great deceivers of the righteous.

The white race is not, and never will be, the chosen people of Allah (God). They are the chosen people of their father Yakub, (the devil).

Hurry and join onto your own kind. The time of this world is at hand.

<hr>

July 18, 1959

THE WHITE RACE'S CLAIM TO DIVINITY

"Jesus said unto them: If God was your Father, ye would love me; for I proceeded forth and came from God; neither came I of myself, but He sent me." (Jesus made no claim to be the equal of God, his sender, in the above words. His coming was not of himself, but of God.) "Why do ye not understand my speech? Because you cannot hear my word." (Because they are the devils, the enemies of truth.) "Ye are of your father, the devil, and the lusts of your father, ye will do. He was a liar and a murderer from the beginning, and abode not in truth, because there is no truth in him. When he speaketh a lie, he speaketh of his own; for he is a liar, and the father of it." (John 8:42, 43, 44.)

According to the Bible, Jesus was talking to Israel (the white race), for it was to that race that Jesus was sent, and not to the world of mankind, as some would have you to believe. Jesus makes it very clear that God, his Father, was not the father or god of Israel, but Israel's (the white race's) father was the devil. Yakub was the father of the white race. Yakub was not a real devil himself, but due to his idea of making devil, made him the father. The devil is not self-created, but the original black man is self-created, and from the black man came all men and colors.

JESUS SAID to Israel: "If God were you Father." The God that Jesus was referring to was the God of Righteousness, whom Jesus called his Father, for if Israel's god had been the same as Jesus' God, Israel would have loved Jesus, the truth and righteousness - which Jesus was teaching; for Israel and Jesus would have been brothers if both had been from the same father. Therefore, Jesus could not convert or save Israel from her sins, for the two (Jesus and Israel) had two different gods as their fathers. Israel's father (god) was a liar and murderer, while Jesus' Father (God) is the Father of Truth, Righteousness, Justice and Equality.

Can the white people truthfully claim to be descendants from the Divine Supreme Being, the God of Righteousness? Can they be the chosen people of the God of Righteousness? Can they see the hereafter, while being the children of the devil? Jesus said: "Israel could not hear his word." They could hear, but they could not believe the word of truth and righteousness which Jesus was teaching, for nature did not give them such divine attributes. Since by nature they were created liars and murderers, they are the enemies of truth and righteousness, and the enemies of all those who seek the truth, and the bearers of truth (the Prophets).

ALLAH SAID to me that their father, Yakub, taught the first lie, and was the first murderer. He taught the nurses (while grafting the white race from the black nation) to kill all black babies and save the brown babies, and to graft the brown into its last stage, which is white. He also told the nurses to lie to the mothers of the black babies (and the white race is still lying to the black women) and tell the mothers of the black babies that they had given birth to an angel, and to allow the nurse to take it to heaven, so that when the mother dies, she will have a room in heaven with her baby. But, the nurse was to kill the black baby or give it to a cremator to be burned to death. That was the beginning of lying and murdering.

The white race is still trying to get rid of the black baby, and they have the black mothers helping them rid the earth of black people. They teach hatred of the black, and the black hate the black; while the black is the best in the eyes of Allah (God). Without Allah's help, not one of us will be saved in a world where the black man and his woman have become the lovers of the devils (the white race). Jesus said in the above chapter and verse that they (the white race) "abode not in the truth." This, all of the so-called Negroes know to be the truth of white people, whom they have been among for 400 years. Can the white race be the divine chosen people of God?

Theodore Fitch of Council Bluffs, Iowa, author and writer of his book titled, "Our Lord's Plan for the White Race," falsely claims the Bible prophecies which are really referring to the American so-called Negroes, to be for the white race. The symbolic lost sheep of the Bible which must be found and restored are the Negroes, and not white Israel.

(To be continued next week).

Hurry and join onto your own kind. The time of this world is at hand.

THE WHITE RACE'S FALSE CLAIM TO DIVINITY

THE devil's struggle against us, their power, and authority, is now slipping since the appearance of Allah. Now they have begun to spread false teachings to trap the so-called Negroes. As soon as truth comes to them, they are prepared to try to crush it and keep their 400-year-old slaves dumb. It is actually a race between God and the devil to win the American so-called Negroes. Allah wants to sit the Negroes in heaven and the devil wants to keep them in hell. As it is written of them: "And the serpent (the devil) cast out of his mouth (false) water as a flood after the woman, (the Messenger of Allah and his followers) that he might cause her to be carried away of the flood." (Rev. 12:15). Here, you have that the devils will flood the people with false teachings to try to prevent the progress of the truth. But the falsehood is destined to come to naught, for God has revealed to me the truth - it is the salvation of my people. With it, I will fight the world of satan and his followers until they submit and are destroyed. (The white race hates the truth that is now making them manifest for fear of losing the Negroes).

The Lord God of Islam is my defense. He will defend me against my enemies. He loves me and I love Him because I seek to do His will, and He knows that I love my people, whom He loves, and has come to deliver us from the power of the devils, that we may become His servants, and dwell in His presence in peace and security.

THE DEVILS SAY to you that they are better than you and I. Really, they are after the so-called Negroes whom they have crushed, made blind, deaf and dumb. They have robbed and experimented on us for 400 years, and all other darker people whom they have come in contact. Now they stand before you saying, "I am better than you." As he says in the Holy Qur-an: "I am better than he; thou hast created me of fire, while him thou didst create of dust." (7:12).

According to the word of Allah to me, the white race was created in haste. (See Chapter 21:37). Their father, Yakub, was in such a hurry to put his new people on earth as rulers, that he married them while very young (15 and 16 years of age). Knowing that they had only 6,000 years to go, he rushed them, so says the word of Allah to me. This makes them hasty, by nature. They have a fiery temperament; while the original black man is meek and humble. They were made to attract the black people. With this attraction, and other actions of evil and filth, they intended to take you to hell with them. As they say: I will certainly lie in wait for them in Thy straight path; I will certainly come to them from before them and from behind them and from their right hand and from their left hand; and Thou shalt not find most of them thankful. And the devil swore to them both; most surely "I am a sincere adviser to you." (7:12, 16, 17, 21).

MR. FITCH, in his book (page 29) states that they the white race are much stronger physically, mentally, spiritually, and morally. I will agree that on average they are larger in stature than we are; but they cannot out-work us if we want to work. They claim 60 per cent more brain space than we. This is not true. They are not as wise as we are. Our father created and made the universe and one of us made them. As we made the present universe, we will build a new universe. Can the white scientists do the same? We played sleep while they worked; now we are awaking and will build a new world which will make yours look like child's play. We have above you seven worlds or heavens, the stars and the moon show the weight of our brains. What do you have that we did not give you? You shall soon come to know who is the wisest and the most powerful.

Hurry and join onto your own kind. The time of this world is at hand.

August 1, 1959

FOR WHERESOEVER THE CARCASS IS, THERE WILL THE EAGLES BE

GATHERED TOGETHER. (MATT. 24:28)

The poor so-called Negroes are the mentally dead carcass of the Nation. The robbers of them, even their own kind, come from every direction to eat (rob) them. Their enemies, (the white slavemasters) bleached them as a dried bone for 400 years. Yet, their own kind seek to grind the bones which are left. They are blind, deaf, and dumb, and every civilized person who finds them soon discovers that they are a prey; and go after them like eagle birds to finish them off. It is a shame and a sin on the robbers of my people. I find robbers of them from black, brown, yellow, red, and white races. They come from all walks of life, from the gamblers and dope peddlers to the religious leaders of all faiths and their members; even to the weak Muslims of America and Asia, not to mention the Christian leaders who have eaten the flesh and left the bones for the foreigners.

THE PRESENCE of Allah (God), Who wants to put flesh again on their bleached bones and life in the body through His word of Truth preached by me and those who follow me, has caused many eagles to come flying; seeking to get a hold on what is left of them. They would like to charge me with grinding the bones of my people, but they cannot. Even after honey-combing my followers with dirty paid stool pigeons, many of them we now recognize and only await the hour to rid ourselves of them. The eagles of prey envy the Shepherd of God among them because the Shepherd will fight for the safety of his sheep, and he has Allah (God) on his side. He is appointed by Allah (God) and Allah has given him the sheep to feed with the bread of truth, and will not give them to anyone else. Some of the eagles (robbers) even seek the help of religious scholars here and there to say that they are the ones who shall or should lead this people to us and God. But, this is not so. You cannot send over or authorize anyone to do this job of giving life to my people, regardless to whom you are, or where you come from. Allah is the Sender of His Messengers.

Many of the eagles (robbers) have nothing to offer but arguments against the Shepherd, telling the sheep that he (the Shepherd) is not the Messenger of Allah and that he is not an Apostle. They say, "He is not teaching Islam, he is teaching hate. He cannot speak or read the Arabic

Language." They so foolishly do not know that the Holy Qur-an and the Bible have all their evil sayings and doings recorded in them. "And those who disbelieve say: You are not the Messenger. Say: Allah is sufficient as a witness between you and me and whoever has knowledge of the Book." (Holy Qur-an 13:43).

MUHAMMAD could not read or write, but was granted the revelations which made up the Book called the Holy Qur-an. He was given the knowledge of it by Allah, Who gave it to him. Take a look at Allah's Servant in the Bible. It says: "Who was more blind, deaf and dumb as my Messenger that I sent? Who is blind as he that is perfect, and blind as the Lord's servant? Seeing many things, but thou observest not; opening the ears, but he heareth not. The Lord is well pleased for this righteousness' sake; he will magnify the law, and make it honourable.

No prophet of the past brought forth judgment unto Truth. Judgment, for truth's sake, comes at the end of this world. Jesus and Muhammad both failed to convert the Jews and Christians, but the last Messenger will not make an attempt to convert them. His preachings are to close the door against the enemies of Allah (God) and His prophets. Judgment follows his message, for only God is left to act after him. He is the end of prophets because there is nothing left for a prophet to do after God has manifested Himself to the world, along with the last Messenger.

Hurry and join onto your own kind. The time of this world is at hand.

August 8, 1959

THE ST. NICHOLAS ARENA NEW YORK CITY

ON Sunday, July 26, 1959 - First - We thank Allah (God) for the safe trip there and return, and for the peace and protection we enjoyed. Second - We thank the people of New York, and especially the nearly ten thousand who greeted us with such warm welcome at the St. Nicholas Arena, 69 West 66th St., Downtown, New York. Thanks to the police department for their presence. Of course, there is very little work for the police officer among us. Wherever we go there is peace. My people are good. This was my second public lecture in New York City. Last July, 1958, was my first. On that visit, we were received by an estimated seven thousand people who jammed the hall for the two days that we were in the city.

Harlem has the most, and best race-minded people in America. There you will find the Black man who wants something of his own for which he can be proud of. They welcome you if you have a sound program for the people. They are a wonderful people. Once Harlem is united into the Brotherhood of Islam, she could command the whole twenty million American dark people. She only needs to rid herself of worthless orators who have no constructive program for this half of a million dark people.

WE, THE NATION of Islam, have been given that constructive program, and by all means, we intend to give it to our people in Harlem, New York. The readiness in the eyes and actions of the people of Harlem tell you and me that these people are now ready for something which they can proudly call their own. If it be the Will of Allah, I will visit my Harlem people again within two or three weeks, for it would be a shame on the part of the Brotherhood of Islam to leave this great half million people to be exploited by hungry want-to-be leaders without a constructive program.

Last Sunday, I wanted to spend my time in making clear to Harlem our program, but having to defend false charges made against me by the enemies of teaching hate - (the white race is, the father of hate) - I did not have time to tell my people all that God wanted me to tell them. The enemies of our people see and know that it is time for the rise of our people, and are seeking every evil and deceitful way to prevent it. The Shepherd must forever be on his guard to show up the wolf, whose only desire is to eat the sheep. Our enemies desire to make the truth, which will free our people from the power of their enemies, and which will sit them in heaven at once, look so dangerous that they will fear to accept it.

GOD HAS FOR our people here in America the greatest blessing that ever was bestowed on any people at any time in the past. He wants to make us the permanent rulers of the earth. He wants to give to us the Kingdom. The so-called Negroes must not follow an Uncle Tom for their leader. They just do not relieve you of the yoke, for their greatest desire is to please the slavemaster and leave you displeased. In this enlightened world of today, the slavemasters' Tom, Boot-lickers, and stool pigeons we cannot use, and must weed them out from among us as other nations have, and still are doing. They are the hold back of our progress among us. Remove them or isolate them and enjoy success. We have a few who are being paid to keep the enemies well informed of all we say. One day they will be out. The poor man in the mud is my friend. His friend is Allah, and myself, and five hundred million Muslims all over the world.

All of you, who failed to get your names on our register Sunday, please send them to me at my address: 4847 South Woodlawn Ave., Chicago 5, Ill.

Hurry and join onto your own kind. The time of this world is at hand.

TRUTH AND JUSTICE FOR THE SO-CALLED NEGROES

Allah (God) has come to us to give to you and me truth and justice and to sit you in heaven at once. But our enemies have ever kept the truth and justice from us and have never, never given justice to the so-called Negroes. To prove their hatred and wicked, unjust rule over us, they are out to prevent that truth and justice from getting to you by using the old trick on us - "divide the Negroes - use one against the other."

The world knows that I am teaching you the truth and, most of all, desire justice for my people in America, with whom I have suffered all of my life. Allah (God) has given to me the key to loosen them from the power and bondage of our ever-relentless, merciless, evil, indecent murderers, our open enemies, the devil slavemasters; so that our people may be free indeed and know their God (our only true friend) and their enemies (the devils), who have deceived them and the world of the black nation.

This truth and justice preached to the blind, deaf and dumb of my people in America is hated by the white race of America, and they would like to fool my people and make them hate me and the truth, which will free them, by teaching them that I am teaching hate. They know that the Negroes are already fools for loving them, and they would be worse fools to love them after having knowledge of them being the real devils.

THIS IS that TRUTH which the white race and their black lovers call hate teachings - THE TRUTH OF GOD AND THE DEVILS. We must know the truth and must have justice for our people. If not, it would be better to commit suicide than to continue to be slowly destroyed by our white slavemasters' children. They make fools and Uncle Toms out of all of our educated professional class of people with a false show of social equality.

We, the so-called Negroes, must and will have what other nations have for themselves - some of this God-given earth that we can call our own, and protection for our wives and children from the murderous and raping hand of the American devils. We love our women and children as other nations love their women and children. We must have good homes to live in and protection for those homes, or die trying to get it. We will never enjoy peace, freedom, justice and equality under our enemies (the white race), for there is no justice and peace in that race.

IN THIS MODERN day and time, we should know that love and unity FIRST among our own kind is the key to power, justice and equality. But envy of those who can do, from those who cannot do, are the hindering causes of the black man. Talid Ahmad Dawud and his TV blues-singing Miss Dakota Staton (who the paper says is Mrs. Alijah Rabia Dawud in private life) and whom the world can hear her filthy blues and love songs and see her immodestly dressed, were successful last week in getting a chance to breathe their venomous poison against me and my followers in this paper and in a local Chicago paper, The Crusader. Mr. Dawud is from the West Indies (Antigua) and was born a British subject. He was known by the name Rannie (sounds like a devil's name). He is jealous of the progress with which Allah (to whom praises are due) is blessing me and my followers, and this jealousy is about to run Mr. Dawud insane. (The Crusader erroneously called him an Imam.) Mr. Dawud and Miss Staton should have been ashamed to try to make fun of me and my followers while publicly serving the devil in the theatrical world. I do not allow my followers to visit such, nor do I allow my wife and the believing women who follow me to go before the public partly dressed. If they would, never would I claim them to be mine any more.

MR. DAWUD has been trying for some time to do me and my followers harm in the Islamic world through the Muslim Embassy in this country and abroad, but he is only hurting himself.

Hurry and join onto your own kind. The time of this world is at hand.

August 22, 1959

JUSTICE FOR THE AMERICAN SO-CALLED NEGROES

MONEY, good homes, friendship in all walks of life await us (on condition that we believe in Allah and stop practicing filth). Our leaders, teachers, scholars and scientists must give and practice his or her wisdom among our people to help elevate them. There are many well-trained professional people among us, such as construction engineers, building engineers, civil, electrical and mechanical engineers, school, college and university professors, artists, draftsmen, biologists, chemists, and many others who are capable, if united and made to devote their time, of uplifting of their own people, could become independent over night.

The average Negro professors love giving their knowledge back to their teacher. It is really a sin that the poor so-called Negroes suffer because of the lack of knowledge of self. Their leaders, hungry for a place among the white race instead of their own race, have brought the Negroes to the present condition. Our very fine doctors and nurses in many fields, tradesmen, salesmen, farmers, mechanics of all kind, just need only one dose of Islam to unite them to become the world wonder people.

THE CLERGY CLASS (Christian preachers) if they only could see the harm that they are doing to their people by teaching the white man's slavery religion called Christianity, and would accept Islam and preach it, would set their people and themselves in heaven at once. They see and know that the white man's Christianity will never get the so-called Negroes out of the power of their 400-year slavemasters.

This Negro clergy class is the white man's right hand over the so-called Negroes. It was proven to be true on Aug. 9, 1959, in Indianapolis. There, we had been promised in advance the use of the Gorham Methodist

Church. The pastor, Rev. Hardin, who from natural fear of the devil more than Allah, changed his mind even before he had knowledge of us and the word of God which he had never before heard, and refused his, and his followers' own salvation. This was due to the lack of love, unity, and true brotherhood among us (the so-called Negroes).

I WAS NOT present, but why did not they try getting acquainted with me and learn what I am teaching before accepting my enemies' version of the truth which I teach? But, fear made him disregard our friendship and brotherhood of the same nation. Would a white pastor of a church who had promised some leader of his race who was preaching love, unity, and white supremacy among his people shut him out because some Negroes are against white supremacists? I should say not!

If the Negroes only knew what evil is now planned by certain whites against them, they would love me. Nothing would please me better than to have a meeting with all leaders of my people, both religious, civic, and political. Such a meeting would clear our misunderstanding of each other. Are you ready for such a meeting? God is with us, and satan is angry, and wishes to keep you away from God and the heaven which God desires to set you and me in.

The Indiana whites are guilty of lynching Negroes. They hate Negroes. Indiana used to be a Ku Klux Klan state. J. B. Stoner, Imperial Wizard, Ku Klux Klan leader, who claims to be the archleader, is trying to stir up trouble for the Muslims, and especially me; but I think and can say with certainty, that if his people try doing such evil to my people who are at peace with Allah and the world, they will baptize themselves into trouble that is not peace. If the Imperial Wizard of the Ku Klux Klan attempts to be carried out on us, I will seek only Allah for our protection. Mr. Stoner knows that seven powers of Allah are ever ready to defend us in this resurrection, and he is not enough for one of the seven!

Hurry and join onto your own kind. The time of this world is at hand.

(Quotes, Testimonies, Commentaries & Expressions of Appreciation)

S. Muhammad Tufail, Islamic Leader from Pakistan

Q. Detractors of the Honorable Elijah Muhammad characterize him and his followers as not being "True Muslims," that they are not "Orthodox Muslims." As an Islamic official, steeped in Islamic jurisprudence, how do you view this commonly made charge?

A. This question is very simple to decide. The Qur-an says: "And say not to anyone who offers you salutation, As-Salaam – Alaikum, Thou art not a believer." That is the minimum requirement for a person to show he's Islamic, to accost you with the Moslem greeting, As-Salaam Alaikum. According to the Qur-an, I must accept him as a Muslim. And then there's the other position of the Prophet. He says, anybody who faces towards Mecca while praying, and he prays like us and he eats the meat slaughtered by us, he's a Muslim. Anybody who says God is one and Muhammad is his Prophet, he's a Muslim. I have read the writings of the Honorable Elijah Muhammad. He clearly accepts that God is one and that Muhammad is his Prophet and the Qur-an is his book.

Q. Do you have any general observations and conclusions to make of the Muslim movement in America?

A. We have been watching the Muslim movement in America with great interest for many years. It is a great movement in this part of the world. It will do a great service not only to their people but to Islam as a whole. There is a tradition of the Prophet that in later times the sun will rise in the West. We interpret this as meaning the sun of Islam will rise in the West.

Q. Do you interpret the fact that a large Muslim movement has come about in America, under the leadership of Mr. Muhammad, as being a sign of the fulfillment of the Prophet?

A. Yes, this may be. Only the future will decide. In the early times, Islam spread towards the East. But in this instance, it is going to spread and dominate in the Western Hemisphere.

Q. Do you have any basic disagreement with any of the teachings of the Honorable Elijah Muhammad?

A. We think that God is the creator and the Lord of all the nations, communities, and peoples of the universe. So, the criterion of judging people is their character, and not their color, race, class or family. We think that the Bible talks of man, not black or white, just man. It is not Arab, it is not African, and it is not white people. It is the whole of mankind. Yet, I can understand that 400 years of slavery has caused this reaction against whites and their domination and all the things they have done to them.

Q. Two of the primary creeds of those referred to here as Black Muslims are separation or repatriation. Do you agree with these demands?
A. I can see the logicality of separation – if by segregation it will help strengthen your community. We separated from India. I don't agree with the Muslims' program of repatriation.

Q. Why?

A. For a Muslim, wherever he is born – that is his country. He must think that is his land. He has a right to it. He must live and die there. (Leaks, Messenger of Allah as Seen by Islamic Leader from Pakistan, 1964)

Muhammad Sami'ullah Naseele Darayai, Bhere, West Pakistan

The West is sick of Pauline Christianity and is longing for a true ideal. The people are falling away from the church. They are looking for something new to take its place. The Honorable Elijah Muhammad, Messenger of Allah, in America is offering the best solution for the West.

Mr. Muhammad has shown America that Islam is the destiny of mankind. That destiny must come to fulfillment sooner or later. Muslim followers of the Honorable Elijah Muhammad carry a great responsibility on their shoulders in that respect and the earlier they awaken to it the better for them.

Islam in this age of struggle for freedom and human dignity under the leadership of the Honorable Elijah Muhammad has a definite and indispensable role to play in the liquidation of racism, colonialism, imperialism and exploitation of all types in the realization of man's age-old dream of peace and plenty. (Darayai, 1964)

Daniel Pipes, Jewish Columnist

In the early 1930's when the Nation of Islam had just come into existence, its founder made the bold prediction that, one day, Islam would replace Christianity as the primary faith of black Americans. At the time, this assertion must have sounded incredible, if not slightly mad; not only was the Islamic faith broadly despised in the United States, but African-Americans who were Muslims numbered at that time only in the dozens.

Today, that 1930's predication no longer seems so outlandish – indeed, it has already been partially borne out. About one million African-Americans now identify themselves as Muslims, and a visit to the black sections of any fair-sized American town quickly confirms the presence not only of an Islamic infrastructure – mosques, schools, halal butchers, stores carrying Islamic clothing – but of an active ambitious drive to propagate Islam. So vital is this movement that the director of a Christian effort to stem its headway has made a memorable prediction of his own: "If the conversion rate continues unchanged, Islam could become the dominant religion in black urban areas by the year 2020."

In the final analysis, it was another man, Malcolm X's mentor, who had the greater impact on establishing Islam among African-Americans. This was the uncharismatic, inarticulate, heterodox, and long-lived Elijah Muhammad.

As Clegg notes: The Muslims were "black" before it became fashionable to be labeled as such, and the Black Power Movement and all subsequent African-American protest styles, from the rhymes of the nationalistic rap group Public Enemy to the raison d'etre of the Million Man March, are undeniably offshoots of the legacy of Elijah Muhammad.

It does not take much imagination to see that, should Islam in fact replace Christianity as the primary religion of African-Americans, this will have vast significance for all Americans, affecting everything from race relations to foreign policy, from popular culture to issues of religion and state. Eric Lincoln, a leading authority of African-American Islam, once wrote that the Nation of Islam might "well change the course of history in the west." Should that come to pass, the credit, or blame, will belong above all to the "squeaky little man teaching hate," Elijah Muhammad. (Pipes, 2000)

Dr. N.S. Hanoka, Turkish Writer

Three years ago, while practicing in Chicago, I found out that there was a Muslim movement in the U.S.A. I was born and brought up in Turkey – lived there the first 20 years of my life – and two years in Cairo, Egypt. Therefore, the knowledge of such a movement intrigued me and I moved to get in touch with their leader, Elijah Muhammad. He invited me to their Temple located on the south side, where I went with my wife, and to my surprise, saw that they were Black Americans.

As time went on, I became better acquainted with Elijah Muhammad, his sons, and many members – learned that he has the only rational and safe method of saving his people from the degrading and inhuman conditions under which they live, especially in the South. Everyone belonging to his movement became a new man, in every sense of the word – fine appearance – disciplined – self-reliant – proud of their race – and eager to free themselves of all shackles and abuses that the white man has practiced and is practicing for the last three hundred years.

This uplift is due to the Muslim religion and the Koran which forbids the use of alcohol and the use of pork – that practices fasting for a whole month each year, and teaches charity. His schools, temples and universities are giving the Black Muslim man, for the first time, a real education which is the only and best road to emancipation.

The Black Muslims do not hate the white man as some of their enemies maintain, but hate the abuses – humiliations, persecutions, jailings, and lynchings – practiced on them. And why blame them? It is now one hundred years since the black man was freed after a terrible Civil War. Is he really free, especially in the South?

In my contact with the Black Muslims, I found them honest, eager to learn, industrious and devoted to their Leader and to each other and to their religion. I found their Leader, Elijah Muhammad, a learned, devoted and dedicated man, inspired and determined to uplift his people from the degradation under which they are living at the present time.

Those who profit by the condition of the Black Man, fear their movement, but so did King George fear the American rebels and George Washington. Elijah Muhammad is to his followers what George Washington was to the American Colonist who wanted to be free from British Colonial Rule. The Black Muslims want to be free from the White Man's rule, abuses and shackles, and the American Constitution guarantees freedom to everyone – it does not exclude anyone on color – race – religion. So Elijah Muhammad is on safe Constitutional, legal and humane grounds. All power to him and his devoted followers! (Hanoka, 1963)

Ruby Dee, Actress

LEAKS: The movement commonly called the "Black Muslims" is probably the most talked about phenomenon in America today. Would you care to express your reaction to the movement?

RUBY DEE: I have heard so much about the Black Muslims and the 'terror' that they have inspired; and I have heard them compared to the Ku Klux Klan and to the Nazis. And I think to myself, over and over, that the Negro has suffered, the deprivations, being at the very bottom of the barrel; the lynchings, not only physically but spiritually.

And I think, here we are in 1963, and the worst white America, who doesn't understand, has to say about the question is, 'here you have the Black Muslims.' How lucky for the United States! That this is the worst that has happened; that the Negro has erupted only in the Black Muslims. I think that's a very lucky state for America.

Were I not black, I would say to myself, when I look at black people, oh! I should think they would have come up with something much more terrible than that.

As it stands, for the most of it, it's a positive organization. One certainly couldn't insult Hitler by comparing them to the Nazis, who murdered six million Jews. The Muslims have not murdered anybody; they have been killed. Some of them. Certainly you couldn't compare them to the Ku Klux Klan. Because they have burned no crosses, no homes; they have deprived nobody of a job; they have not gone out specifically to instill upon white people that you are an inferior being.

I look upon the Black Muslims as another one of the cries in Negro America that say, 'I wanted to love you so much and you wouldn't let me.' And now, I am going to tell you, I don't like you for that. And I am going to say even more than that: I'm going to say, I hate you for that. So there! I'm going to say, I'm going to be a fine human being. So there! I'm going to be clean; I'm not going to drink, and I'm going to get out of jail. So there! And I won't like you because you won't be worthy of it.

I don't even bother to thank about the religious aspect of it. I find it dramatic. I think Elijah Muhammad and Malcolm X are certainly dramatic personalities. They aren't hampered by any thought as to what's proper at the moment; and they haven't hurt anybody. Well, what can one say. It's another example of the black man saying, 'let me out, turn me out, set me free.' (Leaks, World Outlook of Ruby Dee, 1963)

Abdul Basit Naeem, Writer, Businessman

The U.S. Muslim leader teaches of SELF-KNOWLEDGE and SELF-RESPECT – not hate. He exhorts his followers to HELP THEMSELVES – not hinder others. **HE URGES** them to live in RIGHTEOUSNESS (that is to say, in PEACE and complete harmony with the laws of NATURE as established by its Originator and Rightful Master, ALLAH) – not in frivolity and sin. He warns his innocent people against "disintegration" – not integration (as such). It is preposterous (on the part of anyone) to charge him with sedition, subversion or "just pain Un-Americanism" when, in reality, all he is trying to do is acquaint the (so-called) "Negroes" of America with the true meaning of FREEDOM, JUSTICE and EQUALITY and show them the way – through ISLAM – to unlimited human progress.

FURTHERMORE, The Honorable Elijah Muhammad's teachings (as well as the "technology" or techniques employed in imparting them) have already proven effective – and raised scores of thousands of (so-called) "Negroes" in this wilderness from a state of mental death (brought about by their past adherence to "Christianity" – the false religion of their former slave masters"). **THIS BEING A** fact – which no one can deny – I should think the enlightened writers of this land ought to favor (instead of frown upon)what the respected U.S. Muslim leader has done and continues to do on behalf of his people. (Muhammad Speaks, October 1, 1965)

Limitations of space did not permit me to elaborate on the concluding remark in my last week's article, which was: "…The Honorable Elijah Muhammad is perfectly capable of delivering what he promises."

I am sure the Messenger's followers fully understood what my brief statement implied. However, some of the "lost-founds" (so-called "Negroes" who have not as yet joined up with the Nation of Islam) might have found the comment wanting of explanation. These lines are intended to provide just that.

Let me take just one of the many "principal" teachings of the Honorable Elijah Muhammad. He says (and has said this a thousand times): "Follow me and your God (ALLAH) will make you a new people." Let us now see if he is able to deliver on this promise. **Actually, you can just glance at the Muslim men, women and their children – from a distance if you like – and you will know that they are no longer what they used to be (deaf, dumb and blind). When they walk, they walk erect (self-confident and unafraid) no longer do they limp (from prolonged dope addiction or consumption of forbidden foods) or stagger (from drunkenness).** (Naeem, How Pakistani Periodical Views Nation of Islam, 1965)

Fred Hill, President and Founder of the Midwest Mattress Company

"I admire Mr. Muhammad and his people are my people too," Hill says. "It was his philosophy which helped me succeed. I learned a lot from him."

Hill founded the Midwest Mattress Company in 1945 with only $5,000. He soon ran the business up to gross $100,000 per. With a relatively small but highly-skilled staff he produces carefully constructed mattresses and Hollywood beds for the hotels and swank department stores throughout the country. (Hill, 1964)

Wayne Hightower, San Francisco Warriors Professional Basketball Player

"Mr. Muhammad is the first of our race to initiate the idea of a collective enterprise for the black man's interest." (Hightower, 1963)

Cleo Staples, Singer with the Legengary Staple Singers

CHICAGO – Black celebrities have begun to publicly voice their support of the programs of the Honorable Elijah Muhammad and the latest to be added to a growing list is Cleo Staple, a member of the famed Staple Singers.

MS. Staple expressed her admiration for the hospital program of Messenger Muhammad, following a banquet-fashion show sponsored by the "Friends of the Nation of Islam," held in the quiet, elegant atmosphere of the Salaam Restaurant. "I think the banquet and show was for a very fine cause," she commented. "I am hoping that everything will go fast because we really do need a hospital. As for me, I learned a lot about the Messenger's program when I was in the hospital and a Muslim sister was my roommate for two weeks." Ms. Staple pointed out how her whole family supported the work of the Honorable Elijah Muhammad in action and deeds and not just words.

"My mother buys the Whiting H&G fish, five and ten pounds at a time," she said, "And Pop is contacted by the brothers from the Temple in New York whenever we are in town and we participate in any way we can." Adding that her first visit to Salaam Restaurant was with Sister Belinda Ali, wife of Heavyweight Champion Muhammad Ali, Ms. Staple said her family also supports efforts to build a hospital on the South Side of Chicago. Ms. Staple expressed great interest in being more active in participating in the programs of the Honorable Elijah Muhammad here on Chicago's South Side. She said she is a weekly reader of Muhammad Speaks newspaper.

"We have such a hard time just getting a daily newspaper in our apartment building, so I make a special trip to the bank on the corner of 53rd street to get my **Muhammad Speaks** from one of the brothers on the corner there." She said. Ms. Staple said her desire is to continue to participate and help push the Honorable Elijah Muhammad's program in Chicago. (Pamela7X, 1974)

Amy Ashwood Garvey, wife of the late Marcus Garvey

"I have been deeply impressed by Messenger Elijah Muhammad's message of Freedom and Unity in the March 18 issue of Muhammad Speaks, and I wish to compliment him on it.

"The idea of creating Negro markets which can provide food, clothing and housing for them is a noble and humanitarian one. That is what the masses need in Africa today, and you who-live in the greatest manufacturing country in the world have the opportunity to extend such facilities to your brothers in Africa. I sincerely share Messenger Muhammad's desire to see Negroes united in the case of liberating themselves from the shackles of economic and political subservience."

"In fact, I would say that they should even go as far as forming their own political party. The word Negro might soon become obsolete. It is gratifying to see that another dynamic figure has arrived in the arena of world affairs. Please convey to your followers my warm salutations. I am especially happy to note that your people are expressing tremendous interest and love for Africa which of course, you have a right to do. There is no feeling like the feeling of belonging to a country, a people and a nation. I keep praying for you." Very Sincerely yours, Amy Ashwood Garvey (Garvey, 1963)

Julius Hobson, Committee of Racial Equality (CORE)

Core Praises Muslims in D.C. The bold stand of the Honorable Elijah Muhammad against racial injustice and the work of Muslims against crime and delinquency in the Washington area were cited last week by the chairman of the Washington branch of the Committee of Racial Equality. Attending a Muhammad Speaks Award Program, CORE leader Julius Hobson told 500 Muslim and their guests that the Muslim aim to combat the social ills of discrimination, unfair housing and job bias was highly commendable.

"WE WILL come to the support of the Muslims when asked or needed," Hobson said. "And we welcome Muslim support when we are on the picket lines for better jobs and opportunities for our people. Acknowledging the need for unity among Negroes, Hobson asserted that while certain civil rights groups had failed greatly in their efforts to reach the masses, the Muslims have had amazing success."

He said he was particularly impressed by the great number of young people being attracted to the teachings of the Honorable Elijah Muhammad and praised the address made by Minister Isaiah Karriem of Muhammad's Mosque No. 6, Baltimore, Md., guest speaker, as "a great message." (CORE Praises Muslims in D.C., 1963)

Lewis H. Michaux, Garveyite, Owner of Historic Harlem Black Book Store

"THE ONLY difference between black nationalists and Muslims is that we want to return to our home in Africa and Muslims want some separate land here," declared Dr. Michaux. Stating that his organization agreed with all the objectives the Muslims have. Dr. Michaux described the Honorable Elijah Muhammad as a very wise prophet. "He is a seer," said Michaux. "Since I'm not a prophet, I must yield to him regarding the future." (Garvey Group Praises Muhammad, 1963)

World Famous Composer Duke Ellington

"What the Negro needs first is $100 million," world famous composer Duke Ellington said last week in an exclusive interview with Muhammad Speaks. "And that is the advantage your boss (referring to the Honorable Elijah Muhammad) has over the rest of the 20 million. He urges that we get some money together." "Without $100 million there is no voice. There are 20 million Negroes and we don't have $20 million. "MONEY TALKS in our society and economics is the big question throughout the world. Every race on this earth has some money but the American Negro…" This then is the solution to the "race problem" of the famous Duke, who is universally acclaimed as royalty in the realm of American music. "Negroes built America with their labor and they have fought in every war," said Ellington. "AND MUSICALLY, Negroes have made their cultural contribution felt through work songs, spirituals, the blues, jazz, rock and roll and bossa nova," asserted the Duke. (Walker, 1963)

Jim Brown, Heisman Trophy Winner, Professional Football Player, Actor and Community Activist

"Does he (the white man) realize that the black Muslim's basic attitude toward whites is shared by almost 99 per cent of the Negro population?… "I am not one of the Muslims, yet I'm all for them because we need every possible element going for us. (Why Brown Will Not Back Down On the Messenger, 1964)

Edwin Sexton Jr., the first Negro State Senator in Kansas

Senator Sexton praised the Honorable Elijah Muhammad and the Muslims for their success in restoring dignity to the black people of America. "They are doing something the other leaders and preachers have failed to do," Sexton said. He said Kansas Negroes are continuously fighting for their rights, especially in Wichita, where they are badly in need of better schools, housing, and full-time employment. Sexton represents the 27th District of Wichita where he lives with his wife and two daughters, aged 12 and 14. (1st Negro State Senator Comments On Mississippi and Muslims, 1965)

Rev. F.D. Arnold, Methodist Minister

The Rev. F.D. Arnold minister of the Asbury Methodist Church, who has studied in some of the great seminaries of this country, said that what the Honorable Elijah Muhammad teaches about the Bible is true. REVEREND Arnold, who said it would be a privilege and honor to sit and talk with the Messenger, feels that the Negro leaders of this city should recognize Mr. Muhammad and see that he and his followers are called in to share discussions on the struggle for freedom, justice and equality. The Methodist minister said the Honorable Elijah Muhammad had accomplished more than the Christian church in the highest standards of morals, cleanliness, dedication, loyalty, self-pride and determination.

REVEREND Arnold who heads a committee of the Planned Parenthood Association, was asked his opinion of the Messenger's stand on birth control. He replied that he had thought birth control was right and acceptable, but that Mr. Muhammad had given him food for thought on the subject. (Methodist Minister Has High Praise For The Messenger, 1965)

Art Peters, Columnist

He should have expected it. Elijah Muhammad, leader of the Black Muslims, is building two palatial homes in Chicago, reportedly at a cost of about $200,000 each, for himself and members of his family. A lot of people, Black and white, are very uptight about it. In this country, religious leaders in general and Black ones in particular, are expected to live slightly above the poverty level. The president of United Steel or General Motors may wallow in wealth, the board chairman of Lockheed or Penn Central may receive salaries upwards of $100,000 annually while their respective companies go down the drain, but woe unto the religious leader who lives that way.

It is ironic. Countless millions of Roman Catholics around the world are hungry, but there is no hue and cry over the fact that the Pope, the Prince of the Church, lives amid palatial splendor surrounded by the priceless treasures heaped upon him by followers, many of whom don't even own shoes. But, Elijah Muhammad, who preaches a doctrine of strict racial separation and who urges his followers to become economically independent of the white race, is condemned for wanting to live in the same comfort which has been a way of life for the Kennedys, the Rockefellers and the Lyndon Johnsons. In this color conscious society, green money in Black hands is regarded as a very bad color combination. Money is frequently called the root of all evil, but that all depends upon who planted and cultivated the weed. (Peters, 1972)

Mrs. Sallie B. Howard, New York Public School teacher

New York schoolteacher ranks Muhammad No. 1.

Evidently Mr. Muhammad believes that schools are for learning reading, writing and arithmetic – the academic skills that most parents are unable to teach their children. Moreover, he teaches his staff that our Black children can learn anything if properly taught. And they do! Also, I would be remiss if I did not mention that everyone's manners in these schools – from top to bottom – is impeccable.

In these classes, you will find four and five year olds doing work that I only wish our Public School children could master in the third and further grades. At this tender age, these beautifully Black children can read, write, spell, speak Arabic and go right through the twelfth time tables. You will find six year olds executing long divisions such as our poor messed – up fourth and fifth graders are struggling to do at ten and eleven when in reality, many of them barely know their basic number facts. Anyone who doubts the veracity of these assertions he owes it to himself to acquaint himself with both systems. Also he should check those devastating reading scores recently published in the New York Times. New York City's Public School System was the lowest among national ratings. If the Honorable Elijah Muhammad had never done anything other than founded these excellent schools to salvage and educate the minds of our youngsters, that indeed would have been enough proof of "power" to give him the divine right to "harangue" until doomsday – which he probably will have to do anyway if he's to get us all awake.

May I say in closing that I think that it is grossly unfair, cowardly and self-demeaning for us to stand mutely by and hear our Muslim brothers and sisters viciously maligned without so much as demanding to know from where they got their information. (Howard, 1972)

Samuel E. Cuero Rubio, South American

SOUL BROTHER, I'm glad to know the best newspaper all around the world. I got my first Muhammad Speaks by an American friend – a Black seaman. Buenaventura is a land of Black people where they don't know where to go, what religion to follow and so on. I have been talking to people who like Allah's religion. I want to know more and more of Allah's religion because Muhammad is the best way. I'm father of two boys and I want them to believe in Allah and study at Islam. I want somebody to sponsor my two (2) boys. Write me as soon as possible and send me Muhammad Speaks.
Thank you a lot,
Samuel E. Cuero Rubio,
Calle 14 No. 3-09, Buenaventura (Valle)
Colombia, South America. (Rubio, 1972)

Louis Martin , Noted editor-politician

"ELIJAH MUHAMMAD, the head of the Black Muslims, is one of the few, if not the only mass leader in the national Black community who is not regarded as a great orator. He talks softly with almost none of the eloquence one traditionally associates with Black leadership and especially Black religious leadership. Some reporters claim that the Muslim leader literally drives them up the wall when they try to catch his words in a formal speech.

"Organizational leaders, politicians, preachers and most public figures who seek to win mass support for their views and programs seem to live on the public platform. Perhaps no public figure in our time, white or Black, can match the eloquence of the late Dr. Martin Luther King. Yet Elijah Muhammad has managed to build a mass movement in his own quiet way.

"Also unlike most of our leaders, Mr. Muhammad rarely if ever tells the world what he is going to do next. It is the custom of our popular leaders to call a press conference as soon as they get a new thought. The Black Muslim chief never, as the sports writers say, telegraphs a punch. Most of his press coverage seems to follow rather than precede a course of action. "Indeed the intricacies of the Black Muslim structure and hierarchy and the manner in which it functions remain something of a mystery to most of those who have studied the movement.

"Nevertheless, Elijah Muhammad has succeeded in building one of the largest, richest and most cohesive national, organization in Black America. "What is the key to the success of Elijah Muhammad? There are some who would say divine guidance. Others point to his insistence on self-reliance, self-respect and self-motivation which seem to under-gird his religious philosophy. His teachings have been criticized as anti-white, anti-Semitic, anti-Christian and anti-intellectual. However justified this criticism is, the same criticism can be made of some other Black organizations which have gotten nowhere. To be sure other Black organizations which also preach Black pride have failed to match the progress of the Black Muslim movement.

"Perhaps there is no answer to the question that will satisfy everyone. I am intrigued, however, by one aspect of Mr. Muhammad's leadership. He always seems to have his eye on what might be called the basics. He seeks to meet fundamental human needs in a very simple and practical manner. He is a builder and a doer who recognized the appeal of concrete example. "It is no secret that the Black Muslims own and operate more farm land than any Black group in our history. From this vast acreage in many states come produce, poultry, livestock and dairy products that are processed and distributed by the organization to their own stores and restaurants and other outlets.

"The business acumen of Elijah Muhammad and his group is well known. Here are some of their enterprises in Chicago: Good Foods, Inc., Chicago Lamb Packers, Inc., Shabazz Bakery, National Clothing Factory, Your Supermarket and other grocery stores and restaurants. The newspaper, Muhammad Speaks, is printed in their own new million dollar plant. A few weeks ago a multi-million dollar Greek church and school was purchased in Chicago and several homes for his top aides are under construction near the residence of the leader.

"Whatever the number of Blacks employed in the various Black Muslim enterprises, the total must be impressive when you compare it to what others are doing in the Black community.

"I have commented before in the column on the unique character of the Black Muslim movement and wondered out loud about its future. It seems to be a safe bet that as long as Elijah Muhammad's teachings on self-reliance, self-respect and constructive, concrete action, are taken seriously, the Black Muslims are going to grow and prosper. Concrete achievements have a way of speaking for themselves. (Martin, 1972)

Livingston Wingate, Political Leader

Ward was followed to the rostrum by Livingston Wingate who was lavish in his praise of Muhammad's Nation of Islam as a model group of Black progress. "Let me say one word to the Nation of Islam." The articulate lawyer and congressional candidate said, "I think it is perhaps one of the greatest laboratories and testing grounds for the goals which the Black community seeks."

Wingate supported the "Muslim call for Black police" in the Black community because they (the Muslims) recognize that rules of an open society is not applicable to a racist society. He said that in the Nation of Islam, he saw the "greatest design" for a Black morality, discipline, value system which is necessary for a people seeking liberation. Attempting to convey to the audience a sense of what keeps the Muslims cohesive and progressive, Wingate said "They have a value system which is compatible with Black mental and emotional survival. They've given the Black people the greatest ideology, wrapped in a religion. They have really given us something in Black values.

URGING HIS audience to move beyond U.S. media propaganda against Muhammad's Nation of Islam. Wingate said "Now you don't have to like the Muslims" to recognize that they respect their women, taught us cleanliness, taught us about Black hope and other valuable things in an environment where our children are shooting each other every day. "They have given to Black communities what the colleges can't buy and what the universities can't sell," he pointed out and proposed that therefore in order to help the Black scholar, educator and community to benefit more abundantly from the Nation's example and Muhammad's teaching. There should be a course in all the community programs, colleges and universities on what makes the Nation of Islam work.

"I'd tell any organization, don't tell me anything until you tell me what ingredient it is that keeps the Muslims together." He said it is clear that "the greatest organizing element in the Black community is the Muslims."

"Finally I'd like to ask the Nation of Islam to address itself to the most dastard issue of today, claiming that issue to be the American political process, the veteran political and community leader said when the political apparatus abuses its power. The communications media is supposed to blow the whistle.

Implying that the Black community would eagerly listen to Muhammad's advice on the political process, Wingate said. The Muslims are highly respected in the Black community. (Samuel17X, 1972)

Joe Walker, M.S. New York Editor

New York – The Honorable Elijah Muhammad was awarded the National Association of Black Social Workers' (NABSW) National Service Award for 1972, at the Plenary Session, of that organization during its Fifth Annual Convention here. The thousands of social workers present rose to their feet and loudly applauded the announcement of the award to the Messenger of Allah. (Walker J. , 1973)

Theresa Fambro Hooks, Olive-Harvey Public Information Officer

Chicago – More than 550 graduates and 2,000 guests heard the Honorable Elijah Muhammad named as the recipient of a "community award" at Olive-Harvey College graduation last week. THE AWARD WAS given to "The Nation of Islam led by the Honorable Elijah Muhammad." Two other community leaders, Dr. Raymond Lee and Vernon Jarrett, also received awards. Lee is the president of the Southeastern Community Organization and Jarrett is a newspaper-columnist, radio-commentator and television show-host. All three men were given the award for "going beyond and above" ordinary contributions to community development.

When presenting the awards, Mrs. Theresa Fambro Hooks noted that, "It was the decision of the student body, the faculty, the staff and the administration," which chose the awardees. "THE NATION has been an integral part of our community development," Mrs. Hooks noted, "and it is necessary to the further development of our community."

The Nation's Award was accepted by Wali Muhammad, grandson of Messenger Muhammad. Mrs. Hooks, Olive-Harvey public information officer, assisted Olive-Harvey president, Dr. Charles C. Kidd, Sr. in directing the commencement programs. (Samuel17X, College Award To Muhammad, 1973)

David Rothensberg, Executive Director of Fortune Society

Chicago – The executive director of the Fortune Society, which works with ex-convicts told Muhammad Speaks that only the Black media has responded to a society press release attacking biased Anti-Muslim coverage of the Philadelphia prison incident in which two prison officials were slain.

David Rothensberg says in addition to the distortion, "It is a known fact that Muslims are a positive influence in prisons." He said, "I was in Attica and everyone knows that the Muslims saved lives there." Rothensberg indicated that the press release was a direct result of experiences that he and other former convicts have had with Muslims in prisons like Attica that lead the society to attack the white media coverage of the Philadelphia incident.
"The Fortune Society voices objection to media reporting of the killing of two Philadelphia prison officials. In all reports of this tragic news event it was emphasized that the alleged assailants were Black Muslims. "We have never seen such strong emphasis on religious affiliation in past crime stories. Past media stories on similar crime stories have never headlined a person's Catholicism, Protestantism, or Judaism. "Media coverage in this Philadelphia case is distorted and is fanning a dangerous flame.

THE FORTUNE SOCIETY is greatly saddened by this outburst of violence once again in a prison setting. We are saddened both by the death of two prison officials and by the state of conditions which may have driven two men to such desperate acts of violence. (New Yorkers Attack Anti-Muslim Media, 1973)

Mayor Douglas Dollarhide, Compton, California

"The Honorable Elijah Muhammad's program is the only real hope for our people" (Larry5X, 1973)

Mayor Richard Hatcher, Gary, Indiana

Mayor Richard Hatcher from Gary, Indiana, who enjoys a nation – wide reputation as one of the more dedicated Black representatives in American politics, was the final delegate from the U.S. Conference of Mayors to address the assemblage. Mayor Hatcher told the gathering of his abundant respect for the Honorable Elijah Muhammad, "I think that he understands better than anybody else in this country what it's going to take to make Black people free." The Gary mayor said further that in combating white economic control of the city he is implementing a program in close conformity with the Messenger's Teaching. (Larry5X, 1973)

Chicago professionals witness Muslim accomplishments

Enthusiastic response to Muslim guided tours of Southside economic progress.

"I would like to say that just having returned from the hospital after a very, very serious siezure with an illness and operations, this being my first real outing, I might say that today I felt a great spiritual uplift and I saw the fruits of the most Honorable Elijah Muhammad's work. I saw people who were inspired, who were friendly, who were warm, who expressed love and understanding and who had accomplishments beyond my wildest dreams. I came and I saw and I believe that the real answer to our problem is self-help as taught by the Honorable Elijah Muhammad – and I say this from the bottom of my heart. **–Russ Meeks, Search for Truth.**

"Well, I think that it was very impressive, very much impressive – and it's great to see Blacks who are on the move such as the Muslims are – building their own shopping centers, stores, attempting to build hospitals, housing, their own restaurants and what have you. I think it's just great, and I think that there should be more of it and if Muslims or the Muslim religion is the key to Blacks being independent and having their own and control their own communities and destinies, then I think all Black people should be Muslims. – **Roger Phillips, Al Johnson Associates, Public Relations.**

"Oh fantastic! The whole experience – your courtesy, the detail, the freedom with which you showed us everything behind the scenes and all the information we gathered and the Temple is just beautiful "The impression when you walk in the door – that airiness, that light, that glow and then the ladies are so polite; even going through the security business, they are so polite, that nobody could object to it. I expected of course that I would have a wonderful time, but I think that you have topped all my expectations in your arrangements for all of our courtesies; and I think I speak for everybody on the bus when I say that. Thank you. ---**Frances Matlock, National Council of Negro Women.**

"I am more than impressed. I have always had knowledge of some of the workings of the Message of Muhammad over the years, but today after having a full tour and being guided through the exploits and the achievements of what has been made, I'm even more impressed. I certainly appreciated it having been done; it was the greatest thing for my son to be exposed to this – and my daughter, because it's not often in our lifetime that our youth are able to go into business establishments whereas that we can proudly say that from the beginning to the end is all done by Blacks. –**Millard Frazier, Black Beauty Boutiques** (Chicago Professionals Witness Muslim Accomplishments, 1973)

Dr. Matthew Walker, Physician, Meharry Medical College faculty member, community leader and Omega Psi Phi fraternity 'Man of the Year'

Recently, in Nashville, Tenn., Dr. Matthew Walker --- distinguished physician, Meharry Medical College faculty member, community leader and Omega Psi Phi fraternity 'Man of the Year,' --- applauded the great achievements of the

Honorable Elijah Muhammad in the area of drug reform, which he described as the no. 1 blight on Black people in America. "Any group that can solve the most difficult, the most agonizing, the most death dealing problem of America – any group that can solve that problem, can solve any problem." Dr. Walker told the audience at a fund raising banquet sponsored by Muhammad's Temple No. 60. (Muhammad(Charles67X), 1973)

Mayor Johnny Ford, Tuskegee, Alabama

Tuskegee, Ala. – In an unprecedented move, Mayor Johnny Ford of Tuskegee, Alabama presented to the Honorable Elijah Muhammad the key to the City. This ceremony followed a letter to the Messenger of Allah from the mayor himself, which stressed the desire for the Nation of Islam's "industrial entry" into the Tuskegee Macon County area.

Mayor Ford's letter to the Messenger stressed his desire to see the Messenger come into the Tuskegee and Macon County area to build industries, factories, and foundries. And to do whatever the Honorable Elijah Muhammad wanted to do in the way of structuring "Black Economy." It was a letter from the Mayor of Tuskegee telling the Messenger how "very much" he, the mayor, wanted to work with the Honorable Elijah Muhammad and the Nation of Islam in terms of his efforts to structure these businesses in the Tuskegee Macon County area.

Mayor Ford expressed his views on the Nation of Islam by saying, "I believe fully in the philosophy of self-help; of pulling oneself up by one's own boot-straps of economic development, of building and helping ourselves. That philosophy is a most meaningful one; it is the kind of philosophy that other people have adopted," said the mayor. "This is what makes the movement of the Nation of Islam so successful and the leadership of the Honorable Elijah Muhammad so viable." As a result of the productivity of the Nation of Islam, Mayor Ford said that he was just "Gung-Ho" about working with the Messenger "Hand in Hand," to lay an economic foundation in Tuskegee for Black people. (Harold4XandMinisterOscarX, 1973)

Willie D. Cameron, Atlanta Criminal Investigator

Atlanta, Ga. – Willie D. Cameron, a Criminal Investigator in the Atlanta Police Detective Division and President of the Afro-American Police League, revealed to M.S. his knowledge and feelings concerning the conduct of the Nation of Islam in terms of law enforcement relationship.

M.S. – "Do the Muslims annoy you or bother you?"

CAMERON: - "No. Definitely not – because I'm very interested in the Teachings. In fact, I read a lot. I've read two or three books by the Messenger. It gives me greater insight into who I am, where I came from and what my destiny is. I'm very much concerned about that. I'm not a Muslim myself, but I believe very much in the Teachings of Mr. Muhammad."

M.S. – "Would you recommend a hard criminal or drug user just being released from jail to be rehabilitated by the Nation?"

CAMERON: - "My honest opinion about that, is that, I think the Nation of Islam has the best rehabilitation program anywhere in the world. I haven't seen any other agencies with programs anywhere that are as 'thorough' as the Nation of Islam. In fact, I would recommend Black people, in general, to look, take a second look, a more positive look in the direction of the Nation of Islam." (Harold4X, 1974)

Lawyer pays tribute to Muhammad

(Reprinted from the Chicago Woodlawn Observer) By E. Duke McNeil.

More than 40 years ago the Hon. Elijah Muhammad began his work and today millions of black Americans can point with chest filling pride at his accomplishments, and those of his followers. Without question the Nation of Islam is the most successful entity within black America. Their success is all around and the Messenger is, also without questions, the greatest black leader this century has seen in America. Now I am fully aware of the fact that many persons will dispute this statement, and point to several other black leaders, particularly those who strode across the world's stage during the 1950's and 1960's and say that they are as great as the Messenger, and to those person I'll say "Let's look at what he has accomplished and what other black leaders have achieved, and there is no comparison."

In Chicago this fact is painfully obvious. The most successful black economic institution that we have, in a city which boasts of many black institutions, is the Nation of Islam. Crime is a major problem confronting the black community here and across the country. And as we examine those blacks who are counted among the criminal ilk, the Black Muslims are conspicuously absent. I read recently where Deputy Chicago Police Superintendent, Sam Nolan stated: "Wherever Muslims go crime goes down."

Now with food shortages becoming a significant factor of everyday life, the Messenger has imported 2 million pounds of fish from Peru, to be sold to black Americans. Now I don't know about you, but it's hard for me to visualize that much fish in my mind. But at the same time one easily can imagine what this can mean to feed hungry black people. For more than 40 years now the Messenger has been telling black people in America, they must get it together for themselves. The beauty and truth of this admonition has been demonstrated for us most forcefully by the current occupant of the White House. After the Great Society and the War on Poverty got started, black people were lulled into a sense of false security about what they had and were going to get.

It took Richard Milhouse Nixon exactly one sweep of his pen to eliminate everything black folks thought they had and a helluva lot they didn't. The report is in now and it is very, very clear that it is "every man for himself time," and God pity those unfortunates who still feel that the way to get it together is making sure you shout the loudest. Black Muslims walk tall and proud, and they have reason to. There is no other institution which has done as much for black people, those who belong to the nation, and those who don't, than any other single institution in America. (McNeil, 1974)

Squire Lance, Special Assistant to the Governor

"It gives me great pleasure on behalf of Illinois Governor Dan Walker, to proclaim this day, March 29, 1974, as the Honorable Elijah Muhammad Day." (Thank You: Sincere Words Praising Messenger Muhammad, 1974)

Mayor Richard Hatcher, Gary, Indiana

"I thought it was a beautiful program. I think the beautiful thing was to see a variety of Black people here tonight; A lot of people who I have not seen previously supporting the Honorable Elijah Muhammad...I support Him absolutely. So I was very pleased and honored to be here." (Thank You: Sincere Words Praising Messenger Muhammad, 1974)

Curtis Mayfield, Musician

"We're here in honor of a man to be respected. In honor of a man who is very much deserved of the praises given to Him for His many deeds that most of us know very little about. I'm here, joining the others to give respect to a very beautiful man that I've seen do a lot with my brothers, people who I lived with; as a matter of fact – people that I am. He has most definitely been a positive influence...I've got to respect this man for His works." (Thank You: Sincere Words Praising Messenger Muhammad, 1974)

Mayor Richard J. Daley, Chicago,Illinois

PROCLAMATION:

"WHEREAS, on the evening of Friday, March 29, 1974, a citizens' committee will hold a testimonial dinner at the Conrad Hilton Hotel to honor the Honorable Elijah Muhammad; and

"WHEREAS, mutual respect and brotherhood are essential for people to live in harmony everywhere; and

"WHEREAS, the Honorable Elijah Muhammad has exhibited strong leadership to provide quality education, to establish prosperous businesses, to organize recreational activities and to develop good citizenship in the community; and

"WHEREAS, the proceeds from this testimonial dinner will be used to support the construction of a 300 bed hospital on the South Side:

"NOW, THEREFORE, I, Richard J. Daley, Mayor of the City of Chicago, do hereby proclaim March 29, 1974 to be HONORABLE ELIJAH MUHAMMAD DAY IN CHICAGO and call upon all citizens to take cognizance of the special events arranged for this time."

Dated the 27th day of March, 1974. (Thank You: Sincere Words Praising Messenger Muhammad, 1974)

Robert Wallace, Vice President of the Board Exchange National Bank

"I'm happy to join the many business and civic leaders of Chicago in congratulating the Honorable Elijah Muhammad here tonight. The hospital which we all support by our presence represents still another solid extension of His national leadership in promoting Black achievement.

"Exchange National Bank of Chicago takes pride in its' business association with the Nation of Islam. Of course, no bank can lend you its depositors' and stockholders' money to make loans of the heart. Loans must stand the test of credit worthiness. "The fact is that we do business with the Black Muslims because they are reliable, responsible customers who pay their bills. I well remember the day, five years ago when Eugene Dibble introduced me to the Honorable Elijah Muhammad – when we began discussion about financial arrangements to purchase the Temple on Stoney Island Avenue. "Being a careful banker, I did some checking on my own; I read The Black Muslims In America, a PhD. Dissertation by Dr. Eric Lincoln; I also checked with suppliers and contractors I found that the Black Muslims treat financial obligations with the highest priority-as a matter of pride.

"I believe that the Black Muslims' record should make all banks and financial institutions want to business with them. I'll be glad to answer their question; some of these questions are as follows: "Don't Muslims favor racial separation?" Yes, but for positive reasons they want to develop themselves without outside help." "But don't the Muslims talk about the white devil?" I tell'em if the shoe fits wear it. But I say to them they are really talking about 300 years of discrimination." "Don't Muslims make trouble?" They sure will if they're attacked. Then you can be sure they will defend themselves and do it well. The Black Muslims oppose the use of alcohol and narcotics; they are hard-working law-abiding citizens, proud of their accomplishments and proud of their Black heritage; what more can you ask?" (Thank You: Sincere Words Praising Messenger Muhammad, 1974)

Augustus Adair, Executive Director, Congressional Black Caucus

"I am here to represent not only the 16 Black members of the House of Representatives, but myself. It is very clear that the Honorable Elijah Muhammad does not need a testimonial; he deserves one." (Thank You: Sincere Words Praising Messenger Muhammad, 1974)

Kim Weston, Entertainer

"I'm interested in helping Black people and so is the Honorable Elijah Muhammad...and Black people really need a hospital. I think it's my responsibility to help in any way I can." (Thank You: Sincere Words Praising Messenger Muhammad, 1974)

State Sen. Charles Chew

"One of the best programs I have ever attended...I want to go on record as totally supporting the program of the Honorable Elijah Muhammad. I bought table number one when they gathered for this occasion." (Thank You: Sincere Words Praising Messenger Muhammad, 1974)

Dick Gregory, Comedian and Activist

TO THE HONORABLE ELIJAH MUHAMMAD
CHICAGO, IL 60649

PEACE BE WITH YOU MY BROTHER. ALL OF US SUPPORT YOUR EFFORTS TO PROVIDE FOR THE MEDICAL NEEDS OF OUR PEOPLE EXEMPLIFIED BY THE HOSPITAL PROJECT WHICH I WARMLY INDORSE. BY SUCH ACTIONS YOU BRING SUCCOR TO THE MANY. REGRET I CANNOT BE THERE IN PERSON TO HONOR THIS WORK

BUT I AM WITH YOU IN SPIRIT. (Thank You: Tributes Acknowledged, 1974)

Ralph David Abernathy, President, SCLC

TO MUHAMMAD ALI
CHICAGO, IL 60649

I REGRET DUE TO PREVIOUS COMMITMENTS I CANNOT JOIN WITH YOU IN PERSONALLY PAYING TRIBUTE TO THE HONORABLE ELIJAH MUHAMMAD ONE OF THE TRULY GREAT LEADERS OF ALL TIMES. THIS MESSENGER HAS DONE SO MUCH FOR SO MANY IN BREAKING THE SHACKLES OF FEAR AND IGNORANCE WHICH HAVE IMPRISONED BLACK PEOPLE FOR SO LONG. MY WISHES ARE THAT HIS DREAM OF BUILDING A HOSPITAL FOR OUR PEOPLE ON THE SOUTH SIDE OF CHICAGO WILL BECOME A REALITY. YOU HAVE MY BEST WISHES AND SUPPORT. (Thank You: Tributes Acknowledged, 1974)

Mayor Kenneth A. Gibson, Newark, New Jersey

TO THE HONORABLE ELIJAH MUHAMMAD
CHICAGO, IL

DEAR HONORABLE ELIJAH MUHAMMAD, MY SINCEREST REGRETS FOR NOT BEING ABLE TO ATTEND THE TESTIMONIAL DINNER IN YOUR HONOR. CERTAINLY THE NATION OF ISLAM HAS PROVEN TO ALL PEOPLE THAT WHICH CAN BE ACCOMPLISHED BY ECONOMIC UNITY. I WOULD WISH TO HAVE THESE THOUGHTS EXPRESSED IN PERSON BUT IT WAS IMPOSSIBLE TO GET A FLIGHT TO CHICAGO IN TIME FROM NEWARK. OUR CITY HAS BECOME A BETTER PLACE BECAUSE OF THE REALISTIC ECONOMIC ACTIVITIES OF YOUR ORGANIZATION HERE. YOUR WORK IN THE FIELD OF EDCUATION IS WELL KNOWN OF YOU. THERE IS NO DOUBT IN MY MIND THAT IF THE NATION OF ISLAM HAS SET OUT TO BUILD A HOSPITAL, A HOSPITAL WILL BE BUILT. SO ALL THERE IS LEFT FOR ME TO SAY

IS THAT I WISH YOU AN EARLY COMPLETION OF YOUR HOSPITAL. SINCERELY. (Thank You: Tributes Acknowledged, 1974)

Ralph H. Metcalfe, Member of Congress

AS PREVIOUSLY STATED IN MY CORRESPONDENCE TO MUHAMMAD ALI, GENERAL CHAIRMAN, THAT BECAUSE OF A SPEAKING COMMITMENT OF LONGSTANDING, I WILL BE UNABLE TO ATTEND THE TESTIMONIAL DINNER PAYING TRIBUTE TO THE HONORABLE ELIJAH MUHAMMAD.

THROUGH HIS INGENUITY AND DEDICATION, THE NATION OF ISLAM HAS PROSPERED AND HAS BEEN A GREAT FORCE IN DEVELOPING SELF-RELIANCE, PERSONAL PRIDE AND THE MANY INNOVATIVE BUSIENSSES AND PROGRAMS TO MAKE ALL BLACK PEOPLE PROUD OF THEIR HERITAGE.

MY CONGRATULATIONS TO YOU, MUHAMMAD ALI AND THE DINNER COMMITTEE FOR YOUR VERY TIMELY TRIBUTE OF THE HONORABLE ELIJAH MUHAMMAD. (Thank You: Tributes Acknowledged, 1974)

John Calhoun, Staff Assistant to the President

FOR THE HONORABLE ELIJAH MUHAMMAD
CARE CONRAD HILTON HOTEL
CHICAGO, IL 60649

I DEEPLY REGRET THAT I AM UNABLE TO ATTEND THE TESTIMONIAL DINNER TONIGHT BECAUSE OF TRAVEL DIRECTED BY THE PRESIDENT.
YOU HAVE MY BEST WISHES FOR A HIGHLY SUCCESSFUL EVENING AS YOU PAY HONOR TO THE HONORABLE ELIJAH MUHAMMAD (Tribute to Honorable Elijah Muhammad , 1974)

Congresswoman Cardiss Collins, Member of Congress

TO THE HONORABLE ELIJAH MUHAMMAD
CONRAD HILTON HOTEL
CHICAGO, IL 60649

LEGISLATIVE BUSINESS HERE IN WASHINGTON WILL PREVENT MY PARTICIPATION IN HONORING THE GREAT AND MOST HONORED ELIJAH MUHAMMAD ON MARCH 29. I KNOW THE EVENING WILL BE A SUCCESS. IN PEACE AND IN HEALTH I AM YOURS TRULY (Tribute to Honorable Elijah Muhammad , 1974)

Vernon E. Jordan Jr. Executive Director National Urban League

TO THE HON. ELIJAH MUHAMMAD
CARE THE DINNER COMMITTEE
CHICAGO, IL

DEAR MR. MUHAMMAD

AN ENGAGEMENT OF LONG STANDING IN MADISON WISCONSIN PREVENTS MY ACCEPTING YOUR INVITATION TO ATTEND YOUR TESTIMONIAL DINNER ON MARCH 29TH. I DO, HOWEVER, WANT TO EXTEND MY PERSONAL BEST WISHES TO YOU AND MY CONGRATULATIONS ON YOUR ALMOST HALF A CENTURY OF PRODUCTIVE LEADERSHIP. (Tribute to Honorable Elijah Muhammad , 1974)

Sam Cornelius, U.S. Department of Commerce Office of Minority Enterprise

"I bring you greetings from the Office of Minority Enterprise and I commend you on this great occasion – In the appreciation of more than 40 years of distinguished service of the Honorable Elijah Muhammad to the Nation of Islam. I also commend you as I understand all proceeds of this dinner go toward your hospital building fund. "Certainly one good business example is your Guaranty

Bank here in Chicago with $9.5 million in assets and I commend you for this great venture. I commend you also as I recently read that the Muslims realized an income of $50 million last year. This is a great determination on your part. Your promise is great and must be achieved if we are to survive. In closing let me urge you to do this: There are many communities who suffer as much, if not more than Chicago, and I would hope that as you embark upon this mission of raising money to build a hospital that you create a record so that other communities across this country will have the opportunity to know how it is done. I commend you and urge you to keep on." (Tributes to Muhammad, 1974)

Mayor Maynard Jackson, Atlanta, Georgia

TO THE HONORABLE ELIJAH MUHAMMAD
CHICAGO, IL

I AM VERY SORRY THAT PREVIOUS COMMITMENTS WILL MAKE IT IMPOSSIBLE FOR ME TO ATTEND THE TESTIMONIAL DINNER PLANNED FOR MARCH 29 IN HONOR OF THE HONORABLE ELIJAH MUHAMMAD. YOUR FINF BORN HAS BEEN A SOURCE OF PRACTICAL HELP AND SPIRITUAL INSPIRATION TO BLACK PEOPLE ALL OVER THIS NATION.

I CONVEY MY BEST WISHES FOR YOUR CONTINUED SUCCESS. (Salute to Messenger Muhammad, 1974)

Dr. Gloria E.A. Toote, Asst. Secretary, Department of Housing and Urban Development

TO THE HONORABLE ELIJAH MUHAMMAD
CHICAGO, IL

THE TRIBUTE TO YOU AND THE LEADERSHIP YOU HAVE GIVEN TO COUNTLESS AMERICANS, ALL REACES AND OTHERS THROUGHOUT THE WORLD IS RICHLY DESERVED.

PLEASE ACCEPT OUR PERSONAL CONGRATULATIONS AND BEST WISHES FOR THE SUCCESS OF THE PLANNED HOSPITAL (Salute to Messenger Muhammad, 1974)

Ralph T. Grant Jr., Executive Director, Action Now, City of Newark, New Jersey

TO THE HONORABLE ELIJAH MUHAMMAD
CHICAGO, IL

I REGRET I CANNOT BE WITH YOU TONIGHT TO SHARE WITH YOU THIS GREAT HONOR WHICH IS DESERVED FOR YOUR MANY YEARS OF HARD WORK TO BETTER THE LIVING CONDITIONS OF MANY. I WISH YOU CONTINUED SUCCESS. (Salute to Messenger Muhammad, 1974)

A.L. Thomas, M.D., President, The Cook County Physicians Associations

TO MR. EUGENE DIBBLE AND THE GUEST OF THE TESTIMONIAL DINNER HONORING THE HONORABLE ELIJAH MUHAMMAD

REGRETFULLY I AM UNABLE TO BE PRESENT AT THE DINNER HOWEVER AS PRESIDENT OF THE COOK COUNTY PHYSICIANS ASSOCIATIONS I HEREWITH PLEDGE THAT THE PHYSICIANS OF THE COUNTY WILL BE FULLY SUPPORTIVE TO PROVIDE MEDICAL ASSISTANCE AS NEEDED AND DESIRABLY TO ASSIST IN THE DEVELOPMENT OF THE HEALTH CENTER BEING PLANNED BY THE MUSLIMS. I AM SURE THAT THE TOTAL COMMUNITY WILL AGREE THAT THE HONORABLE ELIJAH MUHAMMAD HAS BEEN A VITAL FORCE IN THE GROWTH AND DEVELOPMENT OF THE COMMUNITY. WE WELCOME THE OPPORTUNITY TO PARTICIPATE IN THESE EXCITING VENTURES.

UNFORTUNATELY, DUE TO EMERGENCY MATTERS I AM UNABLE TO BE WITH YOU THIS EVENING BUT SEVERAL OF MY COLLEAGUES ARE PRESENT AND IN SPIRIT I AM PRESENT ALSO.

BEST WISHES FOR CONTINUED SUCCESS. (Salute to Messenger Muhammad, 1974)

A.G. Gaston, Black Millionaire

M.S.: What do you think about the Honorable Elijah Muhammad's program?

Gaston: Wonderful! Wonderful! That's my program. Providing something for…that Fish Program was the best thing I ever heard of that I read in the paper about – right. That's a great thing; He's my man, He's all right with me – my philosophy 100 per cent. That's the reason why I wanted to talk with Him when I was up there in Chicago at Jesse Jackson's Expo. He's got the answer to it – He's got the answer to it. Let this Black man get something for himself. Waiting on this white man out there with everything you get you got to go to the white man to get it, that don't make sense. They come to me now. They come in here and say, "Mr. Gaston – "They want to borrow some money – they "scratch" like I used to "scratch." You think about politics. Politics is all right, but that is the most dangerous thing to have – being in politics "broke." A broke politician is terrible; he is a dangerous man. (Harold4X, Pay Yourself First: Black Millionaire Advises, 1974)

N.H. Jackson Assoc. Black Consumer Research Report, Freeport, New York

Black Consumer Research has been surveying and conducting a study to determine the most powerful Black man in America. The focus of this investigation is not to suggest that there are in fact influential Black people in America rather to point out the most influential among the powerless – to discover the one-eyed king in the valley of the blind.

Also of this date our research would suggest that the most influential Black man among the powerless black people in America is the Honorable Elijah Muhammad of Chicago. If we are to accept the definition that power is the ability to influence human behavior, then there is little room left for questioning the fact that Elijah Muhammad is the only Black person in America today, who has the influence to call tens of thousands of well-disciplined Black people to a course of action in a matter of hours. (Research Group Concludes Muhammad Most Influential Black Man In America, 1974)

Compton City Councilman Walter Tucker

Councilman Tucker, himself a steady fish customer, said, "The fish program is wonderful; it is sold for less than in the local markets in our communities which subject us to high priced goods. You really will begin to convert a lot of people when you start feeding them. Muhammad really knows what he is doing. (Lawrence2X, 1974)

The National Association of Black Psychologists (NABP)

In this, the mid-1970s in Nashville, Tenn., the National Association of Black Psychologist (NABP) honored the Honorable Messenger of Allah, Elijah Muhammad, for His Divine works. Contributions to the Economic, Social and Spiritual Development of the Black Community. (Harold4X, Black Psychologists Honor Muhammad's Work, 1974)

Mitchell Ware, Deputy Superintendent of the Chicago Police Department

"That's one of the reasons I've always respected Mr. Muhammad, even before now that they've gained a measure of respectability. When somebody else was trying to condemn Him. I had some pretty close friends who belonged to the Nation. They kept themselves clean, they worked and they looked out for themselves. You have to admire the man for the way those people conduct themselves. (Freelain, 1974)

Mayor Richard G. Hatcher, Gary, Indiana

WHEREAS, The Honorable Elijah Muhammad has for the past forty-three years worked for the development of a positive self-image and self-determination for the Blacks of America; and

WHEREAS, Largely as a result of his teachings, American Blacks are increasingly becoming more independent in the areas of education, medicine and economics; and

WHEREAS, The Honorable Elijah Muhammad has adamantly rejected all attempts to be co-opted either politically or morally; and

WHEREAS, The Honorable Elijah Muhammad has built within the American society an independent national school system in order to enable Blacks to meet the standards of the civilized societies of the world without losing their heritage and in a manner worthy of universal and international recognition;

NOW THEREFORE, I, Richard Gordon Hatcher, Mayor of the City of Gary, Indiana, do hereby proclaim the week of December 15-22, 1974, "HONORABLE ELIJAH MUHAMMAD APPRECIATION WEEK" IN THE City of Gary.

IN TESTIMONEY WHEREOF, I have hereunto set my hand and caused to be affixed the great seal of the City of Gary, in the State of Indiana, this 13th day of … December ….1974.. (Muhammad Week Proclaimed In Gary, 1974)

Ramsey Lewis, Composer/Musician

"The restaurants, universities, Temples, the farms: all this that the Honorable Elijah Muhammad has established makes other Black people very proud," declared Ramsey Lewis in a recent interview. "And this store – it's something else!" He recommended that all Blacks visit the Muhammad Temple of Islam. "It's a beautiful thing, that the Honorable Elijah Muhammad has made it possible that Black can go to the supermarket and know they are contributing to their own community," he said. (Larry14X, Celebrities, Civic Leaders Pay Tribute To Muhammad At Supermarket Anniversary, 1974)

Javad Alamir, Middle Eastern Journalist

Javad Alamir, the most revered and best known of all Middle Eastern journalists, recently predicted that the Nation of Islam "will become the nucleus of a great

Black assembly." HE APPLAUDED the "seriousness" of the Muslims, and described the Nation of Islam as "by far the most progressive of all Black movements in the country." (Larry14X, Iranian Journalist Lauds Nation of Islam,
1975)

Professor Herbert Berg, Introduction to his book Elijah Muhammad and Islam

Moreover, in light of ongoing concerns about a clash between Western and Islamic civilizations, it is ironic that hundreds of thousands—if not millions—of Muslims living in
the United States were directly or indirectly converted to Islam via the uniquely American formulation of this religion by Elijah Muhammad. Approximately 30 percent of the
United States' six to eight million Muslims are African American, making Islam the
second most popular religion among African Americans. Although the vast majority of
these African American Muslims are now Sunni Muslims, many (or perhaps their parents or grandparents) were introduced to Islam through the Nation of Islam, a movement
that was exclusively Black, segregationist, and militant. Its leader for over forty years,
Elijah Muhammad, was therefore arguably the most important person in the development of Islam in America, eclipsing other prominent figures such as Noble Drew Ali,
Wali Fard Muhammad, Malcolm X, Louis Farrakhan, and Warith Deen Mohammed
(originally known as Wallace D. Muhammad). Despite his unrivaled prominence, Elijah
Muhammad is rarely treated as a major figure in Islam. Quite rightly, he has been examined for his influence in the transformation of African American politics, economics, and
psychology. But this book is unique in focusing exclusively on Elijah Muhammad as a
religious figure and, in particular, on his relationship with Islam and other Muslims.
(Berg, 2009)

Edwin C. Berry, Chicago Director, Urban League

A guy like this Moslem leader [Elijah Muhammad] makes a lot more sense than
I do to the man in the street who's getting his teeth kicked out. I have a sinking
feeling that Elijah Muhammad is very significant. (Young, 1959)

James Brown, Businessman and Musician-"Godfather of Soul"

"I am with Messenger Muhammad on fulfilling our needs for hospitals, schools, banks and living complexes. Messenger Muhammad is the pioneer of self-dignity. My sole purpose is to build for my people. All Black people should take a stand and be free of the burden of submitting and catering to our oppressors. Messenger Muhammad is right in accord with the times."

Eric Hoffer, Author, The True Believer

But what of Elijah Muhammad and the Black Muslim movement? Alone of all the Negro leaders Elijah Muhammad has a vivid awareness of the vital need of a new birth in any drastic human transformation, and he alone mastered the technique of staging a new identity. Bacon's dictum that you must change many things if you want to change one thing has particular application to drastic change. If the Negro is to become a new man he must be stripped of his habits, attitudes, opinions, beliefs and even memories. He needs a new way of dressing, a new purpose, even a new religion and a new name. The Black Muslim movement can point to many solid achievements. It has transformed idlers, criminals, junkies and drunkards into clean-living, purposeful human beings.

It is worth remembering that what Elijah Muhammad is doing to the Negro, is, in a sense, a recapitulation of what America has done to the immigrant from Europe: It stripped him of his traditions, habits, tastes, opinions and memories, and gave him a new diet, a new way of dressing, a new language and often a new name. (Hoffer, 1964)

Cynthia S'thembile West, Scholar and Author of Nation Builders: Female Activism in the Nation of Islam 1960-1970

The NOI provided a program that met African Americans at the level of their need. Whether that need included moral, familial, financial, or social challenges, the NOI provided the support structure that developed and strengthened African Americans in those areas. Moreover, the Nation used embodied learning in the process of educating black people. Every lesson, whether it concerned respect and love for self, literacy skills, personal hygiene, or marriage and family, was task oriented. People worked in consort with one another. In fact, as the respondents emphasized, the Nation of Islam was a family, a family that addressed the totality of needs of African American Muslims in Newark, New Jersey. As an organization that stressed and provided for family in the context of self-determination, to position women outside of that structure would have been disruptive. As such, the NOI, led by the Honorable Elijah Muhammad, changed not only the dynamics of interaction between African American men and women in Newark, but also transformed the economic base of that city by teaching blacks how to do for self in a spirit of love and collectivity. This was the overwhelming message communicated by the women interviewed, none of whom perceived themselves as submissive or subordinate to men in the context of their Nation experience.

These Black Muslim women looked at the Nation, and saw love and courage. To them the Honorable Elijah Muhammad was a man who loved his people so much that he designed an institution in which the primacy of women was integral, and every man in the organization was obligated to put himself on the line for them. Black Muslim women saw this as a measure of love and respect for them. (West, 1996)

Dawn-Marie Gibson and Jamillah Karim, Authors, Women of The Nation

Feminist and womanist scholars have described Nation women as guilty of reproducing their own oppression because they accept traditional gender roles, including men as providers and women as homemakers. Yet Nation women have strategically embraced these gender roles in the context of the broader struggle for racial equality. As we have seen, women joined Elijah Muhammad's NOI for its racial uplift message and its community-building activities...

Early Nation women conceptualized their role in the home not as restriction but as a tool for liberation and advancement of their entire community...Elijah Muhammad himself encouraged women's work and education when they benefitted the organization. Former Nation women make it very clear that the emphasis on women's contribution to the home did not mean that women thought themselves inadequate to do the work of men. Rather they were making a choice to commit to the strengthening of their marriages and the raising of their children first. (Karim, 2014)

Bayinnah Jeffries, Author, A Nation Can Rise No Higher Than Its Women

On a national level, African American Muslim women in the original Nation of Islam participated in every stage of the community's development...Akin to mid-management, women occupied roles like national directors of the University of Islam, deans, and supreme captains. Women also occupied local status positions like lieutenants, secretaries, and treasurers. As rank and file, women fundraised, took part in institution building, owned businesses, taught in Muslim school, directed girls' troops, and addressed their duties as wives and mothers. (Jeffries, 2014)

Bill Cosby, Entrepreneur, Comedian, Philanthropist

I'm a Christian. But Muslims are misunderstood. Intentionally misunderstood. We should all be more like them. They make sense, especially with their children. There is no other group like the Black Muslims, who put so much effort into teaching children the right things, they don't smoke, they don't drink or overindulge in alcohol, they protect their women, they command respect. And what do these other people do?

They complain about them, they criticize them. We'd be a better world if we emulated them. We don't have to become black Muslims, but we can embrace the things that work. (Brown, 2013)

Rev. Jesse L. Jackson Sr., Civil Rights Leader, Founder of Rainbow PUSH

I as many of you, sat at the feet of the Honorable Elijah Muhammad and shared and was taught. The Messenger made the message very clear. He turned alienation into emancipation. He concentrated on taking the slums out of the people and then the people out of the slums. He took dope out of veins and put hope in our brains. He was the father of Black consciousness. During our "colored" and

"Negro" days he was Black. His leadership exceeded far beyond the membership of the Black Muslims. For more than three decades, the Honorable Elijah Muhammad has been the spiritual leader of the Black Muslims and a progressive force for Black identity and consciousness, self-determination and economic development. (Simms, 1975)

Julian Bond, Georgia State Senator, Founding Member of Student Nonviolent Coordinating Committee (SNCC)

Elijah Muhammad has presented to Black people in this country a model of thrift, of hard work, of devotion to self, and of cleanliness of mind and body that we don't get in many other places. (Simms, 1975)

Vernon E. Jordan, Former Executive Director of the National Urban League, Businessman

The Honorable Elijah Muhammad is a man of unquestioned talents and leadership ability who has left an indelible mark on his times. Under his guidance, the Nation of Islam developed into a vital and positive force within many communities and services for thousands and thousands of people. (Simms, 1975)

Rev. J. H. Jackson, Former President of the National Baptist Convention USA

He[Hon. Elijah Muhammad] emphasized the elements of self-help, self-respect, and economic independence. He made a distinct contribution not only to his own organization but to the people of this country in that he showed what can be done with a little sacrifice and a little effort. In these particulars, we would do well to emulate his philosophies and his positions. (Simms, 1975)

Rev. Leon Sullivan, Founder Opportunities Industrialization Centers of America

This man [Hon. Elijah Muhammad] and his work were part of a new frontier for Blacks in the United States and for Black people throughout the world. I admired him and I still admire his effort. God bless his spirit (Simms, 1975)

John Lewis, U.S. Congressman, Former Head of Student Non-violent Coordinating Committee (SNCC)

Without question, he [Hon. Elijah Muhammad] aided many young Black Americans to gain dignity and hope and a will to survive. I have great deal of admiration for the sense of discipline he provided for many young Black men and women. (Simms, 1975)

Mayor Richard Daley, Chicago, Illinois

He[Hon. Elijah Muhammad] has been an outstanding citizen who is always interested in helping young people and especially the poor. He always exalted the basic family unit, which is something we should all admire, and he developed an educational system which preaches dignity, self-respect and accomplishment. (Simms, 1975)

Dr. C. Eric Lincoln, Former Chairman of Fisk University's Department of Religious and Philosophical Studies and Author of The Black Muslims In America

Elijah Muhammad gave Blacks new confidence in their potential to become creative and self-sufficient people. In addition, he taught his followers the efficacy and rewards of hard work, fair play, and abstinence. It has been shown beyond a shadow of a doubt that the Muslims who have followed his economic teachings and have in many cases moved substantially ahead in their economic pursuits.

He gave also his people a success formula for home and family life. The rate of delinquency among Muslim children is extremely low. The rate of divorce is quite low. The stability of the Muslim home is an ideal for which the rest of America might strive (Simms, 1975)

Father George Clements, Former Pastor of Chicago's Holy Angels Roman Catholic Church

His teachings of dignity, self-respect, discipline and a sense of responsibility are the great works he leaves behind. And this we admire no matter what our religion. (Simms, 1975)

Ralph Metcalf, Former U. S. Representative 1ˢᵗ District, Illinois

Mr. Muhammad's life is one of peace, harmony and great integrity. He made the Nation of Islam a pillar of strength in Black communities throughout the country. (Simms, 1975)

Abdul Latif Qaisi, Writer, Muslim News International

In spite of legal rights, constitutional safeguards and determination of the Federal authority not all the Negroes in America feel secure or equal in status to the white population. The widespread practice of racial discrimination troubles the soul of America and embarrasses its government at home and abroad. The Black Muslim movement aims to restore dignity and self-confidence to the Negroes who are victims of both racial prejudice and inferiority complex. Because of their racial undertones, phenomenal rise in strength, and demand for a separate homeland they have alarmed the American Government and antagonized the orthodox Muslims. Judging them solely by their character and behavior, honesty, personal and public morality, fearlessness and faith in God-one would be led to hail them as excellent Muslims. The success of the orthodox (Muslims) is only a fraction of what the Muslims in America have accomplished under Elijah Muhammad. (Qaisi, 1962)

Abdul Basit Naeem, Publisher, Writer, Businessman

What then is the truth about Mr. Elijah Muhammad? And what in reality is the nature and ultimate aim of his mission? In my opinion, Mr. Elijah Muhammad, affectionately called by his faithful flock as the Messenger of Allah, is a true sincere and selfless leader of his people whose one and only aim in life is to "take the Message of Islam to each and every one of the more than 20 million men, women and children of my race and kind in the wilderness of North America."

I am convinced that Mr. Elijah Muhammad's mission is God-inspired: I doubt that he could have said and done all that is rightfully attributed to him without the blessings of His Keeper. It takes a man of great valor and tremendous courage to challenge a powerful adversary; Mr. Elijah Muhammad can be said to dwell in the lion's den.

Equally convincing to me is proof of the Islamic nature of his mission and work. If alleviating the plight and misery of a community long considered hopelessly stricken with innumerable ills and providing the members the basis of a NEW LIFE-not after death, in Heaven, but HERE and NOW-cannot be considered an Islamic act, I must, in that case, confess my own ignorance as to what Islam is! (Naeem, The Truth About The Honorable Elijah Muhammad, 1962)

Ismail Abdul-Aleem, Prison Chaplain, Indianapolis

My views have changed significantly over the past couple years. Probably working with men who are in prison and are practicing Muslims, and trying ot cater to their needs has given me a greater appreciation for the work of the early Muslim pioneers who dedicated their lives to the establishment of Islam in our community.

Even without full access to the Qur'an or the life model of Prophet Muhammad, Elijah Muhammad and the members of the Nation sought to address the pressing needs of redefining our existence in this country.

Because of their efforts Islam has become an authentically legitimate African-American religion. Any Black person anywhere in the United States can embrace Islam without fear of losing his identity as an authentic Black man. This is something that is unheard of for white Americans, Latinos, and other ethnic groups.

The Nation of Islam defined Islam in a way that featured resistance to oppression, anti-black bias and addressed the reality of white supremacy and our opposition to it.

The Nation of Islam sought to uplift the downtrodden and those who were the victims of racial oppression.

We must accept the contributions of those before us and seek to use whatever was successful in the transformation of human beings-whose souls have been broken-into God-fearing righteous men and women. (Saahir, The Man Behind The Men, 2011)

Diane Williams, MPH, Native American Social Worker

I tell people again and again and again that I know what I know not because of anything U.C. Berkeley (University of California Berkeley) taught me, but because I learned what I learned in the Nation of Islam. I learned it from the sisters who learned it, basically, from Elijah Muhammad- and it worked!

It changed a people who just like my Indian people, had a terrible diet. Still a lot of work needs to be done in the African American community, but Elijah Muhammad was successful in alerting, millions probably, of African American people about pork and leading a healthier life. (Saahir, The Man Behind The Men, 2011)

Larry Johnson, NBA Basketball Star

Once I heard the teachings of the Honorable Elijah Muhammad; that really touched me. It was something I could relate to and made me do better. Once you have heard the teachings (of the Nation of Islam) and know the knowledge, there is no turning back. (Saahir, The Man Behind The Men, 2011)

Imam Warith Deen Mohammed, Son of Hon. Elijah Muhammad, Leader American Society of Muslims and Mosque Cares, Inc.

I don't owe my cleanliness to my new understanding of what Islam is. I owe my cleanliness to the teachings of the Honorable Elijah Muhammad. I owe my moral obedience to that teaching. I owe my success to the person of that teaching. (Mohammed, 2000)

Muhammad Ali, Heavyweight Champion, International Celebrity

He was my Jesus, and I had love for both the man and what he represented. Like Jesus Christ and all of God's prophets, he represented all good things…Elijah

Muhammad was my savior, and everything I have came from him-my thoughts, my efforts to help my people, how I eat, how I talk, my name. (Saahir, The Man Behind The Men, 2011)

Ronald 6X Bell and Robert 9X Bell, Musicians and Entrepreneurs, Founders of Historic Group Kook & the Gang

Whiting H & G, Hereafter, and Fruitman (songs from their album Light of the World) are meant to reflect a message of unity and seriousness from the Honorable Elijah Muhammad.

-Robert 9X Bell

The Hereafter means Freedom, Justice and Equality and I never knew anything about that until I started following the Messenger. When we first accepted Islam in Jersey City, N.J., the rest of the band was against it. They even tried everything to stop us from coming in. But now Islam is attracting them.

-Ronald 6X Bell

Doug Carn, Jazz Legend

After 3 years as a believer in Islam as taught by the Sunni (Orthodox) Muslims, famed musician Doug Carn recently accepted Islam as taught by the Honorable Elijah Muhammad. Carne said "The things that the Messenger is teaching are things that I really believed in my heart, for a long time. After I started studying, I recognized that the Orthodox sect didn't relate to the Black man in this country-in terms of setting him free as a group. When I saw that Black woman that was once on the streets selling her body wearing the clothes of dignity; when I saw schools; when I saw shiploads of fish coming from Peru; when I saw Muslim governments like Libya and Kuwait offering millions of dollars, there wasn't any doubt who had the command from God. The Black man as a whole has to understand Islam first, and to get it in his bones, and into the bones of his children. We have to clean up before we can do anything. What I can do by coming into the Nation of Islam is add that many more people to the Nation." (Larry14X, 1974)

Dr. Naim Akbar, Clinical Psychologist and College Professor

The under-appreciated, but highly successful social and religious movement directed by the Honorable Elijah Muhammad was another powerful example of the call for African American to develop "self-knowledge," as the necessary prerequisite for changing our lives and changing our communities. Though this call and analysis did not come from the academy as did D. Woodson's, it too fell on deaf ears among the majority of African-American community and was summarily condemned by almost all of the non-African world. The unprecedented reformations, transformations and developments that Elijah Muhammad achieved with his work in the Nation of Islam well demonstrated the highly successful consequence of applied "knowledge of self." Certainly, his approach and his metaphors were highly unusual, but the foundation of his approach was a defiant conviction to be self-determining and committed to the re-education of the African-American person. Though he achieved considerable economic success and institution building, the most impressive outcome was the solid and meaningful personal reform that was brought about in the lives of the adherents to Mr. Muhammad's movement. The fact that his movement was able to take destroyed and misdirected lives that had been thrown away to vice, criminality and personal self-destruction and to convert those lives to responsible and constructive social contributors was nothing short of miraculous. Though the movement was ideologically and structurally very complex, the fundamental concept that guided everything else in the philosophy was the importance of "self-knowledge" as the key to transforming human life. (Akbar, 1998)

James, Baldwin, Author, The Fire Next Time

Elijah Muhammad has been able to do what generations of welfare workers and committees and resolutions and reports and housing projects and playgrounds have failed to do: to heal and redeem drunkards and junkies, to convert people who have come out of prison and to keep them out, to make men chaste and women virtuous, and to invest both the male and the female with a pride and a serenity that hang about them like an unfailing light. He has done all these things, which our Christian church has spectacularly failed to do. (Baldwin, 1962)

Booker Griffin, Writer, The Los Angeles Sentinel

The Nation of Islam is a power that has come. Its appeal is racial and not racist, and it has the strength of independence and pride that is lacking in so-called practical movements. Out of ordeal and stagnation, exploitation and despair the only viable alternative visible to thousands of Black Americans is the Nation of Islam under the leadership of the Honorable Elijah Muhammad. (Smith, 1975)

Prime Minister Michael Manley, Jamaica

I want you to convey back to the Honorable Elijah Muhammad that we are proud of His work. That wherever people are oppressed in the world we unite behind the purpose that inspires His work. And let him know that this prime minister of this proud country would be very honored to welcome Him as our guest at any time. (Smith, 1975)

Lehman Brightman, President United Native American Indian Association(UNAIA)

"It's a privilege and an honor to celebrate this great man," said Lehman Brightman, president of the UNAIA and publisher of the Indian newspaper War Path. In praising the Honorable Elijah Muhammad, Brightman said among the things that the Black man and Indian had in common was a "legacy of hatred, unemployment, bad health and poverty." Brightman said he had come to pay his respects to Messenger Muhammad as well as listen and learn. "This is the beginning of something new for me and ware sharing it," he said. (Indian Leaders Honor Muhammad, 1975)

California Mayors

Mayor Thomas Bradley declared February 4th, as Black Community Fair Day here, in appreciation of the Honorable Elijah Muhammad. The mayor announced the city's tribute to Messenger Muhammad before 20,000 persons who had assembled at the Shrine Exposition Hall. Just 24 hours earlier a similar proclamation was made as Compton Mayor Doris A. Davis declared February 3rd The Honorable Elijah Muhammad Day in the predominantly Black city of Compton, California. The 2 events marked the second time the Messenger had been honored by California mayors. Two weeks earlier, He received simultaneous honors with a day in tribute to His works from Oakland Mayor John Reading and Berkeley Mayor Warren Widener. (LawrenceC.X., 1975)

Cesar Chavez, Leader United Farm Workers Union

"We told our people, 'It's got to be done like the Muslims do it. It's got to be done person to person.' Of all the movements we know of, we have a lot of respect for you, because you have a lot of people doing things." he said referring to the constructive program of the Most Honorable Elijah Muhammad and its effect on his energetic followers. (Charles20X, 1972)

Acknowledgements

All praise is due to Allah, who appeared in the person of Master W. Fard Muhammad, to whom praise belongs forever. It is my prayer that Allah is pleased with this work

Working with the words of the Most Honorable Elijah Muhammad has been a joy and I thank Him for all of his tireless labor to put into writing and communicate to the world the precious wisdom and insight that he received directly from Master W. Fard Muhammad. In this series of profound articles of truth we see Him giving to us a great gift that would guide us and be a light for us as this world and its institutions die. It is my prayer that the Most Honorable Elijah Muhammad is pleased with this work.

I especially thank the Honorable Minister Louis Farrakhan for commissioning this work. I thank Him for his enthusiasm and for His patience with me in the completion of it. I thank Him for His guidance, love and encouragement of me. I am so happy to complete this work. It is my hope and intention that it will be of service to the Minister in His ministry of the resurrection of the mentally dead masses. What Allah (God) did in fashioning Him as a helper for the Most Honorable Elijah Muhammad is very evident in the Minister's ability to produce agreement with the teachings among millions of human beings around the globe. It is my prayer that the Honorable Minister Louis Farrakhan is pleased with this work.

I am also very thankful and happy to have had the assistance and labor of some wonderful and talented believers from throughout the Nation of Islam. Mr. Muhammad Speaks An Invincible Truth: The Pittsburgh Courier Archives Project Team includes the following magnificent believers:

Sister Vivian X Lee, New York, New York, manuscript typing, and editing

Sister Ebony Muhammad, Houston, Texas, typing and proofreading

Sister Sonya Muhammad, Houston, Texas, typing and proofreading

Sister Landra Nura Muhammad, Charlotte, North Carolina, typing and proof-reading

Brother Alan Muhammad, Boston, Massachusetts, interior layout and design

Brother Jahleel Muhammad, Detroit, Michigan, cover art and graphic design

Sister Angel Yvonne Muhammad, Indianapolis, Indiana, proofreading and typing

Brother Rodney A. Muhammad, Memphis, Tennessee, proofreading

Brother Abdul Arif Muhammad, NOI General Counsel, Chicago, Illinois, consultation and transcription editing

I thank my wife Sister Tomiko Muhammad for her patience and support during the time we were working on the completion of this project. I would like to also thank the following who offered encouragement and allowed me to access and benefit from their counsel. Brother Ilia Rashad Muhammad (Memphis, TN), Brother Andre Muhammad (Memphis, TN), Brother Cedric Muhammad (Washington, D.C.), Brother Kendrick Muhammad(Charlotte, NC), Brother Jackie Muhammad(Atlanta, GA), Student Minister Anthony Muhammad(Memphis, TN), Student Minister Robert Muhammad(Houston, TX), Student Minister Courtney Muhammad(Utica, NY),Student Minister Rodney Muhammad (Philadelphia, PA), Student Minister James Muhammad (Tampa, FL), Student Minister Amon Muhammad (Durham, NC), and Student Minister Nuri Muhammad (Indianapolis,IN).

I would also like to thank Sister Kim Muhammad from the office of the Honorable Minister Louis Farrakhan.

Many thanks also to believers who encouraged us and provided moral support throughout the various stages of this project: Brother Eric Ahad Muhammad (Phoenix, AZ), Brother Victor Muhammad (Boston,MA), Brother Fred Muhammad (Philadelphia,PA), Brother Derrick 4Muhammad (Memphis,TN) Brother Corey X (Memphis,TN) Brother Charles 2Muhammad (Memphis,TN) Sister Jill Muhammad (Memphis,TN) Brother Student Minister James Muhammad (Rochester, NY), Brother Jackie Muhammad (Atlanta,GA), Brother Dr. Ridgely Muhammad (Bronwood,GA), Brother Sultan Muhammad (Chicago, IL), Brother Bobby Muhammad (Denver,CO), Student Minister Abdul Hafeez Muhammad (New York,NY) and Student Minister Carlos Muhammad (Baltimore, MD).

Bibliography

1st Negro State Senator Comments On Mississippi and Muslims. (1965, February 5). *Muhammad Speaks*, p. 22.

Akbar, D. N. (1998). Know Thy Self. In D. N. Akbar, *Know Thy Self* (pp. 67-68). Tallahassee, FL: Mind Productions & Associates.

Baldwin, J. (1962). *The Fire Next Time*. New York, New York: Random House.

Berg, H. (2009). *Elijah Muhammad and Islam*. New York, New York: New York University Press.

Brown, B. C. (2013, June 9). A Plague Called Apathy. *New York Post*.

Buni, A. (1974). *Biographies: Robert Lee Vann*. Retrieved February 6, 2015, from PBS.ORG: http://www.pbs.org/blackpress/news_bios/vann.html

Charles20X, B. (1972, August 4). Farm Workers' Chavez Speak Of Future Goals. *Muhammad Speaks Newspaper*, p. 5.

Chicago Professionals Witness Muslim Accomplishments. (1973, September 14). *Muhammad Speaks*, p. 14.

CORE Praises Muslims in D.C. (1963, May 24). *Muhammad Speaks*, p. 9.

Darayai, M. S. (1964, May 8). Says Islam Can Save West. *Muhammad Speaks*, p. 3.

Freelain, N. (1974, November 1). Black Police Official Sees Menacing Trend In Society's Lack Of Respect For Others. *Muhammad Speaks*, p. 20.

Garvey Group Praises Muhammad. (1963, June 7). *Muhammad Speaks*, p. 20.

Garvey, A. A. (1963, June 7). Letter to Muhammad from the wife of Marcus Garvey. *Muhammad Speaks*, p. 2.

Hanoka, D. N. (1963, April 1). Muslim Movement In the U.S. *Muhammad Speaks*, p. 9.

Harold4X. (1974, February 5). Atlanta Criminal Investigator Praises Muslim High Integrity. *Muhammad Speaks*, p. 20.

Harold4X. (1974, September 20). Black Psychologists Honor Muhammad's Work. *Muhammad Speaks*, p. 5.

Harold4X. (1974, April 19). Pay Yourself First: Black Millionaire Advises. *Muhammad Speaks*, p. 11.

Harold4XandMinisterOscarX. (1973, December 28). Tuskegee Mayor Pays Tribute To Messenger. *Muhammad Speaks*, p. 4.

Hightower, W. (1963, October 23). One of Basketball's Best Gives Views On Muhammad. *Muhammad Speaks*, p. 15.

Hill, F. (1964, October 23). Soundest Sleep On Beds Built By Son Of Slaves. *Muhammad Speaks*, p. 18.

Hoffer, E. (1964, November 29). The Negro Is Prejudiced Against Himself. *New York Times*, p. SM27.

Howard, S. B. (1972, June 2). New York School Teacher Ranks Muhammad No. 1. *Muhammad Speaks*, p. 29.

Indian Leaders Honor Muhammad. (1975, February 21). *Muhammad Speaks*, p. 15.

Jaap, J. A. (2015, January 17). Pittsburgh Courier. *The American Mosaic: The African American Experience*. 2015, USA: ABC-CLIO.

Jeffries, B. (2014). *A Nation Can Rise No Higher Than Its Women*. Lanham,MD: Lexington Books.

Karim, D.-M. G. (2014). *Women of The Nation*. New York: NYU Press.

Larry14X. (1974, December 27). Celebrities, Civic Leaders Pay Tribute To Muhammad At Supermarket Anniversary. *Muhammad Speaks*, p. 5.

Larry14X. (1974, November 1). Doug Carn popular jazz organist joins growing list of Muslim musicians. *Muhammad Speaks*, p. 6.

Larry14X. (1975, February 7). Iranian Journalist Lauds Nation of Islam. *Muhammad Speaks*, p. 16.

Larry5X. (1973, June 13). Mayors Hail Muslim Progress. *Muhammad Speaks*, p. 5.

Lawrence2X. (1974, June 14). Muhammad: Feeding The Multitudes. *Muhammad Speaks*, p. 11.

LawrenceC.X. (1975, February 28). Compton and L.A. laud Messenger's Work. *Muhammad Speaks*, p. 6.

Leaks, S. (1963, October 11). World Outlook of Ruby Dee. *Muhammad Speaks*, p. 21.

Leaks, S. (1964, May 8). Messenger of Allah as Seen by Islamic Leader from Pakistan. *Muhammad Speaks*, p. 3.

Martin, L. (1972, June 2). Noted Editor, Politiician Hails Muhammad Success. *Muhammad Speaks*, p. 4.

McNeil, E. D. (1974, March 15). Lawyer Tributes Muhammad. *Muhammad Speaks*, p. 18.

Methodist Minister Has High Praise For The Messenger. (1965, December 24). *Muhammad Speaks*, p. 25.

Mohammed, I. W. (Performer). (2000, February 4). *lecture*. Forest Park Community College, St. Louis, MO, USA.

Mosby, D. (1974, March 15). I almost cried when Muhammad left our paper. *Muhammad Speaks*, p. 11.

Muhammad Week Proclaimed In Gary. (1974, December 27). *Muhammad Speaks*, p. 4.

Muhammad(Charles67X), A. (1973, October 5). On Saving The Black Mind. *Muhammad Speaks*, p. 22.

Naeem, A. B. (1962, October 15). The Truth About The Honorable Elijah Muhammad. *Muhammad Speaks*, p. 3.

Naeem, A. B. (1965, July 30). How Pakistani Periodical Views Nation of Islam. *Muhammad Speaks*, p. 16.

New Yorkers Attack Anti-Muslim Media. (1973, June 22). *Muhammad Speaks*, p. 9.

Pamela7X. (1974, December 6). Staple Singers Urge Support For Hospital. *Muhammad Speaks*, p. 5.

Peters, A. (1972, March 17). As Far As Whites Are Concerned Blacks and Green Don't Match. *Muhammad Speaks*, p. 29.

Pipes, D. (2000, June). How Elijah Muhammad Won. *Commentary*, p. 31.

Qaisi, A. L. (1962, September). The Black Muslims. *Muslim News International*, p. 25.

Research Group Concludes Muhammad Most Influential Black Man In America. (1974, May 17). *Muhammad Speaks*, p. 16.

Rubio, S. E. (1972, June 2). South American Ready To Follow Messenger Muhammad. *Muhammad Speaks*, p. 29.

Saahir, M. (2011). The Man Behind The Men. In M. Saahir, *The Man Behind The Men* (p. 240). Indianopolis,IN: Words Make People Publishing.

Saahir, M. (2011). The Man Behind The Men. In M. Saahir, *The Man Behind The Men* (p. 215). Indianapolis, IN: Words Make People Publishing.

Saahir, M. (2011). The Man Behind The Men. In M. Saahir, *The Man Behind The Men* (p. 115). Indianapolis, IN: Words Make People Publishing.

Salute to Messenger Muhammad. (1974, April 12). *Muhammad Speaks*, p. 11.

Samuel17X. (1972, June 30). Candidate Praises Nation of Islam. *Muhammad Speaks*, p. 10.

Samuel17X. (1973, June 22). College Award To Muhammad. *Muhammad Speaks*, p. 5.

Simms, G. (1975, March 13). Leaders Praise Legacy of Elijah Muhammad. *Jet Magazine*, pp. 20-21.

Smith, J. H. (1975). *Civic, Government Dignitaries Honor Muhammad*. Chicago, IL: Nation of Islam.

Thank You: Sincere Words Praising Messenger Muhammad. (1974, April 12). *Muhammad Speaks*, pp. 4-5.

Thank You: Tributes Acknowledged. (1974, April 12). *Muhammad Speaks*, pp. 2-3.

Tribute to Honorable Elijah Muhammad . (1974, April 12). *Muhammad Speaks*, p. 8.

Tributes to Muhammad. (1974, April 12). *Muhammad Speaks*, p. 16.

Udom, E. (1962). *Black Nationalism: A Search For An Identity In America*. Chicago: Unversity of Chicago Press.

Udom, E. (Chicago). Black Nationalism: A Search For An Identity In America. In E. Udom, *BBlack Nationalism: A Search For An Identity In America* (p. 273). Chicago: University of Chicago Press.

Walker, D. (1829). Appeal to the Coloured Citizens of the World. Pennsylvania State University Press.

Walker, J. (1963, June 7). Muhammad Economic Program Cited by Ellington. *Muhammad Speaks*, p. 21.

Walker, J. (1973, May 11). Social Workers Group Honors Muhammad. *Muhammad Speaks*, p. 3.

West, C. S. (1996). Nation Builders: Female Activism in the Nation of Islam, 1960-1970. *The Black Scholar*, 41-48.

Why Brown Will Not Back Down On the Messenger. (1964, October 9). *Muhammad Speaks*, p. 4.

Wiggins, D. K. (1983). The Pittsburgh Courier-Journal and the Campaign to inclue Blacks in Organized Baseball, 1933-1945. *Journal of Sport History*, 5-29.

Woodford, J. (2014). Messaging The Blackman. In K. Wachsberger, *Insider Histories of the Vietnam Era Underground Press* (p. 19). Ann Arbor: University of Michigan Press.

Young, M. (1959, November). Mr. Muhammad and His Fanatic Moslems. *Sepia*, p. 25.

Index

Adam, 25, 37, 47, 89, 105, 135, 141, 152, 156, 157, 158, 171, 180, 200, 227, 238, 240, 241, 242, 246, 273, 281, 292, 295

Aegean, 233, 244, 246

Africa, xvi, xx, xxii, 51, 60, 61, 62, 79, 81, 83, 108, 116, 118, 217, 265, 279, 290, 295, 309, 310, 311, 316, 317, 342, 343, 345, 349, 350, 352, 358

America, xiv, xv, xvi, xvii, xx, xxi, xxiii, xxvi, xxxiv, xxxv, xxxvii, xxxviii, xlii, xliv, xlvii, xlix, li, 1, 12, 17, 20, 21, 22, 24, 27, 30, 32, 33, 34, 48, 49, 50, 62, 65, 66, 67, 68, 69, 75, 81, 82, 83, 84, 85, 87, 92, 94, 96, 97, 101, 103, 107, 108, 116, 124, 126, 135, 140, 142, 143, 149, 153, 154, 157, 160, 161, 170, 174, 184, 185, 188, 191, 196, 198, 205, 206, 207, 211, 212, 213, 214, 216, 217, 218, 219, 221, 223, 224, 225, 228, 229, 230, 232, 234, 235, 242, 243, 251, 252, 255, 256, 257, 258, 259, 260, 262, 263, 264, 265, 266, 268, 270, 271, 280, 285, 286, 289, 290, 291, 293, 295, 301, 303, 304, 308, 309, 310, 312, 313, 314, 318, 321, 322, 328, 329, 330, 332, 339, 341, 342, 343, 346, 347, 348, 359, 360

angel, 13, 32, 33, 35, 114, 122, 136, 200, 201, 232, 259, 260, 269, 293, 298

apostle, 28, 69, 109, 128, 129, 131, 240, 267, 287

Arab, xlii, 7, 15, 33, 51, 62, 63, 66, 111, 122, 180, 193, 204, 246, 252, 309

Armageddon, 48, 52, 57

Armstrong, 100, 101, 277, 292, 293

Asiatic, 5, 89, 116, 144, 190, 213, 215, 266

beast, 14, 44, 45, 46, 47, 84, 122, 231, 232, 233, 234, 235, 236, 237, 240, 241, 242, 243, 244, 246, 247, 252, 253, 255, 256, 261, 262, 265, 266, 267, 268, 269, 271, 272, 273, 282, 286

believe, xvii, xxix, xxxi, xl, li, 7, 8, 12, 25, 28, 38, 41, 42, 46, 53, 56, 57, 61, 62, 64, 65, 67, 69, 70, 71, 73, 77, 78, 82, 85, 86, 88, 89, 90, 91, 93, 100, 105, 106, 117, 123, 125, 126, 130, 131, 132, 142, 153, 154, 158, 162, 163, 166, 168, 172, 173, 174, 175, 176, 177, 179, 181, 183, 184, 185, 189, 190, 192, 196, 197, 198, 202, 205, 207, 208, 212, 216, 220, 222, 223, 226, 227, 228, 230, 231, 234, 235, 237, 257, 258, 260, 262, 267, 268, 274, 277, 278, 279, 280, 283, 284, 286, 292, 293, 297, 298, 306, 321, 326, 328, 329, 332

believers, xxx, xxxviii, xliii, 7, 12, 27, 41, 42, 53, 57, 64, 68, 70, 71, 86, 94, 159, 162, 168, 171, 181, 212, 213, 222, 225, 226, 236, 240, 267, 269, 283, 355

brains, 122, 125, 142, 147, 148, 209, 227, 234, 300, 345

brother, xxxi, xxxiii, xxxviii, xl, xliii, xlvi, 15, 28, 48, 53, 63, 68, 71, 78, 92, 95, 101, 115, 125, 130, 142, 153, 199, 211, 219, 221, 224, 228, 239, 251, 271, 278, 285, 291, 293

Buddhism, 26, 28, 61

Caucasian, 40, 253, 262

Chicago, xix, xxi, xxii, xxiii, xxviii, xxxii, xxxiii, xxxiv, xxxv, xxxvi, 5, 14, 50, 53, 113, 133, 304, 305, 311, 316, 319, 322, 324, 325, 326, 329, 330, 331, 332, 337, 339, 340, 342, 347, 356, 358, 359, 360

children, xlix, 1, 2, 3, 9, 13, 15, 21, 32, 38, 54, 65, 76, 98, 102, 110, 114, 126, 130, 134, 136, 153, 176, 182, 185, 190, 199, 206, 207, 208, 209, 211, 214, 216, 219, 221, 224, 226, 236, 247, 253, 262, 281, 284, 289, 290, 291, 298, 305, 315, 320, 323, 345, 347, 348, 351

China, 108, 295

chosen, xlviii, 26, 43, 62, 76, 80, 111, 124, 160, 169, 178, 183, 203, 292, 293, 296, 297, 298

Christ, xxix, 108, 136, 137, 138, 146, 157, 169, 179, 205, 350

church, 6, 11, 15, 39, 46, 73, 78, 81, 209, 219, 307, 310, 319, 322, 352

civilization, 2, 19, 20, 21, 22, 30, 48, 62, 69, 81, 82, 97, 146, 192, 220, 247, 342

cockatrice, 274

constitution, 100

Cushan, 194

David, xiv, xx, xxvi, xlix, 35, 114, 136, 137, 169, 180, 211, 212, 325, 334

dead, 6, 10, 25, 39, 42, 46, 52, 64, 71, 72, 73, 79, 82, 86, 92, 97, 99, 119, 120, 123, 125, 126, 127, 129, 136, 137, 140, 144, 158, 171, 176, 178, 221, 224, 231, 237, 263, 266, 267, 268, 269, 276, 287, 301, 355

death, xxxvi, 5, 11, 14, 21, 22, 28, 37, 40, 42, 44, 47, 49, 53, 57, 62, 67, 71, 75, 81, 84, 85, 92, 95, 102, 105, 106, 108, 110, 111, 115, 118, 120, 121, 123, 126, 127, 128, 130, 131, 132, 135, 136, 152, 153, 154, 159, 167, 168, 176, 178, 180, 186, 197, 203, 231, 247, 249, 253, 256, 257, 258, 271, 273, 274, 279, 280, 282, 286, 287, 298, 314, 326, 328, 349

demon, 232, 281

Detroit, xxxiii, 5, 109, 356

devils, 2, 12, 14, 24, 27, 31, 33, 35, 39, 41, 43, 45, 53, 54, 61, 62, 64, 69, 73, 74, 75, 78, 80, 81, 85, 87, 93, 94, 96, 98, 101, 102, 103, 104, 105, 106, 107, 108, 109, 112, 115, 118, 119, 122, 124, 125, 128, 129, 131, 133, 134, 135, 138, 139, 140, 144, 145, 146, 149, 152, 153, 156, 157, 160, 162, 175, 176, 181, 183, 185, 186, 187, 188, 190, 191, 192, 194, 195, 196, 197, 200, 205, 206, 207, 208, 216, 218, 219, 222, 223, 224, 225, 230, 231, 232, 238, 240, 244, 245, 246, 247, 249, 250, 252, 254, 255, 256, 257, 261, 267, 269, 272, 273, 274, 278, 279, 280, 281, 282, 283, 284, 286, 287, 289, 291, 293, 294, 295, 296, 297, 298, 299, 304, 305

dragon, 79, 232, 233, 239, 240, 242, 243, 270

earth, xiv, 1, 6, 8, 11, 13, 14, 18, 20, 24, 26, 28, 30, 32, 33, 35, 36, 38, 39, 41, 42, 43, 46, 47, 48, 49, 50, 51, 52, 61, 62, 63, 64, 65, 73, 75, 79, 80, 83, 84, 85, 86, 88, 89, 93, 94, 97, 99, 100, 101, 104, 108, 118, 119, 120, 124, 136, 139, 140, 141, 143, 145, 146, 147, 148, 149, 150, 152, 153, 154, 158, 160, 161, 162, 166, 167, 168, 173, 174, 181, 188, 191, 193, 194, 197, 198, 206, 207, 208, 209, 211, 215, 217, 218, 221, 222, 223, 224, 225, 229, 230, 234, 235, 241, 242, 243, 245, 247, 250, 251, 253, 254, 256, 257, 259, 260, 262, 263, 264, 265, 266, 270, 271, 275, 276, 277, 278, 279, 280, 284, 286, 287, 293, 295, 296, 298, 300, 303, 305, 318

Egypt, xliv, xlvii, xlviii, xlix, 7, 51, 87, 116, 117, 118, 120, 126, 175, 184, 187, 203, 269, 311

Eliphaz, 193

Emmanuel, 136

enemy, xiv, xv, 5, 6, 11, 13, 25, 35, 39, 45, 49, 52, 64, 74, 92, 94, 106, 131, 135, 142, 147, 160, 166, 169,

174, 178, 182, 198, 199, 208, 214, 215, 226, 228, 231, 232, 242, 243, 244, 249, 259, 265, 269, 273, 278, 279, 280, 283, 287, 288, 289, 296
England, 33, 35, 235
English, xxxvii, xliv, xlv, xlvii, xlviii, xlix, l, li, 7, 23, 96, 107, 108, 114, 162, 163, 202, 232, 237, 238, 260, 263, 264
Esau, 193
Europe, xxi, 24, 38, 40, 50, 62, 81, 82, 216, 220, 246, 247, 249, 252, 253, 260, 265, 295, 343
European, 47, 68, 134, 202, 205, 207, 208, 215, 235, 242, 243, 265
Ezekiel, 71, 84, 86, 143, 145, 146, 147, 148, 150, 229, 256
Fard, xxxii, xxxiv, li, 2, 9, 17, 22, 28, 36, 107, 133, 137, 155, 164, 242, 342, 355
Farrakhan, Honorable Minister Louis, i, xii, xiv, xv, xxviii, xxix, xxx, xxxi, xxxii, xxxiii, xxxiv, xxxv, xxxvi, xxxvii, xxxviii, xxxix, xl, xli, xlii, xliii, xliv, xlix, li, 342, 355
Florida, 282
future, xxiii, xxvi, xxxii, li, 11, 43, 68, 72, 82, 111, 116, 123, 129, 130, 131, 132, 158, 168, 171, 180, 185, 207, 208, 211, 213, 233, 240, 263, 264, 285, 309, 318, 323
Ghana, 79, 217
grafting, 101, 121, 133, 197, 250, 295, 298
Greenwood, MS, 14, 50, 53, 113, 133
Harlem, xxxiii, xxxv, xlii, 303, 317
Hebrew, xliv, xlviii, 7, 45, 62, 177, 184
hillsides, 40, 220, 246, 252, 253
history, xiii, xvi, xix, xx, xxi, xxvi, xxvii, xliv, xlvii, xlix, li, 8, 12, 18, 19, 21, 38, 50, 62, 66, 67, 83, 84, 101, 106, 107, 108, 110, 118, 123, 124, 126, 128, 129, 130, 131, 144, 146, 156, 157, 158, 178, 184, 197, 200, 216, 218, 220, 232, 233, 234, 238, 243, 244, 247, 250, 252, 253, 255, 256, 262, 263, 264, 291, 296, 311, 322
hog, 22, 23, 36, 38, 39, 211
hypocrite, 45, 283
Iblis, 156, 157, 232
Illinois, 14, 211, 331, 347, 348, 356
Imam, xvi, 44, 164, 202, 305, 350
injustice, xiv, xv, 16, 48, 79, 82, 100, 104, 142, 214, 228, 247, 259, 276, 277, 288, 289, 317
Isa, 7, 8, 23, 39, 107, 111, 116, 118, 126, 158, 179, 188, 216
Ishmael, 30, 35, 212
Islam, i, xvi, xvii, xviii, xxi, xxii, xxiii, xxvi, xxvii, xxviii, xxxv, xxxviii, xxxix, xli, xlii, li, 2, 5, 6, 10, 11, 12, 14, 15, 16, 22, 24, 25, 26, 27, 28, 29, 31, 33, 34, 35, 40, 41, 42, 43, 45, 47, 48, 49, 52, 53, 56, 57, 58, 60, 61, 62, 63, 64, 65, 66, 67, 68, 69, 71, 72, 73, 75, 76, 77, 78, 80, 81, 82, 84, 86, 87, 88, 90, 91, 92, 93, 94, 95, 96, 98, 99, 100, 102, 103, 104, 105, 110, 111, 115, 118, 119, 128, 129, 133, 140, 141, 145, 152, 153, 159, 160, 161, 162, 163, 169, 170, 172, 174, 176, 179, 180, 181, 184, 185, 186, 188, 197, 198, 199, 202, 203, 204, 210, 211, 212, 213, 214, 218, 219, 220, 223, 224, 225, 226, 227, 231, 235, 239, 240, 246, 249, 251, 252, 253, 256, 258, 259, 267, 268, 269, 270, 277, 278, 279, 280, 282, 284, 285, 286, 289, 291, 296, 299, 301, 303, 306, 308, 309, 310, 311, 314, 315, 321, 323, 324, 328, 329, 330, 332, 336, 341, 342, 343, 344, 345, 346, 348, 349, 350, 351, 352, 353, 358, 359, 360
Israel, 21, 57, 86, 115, 118, 126, 169, 204, 292, 293, 297, 298, 299
Jacob, 35, 136, 233, 240, 292

James, xix, xx, 7, 35, 44, 155, 200, 230, 264, 343, 352, 356
Jehovah, 57, 108, 146, 175, 177, 203
Jerusalem, 85, 117, 119, 121, 155, 199, 249, 257
Jesus, xiv, xxviii, li, 2, 6, 7, 8, 9, 12, 13, 23, 25, 28, 35, 52, 53, 54, 57, 60, 62, 63, 64, 66, 67, 68, 70, 71, 72, 73, 75, 76, 78, 81, 82, 86, 88, 89, 91, 92, 105, 106, 107, 108, 109, 110, 111, 112, 114, 115, 116, 117, 118, 119, 120, 121, 123, 124, 125, 126, 127, 128, 129, 130, 131, 132, 135, 136, 137, 138, 139, 140, 144, 146, 150, 153, 155, 156, 157, 158, 159, 161, 170, 171, 176, 177, 179, 180, 182, 183, 184, 186, 187, 192, 194, 197, 199, 202, 204, 212, 224, 227, 233, 235, 237, 247, 249, 255, 260, 262, 271, 276, 278, 279, 280, 291, 293, 297, 298, 302, 350
Jonah, 35, 169, 212
justice, xiv, xxvi, 1, 16, 27, 44, 68, 69, 76, 79, 80, 82, 85, 87, 92, 93, 95, 96, 110, 124, 128, 142, 156, 157, 172, 181, 186, 190, 203, 206, 208, 213, 214, 216, 218, 219, 221, 223, 228, 229, 230, 232, 233, 240, 247, 257, 261, 266, 273, 274, 281, 282, 288, 289, 290, 291, 304, 305, 319
Kashmir, 132
knowledge, xiii, xxiii, xliv, 2, 3, 5, 6, 10, 11, 13, 15, 17, 18, 19, 20, 21, 22, 23, 24, 33, 34, 35, 36, 37, 38, 45, 47, 48, 51, 52, 54, 55, 56, 62, 64, 69, 72, 73, 74, 76, 80, 86, 90, 91, 94, 95, 97, 99, 103, 104, 105, 106, 108, 116, 118, 123, 124, 128, 130, 131, 133, 134, 138, 141, 144, 146, 159, 168, 175, 178, 180, 184, 186, 188, 190, 191, 195, 197, 198, 199, 200, 201, 203, 207, 208, 215, 217, 219, 223, 226, 229, 233, 235, 236, 237, 238, 239, 242, 243, 244, 246, 247, 252, 254, 260, 269, 270, 271, 273, 274, 277, 284, 285, 291, 292, 294, 295, 296, 302, 304, 306, 307, 311, 327, 329, 350, 352
Lazarus, 5, 32, 64, 129
Lord, xiii, xxvi, xxxviii, li, 4, 12, 25, 26, 31, 35, 39, 42, 57, 60, 65, 71, 73, 89, 101, 105, 114, 127, 137, 143, 146, 150, 156, 160, 167, 170, 171, 173, 175, 176, 179, 186, 188, 192, 198, 200, 201, 202, 204, 206, 212, 222, 228, 237, 244, 250, 251, 254, 264, 267, 271, 273, 292, 294, 296, 298, 299, 302, 309
love, xii, xxx, xxxi, xxxiii, xlvi, xlvii, 3, 4, 6, 10, 13, 14, 16, 17, 26, 27, 37, 43, 45, 46, 48, 54, 60, 69, 71, 74, 76, 79, 82, 87, 93, 94, 95, 96, 97, 100, 102, 103, 104, 105, 106, 107, 110, 111, 112, 124, 129, 131, 132, 133, 134, 141, 144, 152, 154, 161, 168, 174, 183, 186, 190, 198, 199, 202, 205, 207, 208, 210, 212, 213, 215, 216, 219, 222, 223, 230, 237, 239, 243, 249, 250, 251, 254, 258, 259, 262, 266, 269, 270, 271, 272, 273, 276, 277, 278, 279, 281, 285, 286, 287, 289, 292, 297, 299, 304, 305, 306, 307, 313, 317, 326, 343, 344, 350, 355
Malachi, 65, 130
Malcolm, xv, xvi, xxii, xxxii, xlii, xlvi, 60, 64, 65, 311, 313, 342
Mary, 9, 28, 78, 107, 112, 113, 114, 115, 116, 123, 124, 126, 127, 132, 133, 136, 158, 159, 190, 197, 237
Mercury, 109
Messenger, xiii, xv, l, 42, 43, 79, 102, 105, 109, 125, 129, 141, 173, 180, 222, 234, 240, 267
Messiah, xxix, xxx, li, 107, 146, 179
Minister, xii, xiv, xv, xxviii, xxix, xxx, xxxi, xxxii, xxxiv, xxxv, xxxvi, xxxvii, xxxviii, xxxix, xl, xli, xlii, xliii, xliv, xlv, xlvi, xlvii, xlviii, xlix, li, 60, 64, 65, 217, 317, 319, 353, 355, 356, 359
ministry, xii, xxviii, xxxviii, xxxix, xlv, xlvii, 108, 110, 131, 136, 235, 355
moon, 29, 42, 51, 89, 149, 194, 300

Moses, xliii, xliv, xlviii, xlix, li, 6, 7, 8, 9, 10, 11, 23, 25, 35, 38, 45, 47, 52, 57, 60, 62, 63, 68, 70, 82, 87, 88, 107, 108, 110, 111, 113, 115, 118, 126, 127, 131, 132, 138, 157, 175, 177, 179, 180, 184, 187, 194, 197, 200, 201, 202, 203, 204, 212, 215,220, 226, 240, 247, 252, 269, 274, 279

mother, xlvii, xlviii, xlix, l, 13, 89, 108, 109, 110, 116, 122, 123, 124, 126, 127, 128, 130, 132, 148, 190, 199, 213, 243, 261, 262, 298, 316

Muhammad, i, xii, xiii, xv, xvi, xvii, xviii, xix, xxi, xxii, xxiii, xxiv, xxvii, xxviii, xxix, xxx, xxxi, xxxii, xxxiii, xxxiv, xxxv, xxxvii, xxxviii, xxxix, xl, xli, xliii, xlv, xlvii, xlix, li, 2, 7, 8, 9, 17, 22, 24, 25, 26, 28, 30, 33, 35, 36, 43, 44, 45, 50,53, 54, 56, 58, 60, 62, 63, 64, 65, 66, 82, 89, 91, 94, 97, 102, 107, 108, 109, 110, 111, 113, 119, 126, 128, 133, 137, 138, 141, 144, 146, 152, 155, 157, 162, 163, 165, 167, 174, 176, 179, 180, 181, 194, 201, 202, 203, 204, 211, 212, 215, 238, 242, 245, 249, 252, 253, 271, 279, 283, 292, 302, 308, 309, 310, 311, 312, 313, 314, 315, 316, 317, 318, 319, 320, 321, 322, 323, 324, 325, 326, 327, 328, 329, 331, 332, 333, 336, 339, 340, 341, 342, 343, 344, 345, 346, 347, 348, 349, 350, 351, 352, 353, 355, 356, 358, 359, 360

Musa, xlviii, xlix, 7, 8, 9, 38, 110, 111, 131, 179, 204, 212, 252

nation, xv, xxiv, xxvi, xxxiii, xli, xlii, xlix, 3, 5, 7, 8, 10, 13, 14, 17, 18, 19, 20, 21, 27, 29, 33, 35, 36, 43, 44, 51, 53, 54, 60, 62, 72, 76, 78, 80, 81, 82, 83, 84, 89, 96, 97, 98, 99, 100, 101, 102, 103, 104, 105, 106, 111, 116, 118, 121, 122, 123, 124,129, 132, 133, 144, 146, 147, 150, 152, 156, 157, 161, 162, 169, 176, 178, 180, 182, 184, 188, 190, 194, 205, 208, 215, 216, 217, 220, 221, 224, 229, 233, 234, 237, 240, 242, 244, 250, 251, 253, 255, 259, 260, 261, 265, 266, 267, 270, 276, 277, 278, 281, 284, 286, 287, 288, 289, 292, 293, 294, 296, 298, 304, 307, 317, 326, 330

Noah, 3, 9, 10, 25, 35, 47, 60, 68, 70, 88, 138, 148, 150, 184, 200, 205, 212

obligatory, 164, 172

Pacific, 108, 250, 265, 291

Palestine, 45, 107, 117, 119, 155, 279

paradise, 169, 203, 273

Paran, 193, 194

peace, xviii, 6, 8, 13, 24, 26, 27, 28, 35, 39, 40, 41, 45, 48, 49, 50, 55, 60, 61, 63, 64, 67, 69, 72, 76, 77, 80, 89, 94, 96, 109, 110, 130, 136, 146, 152, 161, 179, 186, 207, 208, 213, 216, 218, 219, 220, 221, 222, 223, 230, 231, 235, 253, 254, 261, 267, 268, 271, 275, 276, 279, 283, 285, 293, 296, 299, 302, 305, 307, 310, 348

Pelan, 43, 122, 233, 246

Pharisees, 10, 136

Pittsburgh, i, xvii, xix, xx, xxi, xxii, xxiii, xxiv, xxvi, xxvii, xxviii, xxix, xxxv, xxxviii, xl, xliii, xlvii, 355, 358, 360

power, xxvi, xxxvii, xliv, xlix, 3, 6, 15, 33, 34, 38, 40, 44, 52, 57, 67, 80, 81, 82, 86, 95, 98, 100, 105, 110, 135, 136, 137, 138, 139, 140, 142, 143, 145, 146, 149, 150, 152, 156, 157, 172, 174, 176, 181, 183, 186, 187, 193, 212, 215, 220, 226, 227, 229, 232, 233, 234, 235, 236, 243, 244, 247, 249, 251, 260, 265, 266, 267, 269, 277, 278, 285, 291, 299, 303, 304, 305, 306, 312, 320, 324, 339, 353

prayer, xxx, 29, 30, 31, 71, 82, 159, 162, 163, 164, 165, 166, 167, 168, 169, 170, 171, 172, 173, 174, 175, 187, 224, 258, 355

preacher, xxxiii, xxxiv, 36, 37, 107, 226, 292

prophecy, 22, 31, 43, 45, 49, 77, 107, 140, 141, 149, 158, 169, 184, 193, 195, 205, 230, 235, 261, 266

prophet, xlviii, 6, 10, 12, 26, 35, 52, 61, 62, 63, 82, 92, 109, 111, 114, 115, 116, 118, 126, 127, 130, 132, 137, 138, 153, 157, 159, 169, 170, 171, 176, 180, 193, 203, 205, 224, 231, 234, 237, 242, 249, 260, 279, 287, 296, 302, 318

prophets, xiii, xv, 5, 6, 7, 8, 22, 23, 24, 30, 35, 47, 48, 56, 60, 61, 63, 68, 70, 71, 75, 80, 82, 83, 86, 88, 93, 94, 102, 105, 106, 110, 115, 118, 123, 126, 127, 132, 135, 137, 138, 140, 141, 150, 153, 154, 166, 167, 176, 177, 178, 180, 182, 183, 184, 186, 187,189, 191, 195, 197, 202, 212, 215, 225, 226, 230, 236, 240, 241, 242, 245, 249, 251, 252, 255, 272, 273, 279, 296, 302, 350

religion, xxxviii, xli, xlii, 2, 5, 6, 7, 11, 12, 14, 15, 16, 20, 21, 25, 26, 27, 28, 29, 31, 33, 35, 41, 45, 46, 47, 48, 50, 52, 53, 57, 58, 60, 61, 62, 64, 67, 68, 69, 70, 71, 72, 73, 75, 76, 77, 78, 79, 80, 81, 82, 84, 86, 87, 88, 90, 91, 92, 94, 95, 96, 98, 100, 102, 103, 104, 105, 110, 118, 128, 129, 141, 145, 150, 152, 153, 154, 157, 158, 159, 160, 161, 166, 169, 170, 171, 172, 176, 177, 181, 184, 185, 186, 188, 191, 196, 198, 199, 202, 203, 205, 206, 209, 210, 211, 212, 213, 214, 216, 218, 219, 220, 223, 224, 225, 226, 227, 231, 235, 237, 239, 240, 241, 245, 246, 251, 252, 256, 258, 262, 267, 268, 269, 270, 271, 272, 273, 275, 277, 278, 279, 280, 282, 284, 285, 306, 310, 311, 312, 314, 321, 323, 327, 342, 343, 347, 349

representative, xxxv, xlv, 6, 154, 203

resurrection, 10, 11, 46, 76, 93, 103, 127, 136, 139, 140, 178, 268, 280, 296, 307, 355

Rome, 81, 121, 155, 199, 212, 233, 234, 252, 279

Roosevelt, Theodore, xxxvi, 266

Russia, 234, 235

salvation, xlviii, 3, 5, 10, 11, 16, 21, 33, 48, 68, 85, 86, 92, 95, 97, 100, 101, 106, 125, 128, 139, 143, 145, 160, 168, 169, 182, 186, 191, 194, 195, 196, 198, 212, 227, 229, 256, 270, 274, 277, 285, 292, 299, 307

Saviour, xxi, xxxii, xxxviii, xlvi, 94, 118, 143, 161, 229, 269, 292

scripture, xiii, xiv, xxv, xxvii, 5, 35, 79, 91, 118, 119, 133, 138, 144, 180, 203, 204, 212, 229, 272, 273, 287

serpent, 89, 135, 232, 237, 238, 239, 240, 241, 242, 243, 245, 246, 247, 252, 253, 270, 273, 274, 299

Shaitan, 122, 232, 238, 281

Sharrieff, 34, 35, 40, 56, 60, 86, 101, 104, 105, 106, 107, 108, 250, 251

sheep, xiv, xv, xvi, 10, 43, 128, 142, 144, 168, 169, 206, 207, 210, 227, 228, 231, 264, 279, 289, 293, 299, 301, 303

slavemasters, 21, 64, 66, 67, 68, 76, 78, 86, 90, 92, 94, 95, 144, 155, 175, 176, 177, 182, 184, 196, 301, 303, 304, 305, 306

slavery, xiv, 2, 3, 6, 10, 14, 21, 24, 27, 28, 32, 33, 37, 42, 52, 67, 75, 78, 96, 105, 118, 184, 186, 208, 236, 260, 275, 278, 280, 288, 290, 291, 306, 309

Sodom and Gomorrah, 32, 138, 148, 205

Solomon, xlix, 35, 169, 212

spirit, xv, xlvi, xlvii, li, 8, 25, 41, 42, 55, 56, 70, 104, 132, 133, 135, 139, 140, 143, 159, 171, 173, 188, 189, 191, 192, 193, 194, 195, 196, 197, 212, 229, 232, 242, 254, 260, 261, 279, 344, 346

Stoner, J.B., xxiii, 81, 82, 307

suffer, xii, 4, 6, 14, 50, 66, 92, 101, 120, 126, 134, 145, 184, 209, 218, 220, 224, 231, 233, 268, 282, 289, 306, 337

teach, 2, 10, 11, 14, 19, 22, 23, 24, 33, 34, 37, 38, 47, 48,
51, 62, 64, 68, 74, 75, 81, 90, 96, 100, 105, 107, 108,
114, 115, 117, 118, 119, 128, 134, 138, 142, 144, 162,
174, 177, 183, 186, 189, 190, 191, 193, 195, 197, 200,
202, 225, 228, 231, 276, 277, 285, 294, 295, 298, 307,
320
teaching, xxxv, xxxvi, 1, 2, 6, 10, 13, 19, 23, 24, 28, 37,
38, 48, 52, 62, 88, 89, 93, 94, 100, 102, 104, 105, 110,
117, 118, 119, 122, 124, 125, 129, 131, 134, 153, 171,
174, 178, 189, 190, 191, 196, 197, 198, 205, 221, 236,
246, 250, 251, 252, 270, 272, 275, 277, 278, 287, 293,
297, 298, 301, 303, 304, 306, 307, 311, 324, 344, 345,
350, 351
Teman, 193
time, xv, xvii, xviii, xx, xxii, xxiv, xxviii, xxx, xxxi,
xxxiv, xxxv, xxxviii, xli, xlv, xlvi, xlvii, xlix, li, 2, 3,
4, 5, 6, 14, 16, 17, 18, 21, 22, 23, 24, 32, 35, 36, 40,
42, 43, 47, 48, 49, 52, 55, 62, 69, 70, 72, 73, 76, 77,
79, 82, 86, 87, 92, 93, 96, 97, 100, 106, 111, 112, 113,
114, 116, 118, 119, 121, 123, 124, 129, 131, 133, 138,
140, 141, 143, 144, 145, 146, 147, 148, 149, 150, 152,
153, 154, 156, 157, 158, 159, 162, 164, 166, 167, 168,
170, 171, 173, 175, 176, 177, 178, 179, 180, 181, 183,
185, 187, 188, 189, 190, 191, 192, 193, 194, 195, 196,
197, 198, 199, 201, 203, 204, 205, 206, 207, 208, 209,
211, 213, 215, 216, 218, 220, 222, 224, 225, 226, 227,
229, 231, 233, 234, 235, 237, 239, 241, 244, 245, 246,
247, 249, 250, 251, 252, 253, 254, 255, 257, 259, 261,
263, 264, 266, 267, 268, 269, 271, 272, 273, 274, 276,
277, 278, 279, 281, 282, 283, 284, 286, 287, 289, 291,
293, 295, 296, 297, 299, 300, 302, 303, 304, 305, 306,
307, 310, 311, 312, 316, 318, 320, 321, 327, 330, 332,
351, 353, 356
unite, xlviii, 48, 57, 63, 65, 67, 94, 95, 96, 99, 100, 101,
130, 161, 202, 209, 212, 223, 239, 271, 276, 277, 278,
280, 281, 284, 285, 289, 306, 353
Washington, xvi, xxxvii, 95, 100, 209, 290, 312, 317,
356
wicked, xiii, xlix, li, 4, 10, 19, 26, 27, 28, 30, 32, 43, 46,
50, 55, 72, 75, 78, 82, 84, 133, 135, 137, 141, 155,
162, 176, 178, 188, 192, 194, 197, 199, 205, 206, 215,
216, 232, 242, 245, 256, 258, 269, 270, 280, 287, 304
work, xii, xiii, xv, xvii, xxvii, xxix, xxx, xxxi, xxxv,
xxxvii, xliii, xlix, li, 3, 4, 6, 16, 22, 31, 35, 43, 64, 65,
84, 85, 86, 88, 89, 93, 95, 100, 106, 109, 111, 126,
129, 132, 137, 140, 144, 158, 163, 180, 188, 196, 199,
208, 215, 216, 217, 223, 234, 245, 249, 256, 257, 259,
263, 266, 272, 275, 277, 279, 292, 300, 302, 316, 317,
318, 320, 324, 326, 328, 329, 344, 345, 346, 347, 349,
350, 352, 353, 355
Yacub, 24, 38, 43, 61, 71, 72, 102, 105, 121, 122, 179,
182, 195, 197, 213, 231, 233, 236, 244, 245, 246, 249,
251, 252, 265, 268, 292, 293, 294, 295, 297, 298, 300

www.ingramcontent.com/pod-product-compliance
Lightning Source LLC
Chambersburg PA
CBHW050559270326
41926CB00012B/2113